iSpeak

What makes *iSpeak* special?

iSpeak offers instructors **unmatched content and currency** in a *succinct magazine format*. With its unique emphasis on **vital personal, social, and political themes**, *iSpeak* helps students **develop strong speech topics** and prepare successful public speaking presentations.

Connect Public Speaking

iSpeak is an integrated program that helps students practice, build confidence, and achieve success in public speaking. Connect Public Speaking provides students a wealth of resources to prepare and plan speeches, while LearnSmart—McGraw-Hill's proven adaptive learning system—guides them toward mastery of key course concepts. Additionally, Connect's highly flexible Speech Capture tool saves instructors valuable time in managing assignments and evaluating student speeches.

ISPEAK, FIFTH EDITION

Published by McGraw-Hill, a business unit of The McGraw-Hill Companies, Inc., 1221 Avenue of the Americas, New York, NY, 10020.
Copyright © 2014 by The McGraw-Hill Companies, Inc. All rights reserved. Printed in the United States of America. Previous editions © 2012, 2011, 2010, and 2009. No part of this publication may be reproduced or distributed in any form or by any means, or stored in a database or retrieval system, without the prior written consent of The McGraw-Hill Companies, Inc., including, but not limited to, in any network or other electronic storage or transmission, or broadcast for distance learning.

Some ancillaries, including electronic and print components, may not be available to customers outside the United States.

This book is printed on acid-free paper.

2 3 4 5 6 7 8 9 0 RMN/RMN 1 0 9 8 7 6 5 4

ISBN 978-0-07-803688-0
MHID 0-07-803688-7

Senior Vice President, Products & Markets: *Kurt L. Strand*
Vice President, General Manager: *Michael Ryan*
Vice President, Content Production & Technology Services: *Kimberly Meriwether David*
Managing Director/Director: *Susan Gouijnstook*
Executive Director of Development: *Lisa Pinto*
Content Development Editor: *Elizabeth Murphy*
Editorial Coordinator: *Jamie Daron*
Marketing Manager: *Clare Cashen*
Director, Content Production: *Terri Schiesl*
Project Manager/Content Project Manager: *Anne Fuzellier*
Buyer: *Carol Bielski*
Senior Designer: *Lisa King*
Cover Image: *© Hill Street Studios/Blend/Glow Images*
Photo Researcher: *Lili Weiner*
Media Project Manager: *Katie Klochan*
Typeface: *10/12 Janson Text LT Std*
Compositor: *Lachina Publishing Services*
Printer: *RR Donnelley*

All credits appearing on page 307 of the book are considered to be an extension of the copyright page.

Library of Congress Cataloging-in-Publication Data

Nelson, Paul E. (Paul Edward), 1941- author.
  iSpeak : Public Speaking for Contemporary Life / Paul Nelson, North Dakota State University ; Scott Titsworth, Ohio University-Athens ; Judy Pearson, North Dakota State University. — FIFTH EDITION.
    pages cm
  Includes bibliographical references and index.
  ISBN 978-0-07-803688-0
1. Public speaking. I. Titsworth, Scott, author. II. Pearson, Judy C., author. III. Title.
  PN4129.15.N46 2013
  808.5'1—dc23

2012039695

The Internet addresses listed in the text were accurate at the time of publication. The inclusion of a website does not indicate an endorsement by the authors or McGraw-Hill, and McGraw-Hill does not guarantee the accuracy of the information presented at these sites.

www.mhhe.com

Contents

[Part One] Preparing Your Presentations

2

PREPARING YOUR FIRST PRESENTATION 24

SELECTING A TOPIC AND PURPOSE 44

ANALYZING THE AUDIENCE 62

[Part Two] Selecting and Arranging Content

6

ORGANIZING AND OUTLINING YOUR PRESENTATION 118

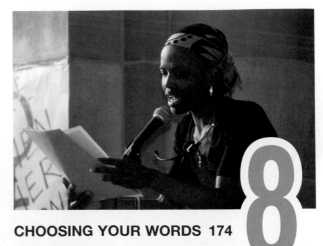

DELIVERING SPEECHES 150

CHOOSING YOUR WORDS 174

VISUAL RESOURCES AND PRESENTATION TECHNOLOGY 194

[Part Three] Types of Presentations

10

PRESENTING TO INFORM 214

11

PRESENTING PERSUASIVE MESSAGES 238

SPEAKING ON SPECIAL OCCASIONS 260

[Appendix]

WORKING AND PRESENTING AS A GROUP 276

1

GETTING

The purpose of this chapter is to help you face your fears, manage your anxieties, and launch your learning about effective public presentations. It also will remind you of the role public speaking plays in a democratic society and will encourage you to view the public speaking course as a way to learn how to be a fully functioning member of your local community. Toward the end of the chapter, you will learn unique characteristics of public presentations, tips for effective talks, and techniques for avoiding problems with your audience.

STARTED

Almost anyone who becomes successful for almost any reason will be asked to speak to others about his or her experience. Danny Wong, for instance, attends Bentley University (Massachusetts), where he studies communication. As a high school student in Brooklyn, Danny co-founded an online custom dress-shirt company called Blank Label that he still runs from his college dorm room. The operation has been such a success that it's been featured in *Forbes*, *Bloomberg Businessweek*, and *The New York Times* among other publications.

Naturally, everyone in the business world wants to know what contributed to Danny's success, and the young entrepreneur has told his story to the media in speeches and interviews a number of times. He attributes his achievements to the opportunity to attend a strong high school, to his efforts to build a network of contacts, and to reading everything he could find about how to start a small business. Asked what advice he would offer aspiring entrepreneurs, Danny recommends having realistic expectations and realizing that success requires a lot of "determination, dexterity, and sacrifice."

Whether or not you imagine yourself becoming a successful entrepreneur like Danny, over the course of your life you are likely to confront many situations in which public speaking skills can make the difference between success and failure. This book encourages you to explore the issues you care about so you can share your views with others in class and throughout your life. This chapter will help you see public speaking as an exciting and positive experience and will lead you to choose vital and appropriate topics.

Blank Label

DESIGNED BY YOU, STITCHED BY US

Speaking Excites

If you are reading this sentence, you are taking a class in which you are expected to deliver presentations. Which of the following comes closest to how you feel?

Student 1: I'm eager to get in the spotlight, take center stage, and perform. I'll give a speech that will dazzle my classmates with its brilliance. I am so pleased that I am required to do something that will make me very happy.

Student 2: I'm so scared that I think I'm going to die from fright before I ever get to the front of the room to give a speech.

Yes, these two are extreme cases, but in fact most students face a public speaking class with mixed emotions.

Typically, students who have been active in debate, individual events, theater, and musical performances are more like Student 1. Similarly, students who have worked full-time in responsible jobs, are married, have raised kids, or have served in the armed forces seem more likely to have confidence. Perhaps they already know more than most people about some subjects, and they are not worried about sharing their experiences.

The less you have interacted with people, the more likely you are to be worried about public speaking—like Student 2. People who grew up in families, cultures, and communities that value verbal communication may have been encouraged to hone their skills through such activities as debating, acting, volunteering, performing, or working. If you grew up in a family where "silence is golden" or "children are to be seen but not heard," then you may have been discouraged from developing presentation skills.

Almost anything that you do for the first time has an element of risk: the few lines you had to say in front of the class in grade school, the first date, the first kiss, the first job interview, or the first request for a raise. Interestingly, many people who claim to be afraid of public presentations probably like other experiences that scare them—for example, skiing down a steep slope, parachuting from a plane, swimming in riptides, or driving too fast. Look on your public speaking class as an opportunity to give yourself a thrill, just like many other first-time experiences. You will suffer no bruises or head traumas, but you will feel excitement.

What's the Worst-Case Scenario?

One way to face fear is to consider, "What is the worst thing that can happen?" Beginning speakers have great imaginations, especially when they fantasize about everything that could go wrong. Let's consider the possibilities:

Will you die? Comedian Jerry Seinfeld had an opening monologue in which he said, "The number two fear people have is death. The number one fear is public speaking. This means if you go to a funeral, you would rather be the person in the coffin than the person delivering the eulogy." The authors of this book have more than 90 years of combined teaching experience. We have heard thousands of classroom speeches. So far, not one student has died while speaking. Nor have we ever heard of one who did.

Will you faint? One of the authors used to carry a smelling salts capsule (the kind used to revive people when they faint), just in case a student fainted while delivering a speech. After several thousand student speeches, the gauze-wrapped capsule started to get very dirty, but not from ever using it. The author finally threw the capsule away. None of the authors has ever seen a student faint.

Will you shake, sweat, look down, and feel your mouth go dry? Probably. Most beginning speakers feel these symptoms of anxiety, but they feel them less as they speak more. Were you as nervous on your third kiss as you were on your first? Well, you will not be as nervous on your third speech as you were on your first. By the time you complete this class, you will be more confident than you ever were before.

Will you blush, flush, stammer, and trip over your tongue? You might. You cannot help blushing and flushing. They are natural responses that disappear as you become more comfortable. Sometimes, even experienced speakers stammer a bit and mess up on a word. You shouldn't be very concerned even if you do have minor difficulties. Even the pros trip over a word now and then.

Will you forget what you were saying? Could happen. In front of 1,200 students, one of the authors used to move 40 feet from the lectern that held his notes and then forget what he was trying to explain. He would ask the class what they thought he was trying to prove, and someone in the front row always knew. In your presentations, you will likely have note cards that can help you if you get stuck. If you don't act overly concerned about an error, your audience won't be concerned either.

"Often your speech class is the only class in which you get to express your opinion about an important issue, and it may be one of the very few in which the teacher actually knows you."

Will you survive the course? Chances are excellent that you will complete the course, learn how to reduce your fears, learn how to focus on the message and the audience, and perhaps even want to speak in the workplace or community. The vast majority of public speaking students like the course and understand its importance—after they have completed it. In fact, our experience is that students often claim they entered the class "dreading" it, but quickly discovered that public speaking was one of their most interesting and enjoyable classes. Often your speech class is the only class in which you get to express your opinion about an important issue, and it may be one of the very few in which the teacher actually knows you. In the next section, let's address how public speaking will be one of the most useful courses you will take.

Why Study Public Speaking?

Democracy

Studying public communication can help you exercise your constitutionally guaranteed freedom of speech. In many countries, citizens are afraid to say anything about their leaders, their government, and public policies. In some countries, you can be killed for expressing your views. But the United States has a Bill of Rights that invites citizens to communicate their opinions and ideas. Freedom of speech is essential to a democratic form of government. Being a practicing citizen in a democratic society depends on knowing about current issues and being able to address them in conversations, in speeches, and through social media. Citizenship also involves being able to critically examine messages from others. Your public speaking course can help you become a fully functioning member of your local community and our democratic society at large. Democracy presents many opportunities, but it thrives only when everyday citizens embrace its freedoms as responsibilities to actively uphold.

To apply this concept of freedom of speech to civic engagement, you should think of individuals in your school, neighborhood, or community who take risks by speaking out. Which parent dares to confront the school board about some new rule? Which student takes the initiative to attack bullying by texting, tweeting, and blogging about the problem? Or which manager tells workers about the new merger, the workforce reduction, or the laying off of employees? All of these instances take some daring, but all are practical examples of how an individual can use public speaking to clarify a rule, fight for a cause, or reveal an unfortunate turn of events like the closing of an industrial plant.

Life Skills

Studying public speaking can teach you important life skills. This course involves learning skills that every person will use at some point—skills such as critical thinking, problem solving, decision making, conflict resolution, team building, and media literacy. Studying communication early in your college career can enhance your success throughout college. Consider the centrality of oral communication to all of your classes. You regularly are requested to answer questions in class, to provide reports, to offer explanations, to send meaningful messages, and to make presentations. In addition, your oral and written work depends on your ability to think critically and creatively, to solve problems, and to make decisions. Most likely, you will be engaged in group projects where skills such as team building, conflict resolution, and presentation will be keys to success. These same skills will be essential throughout your life.

One of the most important life skills that you can apply immediately and every day is critical listening. Because you hear many more speeches than you give, you can frequently apply your brainpower to what other speakers say: Is the speaker telling the whole story, or is important information being omitted? Is the speaker promoting a community action that makes sense (building a new stadium, a halfway house for addicts, or a new mall), or should opposing views be heard? Civic engagement means taking a critical look at which projects will do a community the most good. Maybe the new stadium will be an economic asset, but will that project also wipe out a neighborhood or two that deserve a hearing on this matter?

Work and Career

Studying public speaking can help you succeed professionally. Michael Phillips, in his blog *Corporate Heights,* lists "Communication Skills"—written and oral—as a transferable asset that can help you progress up the employment ladder for a lifetime.[1] A look at the job postings online will give you an immediate understanding of the importance of improving your knowledge and practice of communication. The following examples from advertisements on Monster.com are fairly typical:

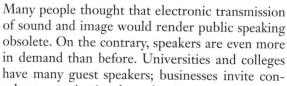

- A job opening for a truck driver's assistant says the candidate must "maintain customer relationships."
- Another job opening for assistant manager requires the "ability to motivate and develop unit managers and staff."
- And yet another for a senior manager in public relations requires "strong writing and oral communication skills."

The higher you go on the employment ladder, the bigger the demand for strong communication skills. The truck driver's assistant has to know how to communicate with customers; the assistant managers need to motivate and develop other managers; and senior managers have to communicate well with people inside and outside the company. Personnel managers typically identify effective speaking and listening as the most important reasons for hiring the people they do. Your communication skill set will continue to be important throughout your career and will always be a factor in upward mobility and successful entrepreneurship.

Do People Really Speak Anymore?

Many people thought that electronic transmission of sound and image would render public speaking obsolete. On the contrary, speakers are even more in demand than before. Universities and colleges have many guest speakers; businesses invite consultants, motivational speakers, successful executives, and salespeople to speak; and every academic and business conference pays speakers to attract members to their conventions. Speaking is very big business.

Sure, ex-President Clinton earns $50 million a year in speaker fees, but, you are probably thinking, I'll never be an ex-president. The truth is you don't know at this point if people will want to pay you to speak.

Chances are excellent that you too will have opportunities to speak publicly. Peggy Noonan—speechwriter for Republican presidents and a TV political commentator—says:

> As more and more businesses become involved in the new media technologies, as we become a nation of fewer widgets and more Websites, a new premium has been put on the oldest form of communication: the ability to stand and say what you think in front of others.[2]

What if you could hear or see your favorite entertainer (1) on radio, (2) on TV, (3) on a "live" transmission via a large screen, or (4) in person? Which would you choose if cost and distance were not an issue? Why do we want to see politicians, athletes, and entertainers in person? We are so overexposed to people on film and video that seeing an important individual in person becomes much more special. More than ever we want to see a flesh-and-blood person talking to us.

What Is the Presentation Process?

Early in this course you need to grasp the big picture of the communication process with its component parts. Presenting is just one kind of communication context that can include many others, such as interpersonal communication, group communication, computer-mediated communication, and the many ways you can communicate with others on your cell phone and your iPad. All of these contexts involve the seven components described in the next section. Just as you are unlikely to understand the particulars of an automobile without understanding how horsepower, octane, torque, and exhaust contribute to speed, you are unlikely to understand the particulars of public presentations without knowing how the parts interact with each other.

What Are the Seven Components of the Communication Process?

Some basic elements are present in practically all public speaking and communication situations:

1. A source, presenter, or speaker who utters the message.
2. A receiver, audience members, or classmates who listen.
3. A message: your words and ideas adapted to that audience.
4. A channel, or means of distributing your words.
5. Feedback: responses from the audience.
6. A situation: the context in which the presentation occurs.
7. Noise: any form of interference with the message.

Let's look more closely at the components of the communication process.

Source

The **source** is *the person who originates the message*. Who the sender is makes a difference in determining who, if anyone, will listen. Suppose you were walking down a street in New York City without your iPod in your ears. You would hear cell phone conversations, people hailing taxicabs, and vendors selling everything from bagels to baklava. Would you listen to the messages they are sending? Some of the talented singers, dancers, and instrumentalists might attract your attention, but few of the many contenders for your eyes and ears would succeed. Huge fallout occurs, even in the classroom, between the source's intent (your teacher wants you to listen) and the actual successful transmission of the message (as, for instance, when you are busy updating your Facebook page). In the lecture hall, some teachers capture your attention and leave you wishing for more ideas. Occasionally you hear delivery-challenged professors who put you to sleep in spite of their bright ideas. A source is useless without a receiver, and a speaker is useless without an audience that listens.

The source of a message has to be ethically responsible. You cannot say anything to anybody just because speech is free and its use is guaranteed. You can face charges if you incite a riot, cause a panic, or slander someone who is not a public figure. Some campuses have rules against hate speech. Our freedom of speech is linked to the principle of responsibility that says you are acting unethically, immorally, and possibly illegally if your message is damaging to individuals or the community in some irresponsible fashion.

Receiver

The **receiver**, listener, or audience is *the individual or group that hears, and listens to, the message sent by the source*. All individuals are unique. Receivers are individuals who have inherited certain characteristics and developed others as a result of their families, friends, and education.

The best speakers can "read" an audience; through analysis or intuition, they can tell what an audience wants, needs, or responds to. This sort of group empathy allows some speakers to be seen as charismatic: They seem to exhibit what the audience feels. Even a beginning speaker can learn to see the world through the audience's eyes. Nothing helps more in the classroom than to listen carefully to your classmates' speeches, because every speech will reveal as much about the speaker as about the issue being discussed. Few speakers outside the classroom are able to hear each individual in the audience reveal herself or himself through a speech, a unique opportunity to analyze your listeners. The great benefit of speaking is that you get to respond with and to your audience, adapting and supporting your message in a way you cannot do in any other form of communication.

Message

Verbal and nonverbal messages are an integral part of the communication process. What else links the source and the receiver? Both source and receiver sense the **message**: *the facial expressions seen, the words heard, the visual aids illustrated, and the ideas or meanings conveyed simultaneously between source and receiver*. **Verbal messages** are *the words the source chose for the speech*. **Nonverbal messages** are *the movements, gestures, facial expressions, and vocal variations that can reinforce or contradict the words*, such as pitch or tone of voice that can alter the meaning of the words. Text messages are often misunderstood because they leave out nonverbal cues.

Channel

The **channel** is *the means of distributing your words, whether by coaxial cable, fiber optics, microwave, radio, video, or air*. In the public speaking classroom, the channel is first of all the air that carries the sound waves from the mouth of the source to the ear of the receiver. The type of channel might not seem to make very much difference, but messages have decidedly different impacts depending on whether they are heard from your mouth, seen on Microsoft PowerPoint, viewed on a laptop, or heard on an iPod.

Some public speaking students discover the differences among channels when their teacher videotapes their speeches. Watching yourself electronically reproduced is not the same as watching yourself in a live performance because channels are themselves part of the message. Do you perceive a professor in a classroom the same as you do an instructor of an online course? Probably not. The channel makes a difference. Or, as Marshall McLuhan famously expressed, "The medium is the message."

Feedback

Feedback includes *verbal or nonverbal responses by the audience*. During a public speech, most of the audience feedback is nonverbal: head nodding, smiling, frowning, giving complete attention, texting while pretending to listen. All this nonverbal feedback allows the speaker to infer whether the message is being communicated to the listeners.

The question-and-answer session is a good example of verbal feedback in which the audience has an opportunity to seek clarification, to verify the speaker's positions on issues, and to challenge the speaker's arguments. In any case, feedback, like the thermostat on a furnace or an air conditioner, is the speaker's monitoring device that continuously indicates whether the message is effective.

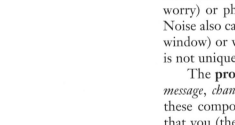

Situation

Communication occurs in a context called the **situation**—*the time, place, and occasion in which the message sending and receiving occurs*. The situation can determine what kind of message is appropriate. Only certain kinds of messages and speakers are acceptable at funerals, debates, elementary school meetings, bar mitzvahs, court hearings, and dedications. In the classroom, the situation is a room of a certain size, containing a number of people who fill a specified number of seats. The physical setting can mean that you can talk almost conversationally or that you must shout to be heard.

To apply this idea of situation in public speaking, and to link the idea to civic engagement, think of how often in your experience a speech is expected. Does a politician ever make a public appearance without a speech? How often does a graduation occur without a student or guest speaker? Do you expect words to be spoken at religious services? A uniting feature in all human communities is the ritual presentation that we expect to hear to commemorate the specific occasion.

Noise

Another component of the communication process is **noise**, *interference or obstacles to communication*. Noise can be internal, in which case it can be mental (daydreaming or worry) or physical (headache or illness). Internal noise is unique to the individual. Noise also can be external, in which case it can be auditory (a jackhammer outside the window) or visual (sunlight in your eyes). External noise can affect one or many and is not unique to the individual.

The **process of communication** is *the dynamic interrelationship of source, receiver, message, channel, feedback, situation, and noise*. In actual, real-life presentations, all of these components function simultaneously and continuously. For example, let's say that you (the source) are trying to convince fellow workers (the receivers) that they should unionize (message). You argue first that the union will result in higher pay (message). The audience appears unimpressed (feedback), so you argue that the union will bring such benefits as better working conditions (message). They doze (feedback). Finally you argue that the workers will get better medical and dental plans for their families, reducing their out-of-pocket health expenses (message). This argument gets attentive looks, some questions, and considerable interest (feedback). The audience has influenced the source and the message through feedback.

"The speaker conveys a message through words and action, but the audience gives meaning to that message through its own thought processes."

The speaker conveys a message through words and action, but the audience gives meaning to that message through its own thought processes. Audiences interpret messages; they construct messages of their own from the words they hear; and they carry with them their own version of the message. Politicians slather their presentations with abstractions that audiences interpret in their own ways. The more abstract the language, the greater are the possible interpretations. "I stand for family values," says a politician. The listeners from a variety of different kinds of families can interpret this message to mean that the politician is embracing their particular family.

The process of communication is a transaction between source and receivers that includes mutual influence, the interpretation and construction of meaning, and the development of an individualized message that includes how others respond. What is **communication**? *A transaction in which speaker and listener simultaneously send, receive, and interpret messages.* In public speaking, the temptation is to see the action as predominantly one-way communication: The speaker sends words to the audience. However, in many public speaking situations, the audience influences the speaker through continuous feedback, sometimes with words and actions and sometimes almost subconsciously.

To demonstrate the powerful effect of the audience on the speaker, a teacher challenged his class to influence his behavior. One rule was that the moment he knew they were trying to influence him, the game was over. The class had to figure out what they could do to encourage some kind of behavioral change. After 10 weeks, the teacher had not caught the class trying to influence him. They had documented, however, that, when the experiment began, the teacher stroked his chin once or twice each class period. They decided that the teacher would feel rewarded if they paid more attention, asked questions, and showed interest whenever this behavior occurred. Every time the teacher touched his chin, the class subtly rewarded him with their interest, attention, and questions. By the end of the 10-week course, they had the teacher touching his chin more than 20 times each class session—and the teacher was totally unaware of this influence.

The point of this anecdote is that audiences do influence speakers. In a public rally against gang proliferation and violence, they might do so with the words they yell, the movements and noises they make, or even with the signs they hold. In class, audience influence could be the sight of heads nodding or eyes glazing over. The fact is that speakers influence audiences, audiences influence speakers, and speakers and audiences influence each other continuously in public speaking situations. See Figure 1.1 for a model of the presentation process.

Why Is Public Speaking a Unique Form of Communication?

Public speaking has some unique features that are important for you to know. However, in some ways, public speaking is like enhanced conversation. Teachers often praise students for using conversational, everyday language with their classroom audiences. When you meet someone for a friendly conversation, you normally greet (introduction), talk about something (body), and say goodbye (conclusion). Classroom presentations tend to be about serious issues, but so do many conversations. Yet, the language of conversation has fewer rules—you can say just about anything in any manner to a close friend—and conversation has turn-taking, which is usually reserved for the question-and-answer portion of a presentation. In contrast to everyday conversation, the language of presentations is more carefully chosen to appeal to a larger group. However, both in conversation and in presentations you basically are trying to get some message across to another person. Here are some additional unique features of public presentations, especially classroom speeches.

Brief. Public speaking presentations typically are short. Ronald Reagan, who was called "The Great Communicator," once said that no speech should last more than 20

Figure 1.1   **The presentation process shows a speaker and an audience simultaneously sending and receiving messages while constructing meaning.**

minutes. He meant that 20 minutes is about all an audience can tolerate. Most of your speeches will be considerably shorter.

Simple. You cannot say much in five minutes, especially when you consider that the introductory portion of the speech often takes one minute and the conclusion takes about half a minute. How much can you say about any subject in the remaining three-and-a-half minutes? Complex topics must be simplified, complicated topics may have to be covered in parts, and deep topics may have to be introduced rather than thoroughly vetted. In his Gettysburg Address in 1863, U.S. President Abraham Lincoln delivered a "deep speech" in about three-and-a-half minutes.

Limited. Even though bulleted lists are common and most everyone knows "The Top Ten Reasons" format, you need to limit your speech to very few main points—usually two or three. Why? Because people do not remember much. Even if you ask your audience, "What were my three main points?" you will be lucky if they remember one or two. Can you remember a politician's position on global warming, stem cell research, hate crime, or literacy? Probably not. We tend to remember brief declarations such as "No more taxes," "No more war," and "Jobs for all."

Important. You need to have something important to say. A beautifully delivered speech about a trivial topic is still an empty shell, but an important or timely topic can have impact even if the delivery is uninspiring. We listen carefully to messages that are important to us.

What Topics Should You Talk About?

In a public speaking class, some topics work better than others. The following are some practical guidelines to help you think of topics.

Choose vital topics. This book encourages students to select topics on important issues. Among these important topics are the ones in the list on this page.

From any of these broad areas of concern, you could generate dozens of possible topics for your speeches—topics that you can make interesting and relevant to you and your classmates.

Choose current topics. Audiences prefer speakers who talk about issues that are affecting them right now. The speaker who can figure out what important issues are of concern to the audience at the moment will have a topic that wins the hearts and minds of the audience.

Choose topics that improve the audience. What can your audience do to change policies (democracy), increase their buying power (economics), improve their classes (education), or increase their social media competence (technology)? Any of these vital topics can improve audience lives and make you a valued source of information and ideas.

You can learn to be an effective speaker by choosing vital topics, selecting a current topic, and picking a topic that improves the audience, the community, and/or the country or world.

Democracy
Environment
Technology
Education
Diversity
Ethics
Health
Economy

What Should You Avoid in a Presentation?

Communication teachers believe in freedom of speech. We think that Americans should be allowed to talk about almost anything. All freedoms have limits, however. Although you can talk about almost anything in this country, here are some suggestions for topics and approaches to avoid in the classroom.

Avoid exhausted topics unless you have a new approach. Remember, your speech teacher hears many speeches. Some topics have been talked about so often without making much headway that hearing them again makes the teacher's head throb. Gun control and abortion rights are a couple of examples. But exhausted topics like gun control and abortion rights can gain new life when discussed in the context of an upcoming presidential election, or an event in the news that lends the topic currency.

Avoid illegal items lest you end up suspended or in jail. Most campuses do not allow alcohol, drugs, weapons, or bombs. So do not advocate using them, especially by showing them in class. On the other hand, you can argue that something currently illegal ought to be legalized: assisted suicide, medical marijuana, or a drinking age of 18. If you have doubts about the legality or appropriateness of your topic, then you should get your teacher's opinion before you speak.

Avoid insulting your audience. Because one of the goals of this course is to teach you how to influence others through public speaking, you need to be careful what you say about others. Ethnic slurs, cultural slights, racial epithets, street lingo, swearing, and attacks on religious beliefs of others may be legal, but they certainly are unwise choices. Saying something in a classroom speech that would get you in trouble on the street or in a bar requires careful consideration on your part. You can avoid insulting your audience by always approaching them with an attitude of respect.

Plagiarism: Serious Warning about Cheating

Teachers across the country are reporting an increasing number of students who get in serious trouble because they commit **plagiarism**, *the intentional use of information*

from a source without crediting that source. Scholars regard plagiarism as a form of stealing, the theft of someone else's words or ideas. Because we do not want you to get into any difficulty over this offense, this warning reveals the problem and the solution.

The problem is taking someone else's words or ideas and claiming them as your own by not including a footnote or endnote in writing or an oral citation or oral footnote in speaking.

For example, a student giving a presentation about the Supreme Court's first decision on Arizona's controversial immigration law finds on the Internet this passage from the *Los Angeles Times*: "The Supreme Court gave a big boost to proponents of stricter state laws against illegal immigration by upholding Arizona's 'business death penalty' for employers who repeatedly hire undocumented workers."[3] The student also finds on the Internet this direct quote from *The New York Times*: "The Supreme Court is set to hear arguments next week challenging the most controversial sections of an Arizona immigration law, known as SB 1070, which seeks to push illegal immigrants out of the state by making it hard for them to go about their lives and earn a living."[4] The student takes these two quotes to create this one for the presentation (the plagiarized words are in italics):

> *Proponents of* Arizona's continuing effort *to push illegal immigrants out of the state by making it hard for them to go about their lives and earn a living got a big boost when the Supreme Court upheld the business death penalty for employers who repeatedly hire undocumented workers.*

By mixing the words (all in italics) of two sources, neither of which is identified, this student commits plagiarism. The student could have avoided plagiarism by saying in his presentation: "According to *The New York Times* of April 18, 2012, Arizona's new immigration law "seeks to push illegal immigrants out of the state. . . ." And a new Supreme Court decision encouraged those who favor strict immigration policies by upholding a "business death penalty" that punishes employers "who repeatedly hire undocumented workers," according to the *Los Angeles Times* of May 26, 2012.

The following are acts of plagiarism.

- Copying part or all of another person's speech or outline as if it were your own.
- Copying part or all of a speech or outline lifted from the Internet.
- Paraphrasing (putting someone else's words into your own words) without citing a source.

If you are unsure about whether something requires a verbal citation or a footnote, you should ask your teacher.

Every college and university has a student code of conduct that reveals the punishments for plagiarism. They often range from flunking the assignment to failing the course to being expelled. Many colleges and universities supply their faculty with software for detecting plagiarism. Finally, cultural differences occur in this issue, so international students need to be aware that colleges and universities in the United States abide by a strict interpretation of the rules against plagiarism. Do your own work, and credit others when you use their words or ideas.

Tools for Detecting Plagiarism

Some instances of plagiarism occur because of a lack an understanding of how to properly provide source citations; others result from simple errors of omission—you literally forget to cite a source and do not catch that error in the revision process. Teachers are quite good at sensing when the wording of a particular sentence or section of an outline comes from another source. Using tools on the Internet, you can easily check your work for material that could be identified as plagiarism. If you go to **dustball.com**, you can copy and paste your entire outline into a search engine and the site will compare your wording to sources on the web. The analysis will flag phrases that could potentially be considered plagiarism; you can then carefully review the phrase or phrases to determine whether proper citations were included. This tool can assist you in avoiding errors and misunderstandings.

iConnect

Becoming an Effective Speaker

You play the most important role in making a presentation. You choose the message, you analyze the listeners, you organize the message, and you deliver the message. A presentation is always a dance, however, in which the speaker (one dance partner) uses a message (the music) to influence the listener (the other dance partner).

The Speaker's Source Credibility

Some students think they must receive a complete makeover before they can be public speakers. They may see themselves as shy, fearful of audiences, or just cautious in front of a group. They may think they have to look and sound like an entertainer, a famous preacher, or a broadcaster. Actually, the notion of a complete makeover is not possible or desirable. If all speakers looked and sounded alike, then we would grow weary of hearing them speak. If you are not funny now, this course is unlikely to make you humorous. If you are not a live wire now, this course is unlikely to make you crackle with energy. And if you lack charisma, this course is unlikely to turn you into the most popular person in the room. If you really concentrate on communicating your message to your audience in a caring and conversational manner, then you will not have to worry about how you look.

A beginning speaker can develop three areas that have been the cornerstones of public speaking for well over 2,000 years. The ancient Greek philosopher Aristotle called them *ethos*, *logos*, and *pathos*. We call them source credibility, logical argument, and emotional argument. You need credibility (*ethos*) to inspire an audience to listen to an emotional story (*pathos*) that is backed by an argument (*logos*) for change. We will look most closely in this chapter at you—the source—and how "who you are" and "what you are" affect your influence on an audience. Later, in the chapter on persuasion, we will examine logical and emotional argument.

Aristotle
384–322 BCE

Benjamin Franklin
1706–1790 CE

What Aristotle called ethos is called "source credibility" today. Benjamin Franklin likened a person's reputation to glass and china: once cracked it is never quite the same again. He was speaking of **source credibility**, *the audience's perception of your effectiveness as a communicator.* Your effectiveness is not based just on presentation or delivery skills but more on what you know and how effectively you communicate your ideas to the audience.

One means of establishing a relationship with your audience is to use **common ground**—*pointing out what features you share with your audience when you speak on vital topics like the environment, health, and education:* "All of us have noticed that our air quality is poor here," "We students need to balance learning with keeping physically healthy," and "What courses should qualify as general education credits?"

A second means of establishing source credibility is establishing trustworthiness. **Trustworthiness** is *the degree to which the audience perceives the presenter as honest and honorable.* A student in one author's public speaking class came unprepared. Because the assignment was brief (just the introductory portion of his presentation), he listened carefully to the first five speakers and then confidently jumped to his feet to deliver a two-minute introduction full of facts and figures. After his presentation, classmates inquired about his claim that 4,000 people died from eating junk food during the Super Bowl. The student admitted that he had made up all the facts and figures while the other students were delivering their presentations. After that, the class never fully trusted him because he had lied so obviously in his first presentation. Trust is difficult to earn but easy to lose.

A third technique for encouraging your audience to listen to you is to display **competence**, *a thorough understanding of your topic.* For example, an agriculture major might demonstrate her competence in organic gardening by showing how to compost, irrigate, and manage pests. You can accomplish the same purpose by presenting topics about which you have some expertise beyond most people in your class, or topics that you have researched thoroughly.

A fourth feature that encourages your audience to pay attention to you is **dynamism**, *the energy you expend in delivering your message.* Typically, audiences are attracted by movement, gestures, facial expression, and voice variety—all delivery characteristics. Think about this comparison. Would you rather watch a presenter who is difficult

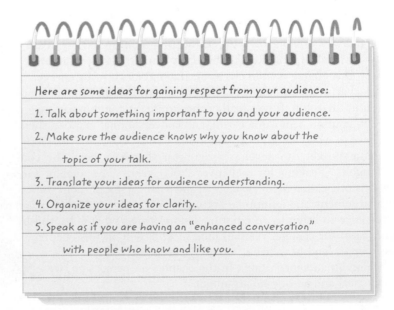

Here are some ideas for gaining respect from your audience:

1. Talk about something important to you and your audience.

2. Make sure the audience knows why you know about the topic of your talk.

3. Translate your ideas for audience understanding.

4. Organize your ideas for clarity.

5. Speak as if you are having an "enhanced conversation" with people who know and like you.

Figure 1.2   **Tips for gaining respect from your audience.**

to hear, rarely looks up from the notes, lacks facial expression, speaks in one tone, and never moves or gestures? Or would you rather watch someone who is lively and maybe even a bit dramatic, someone who can whisper and shout, someone who moves, points, and exclaims during the presentation? Listeners tend to respond favorably to presenters whose manner reflects their sincerity and conviction about the subject matter. For tips on gaining audience respect, see Figure 1.2.

The good news is that you do not have to be a top performer in all aspects of credibility. You might, for example, be exceedingly strong on trustworthiness but not be particularly dynamic, or you might be highly competent but not have much in common with your listeners. Play to your strengths without feeling that you have to be at the top of every dimension of source credibility. You don't need a personality makeover if you just do your best to establish common ground, remain trustworthy, demonstrate competence, and exude some passion for your vital topic.

Listening

Winston Churchill once said these wise words: "Courage is what it takes to stand up and speak; courage is also what it takes to sit down and listen."[5] Audience members decide in seconds what they think of a presenter, and what they think of a presenter may determine whether they are merely **hearing** (*receiving sound waves*) or **listening** (*interpreting the sounds as a message*). Hearing is physiological: You cannot keep from picking up the sounds unless you always leave your iPod on high. Listening is a psychological process: You need to attend to, think about, and interpret meaning from the sounds. For suggestions on listening, see Figure 1.3.

You probably listen differently in different situations: passive listening to background music in your car or home and active listening when the sounds demand full attention. Active listening is characterized by posture (forward lean, head cocked for better reception), facial features (eyes alert and on the source of the message), and movement (hand cupped on the ear, hand taking notes). You might be a passive listener when your teacher is giving examples of a concept you already understand, but you are likely to be an active listener when your teacher says the words, "What I am telling you next will be on the test." Listening actively in conversation can make you a valued friend, mate, or partner.

Listening actively in class is often the difference between the student who earns poor grades and the one who earns good grades. In the public speaking classroom,

1. Avoid Distractions.
   Sit so the presenter is your main focus, in front of the room, away from talkative friends, away from distracting sounds and sights.

2. Actively Engage.
   Watch attentively, write down important points and useful observations, note what is not being said, and ask questions for clarification.

3. Be Thoughtful.
   What are the presenter's main points? Were they supported well? Do you agree with the message? Why or why not?

Figure 1.3 **Tips for listening during a presentation.**

active listening not only allows you to learn from the content of other speakers, but it invites you to learn what delivery skills are most effective with your audience.

How to Reduce Your Fear of Presenting

Effective presenters learn to manage their natural nervousness so that their delivery is not damaged. In fact, they often regard "stage fright" positively. Just as athletes feel an adrenaline rush before a big game and entertainers get "keyed up" before a performance, experienced public speakers know the initial nervousness will pass and likely will be transformed to positive energy. Although most of us feel apprehension when presenting in public, we typically get over this natural nervousness quickly. This is not to say that you will never be nervous. The point is that experienced presenters recognize that some nervousness is natural, and they take strategic steps to minimize the possibility that natural nervousness will become so severe that their delivery becomes less conversational. Let's identify these strategies, because nearly everyone experiences some fear when presenting in front of an audience.

Students with high levels of anxiety practically set themselves up for failure.

Understanding Communication Apprehension

The fear of presenting is called **communication apprehension (CA)**, or *an individual's level of fear or anxiety associated with either real or anticipated communication with another person or persons.*[6] Symptoms of CA include sleeplessness, worry, reluctance before you present, and "interfering, off-task thoughts" while you present.[7] Thinking "off-task thoughts" means losing focus on communicating your message to your audience by concentrating instead on sweaty palms, shaking knees, and "cotton mouth," the feeling that your tongue is swollen and your mouth is as dry as the Sahara. One wit noted that public presenters suffer so often from wet palms and dry mouth that they should stick their hands in their mouths.

What else do we know about CA? Students with high levels of anxiety practically set themselves up for failure. Students high in anxiety exhibit "less audience adaptation, less concern for equipment likely to be available when the speech was presented, less concern about the tools available to aid in preparing the speech, more difficulty in coming up with information for speeches, and greater self-doubts about one's capability as a speaker."[8] On the other hand, CA is not correlated with age, sex, or grade-point average,[9] and students with the highest anxiety in public communication courses "showed the largest improvement in perceived competence."[10]

Reducing Anxiety

What can you do to reduce the anxiety that you are likely to feel before speaking? What thoughts can you think, what actions can you take, and what precautions can you observe to help you shift attention from yourself to your message and your audience? The following six keys to confidence can help you reduce your fear of public speaking.

1. *Act confidently.* Actions can change attitudes. You may act as if you like others before you really do. You dress up for a party, and as a result, act in a certain way. You decide that you are going to have fun at a social event, and you do.

You can use the same strategy when you present by thinking of public speaking as acting. You can say to yourself, "I am going to behave in a confident manner when I speak" and then proceed to act confidently even if you are not. This action is not much different from acting cool on the street, playing the role of the intellectual in class, or pretending you are a sports hero in a game. You are simply acting as if you are confident standing in front of the class. Our students suggest the following: Move to the front of the room as if you own it and act as if the audience respects you and wants to hear your words.

CULTURAL DIFFERENCES IN PRESENTATIONS

Speakers from different countries of origin often behave differently when they speak. After working with African American students at Howard University; working with students from Korea, Malaysia, and Thailand; and frequent visits to Africa and Scandinavia and 40 other cultures, the authors have observed the following: Scandinavian and many Asian women cover their mouths when they smile, laugh, or giggle. Puerto Ricans, Italians, Slovenians, and Israelis tend to use gestures and facial expressions more freely than others. Finns, Swedes, Norwegians, and Native Americans are relatively unexpressive. Many Pacific Rim women are reluctant to speak loudly, and African-American men and women are particularly good at being expressive.

cultural NOTE

2. *Know your subject.* Your first presentation should be about something you know already. This early experience should not require very much research. In fact, many teachers will ask you to talk about yourself. Whether you speak about some aspect of yourself or some other topic, you will be a better presenter if you choose a subject that you know something about.

When LaMarr Doston, a 30-year-old father of three, was assigned to give his first presentation, he could think of nothing about himself that he wanted to share with the class. He was glad that he did not have to do research for the presentation, but he was unhappy that he did not know what to say about himself. After two days of worrying, LaMarr was in his office at work when he thought of what he was going to say: "I am LaMarr Doston, the Fast-Food King."

LaMarr had worked for five different fast-food chains over the years. He worked his way from a mop jockey at one place, to counter server at another, to fry cook at a third, to night shift manager at a fourth, and now morning shift manager at the fifth fast-food chain. LaMarr was good at his work, promoted frequently, commended often, and recommended highly. He seemed to know every job at a fast-food outlet. He was the Fast-Food King.

3. *Care about your subject.* Amanda Carroll gave an introductory presentation about being adopted and bi-ethnic. Amanda had one African American biological parent and one European-American biological parent. As a baby, she was put up for adoption in a small Ohio town and raised by white parents. Amanda was very perceptive. She knew that people wondered about her origins because of her appearance. She satisfied the audience's curiosity and provided an added dimension by discussing the satisfaction of being chosen as a baby by parents who wanted and loved her.

If your teacher wants you to speak on a topic other than yourself, you should make sure that you select a subject that you know and care about. Avoid, in general, politically charged issues, but do select a topic in which you are passionately interested. The more you care about your subject, the more you are going to focus on the message and the audience instead of worrying about yourself.

4. *See your classmates as friends.* No audience is more concerned about your success than your classmates in a beginning public speaking course. They worry about you so much that if you should falter, they break into a sweat. They care how you do. See them as friends instead of uncaring strangers, and your perceptions will help you feel confident in front of the classroom. Our

TABLE 1.1 STATEMENTS OF NEGATIVE AND POSITIVE SELF-ASSESSMENT	
STATEMENTS OF NEGATIVE SELF-ASSESSMENT	STATEMENTS OF POSITIVE SELF-ASSESSMENT
• "I will forget what I am supposed to say."	• "I can prepare well enough to succeed in my presentation."
• "I will turn red when I get nervous."	• "Each time I practiced the presentation I felt better about it."
• "My presentation will be boring."	• "People usually respect my opinion on things."
• "I do not know enough about anything to speak on it."	• "I can come up with something to say about anything."

own students suggest that you begin talking only when you are ready, and that you look at the people in your audience before starting. While speaking, focus on the friendly faces—those who smile, nod, and generally make you feel good about your speech.

5. *See yourself as successful.* If you are an inexperienced presenter, you may need to work at thinking positively about your prospects as a public presenter. You need to think about, and then rehearse in your mind, how you are going to give your presentation. Some people might call this "worrying," but psychologists call it "mental imaging." Whatever you call this mindfulness, you can use it to help you succeed. Consider the difference between the statements of negative and positive self-assessment in Table 1.1. Thinking about your presentation in a positive way will not eliminate all nervousness, but upbeat thinking will keep your nervousness from becoming harmful.

6. *Practice for confidence.* More and better practice reduces nervousness. Indeed, research has demonstrated that this is the case.[11] Our own students recommend having your introduction, main points, and conclusion clear in your head. The more times you practice, the less nervous you will feel. Also, the more closely your practice sessions resemble your actual speaking experience—including an audience, for example—the less nervous you will feel. Although you should not practice your presentation to the point of memorization, you should not overlook the importance of practicing several times over the span of a couple of days.

Make sure that you take every opportunity to stand in front of the class before class begins and as your classmates leave the room. You need to see what the class looks like from the front before you give your speech. Unless you have been a teacher, a business trainer, or have had other opportunities to speak in front of groups, you do not know what an audience looks like from the front of the room. The more you get accustomed to that sight before you give your speech, the more comfortable you will be.

Most college classrooms are empty for some hours during the day or evening. Have some of your friends listen to your presentation as you practice your message in an empty classroom. The experience will be very close to what you will encounter when you actually give your presentation. The practice will make you more confident.

You should be careful not to have unrealistic expectations. Not everyone starts from the same place. People of all ages, cultures, nationalities, and experiences populate colleges today. Some students have been active in the workplace for years. Some have come to college with half a lifetime or more of experience; others have very little experience and may even be uncertain about their command of the English language. Your job in this class is to work on building your confidence, so you can spend a lifetime working on your competence and your effectiveness with audiences in public communication situations. For example, an occasional vocalized pause may not even be noticed if you are involved with the message and the audience, and they are focused on your message. Perfection is not really the goal; communicating effectively is the aim of this course.

For REVIEW >>

SUMMARY HIGHLIGHTS

Speaking Excites

▶ Nearly everyone gets a rush from standing in front of an audience.

▶ Almost always, our fears before speaking turn out to be an exaggeration—nobody dies of heart failure, faints, or falls on the floor.

Why Study Public Speaking?

▶ Your public speaking course can help you become a fully functioning member of your local community.

▶ Being a practiced citizen in a democratic society depends on knowing about current issues and being able to speak about them in conversations, in speeches, and even through the mass media.

Do People Really Speak Anymore?

▶ Despite people's belief that the emergence of electronic transmission of sound and image would render public speaking obsolete, speakers are in demand more than ever before.

What Is the Presentation Process?

▶ The presentation process involves the seven components of communication: a source, a receiver, a message, a channel, feedback, a situation, and noise.

Why Is Public Speaking a Unique Form of Communication?

▶ Public speaking is unique in that time is short, making simplification of your points necessary. This also means that you must choose important topics and limit the number of points you present.

What Topics Should You Talk About?

▶ You should aim to discuss vital topics like those to do with the environment, ethics, technology, or diversity, for instance.

▶ You should also choose current topics, and those that will improve the perspectives and actions of those in your audience.

What Should You Avoid in a Presentation?

▶ You should avoid presenting on exhausted topics, using illegal objects or substances as part of your speech, and insulting your audience with offensive language or tone.

Becoming an Effective Speaker

▶ Some tips for gaining the respect of your audience include addressing topics that matter to them, translating your ideas for their understanding, organizing your ideas for clarity, and speaking as if you are having an "enhanced conversation" with people you know and like.

▶ Effective public speaking also requires good listening skills.

How to Reduce Your Fear of Presenting

▶ You can reduce anxiety by acting confidently, knowing and caring about your subject, seeing your classmates as friends, seeing yourself as successful, and practicing.

1. The means of distributing the message is the component of the communication process known as the
   (A) situation   (C) feedback
   (B) channel   (D) noise

2. Which word best describes communication?
   (A) one-way   (C) transactional
   (B) uncomplicated (D) simple

3. When choosing a topic, you should *avoid* topics that
   (A) are current
   (B) improve the audience
   (C) are overused
   (D) are vital

4. Using a speech, outline, or manuscript from a source other than you, without an oral citation, is termed
   (A) dynamic interaction
   (B) plagiarism
   (C) communication apprehension
   (D) common ground

5. Audience members nodding or asking questions following a presentation are examples of
   (A) plagiarism   (C) feedback
   (B) dynamism   (D) self-assessment

Answers: 1 (B); 2 (C); 3 (C); 4 (B); 5 (C)

pop Quiz

APPLICATION EXERCISES

1. Introduce yourself to your classmates by stating your name and whatever you want them to remember about you. Some ideas: year in school, jobs, armed forces, public service, family, place of origin, travel, languages, talents, special skills, unusual hobbies, different experiences.

2. Talk in groups of three to five students for 15 minutes about what you can do to reduce your apprehension about public speaking. Have one person in each group take notes so the groups can share their best ideas with the class after the discussion. The purpose is to allow you to reduce anxiety and to learn some practices to reduce anxiety.

3. Write down as many ideas as you can remember about how to make an effective public presentation. After writing down as many as you remember, you should open the text and add as many more as you can find. The purpose is to mentally reinforce early in the course some of the guidelines for effective presenting.

KEY TERMS

Channel	Hearing	Receiver
Common ground	Listening	Situation
Communication	Message	Source
Communication apprehension (CA)	Noise	Source credibility
Competence	Nonverbal messages	Trustworthiness
Dynamism	Plagiarism	Verbal messages
Feedback	Process of communication	

2

PREPARING

The title of this chapter is probably a little misleading. Odds are that everyone reading this chapter has already given speeches before: a speech to a club like 4H, a speech as a part of a high school class, or a speech as part of your job. All of these are real and meaningful speaking experiences. However, one of the skills you will learn and practice in this class is adaptation—how you adapt to each unique speaking situation in which you find yourself. In that sense, going back to square one and thinking about your speeches in this class as if they were among your first is probably smart.

YOUR FIRST PRESENTATION

Today, with the rapid dissemination of many social networking services like Facebook, Twitter, LinkedIn, MySpace, and Badoo, you have probably spent a great deal of time communicating with others. Consider your messages on such social networks. Have you ever read a post that paints the writer in a negative light? Have you viewed disclosures that might be troubling to parents or friends? Have you considered how your posts might be seen by potential employers? While social networking is not the primary topic of this text, the connection between the speaking you do and the writing you post on various sites is worthy of discussion. In both public speaking and networking, a consideration of your audience—and the potential long-term positive and negative effects of your messages—is essential.

This chapter helps you reorient your understanding of public speaking by introducing you to the Five Canons of Rhetoric, a useful way of thinking about the process of preparing a speech, as well as tips for preparing your initial presentations in this class.

You have heard dozens of speeches or excerpts from speeches. Humorists like Amy Poehler and Stephen Colbert offered commencement speeches this past spring at Harvard and Northwestern Universities, respectively, that were filled with humor. By contrast, Sheryl Sandburg spoke at Barnard's class of 2011 graduation and delivered this serious message to young women, "Men run the world. We will never close the achievement gap if we don't close the ambition gap." Meanwhile, at the University of Pennsylvania, Denzel Washington told graduates that success cannot occur without failure. Imagine that you were asked to provide a commencement speech for the high school you attended. What would you tell the graduating class? Would you be funny, serious, use stories, or reminisce about your time as a student at the high school? You have many choices to make, and this chapter will get you started on a first speech.

During the past two years, you have probably heard many political speeches by U.S. presidential candidates, as well as people running for other offices. Some of those speakers used logos, or logic, while others used pathos, or emotional arguments. Nearly all of the speakers developed their source credibility by establishing common ground with the audience, by showing that they were trustworthy, by demonstrating their competence, and by being dynamic speakers. We discussed these approaches to establishing your credibility in the last chapter, and you will see that they remain important as we discuss the first speech.

Foundations of Public Communication

This section of the chapter introduces you to the Five Canons of Rhetoric. The Five Canons have been used since the time of ancient Greece to help students of rhetoric and oratory understand the essential principles of preparing and presenting a well-crafted speech. Although their application has been updated to reflect changing times and cultures, their straightforward presentation of the speech preparation process is a perfect place for your study of public speaking to begin.

The Roots of Rhetoric: The Five Canons

Public speaking is essential to the smooth functioning of democracy. Whether or not you agree with people in the major political parties, their speeches do allow candidates for public office to remain significantly engaged in civic life. If you wanted to become civically engaged, how would you do so? You might volunteer in your community, you might donate money, but at some point you will likely feel compelled to give a speech. In fact, one could argue that meaningful civic engagement cannot happen unless one speaks out to persuade or form solidarity with others.

The **Five Canons of Rhetoric** were created by Greek philosophers to help teach civic-minded students ways in which they could use rhetoric and oratory as tools of civic life. Making speeches about the virtues of taxation, declarations of war, and maintenance of infrastructure was just as relevant in 5th-century Athens, Greece, as it is today, and the best way to guide action on these topics is to present compelling public arguments. The Five Canons are a useful starting point for your study of public speaking. Table 2.1 describes the Five Canons and suggests key skills associated with each one.

1. Invention

A common misunderstanding about public communication is that style is more important than substance—how you say your message is more important than what you say. This misunderstanding is a natural by-product of television because we constantly see politicians and other professional speakers talking in carefully edited sound bites. If you attend club meetings, classes, or civic groups, however, you will quickly see that substance is more important because few of us are expert speakers.

The substance of your presentation is directly tied to the **invention** process, which is *the art of finding information*. Invention deals with everything from selecting a topic for your presentation to locating examples, statistics, and other forms of supporting material. From ancient to modern times, speakers have used several approaches to invention.[1] In general, invention attempts to (1) look at a problem from all sides, (2) ask the right questions, (3) select relevant information, (4) find new ways of talking about old topics, and (5) find new analogies and relationships between things.

Mae Lin was asked by her teacher to prepare a speech about an important social issue. Because Mae grew up in California, she was well aware of the Occupy Student

> *"A common misunderstanding about public communication is that style is more important than substance—how you say your message is more important than what you say."*

TABLE 2.1   SKILLS ASSOCIATED WITH THE FIVE CANONS OF RHETORIC

DESCRIPTION OF CANON	KEY SKILLS
1 INVENTION *Finding information for your presentation*	To engage in the invention process you should: • Determine the goal of the presentation. • Determine issues related to your topic. • Determine how you can use ethos, pathos, and logos in your speech. • Predict what your audience wants and needs to know. • Conduct research to supplement your personal knowledge.
2 ORGANIZATION *Selecting an appropriate arrangement and structure for a presentation*	To engage in effective organization you should: • Prepare an introduction. • Organize main points and supporting material for the body of the presentation. • Develop a conclusion that summarizes the presentation and ends with impact.
3 STYLE *Using clear and ornamental language*	To effectively use style you should: • Avoid technical language unless necessary. • Define important terms. • Arrange words using patterns appropriate for oral presentation. • Use metaphors, analogy, and creative language to increase artful ornamentation.
4 UNDERSTANDING *Being able to recall main ideas and details in your presentation*	To effectively use understanding you should: • Prepare a planning outline of your ideas. • Prepare a shortened presentation outline that will help keep you on track during the presentation. • Engage in extemporaneous delivery to maximize eye contact and conversational delivery.
5 DELIVERY *Using effective verbal and nonverbal behaviors to maximize the effectiveness of your message*	To engage in effective delivery you should: • Avoid reading your presentation. • Maintain consistent eye contact. • Be natural with your use of gestures, facial expressions, and movement.

Debt protests that began on both the West Coast and the East Coast. Although Mae was attending a less expensive college in the Midwest, she had several classmates from high school who attended school in California. Their debts exceeded $70,000 and they were told that they had to begin paying them off. The students simply did not know where to turn in light of proposed increases in tuition. Mae decided to interview some of these friends on Skype, by texting them, and even by telephone. Although Mae Lin

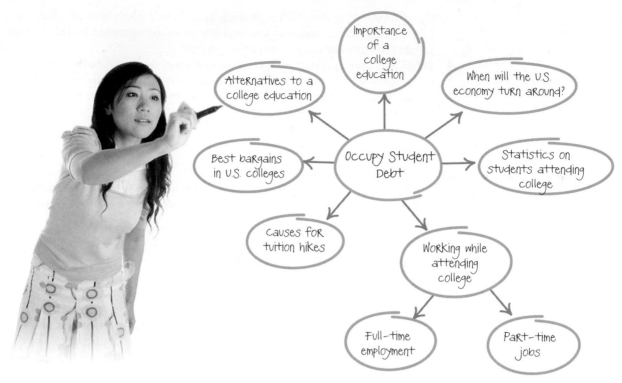

Figure 2.1   **Concept map for Mae Lin's speech about Occupy Student Debt**

was very interested in the topic because of her friends' experiences, she knew that not everyone in her audience would be able to relate to their particular circumstances. So, after doing research, she was able to broaden her approach to include stories about students around the world who were affected by tuition hikes. In so doing, Mae Lin was able to maintain a focus on her friends' stories while at the same time making her speech more relevant to the majority of her classmates.

To follow Mae Lin's lead and effectively engage in the invention process, we recommend that you ask a series of questions about your topic:

1. *What is the goal of the presentation?* Are you primarily trying to teach, persuade, or entertain your audience? Determine what your audience expects and try to approach the topic in a slightly different way. This approach can effectively capture listeners' attention; however, the use of different "angles" should not obscure your intended objective for the presentation.

2. *What general issues are related to your topic?* By brainstorming with a concept map, you can easily identify various subtopics associated with your overall topic. **Concept maps** are *pictures or diagrams that allow you to visualize main and subordinate ideas related to a more general topic.* Narrowing your focus to one or more of the subtopics can help you effectively select relevant information and find new approaches to talking about your topic. This strategy is precisely the one Mae Lin used to talk about Occupy Student Debt. Figure 2.1 provides a concept map related to her presentation. In addition to helping you narrow your focus, a concept map can also assist you in identifying points to include in your preparation outline.

3. *How can you use ethos, pathos, and logos in your speech?* Aristotle's original discussion of invention noted that speakers use three forms of proof to persuade: ethos, pathos, and logos. Ethos refers to the ethical proof, which today we tend to interpret as credibility. Pathos is when the speaker uses emotions to motivate the audience. Logos is the use of logical argument. One of the arts of speaking, according to Aristotle, is finding ways to meaningfully integrate these forms of proof. Although each speech will likely use all three, one may be emphasized more or less depending on the situation and skill of the speaker in carrying out the invention process.

4. *What does your audience need to know and want to know?* Anticipating your audience is a key presentation skill. Taking time to carefully consider your audience is wise because it allows you to adapt your message to their wants and needs.

2. Organization

Organization refers to *the arrangement and structure of a presentation*. As you will learn in detail later in the course, many presentations have an introduction, body, and conclusion. Let's begin by understanding the function of each part of the presentation.

1. *The introduction.* The purpose of the introduction is to set the stage for the whole presentation by providing a central idea or thesis statement and previewing the main ideas to be addressed. Effective introductions find a creative way to introduce the topic—often using a story, example, or audience interaction through questions and answers. Finding ways to establish credibility with your audience is also wise.

2. *The body.* Presentations typically consist of two to three main points. Selecting two, three, or four main points will enable listeners to more easily follow your presentation and remember key ideas. Carefully consider how to arrange your facts, testimony, and other evidence when outlining the body of the presentation. In particular, you should ensure that all main points have adequate supporting materials. You should start your planning process by arranging the body of your presentation because key elements of the introduction and conclusion are dependent on your main and subordinate points.

3. *The conclusion.* Effective presentations develop endings that not only summarize content, but also end with impact by using, for instance, quotations or stylistic devices such as metaphors and similes. Simply stating "That's it" or "I'm finished now" is not an effective way to end your presentation.

Knowing how to arrange presentations is challenging because any topic offers multiple options for arranging ideas and evidence, and no single approach is absolutely correct.[2] In subsequent chapters, we offer multiple options for arranging ideas; for now, we recommend that you focus on developing a distinct introduction, clear main points, and a conclusion that brings closure to the presentation by reviewing key ideas.

3. Style

Strictly speaking, **style** refers to *the use and ornamentation of language*. Most efforts to define the concept of style have focused on using clear language. Avoid the use of jargon, define technical terms that might be unfamiliar to your audience, and use language and phrases you have in common.[3] Clarity also describes the way you arrange words. Avoid long sentences with multiple clauses so listeners can more easily follow your presentation—however, many short sentences in a row can actually cause confusion because the ideas come across as choppy and disjointed. As a practical matter, use conversational language and avoid preparing an elaborate script, because our style of writing often differs substantially from what listeners expect to hear from an oral presentation.

Using clear language, in terms of both words and arrangement, is an important skill. Yet, rhetorical scholar Ray Keesey notes that "clarity of style is the first consideration but it is ornament that, properly speaking, makes rhetoric art."[4] While clarity refers to the ease with which we interpret language, **ornamentation** refers to *the creative and artful use of language.* Using ornamental language is certainly one of the most advanced presentation skills that you can learn.

Fortunately, a few strategies can help you begin:

1. *Target certain areas for ornamental language.* When talking about his hobby of studying hurricanes, Steve used simple stylistic wording to improve clarity. His initial working outline contained this statement for the preview of his presentation:

> Today I will discuss the causes and effects of hurricanes.

Steve's wording became much more effective after he edited his preview for style. After editing his initial ideas, Steve changed his preparation outline to read,

> Today I will talk with you about my hobby of studying hurricanes, one of the most common and most powerful weather phenomena many of us will ever see. Since Hurricane Katrina, the impact of these weather events on our country and the world has received much attention. I hope to teach you about hurricanes by first taking you into the eye of the storm to understand how they form, and then twisting through the path of destruction that they can cause.

As you can see, Steve's stylistic approach is much more effective. Adding ornamental language greatly improves Steve's presentation by engaging the audience's imagination.

2. *Use analogies and metaphors.* Analogies and metaphors help you describe something by comparing it to something else. When introducing herself to the class, Cheri used a metaphor to describe her experience of moving to college. "My trip to college is best described as a train wreck because everything that could have gone wrong did go wrong." Such comparisons add vivid description to otherwise common experiences. Accomplished authors make use of stylistic metaphors and analogies to enhance their novels, and presenters can employ similar strategies to captivate audiences.

3. *Use narratives.* As children, we learn to love stories. Many of us cherish memories of hearing our favorite bedtime story, and this love for narrative lasts well into adulthood. Telling stories based on personal experience or other sources of information naturally adds rich description to the issues we examine during presentations. Your own experiences likely confirm this. Your most interesting teachers probably made ample use of stories and examples to enhance their classes. Effective presenters learn quickly that stories and examples bring language to life through vivid descriptions of lived experiences.

In a commencement address delivered to students at Georgetown University, Wendy Kopp, CEO and founder of Teach For America, used narrative to illustrate how teaching can be an important form of community service.[5] During her presentation she told a story about Joe Almeida, a Georgetown graduate who entered the Teach For America program. She explained that Joe started working for a Washington, DC, high school where students had very low expectations for their educational futures. Despite facing numerous challenges, Joe helped students at his high school envision a better future, as Kopp explained in the following narrative.

But Joe went ahead. And, he threw every bit of himself into the effort to accomplish his goals. Among other things he decided to bring all his kids here to Georgetown to help them envision their future as college-going students. When his school could not pay for all the costs of the trip, Joe just went ahead and raised all the money he needed through bake sales and the like. At year's end, Joe's students had made significant progress in catching up academically and had adopted the mindset that college was in their future. As one student said, "This is the first time anyone's expected me to go to college." A mother said, "I didn't think my son would go to college. Now I know it's possible."

> *"Effective presenters learn quickly that stories and examples bring language to life through vivid descriptions of lived experiences."*

By using the narrative about Joe, Kopp was able to accomplish two important tasks: First, she was able to help audience members identify with her message, because Joe Almeida was a fellow Hoya (that is, a Georgetown alumnus). Second, she was able to present an important piece of evidence using stylistic language and vivid imagery. Such evidence can bring life to a speech in ways that other forms of evidence cannot.

4. Understanding

The fourth Canon of Rhetoric was originally labeled as memory. In ancient Greece, libraries were difficult to find, so speakers relied on their memory to retain historical facts, details of current events, statistics, scientific theories, and other information necessary to develop ideas during a speech. Today, we have readily available external resources to supplement our memory. Now, all information resources on the Internet are literally with you as you walk from class to class.

Rather than relying on memory, the term **understanding** might be a more contemporary way of describing this canon. Although you do not need to memorize details to acquire encyclopedic knowledge in order to be an effective speaker, you do have a responsibility to understand ways of interpreting facts. Whereas the greatest challenge facing our parents and older generations of speakers was finding information, the challenge facing you now is making sense of the hundreds of thousands of resources available to you when researching a topic. Interestingly, communication teachers often refer to the fourth canon as "the lost canon" because the emphasis on memory is largely unnecessary, at least in the way Greek teachers of rhetoric approached the topic. When reframed as "understanding," however, this canon might be the most important.

Developing and using skills of understanding is hard to condense into a list of skills like those found in the other canons. Being able to understand the world around you requires skills developed over a lifetime. Nevertheless, here are some ideas on how you can work toward deeper understanding now as a college student.

1. *A liberal arts education is important.* Courses in your general education program help you develop perspectives and capacities for viewing the world from different perspectives. Rather than viewing your "gen ed" courses as things you have to take before you can focus on a major, view them as opportunities to help you understand your world in more detail and with greater appreciation. Even this term you will learn things in other classes that can help you understand your speech topic(s) in deeper ways.

2. *Be cognizant of current events.* A significant step in understanding the world around you is realizing that it is not simple. Following current events, reading the newspaper, listening to the news, following blogs, and even attending meetings in your community will help you gain an understanding of the systemic nature of our social world. By systemic, we mean that one small thing impacts many others. What happens when teachers are laid off to balance a school district's budget? What would happen if everything in our country was dictated by the free market? What would be the effect of fining companies

who move jobs over-seas? These questions have complex answers, and understanding those answers requires ongoing awareness of the issues. Fortunately, as you teach yourself to be a more complex thinker about the world, the process of understanding new things gets easier.

3. *Talk with others. Understanding is not achieved in isolation. Talking* with others to test your ideas and assumptions is critical in helping you *refine* your ideas and understandings. John Dewey, a noted American social critic and theorist, argued that if we want a more democratic nation

VISUAL RHETORIC GOES GLOBAL

Discussion of the Five Canons of Rhetoric underscores the emphasis on spoken rhetoric. After all, most of the Five Canons provide advice on how to best say something. In fact, the dominant Western view of rhetoric places a nearly exclusive emphasis on the spoken word. Several scholars, however, have documented the role of visual rhetoric. For example, communication scholars Paul Booth and Amber Davisson analyzed how visual imagery in photographs related to Hurricane Katrina created powerful rhetorical statements that help define and provide iconic meanings for important events.[6] Such rhetorical use of visual imagery is not unique to America. Pictures of starving children, cruel treatment to protesters, and the violation of women are common on news programs. Indeed, the Internet, cell phone technology, and other forms of digital media could cause visual imagery to become (if it has not already done so) even more important than the spoken word in terms of rhetorical impact.

we have to start by having a democratic relationship with the people that we live with and next to. Taking time to have meaningful conversation is a first step in such relationships. In large part, your public speaking class gives you an opportunity to practice this exact skill!

4. *Be engaged.* Civic engagement means that you care about your community and the society in which all of us live. Engagement means that you are active in helping, however you choose to define that. As you increase your levels of civic engagement you will have a greater appreciation for and understanding of your surroundings. Take time to volunteer. Use your job as an opportunity to learn about how others work and behave. Care about the future of others as much as your own future. Tell others how you feel about things that are important. All of those steps will keep you engaged and will provide valuable learning experiences.

5. Delivery

Delivery includes *the verbal and nonverbal techniques used to present the message.* Professional speakers and politicians are paid thousands of dollars to present speeches, and we have justifiably high expectations for their delivery. The majority of us, however, cannot call upon such skill. We like to use the analogy of baseball. Watching a major league baseball game is enjoyable because the players are able to perform at a very high level— nearly mistake-free. Yet, we also think that the intimacy and humanness of a minor league, college, or even Little League baseball game makes the experience every bit as enjoyable as a trip to Wrigley Field in Chicago. We can effectively deliver presentations without approaching the skill of a Maya Angelou, Jay Leno, Deepak Chopra, or "Magic" Johnson. In fact, the most effective presenters learn that being perfect in their delivery is far less important than being themselves.

YouTube, Blogs, and Vlogs

Whether you are presenting on a topic of your choice or talking about yourself, preparing your first speech can be a challenge. Fortunately, you are not the first person who has been asked to give a speech early in a public speaking class. In fact, you will be amazed by the number of examples you can find simply by searching the Internet. Using the search terms "best speeches," "speeches of introduction," "introducing another person," "demonstration speeches," "funny speeches," or "impromptu speeches," you can find dozens of examples (and lots of advice) that can help you create your first presentation. Many of these examples will be found on YouTube, as well as blogs and vlogs (video blogs). While there is much that can be learned from watching other people's vlogs, you might also consider creating one of your own as you work your way through your public speaking class. Vlogging can be a real confidence builder!

Although you will learn several techniques for effective delivery later in the course, for now we suggest that you begin working on a couple of skills and avoid some of the worst presentation habits:

1. *Don't read your presentation.* Reading from notes is the single most common bad habit presenters develop. This one habit can literally destroy your ability to be naturally effective in your delivery. Minimize your use of notes by practicing your presentation several times. Each time you practice, try to reduce the number of notes that you need. Effective presenters should be able to deliver a five- to seven-minute presentation with only one 3" × 5" card of notes; this might not be practical for your first presentation, but it should be an objective for which you strive.

2. *Maintain consistent eye contact with the audience.* Your eye contact, rather than your voice, is your "secret weapon" as a presenter. Maintaining consistent eye contact causes listeners to perceive you as more confident, competent, and charming. Glancing at your notes is necessary at times, but always looking down at them causes listeners to question whether you are truly prepared for your presentation. During most of your presentation you should look at your audience rather than at your notes.

3. *Be natural with your nonverbal delivery.* We naturally use our hands, body, and face to communicate messages that complement our verbal statements. Although some presenters plan to use various nonverbal behaviors, most presenters are simply encouraged to follow their instincts and do what comes naturally. Unfortunately, many students develop another bad habit—one related to reading their presentation—which diminishes their ability to be natural: tying their hands to a lectern. We commonly see students clutch the lectern, their notes, or even themselves in a death grip because of the natural apprehension accompanying any type of public performance. If your teacher allows you to use a lectern, we recommend that you place your notes on it for easy reference, but that you stand slightly to the side of the lectern. By doing this, you avoid the temptation to hold on to it.

We have now introduced you to five important areas in which you can develop your public speaking skills. Both accomplished and inexperienced presenters rely on these five foundational skills—sometimes implicitly and sometimes explicitly—to prepare and deliver presentations. We will revisit these skills throughout the book, but you are now armed with enough knowledge to begin preparing your first speech.

Tips for Preparing Your First Presentation

Now that you understand some of the foundational skills used to prepare effective presentations, you should begin thinking about how to translate your knowledge into practice and start preparing your first presentation for the class. Although teachers use a variety of approaches for the first presentation, some general strategies can help you effectively prepare for any presentation.

Tips for Planning Your Presentation

1. *Gather materials.* Especially if your first presentation is prepared entirely in class, having materials to work with is important. You should bring notebook paper to use for taking notes, a couple of 3" × 5" note cards to use for your speaking outline, and two colors of pens to prepare your presentation outline on the note cards. You can use one color to indicate main points and the other to list details or subpoints. See Figure 2.2 for an example.

2. *Carefully review the assignment expectations.* Your teacher may provide you with a written assignment description or may discuss the assignment orally in class. Before you begin working on your presentation—or before you come to class, if the presentation will be prepared in class—take care to review all information about the assignment. Summarizing the key expectations in writing will help you remember exactly what you need to do when you begin working.

3. *Use the invention process to accumulate information.* If your teacher allows you to prepare your first presentation outside of class, you have a full array of resources from which to select during the invention process. In addition to using information from the library or the Internet, think carefully about personal experiences and local sources that may be relevant to your topic. Make sure when you use sources of information that you cite those sources during your speech.

Although listening is important throughout the speech preparation process, it is especially important when you are identifying the topic of your speech. Think of the people you find most interesting. They are probably widely read, and they keep up on the news and current events. They probably take a variety of classes and can share information from those classes with you. As you listen to your classmates and your instructor, try to identify those topics that they might find interesting. Later, when you actually deliver your talk, you should observe your classmates to determine how interested they are in your

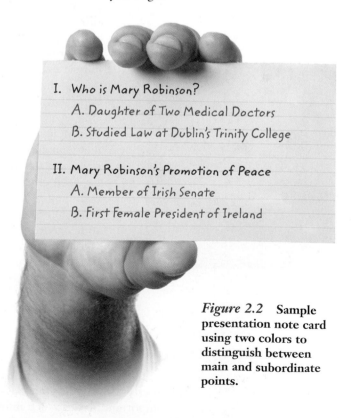

Figure 2.2 **Sample presentation note card using two colors to distinguish between main and subordinate points.**

topic. You should also listen carefully to their speeches because you will gain new knowledge and improve your relationships with others.

4. *Plan to be organized.* Recall that most of your assigned presentations should have an introduction, body, and conclusion. Also remember that most presentations have two to three main points in the body. You can plan in advance by writing headings for these sections on a page in your notebook. Once you begin preparing your presentation, you will simply fill in this template.

5. *Plan to be clear.* Once you have accumulated information during the invention process, the majority of your work should center on developing a clear central idea and main points. Although you may change these points several times as you continue preparing, taking time to plan them first will help you focus your thoughts, and your work will be more efficient. For now, simple wording is most effective; later, you might edit your wording to add style.

6. *When selecting details, focus on quality, not quantity.* Using a well-explained example or statistic is far more important than trying to impress your listeners with the scope of your knowledge. When selecting details to fit under each of your main points, try to select those that are memorable, vivid, and credible. Three quotations from a website such as Wikipedia are far less effective than a statement from a scientific journal or a detailed description of your personal experience because many people view "dot-coms" with skepticism.

7. *Edit for style.* Once you have planned your message, think of ways to "dress up" your style. Can you take the simple wording of your central idea and main points and make them rich by using a metaphor, analogy, or creative wording? Remember that style also involves using clear language. Don't overuse style to the extent that your message is obscured.

8. *If possible, practice, practice, practice.* Some teachers require that the first presentation be prepared and delivered during class, and in such cases, practice is difficult. But you can still practice preparing a speech and delivering it to a roommate or friend. Even if it is on a different topic than the one you deliver in class, you can still rehearse the process. If you are allowed more time to prepare your presentation, plan to practice your talk aloud a minimum of three times.

9. *Plan for effective delivery.* In advance of your presentation, you should carefully visualize what you are going to do when your turn arrives. Remember to minimize your presentation notes and to stand beside the lectern if one is present. As you are delivering your presentation, shift your focus and your eye contact among a handful of people scattered around the room. This practice will help you draw all listeners to your message. Remember that your audience does not expect perfect delivery, especially if your delivery seems natural.

10. *Enjoy the opportunity!* One of the most exciting aspects of a course in public communication is the guaranteed opportunity to talk with peers about topics of interest to you. Such experiences can be exhilarating and even give some students a "rush." If you open your mind to the possibility, we think you can experience a similar feeling. Remember that you are not trying to be a professional public speaker; you are simply trying to meaningfully connect with your listeners. Have fun with the experience!

Common Types of First Presentations

Teachers often use the first classroom presentation to accomplish two primary objectives. First, they usually want you to become familiar with the process of preparing and delivering a classroom presentation. In particular, the first presentation creates an opportunity for you and your classmates to learn more about each other—this knowledge is important because such information will better enable you to adapt future classroom presentations to the specific interests and needs of your audience. Second, teachers typically want you to begin practicing several of the skills necessary for developing and presenting effective presentations. With these two general objectives as a starting point, teachers select from a variety of presentation formats for the first classroom presentation. We provide suggestions for four of the most common types of first presentation assignments: the impromptu presentation, presenting yourself, presenting a classmate, and the demonstration presentation.

Impromptu Presentations

An **impromptu presentation** is *one that does not allow for substantial planning and practice before the presentation is given.* Although you typically are required to develop an introduction, body (with at least two main points), and conclusion, you probably will not be expected to integrate supporting materials such as detailed statistics, quotations, or multiple sources. Teachers typically use this type of assignment to provide you with the experience of presenting ideas to your classmates and to practice thinking on your feet. Impromptu presentations can take many forms. Most of the time, you will have about five minutes to prepare a rough presentation outline. Most teachers will allow you to use a rough presentation outline like the one shown in Figure 2.2.

In a speech before the National Conference of State Legislators in 2009, Joan Detz,[7] a speechwriter, gave several suggestions to politicians who need to master the art of giving a strong, three-minute speech. Among her tips were:

1. *Focus your message and words.* The average American speaks at 140 words per minute. During an impromptu presentation of a couple minutes or slightly longer, you don't have much space to say what you want to say. You should limit your message to one or two specific things.

2. *Think about your audience.* In a short speech, you have to connect quickly and effectively. Irrelevant examples or unclear analysis will cause audience members to tune out because they know the speech will be over quickly. However, if you pull them in effectively, you will likely have undivided attention for the duration of your speech.

3. *Use style.* Light humor, simple visuals, and use of inclusive pronouns like "we" rather than self-centered pronouns like "I" are most effective. Such stylistic choices will grab attention and help audience members connect with you more quickly.

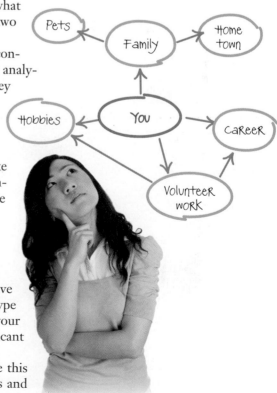

Presenting Yourself

Teachers often use the first presentation as an opportunity to have you introduce yourself to the class. Typically, your task in this type of speech is to prepare a presentation in which you describe your background and other meaningful things about yourself like significant experiences, hobbies, or interests.

Because you will typically have at least one evening to prepare this presentation, your teacher might expect more supporting examples and explanations than for an impromptu presentation.

- *Develop structure.* As you prepare your presentation outline, consider the multiple ways you can organize your talk. One of the more common ways to organize a speech about yourself is the chronological approach, which simply starts at the beginning of your life and continues to today. This approach may be overly familiar, in which case you will want to organize your short talk in another way. Instead, you could use a topical organization where you select a few elements of your life to share. You could also recognize a common thread that explains your life. One speaker observed that every time he failed at something, he did a tremendous amount of learning and went on to succeed at something else. If you have experienced a significant event that dramatically changed your life, you might focus on describing that experience. One student who was a musician discussed an opportunity to play at the Montreux Jazz Festival in Switzerland. Stephen Anderson began his talk very creatively,

> When you think of music in Switzerland, do you imagine this: ["Smoke on the Water" plays]? Almost anybody who has ever tuned into a rock station on the radio has heard this famous riff, but do they know the rich history behind it? I was fortunate enough to spend five days of my summer at the Montreux Jazz Festival, which inspired "Smoke on the Water." Today, I am going to take you all on an imaginary field trip to the glorious, musical party that is the Montreux Jazz Festival. First, we'll have a lesson in the history of the festival, then we'll attend a couple of concerts, and after that, we can poke around the festival's other attractions.

- *Focus on small details.* Because you have time to prepare, you should carefully consider ways that you can use style to improve your creative language use.
- *Be thoughtful.* When selecting stories to tell about yourself, carefully consider which stories will teach the listeners about who you are and persuade them that you are a "credible student." Carefully selecting such examples will allow you to make friends more quickly in class and will tell your teacher that you are serious about doing well in the course.
- *Make content meaningful to the audience.* Although a presentation about you will be naturally interesting, an even better one will find ways to relate your life experiences to those of your listeners. What can they learn from your stories?

Because this assignment asks students to focus on themselves, some students assume that they can easily plan their presentations just before class. However, taking time to carefully develop and organize ideas, paying attention to small details like style, and practicing your presentation can determine whether your presentation is "excellent" or merely "average."

Presenting a Classmate

Some teachers prefer that you present information about a classmate rather than about yourself. The advantage of this approach is that the process more closely follows that which you will use in other presentations; that is, you must consult external sources during the invention process. For this presentation, you are typically asked to interview a classmate and plan a presentation about that person. In many respects, the same suggestions we provided for the self-introduction presentation apply equally well to the peer presentation. Perhaps the one additional skill necessary for this assignment is the need for effective interviewing techniques to use during the invention process.

To gather information, you must interview your classmate. A thorough analysis of interviewing skills is unnecessary for this assignment; however, the following suggestions should help you gain enough information to plan a successful presentation.

- *Plan interview questions.* The most effective strategy for conducting an interview is to preplan some questions, while remaining flexible enough to ask follow-up questions.
- *Record answers.* Effective interviewers will either tape-record or take detailed notes of answers to interview questions. A detailed recording (whether audio or written) will better enable you to select accurate information when preparing your presentation.
- *Start with the basics.* Although basic information such as a person's hometown, major, year in school, and age are potentially the least interesting facts to learn, such information is expected. Begin your interview by learning these basics.
- *Ask questions about more than the basics.* One widely supported concept in communication is that each of us has layers of information that we disclose to others. Our outer layer contains basic information and is commonly revealed to others without much forethought. Subsequent layers include information about our personal beliefs, our personal values, our goals and desires, and our self-concept. These layers of information are revealed naturally as a relationship progresses. For your presentation, you might ask your partner about some of these more personal issues so that you can do a more thorough job of introducing the individual to your class.
- *Look for the novel and unique.* Each of us has characteristics and experiences that make us unique. Although we may find our hobbies or preferences familiar or routine, others may not. Ask questions to learn details that your interview partner may find ordinary but that you think would be interesting to your classmates.
- *Be ethical.* Your short interview with your classmate could be the beginning of a solid friendship. Recognize that some information might come up during the interview that should not be divulged to the class. Moreover, your introduction of your class colleague should be done with respect and consideration.

A sample introductory speech of another person focusing on his virtues and his hobby of gaming was provided recently:

> As I stand here today, I speak, not of a man of talent, but a man of virtue. We have all seen gamers in the past use strategy guides or cheat codes to *artificially* honor themselves with titles of achievement or grandeur. Braden Stevenson has never used either of these methods in his life. Even at a young age, this noble man was proving to many that a game could be beaten, not with hints or tips, but sheer ambition and puzzle-solving skills. At the young age of 5, he had already beaten the first Legend Of Zelda title on his Nintendo Console and from there on he only continued to flourish. As he aged, he began to beat more challenging titles like Myst and Ninja Gaiden. His record time for beating Megaman X is 1 hour and 12 minutes; he's caught all 151 original Pokémon, and it doesn't stop there. With a whopping 116 different game completions under his belt, you know he can tell you how to beat a game every time. Let's hear it for Braden Stevenson!

Effective interviewing skills are valuable for careers in sales, management, health, and even teaching. Our own experience suggests that interviewing and introducing a fellow classmate is one of the more enjoyable presentation experiences you can have in class.

Demonstration Presentations

Another typical first presentation is a more formal informative speech that demonstrates something. A **demonstration presentation** *teaches audience members how something works or how to perform some task.* Students usually pick a topic with which

they have ample experience. At universities in the Midwest, "country students" commonly teach "city students" how things are done "on the farm" in presentations about many rural activities, from bull riding to raising organic vegetables. Students more oriented toward the sciences might illustrate a scientific principle. Kim, for example, used a balloon and tinfoil to demonstrate how black holes develop in space. Yet other students discuss hobbies ranging from making homemade beer to competing in snowboarding competitions.

Demonstration presentations can come across as either interesting or trivial. To prepare an effective demonstration presentation, carefully analyze how you can make your topic relevant to audience members. For example, why would listeners care to learn about snowboarding competitions when most will never engage in the activity? Here are a couple other suggestions for preparing an effective demonstration presentation:

- *Organize logically.* Because even simple processes like recycling can require several steps, it can be challenging to find clear main points for a demonstration presentation. Your main points should divide and organize multiple steps into a few logical categories. To talk about composting, for instance, you might cover the following main points:

  I. Building a compost bin.
  II. "Feeding" the compost bin.
  III. Using compost in your garden.

- *Use visual aids.* One of the most effective ways to increase listeners' interest in your topic is to show them what you are talking about. Displaying diagrams and pictures often does wonders to clarify your explanation of complex or unfamiliar things. Of course, visual aids are also one of the biggest pitfalls for new presenters. In a later chapter, you will learn to effectively plan, create, and integrate visual resources into your presentation. For now, make sure that your visual resources are clear and easily seen, and that you carefully plan when to use them during your presentation.

People running for public office continually illustrate the power of public speaking as a form of civic engagement. They are not equally good at using ethos, pathos, and logos, however. Mitt Romney had a difficult time connecting with the common person in his run for the U.S. presidency. Paul Begala observed, "Romney has amassed a fortune so vast he is expanding his $12 million beachfront mansion and installing an elevator . . . for his cars. For his cars, people. If you're insanely rich, you might have an elevator in your mansion. But a lift for your Lexus?"[8]

President Obama was criticized for being an elite as well: "He is the kind of elite that Democrats love: an academic elite. A professor of constitutional law at the University of Chicago, president of the *Harvard Law Review*, graduate of Columbia University: the egghead trifecta."[9]

Sample Speech for Review and Analysis

In the spring of 2009, CNN awarded several "Hometown Heroes" awards to individuals who have made a difference helping others in their communities. One of those heroes was Anne Mahlum, founder of Back on My Feet, which uses running as a way to help homeless individuals in Philadelphia regain self-confidence and strength. Here is the text of a speech by Jessica Biel, actress and founder of the Make the Difference Network, who introduced Mahlum at the Hometown Heroes awards ceremony (this speech can also be viewed at www.youtube.com/watch?v=DpZrt_t6W70).

Introducing Anne Mahlum

Sometimes an idea is just so crazy it has to work. A young woman from Philadelphia walks into a local homeless shelter and says "I want to take some people running." Right there, in the middle of a place where the forgotten and downtrodden struggle to get through the day, where the outcasts and the addicts sit without their dreams, where the rejected and the ignored believed that the whole world has turned its back on them. In walks a woman filled with such a profound belief that running can be a healing force. She says, "I wanna take some homeless people running," and that's just what Anne Mahlum did. So they laced up their shoes together, they put on their new hats and T-shirts and ran a mile together. They started slow, then the group got bigger and they ran further. And some kept right on running. They kept running toward a new job. They kept running toward a new home. They kept running toward the life they had always imagined. That is why on any given morning before the sun rises you can see a group of runners: professionals, volunteers, and homeless men and women, moving through the streets of Philadelphia stride by stride. And right in the middle of this group is Anne Mahlum, our hero, with her amazing idea.

Notice in this speech how Biel used a series of narratives to tell the basic story of how Mahlum founded Back on My Feet and how that organization aims to help people who are homeless in the Philadelphia area. Biel also used repetition and ornamental language toward the end of the presentation to paint a picture of people running as she introduced Mahlum to the viewers.

For REVIEW >>

SUMMARY HIGHLIGHTS

Foundations of Public Communication

▶ The roots of rhetoric include the Five Canons of Rhetoric.

▶ The Five Canons are invention, organization, style, understanding, and delivery.

Tips for Preparing Your First Presentation

▶ Tips for planning your presentation include
- Gathering materials.
- Reviewing the assignment expectations.
- Accumulating information.
- Organizing materials.
- Being clear.
- Focusing on the quality of details.
- Editing for style, practicing.
- Planning effective delivery
- Enjoying the opportunity.

Common Types of First Presentations

▶ Common types of first presentations are impromptu presentations, presenting yourself, presenting a classmate, and presenting to demonstrate.

1. The invention process involves:
    (A) using clear and ornamental language
    (B) using effective verbal and nonverbal behaviors
    (C) finding information for the presentation
    (D) selecting an appropriate arrangement and structure

2. Which of the following statements regarding organization is true?
    (A) You should avoid using metaphors or similes in the conclusion.
    (B) The body should have five or more main points.
    (C) Not all main points need to have supporting material.
    (D) The introduction should provide the thesis statement and preview the main points.

3. Using language creatively and artfully is referred to as the canon of:
    (A) understanding
    (B) delivery
    (C) organization
    (D) style

4. If you interview a classmate for an introductory speech, you should:
    (A) begin the interview with an in-depth question
    (B) divulge all information, regardless of topic sensitivity
    (C) solely ask questions about the basics
    (D) plan your interview questions

5. The impromptu presentation:
    (A) allows for substantial planning
    (B) should be clearly organized
    (C) includes numerous supporting materials and citations
    (D) should be delivered with minimal eye contact

Answers: 1 (C); 2 (D); 3 (D); 4 (D); 5 (B)

APPLICATION EXERCISES

1. Practice your impromptu speaking skills by preparing short presentations for each of the three quotations that follow. The presentation notes you prepare for each quote should have a thesis statement and two main points. The thesis and main points should develop an explanation demonstrating that the quotation says something about who you are as a person.

    a. " . . . friendship . . . is essential to intellectuals. You can date the evolving life of a mind, like the age of a tree, by the rings of friendship formed by the expanding central trunk."—Mary McCarthy

    b. "You don't need proof when you have instinct."— "Joe" in the movie *Reservoir Dogs*

    c. "Just like a boxer in a title fight, you got to walk in that ring all alone."—Billy Joel

2. You can improve your own skills as a presenter by carefully observing others. Watch a prominent speaker on television or check out a clip on YouTube. Make notes on how the speaker uses nonverbal behaviors like eye contact, gestures, and facial expressions. What did you find effective or distracting about the speaker's delivery?

KEY TERMS

Concept maps	Impromptu presentation	Style
Delivery	Invention	Understanding
Demonstration presentation	Organization	
Five Canons of Rhetoric	Ornamentation	

3

SELECTING A
TOPIC AND

One of the first steps in preparing a presentation is choosing a topic. You may choose to talk about a topic that is familiar to you, or you may use this opportunity to research an unfamiliar topic about which you are curious. In either case, the choice is yours. In this chapter, we will consider selecting a topic and purpose.

PURPOSE

Tim Tolman knew he had spent too much time checking all his friends' Facebook pages when he realized how hungry he was. Shutting down his laptop and heading to the campus cafeteria, he smiled to himself as he remembered what he had recently read about Facebook—headed for a billion active users, the social media site is available in more than 70 languages.[1]

Everyone can think of things that make Facebook appealing. Finding and keeping in touch with friends old and new is as easy as hitting a few keys. Sharing photos and videos is fast and fun. And letting everyone know about good news and big changes in your life is simple when all you have to do is make a single post for all your friends and contacts to find. In fact, millions of people around the world find the social networking site so attractive that they log on to change their status every single day.

On the other hand, Tim mused, quite a few Facebook users forget that everything they post on the site becomes more or less public information. Tim knew about people who had been bullied or harassed online, who had been embarrassed by photos posted by others, and who had run afoul of their employers' policies by posting proprietary or inappropriate information online. Tim read that Facebook removes more than 20,000 profiles each day because of a range of offenses from underage submissions to inappropriate content.[2]

Tim carried his tray over to a table where a couple of his friends were sitting. He had already decided that Facebook would make a great topic for the upcoming speech he needed to prepare for class. He knew his audience would consider it significant and engaging—after all, every one of them had a Facebook page. He believed the vital topic of technology was appropriate for the classroom setting, and that he would be able to find plenty of new information to present.

But he still needed to narrow his topic and determine the purpose of his speech. Did he want to share information about the benefits Facebook could offer or persuade his listeners to pay more attention to the drawbacks of social networking? In this chapter, we will consider how to select a topic and purpose for your speech.

FREE SPEECH, CULTURAL RESPECT, AND CHANGING CONNOTATIONS

In the past, the term "Oriental" was used to describe people, cultures, and products that came from the Far East. More recently, the term "Asian" has come to replace the word "Oriental." Common usage in government documents, newspapers, magazines, and other written materials have supplanted the word "Oriental" with the term "Asian." Imagine that an older speaker who was familiar with the term "Oriental" used the word in his talk to a state legislature. When cautioned about the negative connotation of the word to members of the assembly who had Asian ancestors, the speaker claimed he learned the term "Oriental" as a child and had always used it. He went on to add that his freedom of speech allows him to use this word. He asks sarcastically, "Is the rug in my living room an 'Asian rug'?" How would you respond? Would your response depend on the ethnic makeup of the audience? Why or why not? Which is more important: respect for cultural sensitivity or free speech? Most of us would agree that both are important.

cultural NOTE

Searching for a Topic

The range of topics on which you can speak is almost limitless, but sometimes you might have a difficult time identifying a topic for your speech. The First Amendment to the U.S. Constitution protects the right of free expression saying, in part, "Congress shall make no law . . . abridging the freedom of speech."

Does the First Amendment mean that nothing is off-limits? No: Speakers cannot defame others with falsehoods, they cannot incite audiences to take illegal action, and they cannot threaten the president's life. Consider with your class the obligations associated with the right to free speech. Besides legal obligations (not labeling others, not inciting illegal or dangerous activities), what other obligations do speakers face when granted the right of free speech? Are people obligated to enact their right of free speech?

The First Amendment is often the subject of debate in contemporary society. The development of the Internet, concern for children's rights, differing views on women's rights, and incidents of hate speech by a variety of groups all fuel the sometimes fiery debate about the parameters of the First Amendment. Nonetheless, you are free to speak on almost any topic that you can identify. The authors of this text encourage you to speak on vital topics such as environment, education, health, democracy, ethics, diversity, technology, and economics. Why? Because these vital topics lead you to consider subjects that are important and significant to you and to your audience. Also, by addressing vital issues, you avoid having to listen to speeches on trivial topics like the history of toothpicks, why I wore this outfit today, or why cars have tires. Check with your instructors for any particular expectations they may have. Here are some examples of vital topics:

My experience with welfare	Why people hate taxes
Reducing the federal deficit	Policy on bailouts
Violence and video games	Cheating on the Internet
Bias in American journalism	New restrictions on women's rights
Flunking out of college	The price of prescription drugs
Problems with healthcare	Attracting men to college
Arizona immigration law	Healthcare bill

When your instructor assigns a speech, what do you do? Many beginning speakers put off the assignment as long as possible. You may consider possible topics as you go about other daily activities. How can you jump-start the process so you have more constructive time to plan your presentation?

In this section, we will discuss five methods of searching for a topic: individual brainstorming, categorical brainstorming, conducting a personal inventory, current topic identification, and Internet searching. Some of these methods will be more interesting and useful to you than others. You do not have to use all methods, but you should find one that suits you.

"By addressing vital issues, you avoid having to listen to speeches on trivial topics."

Individual Brainstorming

Brainstorming occurs *when you try to think of as many topics as you can in a limited time*. Without judging them, you simply list all topics that come to mind. Groups frequently use brainstorming when members get together to propose a number of ideas. After the brainstorming process, which should be limited to a specific amount of time (say, five minutes), the group discusses the ideas and selects one or more by assessing their quality.

Individual brainstorming occurs when you, individually, spend a certain amount of time writing down all the possible topics you can think of. After you have completed that phase of the process, you evaluate the topics and choose two or three for further research. Select the one that meets the requirement of being a vital topic that holds your interest and that will be attractive to your audience.

Categorical Brainstorming

Categorical brainstorming is similar to individual brainstorming. The difference is that *you begin with categories that prompt you to think of topics*. For example, you might think about people, places, things, and events. Begin by writing these four categories on a sheet of paper and making four columns. Then, brainstorm topics that fit in the four columns. Table 3.1 provides an example. To localize this activity, use the same categories, but generate a new table using only campus, community, or regional topics.

Conducting a Personal Inventory

Another strategy that might be helpful is conducting a **personal inventory**. *Consider features of your life such as experiences, attitudes, values, beliefs, interests, and skills.*

Write down anything that describes you. Don't worry if your words don't sound like a topic for a presentation. No idea should be discarded at this stage. Later, you will cull this list and identify two or three topics that might work for your presentation. Here are some topics that students identified using personal inventories:

Studying abroad	Laser surgery for better sight
Interning for your senator	The symbols in a powwow
Service learning with hearing-impaired children	Being a Muslim in the United States

Rugby as exercise	Growing up below the poverty line
Free speech in other nations	Preparing for a job interview
Healthcare for veterans	Managing a life-threatening disease
Private versus public education	Volunteering in a mental health facility

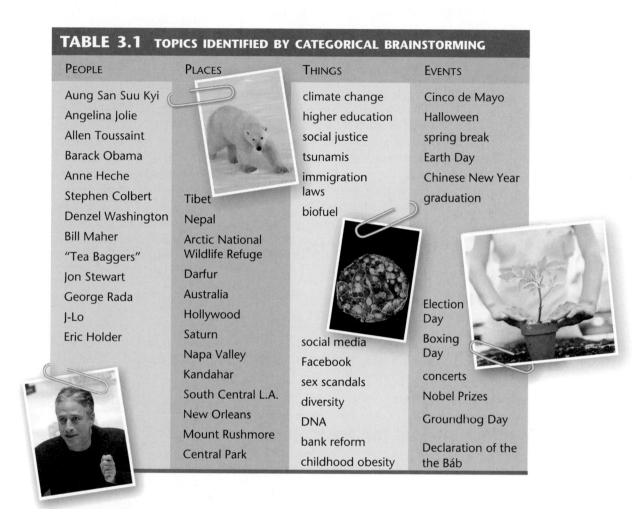

TABLE 3.1   TOPICS IDENTIFIED BY CATEGORICAL BRAINSTORMING

PEOPLE	PLACES	THINGS	EVENTS
Aung San Suu Kyi		climate change	Cinco de Mayo
Angelina Jolie		higher education	Halloween
Allen Toussaint		social justice	spring break
Barack Obama		tsunamis	Earth Day
Anne Heche		immigration laws	Chinese New Year
Stephen Colbert	Tibet	biofuel	graduation
Denzel Washington	Nepal		
Bill Maher	Arctic National Wildlife Refuge		
"Tea Baggers"	Darfur		
Jon Stewart	Australia		
George Rada	Hollywood		Election Day
J-Lo	Saturn		Boxing Day
Eric Holder	Napa Valley	social media	
	Kandahar	Facebook	concerts
	South Central L.A.	sex scandals	Nobel Prizes
	New Orleans	diversity	Groundhog Day
	Mount Rushmore	DNA	
	Central Park	bank reform	Declaration of the the Báb
		childhood obesity	

Current Topic Identification

Another way to approach searching for a topic is to consider topics of interest today. **Current topics** are *items that you discover on Facebook, on a blog, or on a news flash on your iPad.* Most students do not read newspapers or magazines, which remain a treasure trove of topics, but they do watch *The Daily Show* and *The Colbert Report*—shows that report news with a comic twist. Good vital topics are not difficult to find. Student speech topics that originated in current topics include:

Renewable energy	Climate change
Immigration policies	Racial profiling
Disappearing benefits	New election rules
Healthcare costs	Anabolic steroids
Overflowing prisons	Hate crimes

Do-nothing Congress	Hybrid vehicles
Executive compensation	Justice and equity
Same-sex marriage	Genetic privacy
Internet terrorism	Thinspro, pro-anas and pro-mias
Workplace diversity	Sex scandals

Internet Searching

Getting started is most important. Sure, you should think about a proper vital topic, but too many students think too long before they launch their search for information. The search for information contains both a blessing and a curse. The blessing is that never before has so much information about everything been available to so many so quickly. The curse is that same thing: We have access to so much information that selecting what to include has become a major problem. That is why students who earn high grades in public speaking waste no time in selecting a vital topic, narrow it, and then start their research early because they have too much information from which to choose. See Figure 3.1 for tips.

Now that you have identified several topics for a presentation, you will need to comb through them and select one. How can you best succeed in choosing? Here are some general guidelines for topic selection used successfully by public speaking students:

- *Speak about topics you already know.* What subjects do you know about—web design, dieting, or healthy exercising? You will save much time by choosing a familiar topic.
- *Speak about a topic that interests you.* What subjects arouse your interest—politics, social justice, or music? What do you know about? What elective courses do you choose? Selecting a vital topic that interests you will make the research process enjoyable.

iConnect

Social Media as a Tool for Topic Selection

Of course, the Internet is replete with options for speech topics. Using social media, you can not only explore potential topics, you can also determine which topics have widespread interest among people who post, pin, or tweet messages. For example, Pinterest (**http://pinterest .com**) is a social media site where people post information about interests and hobbies ranging from healthy cooking to making art from recycled material. Using Pinterest, you can explore thousands of potential informative speech topics, including valuable tips for creative projects.

Using another site, Project C (**www.clickingcreateschange.com**), you can learn about various non-profit organizations and then vote for your favorite; votes are used to determine how donated funds will be distributed among several community-based groups. Consider using sites like these to gauge people's interest in various causes (organ donation, community food banks, etc.), information that can help you develop engaging persuasive presentations. Although Project C is focused on a particular geographic area, sites like this are becoming more and more common.

When using social media sites to locate topics, you may find interesting posts or other types of information that you want to use in your speech. Remember that social media are like any other source—you should give credit by citing the source in your speech and by providing bibliographic information on your outline. You will learn more about how to do this in Chapter 5.

- Use key words to narrow your search as much as possible.
- Do not just nab the first sources that pop up because much better ones can lie beneath the surface.
- When you locate a valuable source, be sure that you copy the exact site citation to list as a reference (sometimes they are very difficult to relocate later).
- Be sure to use quote marks around anything you lift directly so that you can avoid plagiarism.

Figure 3.1   **Tips for your Internet search.**

- *Speak about topics that are uniquely your own.* If you have done a personal inventory or an individual brainstorm, examine the list for vital topics that might not be shared by others in the class. Consider unusual jobs or personal mental, physical, or situational challenges.

Consider your unique background for ideas to share with the audience.

- *Speak about a vital topic that is important to your local community.* Have you heard the expression "Think globally; act locally"? How can you relate international and national issues and trends to your hometown or present community? How are nondominant people treated in your community?
- *Speak about topics that your audience finds interesting*—finding work, surviving unemployment, or showing how films influence attitudes. What do people in your class enjoy talking and hearing about? Which of their favorite topics could you discuss with some authority? If people tend to talk about certain topics before or after class, consider those ideas for a vital speech topic.
- *Speak about a topic that the audience embraces, but you do not.* Do some members of your class hold ideas that they accept without question, but which you think could be challenged? For example, people in your class might have differing views on politics, cohabiting, marriage, and religion. Try to convince members of the audience to consider your thinking on one of these topics.
- *Speak about a vital topic that is worth your time and effort and the time of your listeners.* Consider the themes that are central to this book: the environment, education, health, democracy, ethics, diversity, technology, and economics.

After you have identified a general vital topic, you need to evaluate it. You must determine if the topic meets standards of appropriateness for the speaker, audience, ethics, and occasion.

Evaluating Topics

Appropriate for You

While you should always keep your attention on the audience, you also need to determine whether a topic is of interest to you. A speech is appropriate for you as a

speaker if you really care about your topic. If you are interested, you can be enthusiastic, and the audience is likely to share your feelings. If you are just fulfilling an assignment, the audience will probably sense your lack of concern.

You should know something about your topic, but you should also have a sincere interest in learning more about the subject. Research is every speaker's obligation. A topic is appropriate for you if you know—or can learn—more about it than most of the people in the audience. Most of us possess only superficial knowledge of most topics. A speaker must learn more about a specific subject than is generally known to an audience. When you have such knowledge, you are said to have subject matter competence.

Appropriate for the Audience

A speech is appropriate for audience members if the content is both interesting and worthwhile to them. The speaker is responsible for generating audience interest. Suppose you are very interested in food and nutrition with the goal of becoming a master chef some day. Even though practically nobody in your class has that interest or goal, you can choose the vital topic of health and relate your knowledge of food and nutrition to our national epidemic of obesity

"Too many students think too long before they launch their search for information."

Also consider whether your topic is worthwhile for the audience. If the audience is already familiar with the topic, be careful about the information you are presenting. Try to present new information about familiar topics; do not repeat what the audience is already likely to know. A presentation about a topic too familiar to the audience—for example, reality television—would probably be uninformative. A presentation about a topic that is too trivial—for instance, your summer vacation at the ocean—will not be worth the audience's time. A proper analysis of your audience should reveal both how interesting and how worthwhile your topic would be for them. In the next chapter, we thoroughly discuss audience analysis.

Appropriate for the Occasion

Finally, consider the topic's appropriateness for the occasion: Is the subject significant, timely, and tailored? A speech topic is *significant* if the content meets the audience's expectation of what should occur on that occasion. In a classroom presentation, for example, a common expectation is that the speech should be on a vital topic of importance to the class, the campus, the community, or the world. Your breakfast preferences, your Saturday night clubbing, or your most recent argument with your kids probably do not warrant publicity; that is, a presentation about them would seem insignificant to a classroom audience.

A speech is *timely* if it can be linked to the audience's current concerns. Say that an election is coming up. That upcoming event can spark speeches about politicians and their policy positions, especially the policies that affect students. Or maybe the state government is trying to legislate more ideas to limit your freedom. On the vital topic of democracy, you can inform your audience about what these new policies will mean to them. Tuition increases, class sizes, shrinking faculties, poor facilities—all of these could be timely concerns on the vital topic of education, concerns that your classroom audience cares about.

1. Do you, as the speaker, have involvement with the topic?
2. Do you, as the speaker, have competence in the topic area?
3. Based on audience analyses, does this topic hold interest for your audience?
4. Based on audience analyses, is the topic worthwhile to your audience?
5. Is the topic significant in terms of the speech occasion?
6. Is the topic timely or appropriate for the speech occasion?
7. Have you appropriately narrowed and limited the topic for the occasion?

Figure 3.2   **Guidelines for topic appropriateness.**

A speech is *tailored* if the topic is narrowed to fit the time allotted for the presentation. To cover the rise and fall of the Roman Empire in a five-minute speech is impossible, but to talk about three ways to avoid obesity through diet and exercise is possible. Most speakers err in selecting too large rather than too small a topic. A narrow topic allows you to complete your research faster; researching too large a topic will require the time-consuming problem of cutting much of the material to meet the time limits of the speech.

Refer to the criteria in Figure 3.2 as guidelines for evaluating your topic for appropriateness.

Purposes of Speeches

Without a map, you do not know how to get to your destination. In public speaking, without a purpose, you do not know what you should say. In this section of the chapter, we consider *purposes* of speeches and the *thesis statement*, which is a kind of short preview of your speech. Speeches have both general purposes and specific purposes. We consider both purposes here.

General Purposes

In the broadest sense, the *general purpose* of many speeches is either *to inform, to persuade*, or *to highlight a special occasion*. In class, your teacher may determine the general purpose of your speech. When you are invited to give a presentation to a particular group, the person who invites you may suggest a purpose. If you are not given a general purpose, you should consider the speech, the occasion, the audience, and your own motivations as you determine the general purpose of your speech.

The general purposes of speaking can sometimes overlap. To understand how informative speaking and persuasive speaking are interrelated, select one or more vital topics and determine how they can be approached as either an informative or a persuasive message. For example, a speech informing the audience about a religion such as Orthodox Christianity is quite different from a speech attempting to persuade the audience to convert. Sometimes, the best we can do is to determine that a particular speech is "mainly informative" or "mainly persuasive." This distinction is more difficult to recognize when engaging complex, multifaceted, or controversial topics. The speaker's intent may be informational, but the audience might perceive the message as persuasive. Can a student inform an audience about gun control without persuading some individuals in the audience that we need more or less regulation of firearms? We tend to classify speech purposes based on speaker intent, but if we classified the speech according to audience effect the achieved purpose could be quite different.

The Speech to Inform

The **speech to inform** *seeks to increase the audience's level of understanding or knowledge about a topic.* Generally, the speaker provides new information or shows how existing information can be applied in new ways. The speaker does not attempt to persuade or convince the audience to change attitudes or behaviors. The informative speech should be devoid of persuasive tactics. The speaker is essentially a teacher. How would the following topics lend themselves to a speech to inform?

Wetlands ecology	Can we prevent oil spills
What is hacking?	What is a social justice?
Wind energy	Does texting result in illiteracy?
Interviewing: best practices	To Twitter or not to Twitter
What does it mean to be Buddhist?	What is the Defense of Marriage Act?

Keep in mind that the main idea behind the informative speech is to increase the audience's knowledge about a topic.

The Speech to Persuade

The **speech to persuade** *seeks to influence, reinforce, or modify the audience members' feelings, attitudes, beliefs, values, or behaviors.* Persuasive speeches may seek change or they may argue that the status quo should be upheld. Persuasive speakers attempt to add to what the audience members already know, but they also strive to alter how the audience feels about what they know and ultimately how they behave. The speaker, in this instance, is an advocate. How would the following topics lend themselves to a speech to persuade?

Reducing binge drinking on college campuses	Does going global mean going broke?
Heart disease has origins in youth	Why families suffer when the economy fails
How hospitals kill	How faith-based organizations help people
Why do we overpay executives?	Why increase state support for education
The conservative cure for high taxes	When do we need big government?
Money problems plague higher education	How can our community help the needy?
Famous Dave's: a successful minority business	What Muslims really believe

Daniel Ramirez, a student, began his persuasive presentation,

> Maybe you have never thought about the safety of your automobile, but after hearing my presentation today, I hope you will. Two months ago, my wife asked me to run some errands in her new car. This automobile purchase was the result of careful research and numerous consultations with *Consumer Reports* magazine. As I sped to pick up a few groceries and two items from the drugstore, nothing was further from my mind than all the investigative work she had done prior to buying the car. But when an oncoming car hit me head on, both air bags deployed exactly as they were designed to do. The engine absorbed the impact of the collision and was driven downward rather than toward the front seat. Amazingly, I walked away without a scratch.

No one in the audience could have doubted that the purpose of his speech was to be persuasive.

The Special Occasion Speech

The **special occasion speech** *is a presentation that highlights a special event.* Special occasion speeches are quite common, but they differ in many ways from the speech to inform or the speech to persuade. Special occasion speeches are presentations designed to welcome, to pay tribute, to introduce, to nominate, to dedicate, to commemorate, or to entertain. The following topics would lend themselves to a special occasion speech.

Honoring a new graduate	Celebrating an anniversary
A eulogy for a friend	A nomination speech
Celebrating a new baby	Dedicating a building
Roasting a retiring officer	An after-dinner thanks
Toasting the bride and groom	Welcoming new members
Introducing a new employee	Initiating members to an honorary

An excerpt from a special occasion speech follows:

Happy Birthday Mom!

> This day means a lot to us, and I thought I'd take a few minutes today to tell you why. The most obvious explanation, of course, is that we all like an excuse for a party! But there's a more important reason. We all want you to know how much we appreciate everything you've done for us. And we all want you to know that we think you have a lot to celebrate. For starters, you've been a great provider. You've been the kind of mother who puts her family first, and does whatever it takes to make...

> **"** Statements of specific purpose guide the entire presentation like a map or blueprint. **"**

Ordinarily a special occasion presentation is short and sweet. Many of these presentations include a story about the person, the couple, or even the building that is being celebrated.

Specific Purposes

The general purpose usually involves nothing more than stating that your goal is to inform or to persuade. The **specific purpose** goes a step further. Here, *you identify your purpose more precisely as an outcome or behavioral objective. You also include the audience* in your specific purpose. For example, a specific purpose statement might be, "My audience will be able to list the five signs of skin cancer." A specific purpose statement thus includes your general purpose, your intended audience, and your precise goal. Some additional examples of specific purpose statements might be the following.

My audience will be able to explain why violence and bullying in elementary schools are on the rise.

My audience will be able to define and identify hate crimes.

My audience will state the benefits of walking.

My audience will learn how to get a voter identification card.

My audience will be able to identify helpful herbs for healthy cooking.

My audience will be able to describe ways to adopt new technologies.

My audience will stop drinking alcoholic beverages in excess.

My audience will identify three reasons to join the health professions.

When developing your specific purpose, consider the following four characteristics of good purpose statements:

1.   They are declarative statements rather than imperative statements (expressing a command, request, or plea) or interrogative statements (asking a question). They make a statement; they do not command behavior nor do they ask a question.

    GOOD: My audience will be able to state some reasons for failing to graduate within four years.

    POOR: Why do students flunk out of college? (A question, not a declarative statement)

2.   Strong specific purpose statements are complete statements; they are not titles, phrases, clauses, or fragments of ideas.

    GOOD: My audience will be able to defend our college's policy on liquor on campus.

    POOR: The importance of liquor policies. (A fragment, not a sentence)

3.   They are descriptive and specific, rather than figurative and vague or general.

    GOOD: My audience will learn how to create a playlist on iTunes.

    POOR: My goal will be to demonstrate the many things you can do with an iPod. (Too general)

4.   They focus on one idea rather than on a combination of ideas.

    GOOD: My audience will be able to distinguish between legal and illegal drugs.

    POOR: I want my classmates to avoid illegal drugs and possibly getting arrested; I also want them to know about legal drugs that may be useful to them as they become increasingly fit. (Focuses on too many ideas)

If your statement of purpose meets these standards, then you are ready to begin creating a thesis statement for your presentation.

Thesis Statement

Similar to the topic sentence or central idea of a written composition, the **thesis statement** is *a complete sentence that reveals the content of your presentation*. It is a forecast of the speech that typically is established early in the presentation. Some examples of thesis statements follow:

- I will show that the economy is improving because unemployment is down, mortgage rates are reasonable, and building permits are up. (On the vital topic of economics)
- America's physical fitness is in jeopardy because many of our kids are overweight, many of our adults are obese, and the weight problem continues to escalate in our population as a whole. (On the vital topic of health)
- I will demonstrate that universities in the United States greatly overproduce law school graduates and greatly underproduce engineers, according to the need for each profession. (On the vital topic of education)

What are some qualities of a good thesis statement? (1) The thesis statement should be a complete statement rather than a fragment or grouping of a few words. (2) The thesis statement should be a declarative sentence rather than a question, explanation, or command. (3) The thesis statement should avoid figurative language and strive for literal meanings. (4) Finally, the thesis statement should not be vague or ambiguous. Let us examine some examples of poorly written thesis statements:

Implementing a job-shadowing program

The immune system is fantastic!

Are you getting enough sleep?

Television destroys lives.

The right to vote

Why are fewer men going to college?

"The thesis statement is a one-sentence forecast of the speech and should be a complete and unambiguous statement."

What is wrong with these thesis statements? The first and fifth are not complete sentences. The second is an exclamation while the third and sixth are questions. The second uses language ("fantastic") that can be defined in multiple ways, while the fourth uses exaggeration to make a point. Some of these topics may also be viewed as trivial. How could we rewrite these ideas into appropriate thesis statements?

A job-shadowing program should be implemented on our campus.

The human immune system is important for homeostasis.

The human need for sleep varies with age and activity.

Excessive television viewing may lead to violent behavior.

Voting is an important element of a democratic society.

A smaller number of men than women are attending college today.

Purposes of speeches are thus general and specific. Although the general purpose is often to inform or to persuade, the specific purpose goes further. The specific purpose includes the goal of your speech as a precise outcome or behavioral objective. The specific purpose reflects considerations of your audience. The thesis statement is a one-sentence forecast of the speech and should be a complete and unambiguous statement.

From Topic Selection to Thesis Statement: A Three-Step Process

Let us finish this chapter by visualizing the three elements that will form the foundation of your presentation. Regardless of the purpose of your speech, all presentations usually require a topic that is appropriate for the speaker and the audience, a purpose that is consistent with the assignment of expectations of the occasion, and a thesis statement that clearly reveals the content of your presentation. Table 3.2 illustrates the three-step process for the three general purposes of speaking: informative, persuasive, and special occasion.

TABLE 3.2 FROM TOPIC TO PURPOSE TO THESIS STATEMENT			
	INFORMATIVE PRESENTATION	**PERSUASIVE PRESENTATION**	**SPECIAL OCCASION PRESENTATION**
STEP ONE TOPIC	Wetlands ecology	The ethics of publicly held companies	An anniversary tribute
STEP TWO PURPOSE	To increase the audience's knowledge of wetlands ecology	To convince the audience that publicly held businesses have community responsibility	To honor the couple on their tenth anniversary
STEP THREE THESIS STATEMENT	Puerto Rico's Caribbean National Forest is a national treasure.	U.S. businesses need to restore trust with the public.	Congratulations to Ann and Mark on a decade of love and happiness.

For
REVIEW >>

SUMMARY HIGHLIGHTS

Searching for a Topic

▶ To search for a public speaking topic, you can use at least five different approaches: individual brainstorming, categorical brainstorming, conducting a personal inventory, current topic identification, and Internet searching.

Selecting a Topic

▶ Speak about topics you already know and that interest you.

▶ Select topics that are unique to you and your interests or that are important to your local community.

▶ Consider your audience's interests. Sometimes, it is worthwhile to speak about topics that your audience embraces and that you do not.

▶ Finally, speak about topics that are worth your time and effort, and the time of your listeners as well.

Evaluating Topics

▶ To evaluate a public speaking topic, determine whether the topic meets the standards of appropriateness for the speaker, the audience, and the occasion.

▶ Identify three general purposes of public speaking.

Purposes of Speeches

▶ The three general purposes of public speaking are to inform, to persuade, and to celebrate a special occasion.

▶ Write a specific purpose for a presentation.

▶ The specific purpose for a public speech includes considerations of your general purpose, your intended purpose, and your precise goal.

▶ Develop a thesis statement for a presentation.

From Topic Selection to Thesis Statement:
A Three-Step Process

▶ After selecting your topic, decide on your speech's purpose. Then, compose a thesis statement, a one-sentence "forecast" of your speech.

pop Quiz

1. Categorical brainstorming is when you:
   (A) find items in the news to discuss
   (B) consider how you spend time
   (C) search on the Internet for a topic
   (D) use one idea to create many

2. When choosing a topic, you should not speak about topics that are:
   (A) uniquely your own
   (B) important to your local community
   (C) uninteresting to the audience
   (D) embraced by the audience

3. The speech that seeks to increase the audience's level of understanding or knowledge about a topic is the speech to:
   (A) persuade to another point of view
   (B) highlight a special occasion
   (C) influence a decision
   (D) inform about a vital topic

4. An example of a speech's specific purpose is:
   (A) "I will inform my audience."
   (B) "The importance of an education."
   (C) "A speech to persuade."
   (D) "My audience will be able to identify three advantages of green tea."

5. The thesis statement:
   (A) avoids revealing the content of the presentation
   (B) is established in the conclusion
   (C) is a complete statement
   (D) uses figurative language

Answers: 1 (D); 2 (C); 3 (D); 4 (B); 5 (C)

APPLICATION EXERCISES

1. Examine the following specific purpose statements. Identify those that are good examples and explain why the others are bad examples.

   a. My audience will be able to explain the current TSA strategies.

   b. What do men want in their personal relationships?

   c. To inform my audience about STDs.

   d. To identify the primary causes of cancer.

   e. My audience will be able to distinguish between moderate and binge drinking.

   f. To explain early baldness in men.

   g. To inform my audience about weekend trips in the region.

   h. To inform my audience about the steps to earning the Eagle Scout Award.

   i. A passion for cooking.

2. Divide a piece of paper into four columns. Write one of the following general topics at the top of each of the four columns.

   a. Job experiences I have had.

   b. Places I have traveled.

   c. City, state, or area I am from.

   d. People who make me angry.

   e. Happy experiences I have had.

   f. Unusual experiences I have had.

   g. Personal experiences I have had with crime.

   h. My involvement in marriage, divorce, or other family matters.

   i. My experiences with members of other groups—the old, the young, other ethnic groups.

   j. The effect of the drug culture on my life.

k. My relationship to local, state, or federal government.

l. My background in painting, music, sculpture, theater, dance, or other fine arts.

m. My feelings about grades, a college education, sororities and fraternities, college requirements, student government, or alternatives to a college education.

n. My reactions to current radio, television, or film practices, policies, or programming.

o. Recent Supreme Court decisions that affect me.

p. My personal and career goals.

Now, write down specific topics under each of the four general topic areas you chose. Spend no more than five minutes on this exercise brainstorming. Next, underline one topic in each of the four columns that is particularly interesting to you. From these four topics, select the one about which you have the most information or the best access to information. Can you adapt the topic to your specific audience?

KEY TERMS

Brainstorming	Personal inventory	Speech to persuade
Categorical brainstorming	Special occasion speech	Thesis statement
Current topics	Speech to inform	

4

ANALYZING

Effective presenters try to learn as much about the members of their audience as they can before communicating. As beginning speakers, we too often focus on our own concerns and interests. We speak on our favorite topics without considering the audience's interests. We use language that we understand without considering that the audience might not understand it. Perhaps the individualistic culture of the United States invites more attention to self and less to audience than might be the case in more collectivist cultures, such as those represented by many Arab, African, Asian, and Latin American countries.[1]

THE AUDIENCE

Ami was deep in thought as she left the community center, her head full of ideas and plans. For her political science seminar in public policy, she had just volunteered to give a talk to the community's senior group in a couple of weeks. Her goal was to help the seniors understand how the government's new healthcare bill would affect them and their health insurance and medical prescriptions. She knew she had a lot of homework to do on the topic before she made her presentation. Today she was concerned with how she could best reach her audience.

"Remember, Ami," the young director of the center had told her, "our members are seniors, but they don't think of themselves as old! Most of them are retired, and some are widowed, but they're active people who travel often and have a lot of outside interests. In fact, some of them are getting out and about with their friends more often now than they did when they were still in the workforce. Please don't underestimate them."

Ami had nodded her understanding and had taken a couple of quick notes.

"On the other hand," the director continued, "they're worried. None of them really understand how healthcare is going to change, and they're going to have a lot of questions for you. That's one reason we're so glad you stopped by today to volunteer. There's a real need for information and reassurance. Now, what else can I tell you about our members?"

What types of the questions do you think Ami should ask the director of the community center about the senior group she's going to address? What would you like to know about them if you were in her place?

Audience Analysis

What is audience analysis? **Audience analysis** is *discovering as much as possible about an audience for the purpose of improving communication with them*. Audience analysis occurs before, during, and after a presentation. Why should a speaker analyze an audience?

Think of public speaking as another version of the kind of speaking you do every day. Nearly always, when you meet a stranger, you size up that person before you disclose your message. Similarly, public speaking requires that you meet and know the members of your audience so you are able to create a message for them. Speakers who do not properly analyze their audiences risk projecting. **Projection** means *acting on the belief that others believe as you do when actually they may not.* Public speaking is not talking to oneself in front of a group; instead, it is effective message transmission from one person to many people in a setting in which speaker and audience influence each other.

Let us consider the wide variety of audiences you might face in your lifetime:

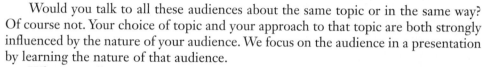

Your classmates	A political group
Fellow workers	A board of directors
Members of a union	A group of children
A civic organization	Community members
A religious group	A school board
Retired people	A committee of professors
A group of friends	A social club

Would you talk to all these audiences about the same topic or in the same way? Of course not. Your choice of topic and your approach to that topic are both strongly influenced by the nature of your audience. We focus on the audience in a presentation by learning the nature of that audience.

When we talk to individuals, we are relatively careful about what we say and how we say it. We speak differently to strangers than to intimates, differently to people we respect than to people we do not respect, and differently to children than to adults. Similarly, we need to be aware of audience characteristics when we choose a topic and when we decide how we are going to present that topic to the audience.

Imagine that you are about to speak to a new audience. How would you learn about the people in your audience? First, you could rely on "conventional wisdom." Second, you could consider a demographic analysis of the characteristics of the people, such as their gender, age, and ethnicity. Let's examine each of these general ways of learning more about an audience.

Conventional Wisdom

Conventional wisdom is *the popular opinion of the time about issues, styles, topics, trends, and social mores; the customary set of understandings of what is true or right.* Conventional wisdom includes what most people are said to think. For many years, *Newsweek* magazine devoted a column to conventional wisdom about people and issues. Sometimes, the president of the United States would receive an arrow up (positive sign) and then would receive an arrow down (negative sign) the next week. The point is that conventional wisdom may change quickly or over time. Let's look at how conventional wisdom relates to audience analysis.

Conventional wisdom is a gross oversimplification often based more on a whim than on deep-seated convictions. Look at the popularity of entertainers: One minute they are on top of the world with hit songs and endless concerts; the next minute they are out of public favor as they face legal charges, seek rehab, or die at their own hands. The healthcare debate is now entering a third decade. During this time, we have listened to thousands of bill-bashing messages sponsored by opponents to the current recommendations. That conventional wisdom by thousands of opponents clashed with another bit of conventional wisdom that embraced Social Security, Medicare, Medicaid, and veterans' benefits—the most socialist of our government programs. An effective speaker needs to know how the wind blows because conventional wisdom is highly variable.

How can a speaker use conventional wisdom? An excellent way to demonstrate your critical thinking ability is to challenge conventional wisdom. If people are becoming too comfortable with government intrusion, then make a reasoned case for why we do not need so much government intervention. If conventional wisdom is against taxation, then inquire how to pay for all the services the public demands. And, if conventional wisdom says no more war, then make a spirited case for a vigorous national defense.

Demographics

What are some aspects of an audience that can affect how they interpret your message? The **demographics** (which literally means "characteristics of the people") of an audience *include gender composition, age, ethnicity, economic status, occupation, and education.*

You can learn the demographic features of your campus or community by getting data from the campus office for institutional research and/or the Census Bureau. From this information, a complete demographic profile of your campus or community emerges. Consider how demographic patterns might be relevant to topic selection and other issues related to audience adaptation.

Gender Composition

Why would a speaker care whether the audience is composed of men, women, or a combination of the two? With some topics, the gender composition of the audience may make no difference at all. With other topics, gender representation may make all the difference in the world. In addition, gender roles have changed dramatically over the past few decades, so assumptions about men's and women's roles must be tempered with a changing reality.

You may need to consider whether your topic is gender-linked or gender-neutral, and modify your treatment of the subject when speaking before generally male, generally female, or mixed-gender audiences. Consider the factors that may cause women and men to react differently to certain topics. For example, women and men may not be equally concerned about issues such as birth control, prostate cancer, abortion, or sports prowess. Be aware that some women and some men feel that women have been victims of discrimination. They will be watchful for signs of discrimination from speakers. Speaking of gender shifts in the workplace may not be greeted with enthusiasm from everyone. Similarly, citing that women now receive the majority of bachelor's degrees and master's degrees might be threatening to men in the audience.[2]

Try to avoid relying on stereotypes to help you determine an audience's needs based solely on gender. For example, if you were a student at Marquette University in Milwaukee, Wisconsin, you might have participated in a service learning project at the Milwaukee Women's Center, which provides a safe haven for women who have been verbally or physically abused. In considering your topic, you might think that this would not be appropriate for your audience because nearly half your class is made up of men. However, you may not know that many of the men in your class are majoring in sociology and have taken classes on gender inequality and that two of the men have actually worked for similar agencies.

Age

The ages of your audience members will also affect your topic selection and the development of your message. For example, you might speak about selecting a career to a younger audience but reserve the topic of cashing in your annuities for an older audience. On the other hand, you might discuss affordable housing with either younger people or older people. However, your approach will be different if you know that your audience consists of 19-year-old undergraduates or members of the AARP, who may be in their 60s and 70s. Considering age is part of audience focus, a primary ingredient in audience analysis.

The 2010 census showed an increase in the over-80 group, an increase in the Hispanic group, a decrease in the proportion of whites, and a dramatic increase in the number of retired individuals. These figures become important in audience analysis because older folks may still read newspapers, while young adults are more likely to actually use the apps on their cell phones, know how to make a DVD, and get their news on the Internet. An effective presenter has to take the audience's level of experience and wisdom into account.

Look at the topics listed in Figure 4.1 and decide which are more appropriate for young adults, middle-aged people, or the elderly. The age of your audience members will affect the topic you choose and how you treat a particular topic. Be wary of stereotyping as you consider the list. Some 70- and 80-year-old people may know as much about social networking, interfaces among phones and computers, and the latest iPad, iPod, and iCloud as do the first-year students at your college.

Ethnicity

Knowing the ethnic makeup and identity of your audience members can make an important difference in your effectiveness. **Ethnicity** identifies *people who are united through "language, historical origins, nation-state, or cultural system."*[3] Ethnic groups preserve communication traditions that affect the way their members speak and listen; some are only partially shared with other groups.

People exhibit and prefer different conversational patterns and expectations because of their ethnic identity. For instance, African Americans and European Americans, while each shares aspects of U.S. culture, have unique styles of communicating. Sometimes dialects differ, sometimes conversational rules and expectations differ, and sometimes interactional styles such as use of argument and discussion differ between the two groups.

As you consider speeches that you might give at work, on campus, or in your community, you recognize that a number of different **nondominant groups**—or *groups that are similar to the larger culture but are distinguished by background, beliefs, and*

Placing your kids in college	Plastic surgery	Competitive sports
Selecting a career	Body piercing	Choosing a major
Managing your time	Enlisting in military service	Animal rights
Saving dollars from taxes	Voting	Health care in hostels
Choosing a college or university	Selecting a tattoo	Domestic violence
Investment opportunities	Cell phones	Downsizing
Social Security reform	Selecting software	Day care facilities
	Traveling in Europe	Community service
		Dating issues

Figure 4.1   **Topics of interest to varying age groups.**

NONDOMINANT GROUPS' BELIEFS ABOUT SPEAKING

Some nondominant groups in the United States have different ideas about public speaking. The Blackfeet Indian Nation in Montana, for instance, values public speaking skills but reserves them for leaders, like tribal elders.[4] Furthermore, Blackfeet see silence as a way to connect with other person—unlike European Americans who tend to dread silence and value a continuous flow of words. To a member of the Blackfeet Nation, public speaking in front of a group can feel like a bold or presumptuous act. This example underscores the importance of knowing the makeup of your audience as you begin to select topics and prepare an approach for your presentation.

behaviors—will be part of your audience. First, list any possible co-cultural groups that may be in your audience. Next, consider the topics that members of that nondominant group might consider important or "vital." Be sure that you avoid stereotypical statements and favor fact-based statements about the nondominant groups in your community or on your campus.

As speakers, we need to be sure that we do not accidentally or needlessly injure or insult audience members who have ethnic backgrounds different from our own. Members of the dominant culture of the United States have had tumultuous relationships with members of smaller nondominant groups. For example, Mexican Americans, Cuban Americans, Puerto Ricans, Vietnamese, and Appalachians are just a few of the groups that have been excluded from many of the privileges members of the dominant culture enjoy. Members of various ethnic groups are sensitive to the discrimination that has limited their people.

Sometimes, even experienced public presenters make errors that are outrageous to members of ethnic nondominant groups. Well-meaning people can accidentally use metaphors, figures of speech, language, or examples that members of nondominant groups find offensive. You can learn to be more sensitive to other groups by practicing your presentation with friends who have backgrounds different from your own or by interviewing and observing other people to determine the kind of language they avoid and the types of examples, analogies, and metaphors they employ.

Economic Status

According to the U.S. Census Bureau, the annual median income for a four-person family is $67,019. However, this number varies by state in the nation. For example, families in Connecticut, Maryland, and New Jersey have the highest median incomes, while families in the District of Columbia, Mississippi, and New Mexico have the lowest. (For more information, see www.census.gov/hhes/www/cincome/4person.html.)

What is the economic status of your audience? Are they primarily wealthy individuals or are they from lower economic groups? People who are wealthier tend to be more conservative, are often older, may have more education, and have probably traveled more than less wealthy people. Wealthy people may be less open to new ideas because they are accustomed to being treated deferentially, with courteous submission to their wishes or judgments. They may be more difficult to persuade because they feel that they have already made good choices. On the other hand, less wealthy people may be more liberal, younger, and may be less educated because of their age. Less wealthy people may be more open to new ideas and may be more easily persuaded because they have less to lose and more to gain.

Some topics are appropriate for more affluent audiences, while other topics are right for less financially successful people. Consider the possible economic differences in your classroom. Do some students have jobs and families? Are some students from affluent families that pay all, or most of, their tuition and expenses? Do other students depend entirely on their own income from large loans and one or more jobs? However, a person's or audience's economic status alone is not sufficient to select or discard a topic.

"As speakers, we need to be sure that we do not accidentally or needlessly injure or insult audience members who have ethnic backgrounds different from our own."

For example, if you attend Ivy Tech, an Indiana community college with 120,000 students on 23 campuses that caters to working adults, you find that the college's strategic plan includes civic engagement and economic development. You can learn about people in need so you can speak with authority about people's economic problems, one of the vital speech topics advocated in this text.

Occupation

Whether you speak in the classroom, in the workplace, or in the community, the kinds of jobs people have are important to audience analysis because occupation influences both delivery and content of presentations.

First, occupations influence the way we talk to each other. Dockworkers are predominantly males who talk to each other at union meetings. Secretaries and administrative assistants are predominantly females who talk to each other at meetings about using new software, new procedures, new forms, and self-development. Sales managers motivate their sales personnel, and managers meet often to face issues. When you present in the workplace, you need to be highly aware of how to present yourself—everything from what you wear to how you talk.

Every business has its own culture that determines everything from what employees wear to work to how they talk to each other. From a communication perspective, language is the important aspect to recognize. Every job has its jargon, but the trouble comes when two sets of jargon intersect. Someone from tech services is supposed to explain to the secretaries how to use the new software system. The secretaries know computers well, but the technology and computer security folks have a language that they use with each other that does not communicate well with others. So, a presenter always has to know how to cross code, how to translate one culture's technical jargon into language compatible with another culture's language. That task is almost always more difficult than it sounds.

For now just remember that every job has its own culture, its own way of talking, and its own language. The effective presenter is a skilled translator: a person who can successfully communicate between cultures.

Education

The most recent information on educational attainment in the United States shows that 85 percent of all adults 25 years of age and older have completed at least high school. More than one in four (27 percent) have received at least a bachelor's degree. Education makes a great deal of difference in earning power. In 2009, adults without a high school diploma earned an average of $21,000 per year; with a high school diploma, the average earnings were $30,000. Those who completed college earned an average of $45,000. If you are interested in tracking these numbers, a good source is the U.S. Department of Commerce, Bureau of the Census, or the National Center for Educational Statistics of the Institute of Educational Services, both of which are available online.

Educational level also differs based on ethnicity and area of the country. Asians and Pacific Islanders have the highest proportion of college graduates (47 percent), followed by non-Hispanic whites (29 percent), African Americans (17 percent), and Hispanics (11 percent). The Northeast region had the highest proportion of college graduates (29 percent), followed by the West (28 percent), the Midwest (26 percent), and the South (25 percent). Even though these percentages seem quite close, the large numbers from which they are derived make them statistically different. (For more information, see www.census.gov.)[5]

Educational attainment is frequently related to economic status and occupation. A person's level of education may tell you very little about his or her intelligence, ambition, or sophistication. However, people with more education tend to read and write more, are usually better acquainted with the news, are more likely to have traveled, and are more likely to have higher incomes. What are some of the implications of educational level for the way you approach your audience?

- People who read and write regularly tend to have more advanced vocabularies, so adjust your language choices to the educational level of your audience.
- People who are receptive to new information need less background and explanation on current issues than those who are not.
- People who have seen more of the world tend to be more sophisticated about differences between people and cultures.

Most important of all, you need to take into account how much your audience already knows about your topic. Knowledge is not necessarily the same as education in analyzing an audience. For example, an auto mechanic might not have a degree from a university, but she clearly would have knowledge about repairing a car, and thus terms relating to auto mechanics would not have to be defined. The opposite, of course, would be true in the case of an educated audience with no background in auto mechanics, for whom all technical terms would require definition.

"Knowledge is not necessarily the same as education in analyzing an audience."

In addition, is the audience likely to have a position on your issue? If so, how might their knowledge level affect your attempt to increase what they know or to change their minds on the issue? For example, if you are talking to a group of older individuals, they may have established opinions on Medicare, Social Security, and the inflated costs of drugs. A younger group of people might not have strong opinions on these matters, but they may care about a poor job market, high bills, and tuition costs.

Worldview

An important point to consider is that every individual has his or her own personal experience that shapes a perspective or point of view about the world. In that way, we are all different from each other. At the same time, we have commonalities, or characteristics, that we all share. In audience analysis, the challenge is to merge perspectives: to discover what we have in common so we can build on that commonality.

In the workplace everyone has had different experiences. Some of your

cultural NOTE

NONDOMINANT GROUPS CAN DISCOURAGE DISCOURSE

Some nondominant groups in the United States do not encourage skills like public speaking because the very act of speaking out is regarded as acting bigger than, better than, or more important than others. One example is the Germans from Russia, a group of ethnic Germans who spent a century in Russia until Stalin killed many and sent the rest to Siberia. Those who escaped to North America live in communities from North Dakota to Texas, basically down the middle of the United States. Even though these hardy individuals are very successful as a group, they are almost absent from the political arena because of their perception that such aspirations could be viewed as acting as though they are better than others. You may know of other cultures and nondominant groups that similarly discourage people in the group from standing up, speaking out, and taking leadership, even in a democratic country.

fellow workers were loved in their family of origin; others may have come from dysfunctional families. Some grew up privileged; others were poor and emerged from tough neighborhoods. But in the workplace, these individuals with such different experiences are in a common cause to advance the goals of their organization. The effective presenter builds on the common goal to seek innovation, advance sales, and improve customer satisfaction. In other words, good audience analysis allows the presenter to transcend differences and to go beyond commonality to new levels of accomplishment. Knowing your audience well can allow you to boost their accomplishments and yours.

Physical Characteristics

Physical characteristics include height, weight, style, fitness, gender display, and obvious disabilities. Imagine that you were going to speak to an audience of the American Federation of the Blind, to a group of individuals in wheelchairs, or to people who had another specific physical disability. How would you adjust your presentation? Most of us would do a poor job of adapting to these situations. Although members of such audiences generally ask that they be treated like those without disabilities, we tend to speak louder, perhaps unnecessarily, enunciate more clearly, or make other changes. We need to guard against language usage that disparages specific people, and we should be sensitive to negative stereotypes that we unintentionally may use. Even if your audience does not include people with physical disabilities, ridding yourself of negative stereotyping is important. People do negative categorizing so routinely that they do not even realize they are guilty of perpetuating myths about individuals with disabilities. For example, in his presentation "Language and the Future of the Blind," Marc Maurer, president of the National Federation of the Blind, discussed one of the stereotypes that he found particularly offensive: the idea that people who are not sighted are incompetent.

Demographics

When it comes time to learn more about your classroom audience, take advantage of online resources that can help you predict your classmates' interests, backgrounds, and values. Did you know that there are websites that list the demographics of most towns and cities in the United States? At **www.city-data.com**, demographic data are categorized according to the characteristics of the town or city you are researching. You can learn about levels of income, education, and crime; the kinds of cars people drive; the length of their commutes; and statistics related to marriage status and sexual orientation. Another useful website, that also is fun to browse, is **www.claritas.com/MyBestSegments**. Simply enter the zip code about which you are curious, and this site will give you information about the largest segments of people in that code. Segments might be labeled "Golden Ponds," "Old Milltowns," "Simple Pleasures," "Traditional Times," and "Young and Rustic," for example. Further exploration of "Young and Rustic" reveals that people in this demographic tend to live in towns or in rural areas, are lower to mid-income, are younger than 55, have households without children, are renters, and have some college education; their ethnic mix includes whites, blacks, and people of mixed races. Use websites like these to prepare relevant and informative presentations specifically designed for your audience.

iConnect

Recently an advertisement appeared from the Carrollton Corporation, a manufacturer of mobile homes. Apparently the Carrollton Corporation was facing fierce competition from other mobile home builders, who were selling their products at a lower price. Consequently, the Carrollton Corporation wanted to show that its higher priced units were superior. In an attempt to convey this impression, the company depicted the blind as sloppy and incompetent. Its advertisement said in part: "Some manufacturers put out low-end products. But they are either as ugly as three miles of bad road, or they have so many defects—crumpled metal, dangling moldings, damaged carpet—that they look like they were built at some school for the blind." What a description! . . . It is not a portrayal calculated to inspire confidence or likely to assist blind people to find employment.[6]

Clearly, you must adjust your language to any perceived physical characteristics of your audience, but going beyond that, rid your presentation of all negative, offensive stereotyping.

Methods of Audience Analysis

Some speakers seem to be able to analyze an audience intuitively, but most of us have to rely on formal and informal means of gathering information. Individuals in advertising, marketing, and public relations have developed complex technological means of collecting information from audiences before, during, and after their message.[7] However, most of us usually collect information about audiences through observation, group identification, interviews, and questionnaires. Table 4.1 summarizes the advantages and disadvantages of these methods of audience analysis.

TABLE 4.1	THREE LEVELS OF AUDIENCE ANALYSIS		
Method	Means	Advantage	Disadvantage
Eyeball or Observation	Scan the audience	Quick and easy	Can be inaccurate and stereotypical
Group Identification	Informant inquiry	Knowing group's values	Presenter as an outsider
In-Depth Inquiry	Interviews and questionnaires	Deeper understanding	Time and effort required

Observation

Observation, or *watching and listening*, reveals the most about the audience before and during the presentation. Looking at audience members might reveal their age, ethnic origin, and gender. More careful observation may reveal marital status by the presence or absence of rings; materialism by conspicuous brand names and trendy jewelry; and even religious affiliation by such symbols as a cross, skullcap, or headscarf. Many people in an audience advertise their membership in a group by exhibiting its symbols.

In the classroom, you have the added advantage of listening to everyone in your audience. Your classmates' speeches—their topics, issues, arguments, and evidence—all reveal more about them than you could learn in a complex questionnaire. Your eyes and ears become the most important tools of audience analysis that you have.

Group Identification

When you speak in the workplace, to a group to which you belong, or to a community organization, you need to meet the expectations of the group. Even in the workplace people, at different levels in the organization may dress differently (bosses are sometimes even called "suits"), talk differently (educational differences), and even think differently (operational vs. visionary leaders). Even in your own workplace, you have to adapt to the specific audience. Outside your own workplace, a key to audience analysis is knowing what a group values so you can adapt your presentation to their expectations.

The easiest way to gain such knowledge is through an **inside informant**, *someone who belongs to the group who can tell you about the group.* You want to know about group values not so you can merely mimic what they already believe but so you can adapt your message for maximum effectiveness. Service groups like Rotary, Lions, and Kiwanis have in common their generosity to causes like defeating polio worldwide, providing glasses for all, and building parks and recreational areas. Religious groups are relatively transparent in their beliefs about many matters, both moral and political. Unless you share some value with a group, you are unlikely to be invited to speak. But for any presentation to a group, you must tailor your message to build on what the group already values. Here are some possible questions to ask of an inside informant:

1. How will this audience respond to my topic?
2. How does my topic relate to what this group values?
3. What are the characteristics of the audience?
4. How long does the audience expect me to speak?
5. What is the setting or the occasion for the presentation?

You really do need to know some answers before you face the audience with your message.

Interviews

Discover information about your audience by interviewing a few members of the group. These **interviews**—*inquiries about your audience directed at an audience member*—should typically occur far in advance of the speech. However, many professional speakers gain some of their most relevant material during the reception or the dinner before the presentation. The competent speaker takes advantage of this time with the audience to learn more about them, their needs, and their interests. Whether it takes place well in advance of the presentation or just before the time you will speak, an interview for information on the audience should focus on the same questions listed in the preceding section on group identification.

When you are conducting an audience analysis for a classroom presentation, you can talk to a few people from class. Try to discover their opinions of your topic, how they think the class will respond to it, and any helpful suggestions for best communicating the topic. Interviews take time, but they are a great way to learn more about your audience.

To make use of the benefits of the interview, arrange to interview at least one person in your community. Consider people who may have information on your topic that will be relevant to your preparation. Next, consider their probable contribution and availability: Your roommate might not offer a unique perspective, and an important elected official may not have any free time in his or her schedule.

Questionnaires

Whereas interviews take more time to execute than to plan, **questionnaires**—*surveys of audience opinions*—take more time to plan than to execute. The key to writing a good questionnaire is to be brief. Respondents tend to register their distaste for long questionnaires by not filling them out completely or by not participating at all.

What should you include in your brief questionnaire? That depends on what you wish to know. Usually you will be trying to discover what an audience knows about a topic and their attitude toward it. You can ask open-ended questions, yes-or-no questions, degree questions, or a mixture of all three—as long as you do not ask too many questions.

Open-ended questions are *like those on an essay test that invite an explanation and discourage a yes-or-no response.* Examples include:

> What do you think should be done about teenage pregnancies?
>
> What do you know about alternative energy sources?
>
> What punishments would be appropriate for plagiarism?

Closed or **closed-ended questions** *force a decision by inviting only a yes-or-no response or a brief answer.* Examples include:

> Should all public schools offer art and music education?
> _____ Yes _____ No
>
> Should a man be allowed paternity leave from his job when his child is born or adopted?
> _____ Yes _____ No

Degree questions *ask to what extent a respondent agrees or disagrees with a statement:*

> I believe that all people deserve housing.
> Strongly agree   Agree   Neutral   Disagree   Strongly disagree

Or degree questions may present a continuum of possible answers from which the respondent can choose:

> Which of the following would be an appropriate punishment for an embezzlement of $5,000?
> $5,000 fine $4,000 fine $3,000 fine $2,000 fine $1,000 fine
> 1 year jail   2 years jail   3 years jail   4 years jail   5 years jail
> How much paternity leave from the workplace do you think men should receive?
> None   One week   Two weeks   One month   Two months   Six months

These three kinds of questions can be used in a questionnaire to determine audience attitudes about an issue. A questionnaire, such as the one in Figure 4.2, administered before your presentation, can provide you with useful information about your audience's feelings and positions on the issue you plan to discuss. All you have to do is keep the survey brief, pertinent, and clear.

Questionnaire: Same-Sex Marriage

1. I think that same-sex couples should be allowed to marry.
   _____ Yes _____ No

2. I think that same-sex couples should be permitted to have legal connections, but should not be allowed to marry.
   _____ Yes _____ No

3. At what point should same-sex couples be allowed to marry?
   _____ Whenever they choose _____ After cohabiting for a year
   _____ After cohabiting for _____ Never
   six months

4. Our society actively punishes gays, lesbians, and same-sex couples.
   Strongly agree   Agree   Neutral   Disagree   Strongly disagree

5. What social support, if any, do you feel should be extended to gay and lesbian individuals? _____
   _____
   _____
   _____

Figure 4.2   **Sample questionnaire.**

Analysis of the Situation

Five factors are important in analyzing the situation you face as a speaker: the size of the audience, the environment, the occasion, the time, and the importance of the situation.

Size of Audience

The *size of the audience* is an important situational factor because *the number of listeners* can determine your level of formality, the amount of interaction you have with the audience, your need for amplification systems, and your need for special visual aids. Larger audiences usually call for formality in tone and language; smaller audiences allow for a more casual approach, a less formal tone, and informal language. Very large audiences reduce the speaker's ability to observe and respond to subtle cues, such as facial expressions, and they invite audience members to be more passive than they might be in a smaller group. Large audiences often require microphones and podiums that can limit the speaker's movement, and they may require slides or large posters for visual aids.

Speakers need to be flexible enough to adapt to audience size. One of the authors was to give a presentation on leadership to an audience of more than 100 students in an auditorium that held 250 people. Only 25 students appeared. Instead of a formal presentation to a large group, the author faced a relatively small group in one corner of a large auditorium. Two hours later, the author was to speak to a small group of 12 or 15 that turned out to be 50. Do not depend on the planners to be correct about the size of your audience. Instead, be ready to adapt to the size of the audience that actually appears.

Environment

You also must be prepared to adapt to environmental factors. Your location may be plagued by visual obstructions such as pillars and posts, an unfortunate sound system, poor lighting, a room that is too warm or too cool, the absence of a podium or lectern, a microphone that is not movable, or a lack of audiovisual equipment. If you have specific audio, visual, or environmental needs, you should make your requests well in advance to the individual who has invited you to speak. At the very least, you will want to inquire about the room in which you are to speak.

Occasion

The *occasion* is another situational factor that makes a difference in how a speaker adapts to an audience. The speaker is expected to be upbeat and even funny at an after-dinner speech, sober and serious at a funeral, full of energy and enthusiasm at a pep rally, and prudent and factual in a court of law. Even in the classroom, a number of unstated assumptions about the occasion exist. You are expected to follow the assignment; not break laws or regulations of the campus, state, or nation; maintain eye contact; keep to the time limit; and dress appropriately for the occasion.

Outside the classroom, the confident presenter learns about the expectations for the occasion. Consider for a moment the unstated assumptions about these public presentation occasions:

- A high school commencement address.
- A persuasive message at a town meeting.
- A talk with the team before a big game.
- A demonstration of how to accurately read blood pressure.
- A motivational talk to your salespeople.
- An informative presentation on groundwater quality issues.
- An announcement of layoffs at the plant.

Each of these occasions calls for quite a different kind of presentation, the parameters of which are not clearly stated but are widely understood. Our society seems to dictate that you should not exhibit levity at funerals, nor should you be too verbose when you introduce another person. The best way to discover information about the occasion and expectations for it is to question the individual or the organization inviting you to speak.

"The speaker is expected to be upbeat and even funny at an after-dinner speech, sober and serious at a funeral, full of energy and enthusiasm at a pep rally, and prudent and factual in a court of law."

Time

A further aspect of any speaking situation that makes a difference to a speaker is when and for how long the presentation is given—the *time*. Time can include the time of day, the time that you speak during the occasion, and the amount of time you are expected to fill. Early morning speeches find an audience fresh but not quite ready for serious topics. After-lunch or after-dinner speeches invite the audience to sleep unless the speaker is particularly stimulating. The optimal time to speak is when the audience has come only to hear the speaker and nothing else.

The time you give the presentation during an occasion can make a big difference in audience receptivity. You will probably find that people are genuinely relieved when a presentation is shorter than expected, because so many speeches are longer than anyone wants. To overestimate our knowledge and charm and how excited an audience is to hear from us is easy. Audiences will be insulted if you give a presentation that is far short of expectations—5 minutes instead of 30—but they will often appreciate a 45-minute presentation when they have expected an hour.

Importance

The final situational factor is the *importance* of the occasion, the significance attached to the situation that dictates the speaker's seriousness, content, and approach. Some occasions are relatively low in importance, although generally the presence of a speaker signals that an event is not at all routine. An occasion of lesser importance must not be treated like one of great importance, and an occasion of greater importance should not be treated lightly.

What are the responsibilities of a speaker in a classroom setting, which is generally viewed as "less important" than many public speaking situations? The classroom talk may be viewed as relatively routine compared with a televised town hall debate. Are the obligations that you have in the classroom different from those that you would have if you were a community leader or activist?

We usually perceive rituals and ceremonial events as high in importance. We see the speaker at a university commencement exercise, the speaker at the opening of a new plant, and the speaker at a lecture as important players in a major event. Speakers at informal gatherings or local routine events are somewhat further down the scale. Nonetheless, a speaker must carefully gauge the importance of an event so the audience is not insulted by his or her frivolous treatment of what the audience regards as serious business.

The Uniqueness of the Classroom Audience

Students sometimes think of the speeches they deliver in public speaking class as a mere classroom exercise, not a real speech. Perhaps this is partly because they know that they have a grade riding on their speech. They may, therefore, be more concerned with the grade than with communicating their message effectively to the class.

Viewing the classroom speech as a mere exercise is an error. Classroom speeches are delivered to people who are influenced by what they see and hear. In fact, your classmates as an audience might be even more susceptible to your influence because of their *uniqueness* as an audience. Table 4.2 illustrates some of the unique characteristics of classroom audiences.

The classmates who make up your audience might have their own knowledge about, and positions on issues, but they are capable of changing their knowledge base and/or positions, too, as they listen and learn. Next, we will look at how you can adapt to your unique audience.

Adapting to Your Audience

This chapter has characterized several tools—observation, informants, interviews, and questionnaires—to use in analyzing your audiences. These tools of analysis and audience demographics will not be beneficial, however, unless you use them for the purpose of audience adaptation. **Audience adaptation** means *making the message appropriate for the particular audience by using analysis and applying its results to message creation.*

In the case of an informative presentation, adapting to the audience means *translating ideas*. Just as a translator at the United Nations explains an idea expressed in English to the representative from Brazil in Portuguese, a speaker who knows about

TABLE 4.2 UNIQUENESS OF THE CLASSROOM AUDIENCE

	CHARACTERISTICS OF THE CLASSROOM AUDIENCE	IMPLICATIONS FOR THE COMMUNICATOR
1	The classroom audience, because of the educational setting in which the presentation occurs, is exposed to messages it might otherwise avoid: the audience is "captive."	May add interactivity to increase interest and engagement.
2	The size of the audience tends to be relatively small (usually 20 to 25 students) and constant.	You can use more personal information and you can avoid microphones and other amplifying devices.
3	Classroom audiences include one person—the professor—who is responsible for evaluating and grading each presentation.	You might need to analyze the professor more carefully as an audience member than you do other members of the audience.
4	Classroom speeches tend to be short.	You must consider topics that can be managed in a brief period of time.
5	The classroom speech is nearly always one of a series of speeches in each class period.	You might keep in mind that visual aids, a dynamic delivery, and stylistic language are even more important than in other situations.
6	The speaker has an opportunity to listen to every member of the audience.	You can learn a great deal about your classmates' opinions, beliefs, and values and do a highly skillful audience analysis.
7	The classroom audience may be invited to provide written and/or oral feedback on the speech.	You can increase your skill as a communicator by carefully heeding any advice or criticism you are given.
8	The classroom speaker has more than one opportunity to influence or inform the audience.	You can show improvement over time.

baud rates, kilobytes, and megabytes must be able to translate those terms for an audience unfamiliar with them. Perhaps you have already met some apparently intelligent professors who know their subject matter well but are unable to translate it for students who do not. An important part of adapting an informative speech to an audience is the skill of *translating* ideas.

Your instructors—from kindergarten through college—are essentially informative speakers. You have heard people communicate informative material for 13 years or more. Consider some of your best instructors. Why were they effective in the classroom? They probably took the time to illustrate their points, instead of simply presenting information as an endless list of facts. This is translation.

Now consider those instructors you would deem poor teachers. What did they do that invites you to rate them lower? Did they talk "over your head" and use sentence structure and language that you did not understand at the time? They may have used examples from events that occurred years before you were born and provided no context for them. They might have used a great deal of jargon that confused you and seemed unapproachable.

In the case of persuasive presentations, adaptation means *adjusting your message both to the knowledge level of the listeners and to their present position on the issue*. Use the tools introduced in this chapter and the audience characteristics you discover to help you decide where you should position your message for maximum effect. Too often, speakers believe that the audience will simply adopt their point of view on an issue if they explain how they feel about the topic. Actually, the audience's position on the issue makes a greater difference than the speaker's does, so the speaker has to start by recognizing the audience's view. For example, if you believe the audience agrees with you, you can place your message early. If you believe they are in disagreement, you may need to proceed more cautiously.

Two students in a public speaking class provided excellent examples of what happens when the speaker does and does not adapt to the audience. Both speakers selected topics that seemed to have little appeal for the audience because both appeared to be expensive hobbies. One of the students spoke about raising an exotic breed of dog that only the rich could afford. The entire presentation was difficult for the listeners because they could not see themselves in a position of raising dogs for the wealthy.

The other student spoke about raising hackney ponies, an equally exclusive business. However, this student started by explaining that he grew up in a poor section of New Haven, Connecticut. His father was an immigrant who never earned much money, even though he spoke six languages. This student came from a large family, and he and his brothers pooled their earnings for many years before they had enough money to buy good breeding stock. They later earned money by selling colts and winning prize money in contests. By first explaining to the audience that he was an unlikely breeder of expensive horses, the speaker improved the chances that the audience could identify with him and his hobby. He adapted his message to the unique audience.

What kinds of messages influence you? Consider the variety of persuasive speakers you have heard—ministers, priests, rabbis, and other clergy; salespeople; teachers and parents; politicians and elected officials of our own and other countries; people lobbying for a special interest group; and people trying to convince you to change your cell phone service or to buy a home gym.

What kinds of appeals work for you—emotional appeals or logical ones? Do you need to believe in the ethical standards of the speaker before you will listen to what he or she has to say? Do you like to hear the most important arguments first or last? Do you tend to believe authorities, statistics, or other kinds of sources? If you use your own experiences and thoughtfully reflect on them, you may be able to understand better how others might respond favorably to you as a persuasive speaker and adapt your message to them.

Audience adaptation occurs before, during, and after a presentation. Central to your ability to adapt to your audience are your listening skills. In the classroom, listening to other speakers reveals information that will be valuable as you prepare your own presentations.

The Importance of Listening

Listening and Public Speaking

Both speaking and listening are essential components of public speaking. In the past, public speaking focused more on speakers and the creation and transmission of messages than on listeners and their active participation in the process. The role of the listener in communication has gained more importance. Indeed, current experts believe that listening is essential to the development of citizenship and a civil society.[8] If you are interested in further exploring the role of listening in a civil society, visit www.listen.org and consider its characterization of listening as the "language of peace."

You learn more by listening than by talking. Every speech you hear and every question asked and answered provides information about the people who will become your audience. Your serving as an audience member during your classmates' speeches provides you with an opportunity to analyze their choice of topics, the way they think, and the approaches they use. In short, being an audience member invites you to analyze your audience throughout the course.

You may not have thought of this fact when you enrolled in a public speaking class, but you will listen to many speeches for every speech you deliver. Over the course of the school term, you will likely hear between 100 and 200 speeches in your public speaking course. You will learn ways to evaluate speeches and ways to improve your own speeches. And you will learn methods of argument that you can employ.

Becoming a Better Listener

How can you improve your listening skills? Consider the many situations in which you listen: when you attend class and listen to an instructor, when you learn how to read to children from the director of the volunteer literacy program, or when you attend a lecture and listen to a visiting speaker. Your purpose is to understand the information the speaker is presenting. You may try to understand relevant information about the speaker and factors that led to the speech, as well as the central idea of the speech itself. Listening requires a high level of involvement in the communication process. The following suggestions, which are also summarized in Figure 4.3, should help you become a more effective listener.

Suspend judgments about the speaker. Suspend your premature judgments about the speaker so you can listen for information. Wait until you have heard a speaker before you conclude that he or she is, or is not, worthy of your attention. If you make decisions about people because of their membership in a particular group, you risk serious error. For example, gay men or lesbian women could be against same-sex marriage, members of fraternities may not be conformists, and artists are often disciplined.

Focus on the speaker as a source of information. You can dismiss people when you categorize them. When you focus on a speaker as a valuable human resource who can share information, ideas, thoughts, and feelings, you are better able to listen with interest and respect. Every speaker you hear is likely to have some information you do not already know. Try to focus on these opportunities to learn something new. Resist categorizing the speaker and dismissing his or her message as a consequence.

Concentrate your attention on the speaker. If you find yourself dismissing many of the speeches you hear as boring, consider whether you are overly egocentric. Perhaps your inclination to find your classmates' speeches boring is due to your inability to focus on other people. Egocentrism is a trait that is difficult to overcome. The wisest suggestion, in this case, is to keep in mind one of the direct benefits of concentrating your attention on the speaker: if you focus on the other person while she is speaking, she will probably focus on you when you are speaking. Even more important, you will come across better as a speaker if others perceive you to be a careful listener. Nothing else you can do—including dieting, using makeup, wearing new clothing, or making other improvements—will make you as attractive to others as learning to listen to them.

Listen to the entire message. Do not tune out a speech after you have heard the topic. More than likely, the speaker will add new information, insights, or experiences that will shed light on the subject. One professor teaches an upper-division argumentation course to 20 students each quarter. She assigns four speeches, but every speech is given on the same topic. In a 10-week period, students hear 80 speeches on the same topic, but every speech contains some new information. The class would be dismal if the students dismissed the speeches after hearing they would all cover the same topic.

Instead of considering the speeches boring, students find them interesting, exciting, and highly creative.

Focus on the values or experiences you share with the speaker. If you find you are responding emotionally to a speaker's position on a topic and you directly oppose what he or she is recommending, try to concentrate your attention on the attitudes, beliefs, or values you have in common. Try to identify with statements the speaker is making. The speaker might seem to be attacking one of your own beliefs or attitudes, but, if you listen carefully, you may find that the speaker is actually defending it from a different perspective. Maximizing our shared ideas and minimizing our differences result in improved listening and better communication.

Focus on the main ideas the speaker is presenting. Keep in mind that you do not have to memorize the facts a speaker presents. Rarely will you be given an objective examination on the material in a student speech. If you want to learn more about the information being presented, ask the speaker after class for a copy of the outline, a bibliography, or other pertinent documentation. Asking the speaker for further information is flattering; however, stating in class that you can recall the figures cited but have no idea of the speaker's purpose may seem offensive.

Recall the arbitrary nature of words. If you find that you sometimes react emotionally to four-letter words or to the specific usage of some words, you may be forgetting that words are simply arbitrary symbols people have chosen to represent certain things. Words do not have inherent, intrinsic, "real" meanings. When a speaker uses a word in an unusual way, or when you are unfamiliar with a certain word, do not hesitate to ask how the word is being used. Asking for such information makes the speaker feel good because you are showing interest in the speech, and the inquiry will contribute to your own knowledge. If you cannot overcome a negative reaction to the speaker's choice of words, recognize that the emotional reaction is yours and not necessarily a feeling shared by the rest of the class or the speaker. Listeners need to be open-minded; speakers need to show responsibility in word choice.

Focus on the intent as well as the content of the message. As you listen to a speaker, focus both on what is said and why it is said—the speaker's intent. Instead of embarking on mental excursions about other topics, focus on all aspects of the topic the speaker has selected. Consider the speaker's background and his or her motivation for selecting a particular topic. Try to relate the major points the speaker has made to his or her stated intentions. By refusing to consider other, unrelated matters, you will greatly increase your understanding of the speaker and the speech.

Be aware of your listening intensity. You listen with varying degrees of intensity. Sometimes when a parent or roommate gives you information, you barely listen. However, when your supervisor calls you in for an unexpected conference, your listening is very intense. Occasionally, we trick ourselves into listening less intensely than we should. Everyone knows to take notes when the professor says, "This will be on the test," but only an intense listener captures the important content in an apparently boring lecture. You need to become a good judge of how intensely to listen and to learn ways to alter your listening intensity. Sitting on the front of the chair, acting very interested, and nodding affirmatively when you agree are some methods that people use to listen with appropriate intensity.

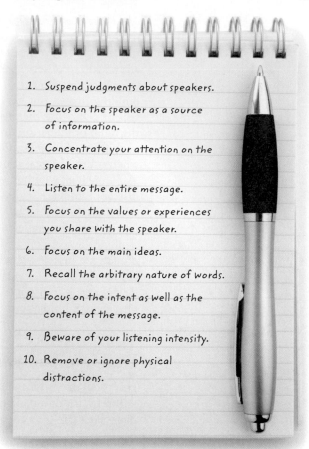

1. Suspend judgments about speakers.
2. Focus on the speaker as a source of information.
3. Concentrate your attention on the speaker.
4. Listen to the entire message.
5. Focus on the values or experiences you share with the speaker.
6. Focus on the main ideas.
7. Recall the arbitrary nature of words.
8. Focus on the intent as well as the content of the message.
9. Beware of your listening intensity.
10. Remove or ignore physical distractions.

Figure 4.3   **Guidelines for becoming a better listener.**

"You need to become a good judge of how intensely to listen and to learn ways to alter your listening intensity."

Remove or ignore physical distractions. Frequently, you can deal with physical distractions—such as an unusual odor, bright lights, or a distracting noise—by moving the stimulus or yourself. In other words, do not choose a seat near the doorway that allows you to observe people passing by in the hall, do not sit so that the sunlight is in your eyes, and do not sit so far away from the speaker that maintenance noises in the building drown out her voice. If you cannot avoid the distraction by changing your seat or removing the distracting object, try to ignore it. You probably can study with the radio or television on, sleep without having complete darkness, and eat while other people are milling around you. Similarly, you can focus your attention on the speaker when other physical stimuli are in your environment.

Consider whether you would be able to concentrate on the speech if it were, instead, a movie you have been wanting to see, a musical group you enjoy, or a play that has received a rave review. One man said that when he had difficulty staying up late to study in graduate school, he considered whether he would have the same difficulty if he were on a date. If the answer was no, he could then convince himself that the fatigue he felt was a function of the task, not of his sleepiness. The same principle can work for you. Consider whether the distractions are merely an excuse for your lack of desire to listen to the speaker. Generally you will find you can ignore the other physical stimuli in your environment if you wish to do so.

Evaluate Your Listening Skills

How well do you listen? Consider a recent experience when you listened to a presentation by another person. Alternatively, use this self-evaluation when you listen to the next classmate give a speech:

1. Did you find something to arouse interest in the speech?
2. Did you find the subject interesting?
3. Did you listen to the message rather than to how it was delivered?
4. Did you listen with a purpose?
5. Did you listen for major ideas and relationships among various points?
6. Did you sit in a place where you could both hear the speaker and listen to the speech?
7. Did you avoid or ignore distractions?
8. Did you subordinate specific words to the total meaning of the content?
9. Did you pay close attention so that at any point you could summarize the speaker's main ideas up to that point in the talk?
10. Did you listen to all the speaker had to say before criticizing it?

Ethics and the Audience

As you prepare to speak to a particular audience, remember ethical considerations, those moral choices you make as a speaker. Audiences expect different levels of truthfulness in different situations. A comedian is expected to exaggerate, distort, and even fabricate stories. A salesperson is expected to highlight the virtues of a product and think less of the competition. A priest, a judge, and a professor are expected to tell the truth. In the classroom, the audience expects the speaker to inform with honesty and to persuade with reason.

Most speakers have a position on an issue. The priest tries to articulate the church's position, the judge follows a body of precedents, and the professor tries to reveal what is known from her discipline's point of view. You, too, have reasons for your beliefs, your positions on issues, and the values you espouse. The general guideline in your relationship with your audience is that you should have the audience's best interests in mind.

Next Steps in Audience Analysis

In this chapter, we talked about audience analysis and audience adaptation. Keep in mind that this process continues as you prepare your presentation. You will apply what you learn about the audience to the research you conduct, the kinds of supporting materials you choose, and the arguments you make. In the next chapter, you will learn about why you will benefit from conducting research for your speech. Armed with the information on audience analysis and adaptation in this chapter, you will be ready to make ethical and informed decisions on using your own experiences, the Internet, and the library for conducting research.

For REVIEW >>

SUMMARY HIGHLIGHTS

Audience Analysis

▶ Audience analysis includes knowing the demographic features of your audience, including gender, age, ethnicity, economic status, occupation, education, and shared experiences.

▶ Situational analysis includes knowing the size of the audience, the environment, the occasion, the time, and the importance of the situation.

Methods of Audience Analysis

▶ You can make observations and consider your group identification.

▶ You can also conduct interviews or use questionnaires to gather information.

Analysis of the Situation

▶ You must consider five factors when analyzing the situations you face as a speaker: the size of your audience, the environment, the occasion, the time, and the importance of the situation.

The Uniqueness of the Classroom Audience

▶ The audience is captive; the size of the audience tends to be relatively small; one person takes responsibility for evaluating the talk, though others may be invited to provide feedback.

▶ The speeches tend to be short, they are one in a series, speakers have the opportunity to listen to every member of the audience, and speakers have more than one opportunity to influence or inform the audience.

Adapting to Your Audience

▶ Remember to make your message appropriate for your audience by using audience analysis and applying the results to the preparation of your presentation.

▶ This might mean adjusting your message both to the knowledge level of the listeners and to their present position on the issue you address.

Listening and Public Speaking

▶ Listening to others is essential as you provide feedback to them and as you determine how to adapt your message.

Ethics and the Audience

▶ Ethical considerations are paramount as you analyze the audience and adapt your message.

▶ It is important to avoid stereotyping when selecting an appropriate topic for an audience.

pop Quiz

1. Gender composition, age, ethnicity, and occupation comprise an audience's:
   (A) situational analysis
   (B) ethical principles
   (C) values
   (D) demographics

2. When speaking to an audience comprised of college first-year students with undecided majors, you should:
   (A) use very specific examples
   (B) avoid including all audience members
   (C) tell generic anecdotes
   (D) use jargon relevant to the communication studies field

3. Mark watches and listens to the audience before he gives his presentation. He is utilizing a method of audience analysis called:
   (A) group identification
   (B) observation

   (C) interviews
   (D) questionnaires

4. "Do you like dogs?" is an example of a(n):
   (A) open-ended question
   (B) closed-ended question
   (C) observation
   (D) environmental factor

5. Justin modified his speech on healthy eating to include nutritional choices that can be made at the local campus dining halls. This is an example of:
   (A) audience adaptation
   (B) worldview
   (C) audience analysis
   (D) observation

Answers: 1 (D); 2 (C); 3 (B); 4 (B); 5 (A)

APPLICATION EXERCISES

1. You have already talked to multiple audiences, especially in informal settings (planning an evening with friends, discussing an adventure with other couples, speaking up at a parent–teacher meeting). How many of these audiences can you recall? How would you describe some of these audiences? Provide as much detail as you can about each of them. Then compare notes with a classmate to see what assumptions you made about your audiences. Remember that one danger in audience analysis is projection.

2. Given the observations listed here, what do you think would be the audience's probable response to a presentation on Social Security issues, world hunger, the erosion of the environment, or changing sexual

   mores? For each statement about the audience, state how you believe they would generally feel about the topic.

   a. The audience responded favorably to an earlier informative speech on race relations.

   b. The audience consists mainly of urban people from ethnic neighborhoods.

   c. The audience consists of many married persons with families.

   d. The audience members attend night school on earnings from daytime jobs in factories and retail businesses.

e. The audience members come from large families.

f. The audience includes many people from developing countries.

g. The audience consists of people from ages 18 to 29.

3. Determine answers to the following questions for your class:

a. What is the age range of the members of the class audience?

b. What are the economic backgrounds of the class?

c. Describe classmates with any obvious disabilities.

d. What styles of clothes do the audience members wear?

e. Describe other features of the students' appearance such as style, gender-display, and fitness.

f. How much do class members interact before and after class?

g. How much time do classmates spend on Facebook?

h. What interests or hobbies do the students discuss?

i. Describe other behavior, both verbal and nonverbal, of the class members.

j. Are various ethnic groups or nondominant groups represented?

What are the implications you might draw from these observations? How should you adapt your speech based on these observations?

4. The audiences you face today may not be identical to the audiences you will face in the future. Review the list of audiences on page 65, and add to this list three audiences to whom you foresee yourself presenting in the next 10 years.

5. Listen to a speech in the classroom, on the Internet, or elsewhere on campus. Using a scale of 1–5 (1 = poor; 5 = excellent), rate your ability to listen on the following dimensions:

a. Suspending judgments

b. Regarding the speaker as a source of valuable information

c. Concentrating on the speaker

d. Listening to the entire message

e. Focusing on shared values and experiences

f. Focusing on the main ideas

g. Focusing on the intent of the message

h. Removing or ignoring physical distractions

KEY TERMS

Audience adaptation	Demographics	Observation
Audience analysis	Ethnicity	Open-ended questions
Closed or closed-ended questions	Inside informant	Projection
Conventional wisdom	Interviews	Questionnaires
Degree questions	Nondominant groups	

5

FINDING
INFORMATION

This chapter will help you find information you will use to prepare presentations. You will learn various strategies you can use—including personal experience, interviews, the library, and the Internet—to find information. You'll also learn how to evaluate sources of information and use different types of supporting material found in presentations.

AND SUPPORTING
YOUR IDEAS

Gary Wolf, a contributing editor at *Wired*, likes numbers. In particular, Wolf enjoys the challenge of finding increasingly unobtrusive ways to monitor and capture the numerical data that reflect his physical health. When he walks, he can monitor his heart rate; when resting, he tracks his blood pressure and body temperature. Much of these data, as Wolf points out, can be measured by sensors much smaller than a piece of pocket change and can be interpreted and displayed on devices as handy as a computer or smartphone.

In his TED talk, "The Quantified Self," Wolf explains how our ability to monitor our physical health can lead to new levels of self-knowledge. According to Wolf, your heart rate, blood pressure, and blood glucose levels represent an intricate narrative of causes and effects that, taken together, characterize your general health and reveal significant details about who you are. As a viewer or audience member, you might expect Wolf's fascination with numbers to be portrayed in graphs, charts, and detailed analyses. Instead, Wolf uses numbers to quantify self-knowledge— examples of which would be difficult to portray in a pie chart or graph.

Numbers are just one example of supporting material that you can use in speeches. In this chapter, you will learn to locate, evaluate, and use supporting material so that your presentations are well documented and compelling.

Why You'll Benefit from Research

You just read about Gary Wolf, who relied on examples to make complex topics easier to follow. Gary's presentation emphasized the stories behind numbers used to quantify our health. If you were giving a speech on the importance of monitoring your own health, what types of supporting material would you use?

In Chapter 2, you learned about the metaphorical lifeblood of speechmaking— the invention process. As you recall, invention involves taking ideas and giving them substance through supporting materials like narratives, quotations, statistics, and so on. Whereas other chapters have taught you how to brainstorm and then narrow your ideas, this chapter is specifically focused on research, the process of finding and using evidence to support your ideas.

Good research is essential to good speaking. To be more specific, you must find a variety of high-quality sources and then think carefully about how to best integrate information from those sources into your speech. For any given speech topic—take

TABLE 5.1 RESEARCH AND THE PRESENTATION PREPARATION PROCESS

	PREPARATION STEP	BENEFIT OF RESEARCH
1	Topic selection	Research helps you discover and narrow topics.
2	Organizing ideas	Research helps you identify main and subordinate points.
3	Supporting ideas	Research provides facts, examples, and definitions to give substance to your points.
4	Preparing introduction and conclusion	Research may reveal interesting examples, stories, or quotes.
5	Practice and delivery	Because your speech is well researched, you will feel more confident and will seem more credible.

coal mining, for example—you can obtain information from a variety of sources ranging from personal experiences and interviews to magazines, academic journals, and government documents. There are even YouTube videos showing the technique of mountain top removal in certain regions where coal mining takes place.

The process of research can be broken down into three basic steps:

1. Use a wide variety of resources to locate high-quality information.
2. Analyze the credibility of those resources to select the best possible evidence for use in your speech.
3. Integrate that evidence in ways that advance your own arguments, positions, and explanations.

Indeed, these three steps are not limited in importance to public speaking; in our information-saturated world, they are in fact becoming critical life skills. Regardless of whether you are making arguments with friends and colleagues or teaching a group of people how to do something, supporting material provides the basis for ideas, thoughts, and positions that you develop. When presenting a formal speech, think of your speech as a series of main points and subpoints that form the basis of your positions. Each of those points and subpoints need to have the adequate support or your position will fail. More broadly, Table 5.1 shows that effective research can positively affect nearly every element of your speech.

Finding Sources of Information

Effective speakers achieve success through well-crafted presentations that contain compelling evidence and support. Advances in technology—in particular the Internet and online databases—help smart researchers find high-quality information very quickly. Not all research, however, requires a broadband connection. In this section, you will learn about a variety of research tools, ranging from your own knowledge to highly specialized databases.

Personal Experience

Your **personal experience**, *your own life as a source of information*, is something about which you can speak with considerable authority. One university has developed an initiative to recruit veterans who are leaving military service. Professors there have noticed how this influx of veterans has affected the types of speeches given in public speaking classes. Now, audience members are likely to hear informative speeches about survival skills, communicating with family members from around the world, and the effects of post-traumatic stress disorders. In all of these cases, student-veterans are able to draw from significant personal experience to provide rich explanations and examples while also solidifying their credibility as speakers on these topics.

Before basing your presentation on personal experience, however, you should ask yourself critical questions about the usefulness of this information. Some of your experiences may be too personal or too intimate to share with strangers or classmates. Other experiences may be interesting but irrelevant to the topic of your speech. You should evaluate your personal experience as **evidence**, *data on which proof may be based*, by considering the following questions:

1. How typical was your experience with the topic?
   a. Was your experience so typical that it will bore the audience?
   b. Was your experience so atypical that it was a chance occurrence?
2. Was your experience so personal and revealing that it will make the audience feel uncomfortable?
3. Was your experience one that audience members will be able to relate to in terms of emotions or feelings?
4. Will your audience be able to learn from your experience to change their own attitudes, behaviors, or ways of thinking?
5. Does your experience really provide proof of anything?

Considering the ethics of using your personal experience is also important. Will it harm others? Is the experience firsthand (your own), or is it someone else's experience? Retelling the experiences of a friend or even family member is questionable because secondhand information is easily distorted. Unless the experience is your own, you may find yourself passing along incorrect information. Also, personal experience is different from personal opinion. While carefully selected personal experiences can potentially provide excellent illustrations of the points you are making, personal opinion needs to be well supported with other types of evidence.

Library Resources

A second source of information is all the resources that are available at your school's library—magazines, journals, newspapers, books, videotapes, government documents, and other materials. Be sure to check with a **reference librarian**, *a librarian specifically trained to help find sources of information*, if you are unfamiliar with resources available at

your library. The reference department in your library has many useful sources. In addition to specialized encyclopedias, there are specialized dictionaries, yearbooks, books of quotations, biographical sketches of prominent individuals, and atlases. A reference librarian can quickly help you determine whether these specialized reference resources are helpful for your presentation topic.

Most libraries offer a number of indexes you can use to locate sources of information. Indeed, modern libraries offer so many options for finding information that the most difficult task is often knowing where to begin. Library websites typically offer two general options for locating information: the holdings database and electronic periodical indexes. You might need to consult with a librarian or with other students to learn how to access them.

The Holdings Database

Libraries are organized using a **holdings database**, which *indexes all books, journals, periodicals, and other resources owned by the library.* The holdings database is a common starting point for finding information, and it organizes materials by subject, author, title, and call number. The call number is used to find the physical location of resources in the library. Most databases also provide links to electronic versions of resources if they exist. When you search for a topic using the holdings database, you can begin by typing in a keyword for your topic. Depending on how broad or narrow your keyword is, the database will return a list of subtopics or a list of resource titles (e.g., books, reference resources, etc.) relevant to your topic. For example, if you type in a keyword such as "alternative energy," the database might return several books with that phrase in the title. Figure 5.1 illustrates the information you might see if you click on one of those resources, in this case a transcript of hearings before the U.S. Senate Committee on Energy and Natural Resources. Notice that the holdings information shows the exact title, call number, and publication information for the book as well as telling you that the book is "available" for checkout. Each holdings database will look slightly different; however, the same essential information should be present.

Holdings databases are not just for locating books. Most libraries allow patrons to search for titles of periodicals and other resources as well. Although the holdings database will not allow you to search for specific articles in a magazine or technical journal—for that you will use a periodical index—you can use the holdings database to physically locate the source. In some cases, the database will provide a link to an electronic full-text version of the periodical so that you can browse for articles.

Periodical Indexes

Periodicals are *sources of information that are published at regular intervals.* Magazines, newspapers, and academic journals are all examples of periodicals found in your library. Periodicals are a different kind of resource than books. With books, you are

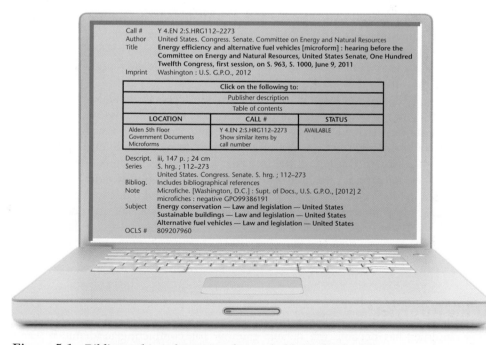

Figure 5.1   **Bibliographic information from a holdings database.**

TABLE 5.2 COMMON PERIODICAL INDEXES

Index Name	Index Description
Academic Search Premier and Academic Search Complete	Excellent for basic research on various topics, the Academic Search Premier provides citations and full-text articles for more than 7,000 scholarly publications ranging from arts and literature to the sciences.
Communication and Mass Media Complete	This database provides citations and full-text articles on topics related to communication and mass media issues.
ERIC	ERIC indexes over 900 scholarly sources covering topics generally related to education.
Humanities Abstracts	Humanities Abstracts cites articles from over 500 periodicals relevant to various humanities topics like the arts and literature.
Lexis-Nexis	This substantial database provides full-text articles from newspapers and magazines as well as transcripts of news broadcasts, legal cases, and testimony before Congress.
Medline	A premier index for medical issues, this database offers citations and some full-text articles.
Reader's Guide	This source indexes articles from 1901 to the present. Most are from popular U.S.-American magazines.
Social Sciences Index	With citations and full-text articles, this index covers a broad range of social-scientific topics including politics, social psychology, and crime.

typically interested in the entire book, whereas with periodicals, you are usually interested in specific stories or articles rather than the entire issue or edition. For that reason, you must use specialized databases to locate specific articles on your topic. Table 5.2 lists several of the most common databases and describes the types of information for which they are useful.

Although the indexes listed in Table 5.2 provide access to hundreds of thousands of citations, you may wish to consult even more specialized databases to which your library subscribes. If your topic is very specialized, consultation with a reference librarian could point you in the direction of valuable resources. Periodical indexes work like most search engines on the Internet. Effective researchers often use more than one periodical index to find information. For example, if your presentation deals with a medical topic like obesity, starting with a general index such as Academic Search Complete or LexisNexis and then moving to a specialized index such as Medline is an effective approach. Also, not every library has all these databases—a reference librarian can help you find alternatives if your library does not subscribe to a particular database.

The Internet

The Internet has become the default gateway for conducting academic research for students and faculty alike. Whereas in the mid-1990s teachers could make easy distinctions between the Internet and "library research," those distinctions have become increasingly blurred as most libraries now have web-based portals where patrons can access library services from any computer in the world. Besides library resources, the Internet provides unparalleled access to multimedia files (e.g., YouTube), pictures, and other types of information.

Even with the many advantages that it has to offer, you have to be careful when using the web. University of Georgia Professor Joseph Dominick says, "Some have described using the Internet as trying to find your way across a big city without a map. You'll see lots of interesting stuff but may never get to where you're going."[1] The trick to not getting lost while researching on the web is to keep some simple ideas in mind. First, you should remember that there is a difference between "free" and "fee." The best information on the web comes from high-quality sources that cost money. Fortunately, your library likely already pays for several web-based services that you can access. Second, start at a good landmark. Google and other "free" search services are less effective starting points than is the Library of Congress or your university library. Third, verify what you find. If you use a free search service like Google, take extra time to thoroughly verify what you find.

Locating Web Sources

To maximize the variety of sources that you can use in your speech, you will likely spend some time using more common web search tools like Google or Yahoo! The following steps describe a strategy that you can use to improve your web search approach:

1. Begin by using a **search engine**, which is *a website on the Internet that is specially designed to help you search for information*. Although search engines will locate thousands of websites that contain the word or phrase you are searching for, one criticism of search engines is that they return hundreds of irrelevant websites. An alternative to using a search engine is to use a **virtual library**, which *provides links to websites that have been reviewed for relevance and usability*. Table 5.3 provides web addresses for several popular search engines and virtual libraries. Meta-search engines are useful because they combine the results of individual search engines like Yahoo! and Excite.

2. Search engines will allow you to refine and narrow your searches to be more precise. For instance, if you use Google to search for the topic "education reform" (typed without the quotation marks surrounding the phrase), the search engine will return more than 20 million results—quite impressive, but a lot to sift through! By placing quotation marks around the phrase, you can use a phrase search. Searching for "education reform" (typed with the quotation marks), the number of hits is reduced to just over 6 million.

    What exactly happens when searching for a phrase rather than the two terms? When typing the two terms—education and reform—without quotation marks, Google searches for all web documents containing both the terms "education" and "reform." Thus, Google might suggest a webpage with the following sentence: "We need more **education** about how to **reform** agriculture policy in Argentina." In this case, the webpage met your search criteria of having the two terms, but the information is clearly irrelevant to your speech topic. However, when searching for "education reform" as a phrase, Google will only return sources that have the terms "education" and "reform" right

TABLE 5.3 WEB SEARCH RESOURCES

META-SEARCH ENGINES

Google: www.google.com

Dogpile: www.dogpile.com

MetaCrawler: www.metacrawler.com

Bing: www.bing.com

COMMON SEARCH ENGINES

Yahoo!: www.yahoo.com

AltaVista: www.altavista.com

Encyclopedia Britannica Internet Guide: www.britannica.com

Excite: www.excite.com

Lycos: www.lycos.com

HotBot: www.hotbot.com

VIRTUAL LIBRARIES

The WWW Virtual Library: www.vlib.org

Yahoo! Libraries: http://dir.yahoo.com/Reference/Libraries

next to each other, and in that order. While 6 million sources is still a lot to digest, at least your efforts will be more efficient! Examples of ways to better frame your searches are shown in Table 5.4.

Another site that can help you refine your searches is dmoz.org. That site allows you to select links that provide progressively more specific information about a general topic area. This approach, rather than a more conventional search engine, is most useful when you are still trying to explore possible topics and do not yet have search terms or phrases identified. Figure 5.2 shows you what the open directory page of dmoz.org looks like, while Figure 5.3 shows a list of web links for a particular topic.

3. Carefully *evaluate all sources of information* you find on the Internet, especially when you locate the sources through a public search engine rather than your university library's home page. Suggestions for evaluating web sources and other types of information are provided in subsequent sections of this chapter.

4. Print or bookmark good sources so that you can easily reference them while planning your presentation. By bookmarking the webpage, you can easily access the site later without having to retrace the steps of your search. If you are familiar with how to create a PDF of a webpage, you may want to do that as well. Because websites are constantly changing, having a PDF of sources that you use can help you more easily locate or at least verify the existence of a source should the website change.

5. In addition to printing and bookmarking your sources, you can subscribe to an RSS (Really Simple Syndication) feed, which will allow you to receive and save up-to-date information from that site. You can add RSS feeds to your home page or other XML-capable personal webpages. If you plan to research and speak on a topic frequently, subscribing to RSS feeds on highly relevant websites is an effective way to stay up-to-date.

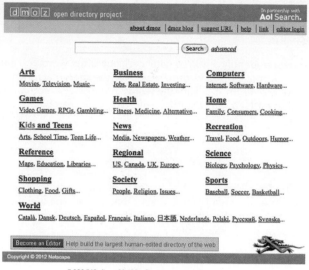

Figure 5.2   **The dmoz.org open directory page.**

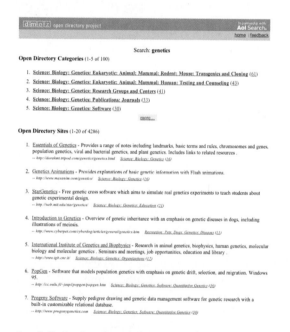

Figure 5.3   **List of web links for the topic of genetics on dmoz.org.**

One of the problems with using the Internet for information is that this medium is unregulated. The information may be biased, or just plain wrong, because no authority monitors the content of the sites. How do you determine what information is accurate and credible? Ultimately, *you* will have to make that decision. Ask yourself whether someone would have reason to present biased information. If at all possible, verify the information through other sources, such as newspaper or magazine articles. If the source is a scholarly article, check for a list of references, and if a list of references is provided, try to determine whether the list is credible by verifying some of the sources. Finally, credible sources often provide the credentials of the individual(s) who wrote the article. If no source is provided, be cautious. In a world dominated by digital information—websites, television, mobile apps, and the like—the most significant problem is not *how to find* information, but rather, how to find *good* information. Learning those skills can affect nearly all aspects of your life.

TABLE 5.4 TOOLS FOR NARROWING YOUR WEB SEARCH

WORD STEMMING

By default, browsers identify any Web page containing the word you entered in the search box. For example, if you want to search for the speech acronym "INFORM," the search engine would return sites with the words informative, information, informal, informing, and so forth. To prevent this result, type your search term with a single quote at the end.

   Example: inform'

PHRASE SEARCH

If you are looking for a phrase, put the phrase in quotation marks. For example, simply typing in *homeless youth* would return all sites that contain the two words "homeless" and "youth" anywhere on the site. Placing the phrase in quote marks will return only sites using the phrase "homeless youth."

   Example: "homeless youth"

BOOLEAN OPERATORS

Boolean operators allow you to specify logical arguments for what you want returned in a list of matching Web sites. When multiple terms are typed in a search box (e.g., "tobacco addiction"), the default Boolean operator is to place "AND" between the terms. Returned Web sites will contain both tobacco AND addiction somewhere on the page. Other Boolean operators include NOT (e.g., "PowerPoint NOT Microsoft"), which will return Web sites with the term before the operator but not sites with the term after the operator. You can also use the operator OR to find sites with one of two possible terms (e.g., "Gauguin OR van Gogh").

PARENTHESES

Using parentheses allows you to nest Boolean search arguments. In the following example, the search argument will look for Web sites containing the terms "media" and "violence" but not "television."

   Example: (media AND violence) NOT television

One additional point to remember is that people have different motives for creating webpages. Some websites intend to provide information, others intend to persuade, and others are profit driven. Some websites try to conceal their true motives—a website might look informative but is actually telling only part of a story to persuade you to purchase a service or product. One way to understand the motive of a website is to pay attention to the server extension. Table 5.5 explains the parts of a web address and the characteristics of web addresses with different types of server extensions. No single type of web address—based on the server extension—is always better than another. All types of sources, web or otherwise, deserve scrutiny.

Other Resources on the Web

In addition to search engines, several reference and primary resources are available. Although this list could change daily, the following sources may be helpful depending on your presentation topic:

- *USA.gov* (www.usa.gov). A topical guide and search engine for all public resources on the web from the U.S. government.
- *Fedstats* (www.fedstats.gov). A government website providing access to statistical information from more than 100 federal agencies.
- *SearchGov* (www.searchgov.com). This search engine provides access to federal, state, and local government websites. The site also provides links to commonly accessed websites and the ability to search military websites.

TABLE 5.5 BREAKING DOWN WEB ADDRESSES

ELEMENTS OF A WEB ADDRESS

http://iwin.nws.noaa.gov/iwin/iwdspg1.html

Server   Server extension   Exact location on server

COMMON SERVER EXTENSIONS

EXTENSION	DESCRIPTION	EXAMPLES
.ed	Primarily college and university websites	www.ohio.edu Website for Ohio University
.com	Primarily commercial or for-profit website	www.mhhe.com Website for McGraw-Hill Higher Education
.gov	Government websites	www.ed.gov Website for the U.S. Department of Education
.net	Primarily Internet service provider public sites; sometimes used as an alternative when a ".com" name has already been taken	www.maui.net Website for island of Maui
.org	Primarily not-for-profit organizations	billofrightsinstitute.org Website sponsored by the public charity, Bill of Rights Institute www.helping.org A resource site for volunteerism and nonprofit organizations

- *The CIA World Factbook* (www.cia.gov/cia/publications/factbook/). You do not have to be a secret agent to access the resources of CIA headquarters in Langley, Virginia. The CIA World Factbook contains detailed information about every country in the world as well as "global" statistics like the total landmass in the world, the global economy, and the current estimated population of Earth.
- *Reference Resources at Yahoo!* (http://dir.yahoo.com/Reference/). If you need a dictionary, a thesaurus, an almanac, quotations, or other reference resources, Yahoo! has an excellent set of links to browse.

Even for specialized topics such as multiculturalism, co-culture, or ethnicity, the Web is an excellent resource. If you need to research various cultural issues, try these sources:

- *Yahoo! Regional* (http://dir.yahoo.com/Regional/). This Yahoo! directory provides links to information on various countries and regions of the United States.
- *The WWW Library—Native Americans* (www.hanksville.org/NAresources/). This site provides links to information about Native Americans on the web.
- *Black History Quest* (http://blackquest.com). Resources on African American history and culture.
- *Latin American Network Information Center* (http://lanic.utexas.edu). Information on Latino history and culture in the United States.
- *Asian-Nation* (www.asian-nation.org). This web portal provides links to resources addressing Asian American history and culture.

Engaging Social and Digital Media

Chances are you have been to a museum and viewed the impressive array of artifacts that museum curators place out for display. Did you know that curation is becoming a hot topic on the Web as well? **Content curation** is *the process of finding and sorting through large amounts of information on the web and organizing it for public display around a specific theme.* For instance, one of the authors of this textbook uses Scoop.it to curate information on the topic of classroom communication and technology. On that curation site, you can read more than 75 articles and webpages directly related to that topic—pages carefully selected because they highlight a particular issue or discuss it in a novel way. In fact, you have likely already acted as a content curator. Facebook is really nothing more than a content curation site organized around ourselves (although you can also use Facebook to create pages about socially relevant topics). In addition to Scoop.it, you can also curate on other sites like Storify and BagTheWeb.

As a public speaking student, you can use content curation in two ways. First, if you find topics on a content curation site, you may be able to use that site to quickly find very high-quality sources selected by an expert on the topic. Still, you should take care to verify information found in those sources. Second, you may become an expert and begin curating content over your speech topic. As you progress through school, you could use the same topic for multiple projects and be able to make the most of your curated information.

The Wikipedia Controversy

The National Communication Association is the largest scholarly organization in the field of communication. One of the services offered by NCA is a listserv called CRT-NET (Communication Research and Theory Network). Periodically, there are discussions in CRT-NET about the use of Wikipedia in speeches. On one side of the controversy, professors argued that Wikipedia is largely unregulated and nothing more than an encyclopedia—a type of source that is discouraged in speeches

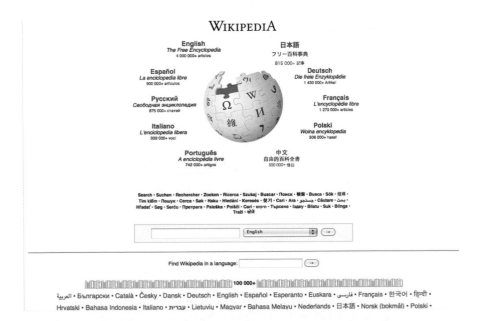

regardless of whether it is from the Internet or found in a library reference department. Others argue that Wikipedia reflects a type of source unique to the Internet—a user-created dialogue where information is democratically created and shared. The debate about using Wikipedia in a speech or paper is important because issues in the debate highlight how information available on the Internet changes more rapidly than our accepted norms and standards can adapt. You should discuss with your teacher the accepted guidelines for using Wikipedia and, for that matter, other web resources, in your class. Remember that although you can learn about general standards for source quality in this chapter, each audience may have slightly different expectations. Good speakers learn to adapt to what their audiences expect.

Interviews with Others

Another important source of ideas and information for your speech is other people. With its numerous faculty, staff, and students, your campus has many experts on particular subjects. Your community, likewise, is populated with people who have expertise on many issues: government workers on politics; clergy on religion; physicians, psychologists, and nurses on healthcare; engineers on highways and buildings; and owners and managers on industry and business.

Think of your own interests. Do you like to listen to music? If you could interview your favorite artist, what would you ask? If you could speak to the president, what would you want to know? We have a natural tendency to want to ask others questions about things for which we lack information. Likewise, when we can hear the results of those interviews by others, we are captivated. In fact, major segments of our entertainment industry are geared toward allowing us to watch others being interviewed. Starting with early morning news programs and ending with late-night variety shows, interviews with celebrities and other notable individuals provide nonstop entertainment options. You can invoke this same intrigue with your presentation.

"Good speakers learn to adapt to what their audiences expect."

You will discover that interviewing is an efficient way to gather information on your topic. The person you interview can furnish ideas, quotations, and valuable leads to other sources. First, however, learn when and how to prepare for the interview, conduct the interview, and use the results.

Preparing for the Interview

Most students are surprised that important people at their university or in their community are more than willing to talk with them about their presentation. Because the person is doing you an important favor, you have a responsibility to carefully prepare for the interview. Following these suggestions will help ensure that your interview is productive:

- *Start early.* Professionals have calendars that, believe it or not, are even more packed than most college students' calendars. You should contact potential interviewees at least one week in advance so that the two of you can find a mutually agreeable time for the interview.
- *Determine the purpose for the interview.* Using your source to find out information easily obtained from other sources like the library or the Internet is a waste

of time. Use your interview to gather important analysis, clever quotations, and personally relevant stories.

- *Do your homework.* You must have some understanding of the topic to know the right questions to ask. Taking time to carefully research your topic before the interview will enable you to ask good questions.
- *Plan questions in advance.* Effective interviewers take time to plan primary questions—questions that introduce new areas of discussion—in advance of the interview. Throughout the give-and-take of the interview, you can ask impromptu or probing questions to clarify and elaborate on answers to your primary questions.
- *Gather equipment.* The best strategy for interviewing another person is to record the interview so that you can replay it to select quotes. You cannot write fast enough to take detailed notes, and interviewees will likely get frustrated if you keep asking them to repeat their statements. Of course, you should get the person's permission to record the interview before you begin—most will be more than happy to allow this.

Conducting the Interview

Once you have scheduled and prepared for the interview, your next task is to conduct it professionally. You will find this task to be fun and engaging. Besides dressing professionally and being on time, keep in mind the following:

- *Be polite and respectful.* Interviews rarely start with the first question. Instead, expect the interviewee to express curiosity about you and your project. Be perfectly frank about your purpose, the assignment, and the audience. The interviewee is doing the verbal equivalent of a handshake with the questioning.
- *Be careful about the tone of your questions and comments.* You are not in the role of an investigative reporter performing an interrogation. Instead, you are seeking information and cooperation from someone who can help you. Your tone should be friendly and your comments constructive.
- *Be flexible.* Even though you have prepared questions, you may find that one response may answer several of your planned questions or that your preplanned order is not working as well as you expected. Relax. Check off questions as you ask them or as they are answered. Take a minute at the conclusion of the interview to see whether you have covered all of your questions.
- *Practice active listening.* Show an interest in the person's answers. If you are recording the interview, you should provide nonverbal feedback and concentrate on generating follow-up questions to gain even more valuable information. Be alert to nonverbal cues revealed by the interviewee, including those indicating that it is time to conclude the session.
- *Remember to get the basics.* Make sure that you have the accurate *citation information*: your interviewee's name and title; the name of the company, agency, or department; and so on. You will be citing this person's words and using oral footnotes to credit him or her, so you need correct source information.
- *Finally, remember to depart.* Give your interviewee an opportunity to stop the interview at the designated time. The interviewee—not you—should extend the interview beyond that, if anyone does. The interviewee will appreciate your gracious good-bye and gratitude for granting the interview. As a parting gesture of good will, thank the secretary, or anyone else who has helped you, as well.

Using the Interview

After you have conducted the interview, you should immediately take time to listen to the recording and type out quotations or ideas from the interview for use in your speech. Later in this chapter, you will read about different types of supporting material, including examples, quotations, and statistics. In reviewing notes from an interview, you will be looking for these types of materials to include in your speech. In that sense, an interview transcript is very similar to a newspaper article or book in how you process and use the information. Don't let your memory of the interview grow cold. The longer you wait, the more likely you are to forget how you wanted to use information from the interview.

Evaluating and Using Sources of Information

The University of California library has developed a very thorough guide for evaluating sources that you find on the Internet. If you visit the UC website (www.lib.berkeley.edu/ TeachingLib/Guides/Internet/Evaluate.html), you will learn effective tips for making sure that any Internet sources that you use are reliable, trustworthy, and credible. In addition to carefully analyzing Internet sources, you should carefully consider any source before including the information in a speech, presentation, or paper. This section explains how you should evaluate sources and cite them correctly in your outline and presentation.

Criteria for Evaluating Sources

Just finding sources does not ensure that you have effectively researched your presentation. You must carefully evaluate each source for its credibility and usefulness. Your credibility as a speaker is directly tied to the credibility of the sources you use.

Taking great care to carefully evaluate sources that you use can dramatically improve the chances of success for your speech. The *Style Manual for Communication Studies*[2] recommends that you use the following criteria when evaluating sources:

1. *Is the supporting material clear?* Sources should help you add clarity to your ideas rather than confusing the issue with jargon and overly technical explanations.

2. *Is the supporting material verifiable?* Listeners and readers should be able to verify the accuracy of your sources. Although verifying information in a book is easy—the book can be checked out and read—verifying information obtained from a personal interview with the uncle of your sister's roommate is not.

3. *Is the source of the supporting material competent?* For each source, you should be able to determine qualifications. If your source is a person, what expertise does the person have with the topic? If your source is an organization, what relationship does the organization have with the issue?

4. *Is the source objective?* All sources—even news reports—have some bias. The National Rifle Association has a bias in favor of gun ownership; Greenpeace has a bias in favor of environmental protection; TV news programs have a bias toward vivid visual imagery. What biases does your source have, and how might those biases affect the way these organizations or people frame information?

5. *Is the supporting material relevant?* Loading your speech with irrelevant sources might make the speech seem well researched; however, critical listeners will see through this tactic. Include only sources that directly address the key points you want to make.

As a presenter, you have a key ethical obligation to carefully evaluate all sources that you use in your speech. These criteria are not "yes or no" questions. Sources will meet some criteria well and fail others miserably. Your job as the speaker is to weigh the benefits and problems with each source and determine whether to include the source in your speech. Moreover, these criteria assume that you will take time to find out information about each source that you are using. Understanding who the author or sponsoring organization is, whether the site bases claims on supporting material or on opinion, and how recently the site has been updated are all important factors to consider. As stated previously, but worth restating over and over, the ability to carefully evaluate sources of information is a critical life skill that must be practiced and refined. The same effort that we put into practicing other common activities like driving safely, being healthy, and performing well on our jobs should be expected whenever we seek and use information from others.

Citing Sources of Information Correctly

Once you find source material, you must provide references for the source both on your outline and in your speech. **Bibliographic references** are *complete citations that appear in the "references" or "works cited" section of your speech outline (or term paper)*. Your outline should also contain **internal references**, which are *brief notations of which bibliographic reference contains the details you are using in your speech*. Internal references will be integrated into the body of your outline, or in the case of a paper, into sentences and paragraphs. These internal references specify where, exactly, specific sources are being integrated. Internal and bibliographic references help readers understand what sources were used to find specific details like statistics, quotations, and examples. Most teachers require students to use a specific style guide for formatting bibliographic and internal references. The two most common types of style guides are the American Psychological Association (APA) and the Modern Language Association (MLA). Figure 5.4 provides sample citations for five types of sources following APA and MLA styles.

APA

Newspaper
Zibel, A. & Webber, T. (2009, July 17). Joblessness helping fuel foreclosure crisis. *Boston Globe*, p.9.

Academic Journal
Condit, C. M. (2008). Race and genetics from a modal materialist perspective. *Quarterly Journal of Speech, 94*, 383–406.

Book
Sala, O. E., Meyerson, L. A., & Parmesan, C. (Eds.). (2009). *Biodiversity change and human health: From ecosystem services to spread of disease.* Washington DC: Island Press.

WebPage
Kelly, R. (2008, July 5). *Civic engagement.* Retrieved 20 July, 2009, from Faculty Focus web site: http://www.facultyfocus.com/articles/philosophy-of-teaching/best-practices-in-teaching-civic-engagement-2/

Personal Interview
Striley, K., Phalen, S., & Weiderhold, A. (2009, August 1). Personal interview. Athens, OH: Ohio University.

MLA

Newspaper Article
Zibel, Alan, and Tammy Webber. "Joblessness Helping Fuel Foreclosure Crisis." *Boston Globe* 17 July 2009: 9. Print.

Academic Journal
Condit, Celeste M. "Race and Genetics from a Modal Materialist Perspective." *Quarterly Journal of Speech* 94.4 (2008): 383–406. Print.

Book
Sala, Osvaldo E., Meyerson, Laura A., and Camille Parmesan, eds. *Biodiversity Change and Human Health: From Ecosystem Services to Spread of Disease.* Washington DC: Island Press, 2009. Print.

WebPage
Rob Kelly. "Civic Engagement." *Faculty Focus.* Maginta Publications, 5 Jul. 2008. Web. 20 Jul. 2009.

Personal Interview
Striley, Katie, Phalen, Steve, & Anna Weiderhold. Personal Interview. 1 Aug. 2009.

Figure 5.4   Five sources following APA and MLA styles.

In addition to citing sources in your outline, you must also provide verbal citations during your presentation. Unlike the readers of a paper or presentation outline, audience members are less concerned with page numbers and titles of articles. Rather, an **oral citation** tells listeners *who the source is, how recent the information is, and the source's qualifications.* The examples listed in Table 5.6 illustrate how to orally cite different types of sources. Notice how the examples provide information about the sources as well as the key point being made by the source. These example statements could be followed by direct quotations or more detailed explanations.

Oral source citation is a skill unique to public speaking. Although written style guides like APA and MLA offer specific rules for how to internally cite sources in a written document, use of oral citations is more fluid and must be adapted to the audience, occasion, and source being used. Generally speaking, oral citations emphasize the credibility of the source being used. To capitalize on the credibility of your sources, you should emphasize their qualifications, the timeliness of the information, the reputation of the outlet, and other characteristics of the source that will make them more credible from the perspective of your audience. The goal of oral source citations should be to build the credibility of your sources, which in turn will build your credibility as a speaker.

Identifying Appropriate Supporting Materials

Cathy Davidson's 2011 book, *Now You See It: How the Brain Science of Attention Will Transform the Way We Live, Work, and Learn*, makes a compelling argument that all aspects of our lives are changing as a result of digital technology like the Internet, role-playing and simulation games, multimedia, mobile apps, social networking, and a host of other technologies. Davidson argues that for decades we have told students that, in order to learn, they have to focus and pay attention to only one thing at a time—the teacher at the front of the room, the textbook chapter they are reading, and so forth. She concludes, however, that this ideal is not realistic. In fact, from the earliest of times, humans have learned to focus simultaneously on many things at once. Veterans who have been trained in combat might call this "situational awareness," or the ability to read all aspects of a situation holistically for threats while also focusing intently on a task at hand. Your attention works the same way. You have the ability to focus intently on one thing while also being aware of your surroundings, including your connection to the world through your mobile device.

TABLE 5.6   EXAMPLES OF ORAL CITATIONS

Type of Source	Example
Newspaper article	"Jayne O'Donnell, writing in the September 6th edition of *USA Today*, pointed out that lead paint tastes sweet, which makes the poison particularly dangerous to young children who are more likely to suck on tainted toys."
Research study	"A 2009 study published in the ***Howard Journal of Communication*** argued that government messages about natural disasters need to be adapted to have meaningful outcomes for non-whites, people who live in poverty, and other marginalized populations."
Webpage	"A story on the American Red Cross website, published on February 9, 2009, described how a teacher at the Decatur Area Technical Academy in Decatur, Illinois, used volunteering for the Red Cross as a way to help her students understand the importance of community responsibility."

Of course, modern mobile technology has only increased the strain on our attention. While the need for humans to monitor their surroundings for predators has largely disappeared, our attention is divided among new urgencies like texts from friends, tweets about topics of interest, emails, status updates, and many others. As a speaker you must recognize this fact and adapt accordingly. Part of this adaptation must be through your speech delivery. You will learn techniques for effective delivery in Chapter 7. However, another way to adapt to your audience's split attention is through the use of highly effective supporting material. By using compelling examples, illuminating statistics, emotional narratives, and other forms of support, your presentation will be more effective at maintaining audience members' attention even in light of multiple, competing stimuli.

The remainder of this chapter teaches you about various types of **supporting material**, or *information you can use to substantiate your arguments and clarify your position*. As you learn about examples, surveys, testimony, statistics, analogies, and definitions, think about how the ways that you locate and use such information might help grab and maintain listeners' attention and avoid distractions.

Examples

Examples, *specific instances used to illustrate your point*, are among the most common supporting materials found in presentations of all types. Sometimes a single example helps convince an audience; at other times, a relatively large number of examples may be necessary to achieve your purpose. For instance, if you wanted to argue that your community should combat sources of pollution, you may need to cite several examples to make your case. If you rely on only one example, people who are unfamiliar with that source of pollution may dismiss the example as atypical. By citing several examples, you increase the likelihood that members of your audience will live close to one of those sources of pollution, making your claim more credible.

Be careful when using examples. Sometimes an example is so unusual that an audience will not accept the story as evidence of anything. A student referring to his own difficulty in landing a job as an example of problems with the economy is unconvincing if more general statistics do not support his claim. A good example must be plausible, typical, and related to the main points of the presentation. For key arguments, you may want to "stack" supporting material by using an example along with a statistic, quotation, or other type of support.

Two types of examples are factual and hypothetical. A *factual* example is just that—a fact. It can be verified. A *hypothetical* example cannot be verified. It is speculative, imaginative, or fictional. The example can be brief or extended. The following is an example of a brief factual example:

> According to the August 5, 2005, issue of *The Chronicle of Higher Education*, the time students spent volunteering in 2004 was worth almost $4.5 billion.

Here is an extended hypothetical example:

> An example of how nanotechnology could be used is in the case of oil spills. Suppose that billions of tiny robots, smaller in diameter than a human hair, were released at the site of an oil spill. These robots are programmed to seek out and digest oil molecules into pieces of silt that fall harmlessly to the bottom of the ocean. In less than one day, all evidence of the oil spill has been magically gobbled up by these minuscule workers. Two days later, the robots run out of energy and join the digested oil molecules on the ocean

floor. In their short life span, these nano-machines saved countless creatures from an ugly death and prevented millions of dollars in destruction.

The brief factual example is *verifiable*, meaning the example can be supported by a source that the audience can check. The extended hypothetical example is *not* verifiable and is actually a "what if" scenario. Explaining to the audience that an example is hypothetical is important. Presenting a hypothetical example as a *real* example is unethical, and your credibility will be questioned if the audience learns that they were misled.

Narratives

Whereas examples provide specific illustrations, **narratives** provide *an extended story showing how another person experienced something*. In speeches, narratives serve important roles in helping audience members learn information and emotionally connect with your ideas. If you recall from your childhood, children's stories are often written in ways that teach readers about values, norms, and ways people can relate to one another. As we grow older, we still rely on others' stories to learn scripts for life events, a process that social psychologist Albert Bandura calls vicarious learning. Using narratives in your speech will literally allow audience members to learn from the experiences of others through vicarious learning. For instance, if you were giving a speech on the topic of spirituality, you might tell the story of someone who was able to combat addiction by turning to spiritual guidance and practices.

In addition to helping audience members learn, narratives also integrate emotion into a presentation because they humanize topics. Three communication professors recently created a documentary illustrating how Dr. Peter Anderson, a specialist in pediatric oncology at M.D. Anderson Cancer Center in Houston, uses narrative to help guide his interaction with patients. While interviews with Dr. Anderson serve as a foundation for much of the documentary, stories about several children who had cancer are interwoven into the program. Those stories provide human faces and authentic emotion for the story of how cancer disrupts lives as well as the important ways that Dr. Anderson tries to help his patients. Narratives provide the basis for emotional connection, empathy, and relevance for many topics.

Although narratives are important parts of speeches, you should keep in mind a few things about how to use them effectively. First, good narratives are sometimes hard to find. Although you may find narratives through library research, better narratives might be collected through interviews, observations conducted while volunteering, and other forms of personal contact. Second, you should be careful in how you present narratives in your speech. Narratives are personal stories and should not be presented as a generalized account of something or even a definitive illustration of an experience. While narratives provide compelling accounts of personal experiences, they do not necessarily illustrate how things generally work. Finally, you should use narratives in ethical ways. You should never reveal private information without permission and you should not rely overly much on the emotional nature of narratives.

Surveys

Another type of supporting material commonly used during presentations is a **survey**, *a study in which a limited number of questions are answered by a sample of the population to discover opinions on issues*. You will most often find surveys quoted in magazines or journals. In comparison to narratives and examples, surveys provide a very different type of support. Whereas a narrative tells one person's experience, a survey provides a summary of hundreds or thousands of people's experiences. When speaking on the topic of binge drinking, one person's narrative may have an emotional impact on audience members. A survey showing that more than 60 percent of college students binge drink at least once a week can illustrate the broad magnitude of the problem. As with personal experience, you should ask some important questions about the evidence found in surveys:

1. How reliable is the source? A report of a survey in a professional journal of sociology, psychology, or communication is likely to be more thorough and more valid than one found in a local newspaper.

2. How broad is the sample used in the survey? Was it a survey of the entire nation, the region, the state, the city, the campus, or the class?

3. How was the survey conducted? Surveys only administered over the telephone may have a different type of sample than surveys conducted through social networking sites. Depending on the topic of the survey, these differences in respondents could dramatically skew results. Better surveys will be random so that anyone has an equal chance of being included in the sample.

4. Who performed the survey? Was the survey conducted by a nationally recognized survey firm, such as Lou Harris or Gallup, or was it by the local newspaper editor? Was the survey created by professionals or one of your peers?

5. Why was the survey conducted? Was it performed for any self-serving purpose—for example, to attract more readers—or did the government conduct the survey to help establish policy or legislation? The source of the survey may have a bias that could potentially lead to misleading results or interpretations.

Testimony

Testimonial evidence, a third kind of supporting material, consists of *written or oral statements of others' experiences used by a speaker to substantiate or clarify a point.* Testimonial evidence shows the audience that you are not alone in your beliefs, ideas, and arguments. Other people also support you, and their statements should help the audience accept your point of view. The three kinds of testimonial evidence you can use in your speeches are lay, expert, and celebrity.

Lay testimony is a *statement made by an ordinary person that substantiates or supports what you say.* In advertising, this kind of testimony shows ordinary people using or buying products and stating the fine qualities of those products. In a speech, lay

cultural NOTE

ADAPTING EVIDENCE TO MALE AND FEMALE AUDIENCE MEMBERS

Decades' worth of research and popular press books point to a cultural difference between men and women. Whether men are from Mars and women from Venus, researchers and commentators alike identify differences in communication styles between the sexes. An article published in a recent issue of the *European Journal of Communication* pointed to differences in how men and women potentially interpret evidence. Whereas men tend to be persuaded more by appeals that will help them directly, women tend to be more persuaded by appeals that will help others. How might this affect you? Rarely will you find that your audience is full of only men or women. So, picking one type of appeal may not be fruitful. However, you can always mix your appeals. By using a narrative of someone you can illustrate how others will be positively affected by the information you provide, thus appealing to women in the audience. By using a well-crafted hypothetical example, you may be able to show how males in the audience could directly benefit from your information. Audience adaptation does not mean that you should cater to one audience group and ignore the other; by using evidence strategically you might be able to appeal to both.[3]

testimony might be the words of your relatives, neighbors, or friends concerning an issue. Such testimony shows the audience that you and other ordinary people feel the same way about an issue. Other examples of lay testimony are parents speaking about curriculum changes at a school board meeting or alumni attesting to the positive qualities of their college at a recruiting session.

Expert testimony is a *statement made by someone who has special knowledge or expertise about an issue or idea.* In your speech, you might quote John McCain about the war in Iraq, the surgeon general about healthcare, or the president of the Sierra Club about the environment. The idea is to demonstrate that people with specialized experience or education support the positions you advocate in your speech.

Celebrity testimony is a *statement made by a public figure who is known to the audience.* Celebrity testimony occurs in advertising when someone famous endorses a particular product. In your presentation, you might point out that a famous politician, a syndicated columnist, or a well-known entertainer endorses the position you advocate.

Although testimonial evidence may encourage your audience to adopt your ideas, you need to use such evidence with caution. An idea may have little credence even though many laypeople believe in it; an expert may be quoted on topics well outside his or her area of expertise; and a celebrity is often paid for endorsing a product. To protect yourself and your audience, you should ask yourself the following questions before using testimonial evidence in your speeches:

- Is the person you quote an expert whose opinions or conclusions are worthier than most other people's opinions?
- Is the quotation about a subject in the person's area of expertise?
- Is the person's statement based on extensive personal experience, professional study or research, or another form of firsthand proof?
- Will your audience find the statement more believable because you got the quotation from this outside source?

Numbers and Statistics

To use numbers and statistics effectively, you must develop basic skills in **numeric literacy**, or *the ability to understand, interpret, and explain quantitative information.* Being literate with numbers does not mean that you have to be an expert in math. Your ability to look at a basic budget spreadsheet, calculate gasoline mileage, interpret your bank statement, or even fill out your yearly taxes are all examples of the type of day-to-day math skills that can help you use this type of evidence in a speech. Finding a set of numbers—what a researcher might call a data set—can help you generate compelling evidence for your audience. Generally speaking, numbers help speakers accomplish the following outcomes:

- *Precisely describe objects, concepts, and ideas.* Using descriptive statistics, you can give very precise details about points you are making in your speech. How large is the national debt? How many people are without medical insurance? How many tornadoes developed in the United States last year? What percentage of Americans has college degrees? All of these are questions that can be answered with precise

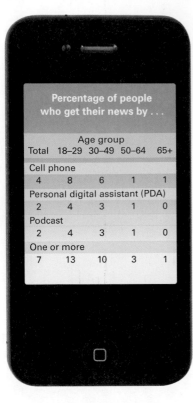

Percentage of people who get their news by . . .				
		Age group		
Total	18–29	30–49	50–64	65+
Cell phone				
4	8	6	1	1
Personal digital assistant (PDA)				
2	4	3	1	0
Podcast				
2	4	3	1	0
One or more				
7	13	10	3	1

descriptive statistics. Because numbers are easier to interpret and understand in written form, speakers often need to simplify values for listeners. For example, instead of saying "There were 323,426 high school graduates," say, "There were more than three hundred thousand graduates." You can couple descriptive statistics with meaningful comparisons to make them clearer. For instance, you could say, "There were more than three hundred thousand graduates, which is about the same population as the city of Lancaster."

- *Show relationships.* Researchers are often interested in using statistics to determine relationships between things. The precise term for this is "statistical correlation." For instance, you could probably guess that there is a statistical correlation between age and reading ability, family income and education level, and city population and crime. Although most of these correlations will be found through research, you may have enough experience to determine statistical relationships on your own. For instance, if you are a small business owner or employee, you might be able to determine whether there is a correlation between advertising expenses and sales or even various factors associated with employee productivity. In fact, common spreadsheets like Microsoft Excel or Apple's Numbers allow easy calculations of correlations.

  When using correlations you should take care to carefully explain them to audience members. A line graph or scatterplot (discussed more in Chapter 9) is an effective visual aid to illustrate correlations and relationships. Also, be careful to avoid the assumption that correlation means causation. For instance, there is a correlation between outside temperature and crime—the higher the temperature the higher the crime rate. Hotter weather does not cause people to commit crimes, but more people are outside in the summer, increasing their susceptibility to being victims.

- *Show differences.* In addition to showing relationships, numbers and statistics can also be used to show differences. What percentage of men and women graduate from high school? Do most people get their news from television, newspapers, radio, or the Internet? Are Democrats or Republicans more likely to affiliate with the Tea Party Movement? These are all questions that require numbers to show differences between groups of people. Another question of difference can relate to objects. Which auto manufacturer has the best gas mileage for family sedans? What type of computer operating system is most attacked by computer viruses? These types of questions often use descriptive statistics, but disaggregate those statistics by groupings. Bar charts are commonly used to visually illustrate this type of information.

- Assume that you are preparing a speech on the rise in popularity of mobile Internet devices. As part of your speech, you decided to survey eight people in your workplace to generate statistics relevant to your topic. Table 5.7 shows a summary of the results.

Using results from the survey, what can you learn? From a descriptive standpoint, you could count the number of males and females, count how many people use each type of mobile Internet device, and calculate averages for both age and hours spent online each day. Do you think there is a relationship between age and hours spent online? If you create a line plot with age on one axis and hours online on the other, you will see that older members of the sample tend to spend less time online than those who are younger. What about differences? If you calculate the average age for Droid and iPad users, and compare those averages to the age for the iPhone and netbook users, you will conclude that iPad users tend to be younger, followed by iPhone users, and then Droid and netbook users. You could use a bar graph to illustrate those differences. Using a similar approach, what is the average number of hours spent online by males and females?

Knowledge of simple statistics can help you draw important conclusions from numeric data. You will likely find many statistics already calculated for you in research

TABLE 5.7 SURVEY RESULTS FOR MOBILE INTERNET SURVEY			
SEX	TYPE	AGE	HOURS ONLINE PER DAY
Male	Droid	43	2
Male	iPhone	23	5
Female	iPad	18	7
Male	Droid	21	5
Female	netbook	32	1
Female	iPad	26	3
Male	iPad	21	5
Male	Droid	30	2

you uncover on your topic. Such information adds important detail and shows that you have carefully researched your topic. As with other types of supporting material, you should cite sources for statistics you use during your presentation.

Analogies

Another kind of supporting material is the analogy. An **analogy** is *a comparison of things in some respects, especially in position or function, that are otherwise dissimilar.* For instance,

> Sometimes, when I'm wearing jeans on campus, I feel like a chameleon. Not because I blend in with the scenery, trees, limbs, rocks, or foliage, but because I blend in with other people—everybody wears jeans.

While providing clarification, an analogy is not a proof, because the comparison inevitably breaks down. Therefore, a speaker who argues that American society will fail just as Roman society did can carry the comparison only so far because the form of government, the time in history, and the institutions in the two societies are quite different. Likewise, you can question the chameleon–human analogy by pointing out the vast differences between the two species. Nonetheless, analogies can be quite successful as a way of illustrating or clarifying.

Definitions

Some of the most contentious arguments in our society center on **definitions**, or *determinations of meaning through description, simplification, examples, analysis, comparison, explanation, or illustration.* Experts and ordinary citizens have argued for years about definitions. For instance, when does art become pornography? Is withdrawal of life support systems euthanasia or humanitarian concern? How you define a concept can make a considerable difference in helping audience members understand your points.

Definitions in a presentation are supposed to enlighten the audience by revealing what a term means. Sometimes you can use definitions that appear in standard reference works, such as dictionaries and encyclopedias, but explaining the word in language the audience will understand is most effective. For example, say you use the term *subcutaneous hematoma* in your speech. *Subcutaneous hematoma* is jargon used by physicians to explain a blotch on the skin, but you could explain it in this way: "*Subcutaneous* means 'under the skin,' and *hematoma* means 'swelled with blood,' so the words mean 'blood swelling under the skin,' or what most of us call a 'bruise.'"

The Ethical Use of Supporting Material

Did you know national statistics show that nearly 40 percent of students report copying sentences and other material from written and electronic sources without giving appropriate credit?[4] Because of statistics like these, coupled with high-profile cases of plagiarism by students, faculty, and even prominent national figures, many institutions are now taking the issue of academic integrity more seriously than ever before. Although you should take care to understand how to act with integrity with any assignment, this obligation takes on special importance in a public speaking class.

Throughout this book, we emphasize various ethical requirements for communication that stem from the National Communication Association (NCA) Credo on Ethics. Let's end this chapter by summarizing the ethical obligations faced by speakers when they use supporting materials:

1. *Speakers have an ethical obligation to find the best possible sources of information.* The Internet and full-text databases certainly provide us with easy research options; however, these tools do not necessarily improve the quality of our research. Yet, your audience depends on you to present the best and most accurate information possible. The best sources of information are sometimes not available online or in full-text form. Selecting a variety of sources including print sources, Internet sources, and possibly even interviews can thus help improve the overall quality of the materials on which you base your presentation.

2. *Speakers have an ethical obligation to cite their sources of information.* In Chapter 1 a stern warning appeared against an offense called **plagiarism** or *the intentional use of information from a source without crediting that source.* A more positive reason for citing sources of information is so anyone in your audience can verify what you say. A verbal citation that reveals your source of information allows others to see for themselves that what you said was accurate.

3. *Speakers have an ethical obligation to fairly and accurately represent sources.* How often have you heard politicians and other public figures complain that the media take their comments "out of context"? To avoid making unfair and inaccurate representations of sources, whether they are newspaper articles, webpages, books, or even interviews, you must ensure that you fully understand the points being made by the source. Remember, for example, that two-sided arguments are often used to present a point. In a **two-sided argument**, *a source advocating one position will present an argument from the opposite viewpoint and then go on to refute that argument.* To take an excerpt from a source where the opposing argument is being presented for refutation and imply that the source was advocating the opposing argument is unethical. As a speaker, you have the liberty to disagree with points made by the sources you consult; you do not have the liberty to misrepresent those same sources.

The act of plagiarizing is often discussed as an issue of ethics—indeed, the Credo on Communication Ethics explicitly states that we have an ethical obligation to credit others' ideas and words. On the other hand, when we have encountered instances of plagiarism, students rarely commit such acts with the intent of being unethical. Research conducted by Melissa Broeckelman-Post[5] found that the most common reasons for plagiarizing were: (1) I have too much work to do and not enough time to finish all of it; (2) I don't have enough time because I procrastinated; (3) I will get a better grade if I cheat; (d) If I don't get a good grade, I will lose my scholarship; and (5) I don't understand the course material/assignment. Nearly all of these reasons revolve around the issue of adequate time management. As a student growing in your skills as a speaker, writer, and researcher, you must give yourself enough time to adequately research, organize, prepare, and revise your ideas.

Although it is tempting to try to expand the NCA credo to provide a definite list of suggestions on what to do or avoid with respect to academic integrity and plagiarism, such "rules" must be co-created between you and your teacher. We encourage you to have discussions with your instructor, either individually or as a class, about the following questions:

1. When should sources be cited?
2. How much information in a speech should come from other sources?
3. How should I determine whether to paraphrase or quote?
4. So long as I cite the source, can I quote/paraphrase as much information from a source as I want to?
5. Do I have to cite sources for information other than quotes (e.g., statistics, pictures, graphics, etc.)?
6. Is working on my speech with other people considered cheating?

Such discussions will provide you with valuable information about the expectations surrounding your assignment and will also allow you to experience firsthand how communication is a tool for shaping the culture in which we live.

In conclusion, locating, understanding, and incorporating supporting material are some of the most important tasks you will undertake as a presenter of information and argument. Good research affects literally every step in the process of preparing and delivering a presentation. Taking care to effectively and ethically use your information will make you a better speaker and will earn the respect of your peers and teachers.

For REVIEW >>

SUMMARY HIGHLIGHTS

Why You'll Benefit from Research

▶ Research is a key aspect of the invention process where ideas are formulated and refined.

▶ Good research skills involve accumulating information from a variety of sources and integrating the best of that information into your speech.

▶ Skills involved in researching for your speech are a necessary component of life in our information-based world.

▶ Research will improve all aspects of your speech preparation, including topic selection, organizing your ideas, supporting your ideas, preparing your introduction and conclusion, and delivering your speech.

Finding Sources of Information

▶ Personal experience is where you use your own life experiences as support. You should carefully evaluate the effectiveness of your personal experience before integrating it into your speech.

▶ You can use interviews with others to solicit expert opinion, rich personal narratives, and other specific types of support. A good deal of work goes into carefully planning, executing, and integrating an interview into your speech.

▶ Libraries provide access to specialized databases, books, and other topic-specific resources. A reference librarian can assist you in locating and using the resources unique to your library.

▶ The Internet provides access to an enormous array of information. Knowing how to search for information efficiently, how to evaluate information, and how to diversify the sources you use are all critical aspects of using the Internet effectively.

Evaluating and Using Sources of Information

▶ All sources, regardless of their qualifications, deserve scrutiny. When evaluating a source, you should ask if it is clear, if it is verifiable, if it is objective, and if the information is relevant to your argument.

▶ When using any source of information, you must provide proper citation information. Your speech will require bibliographic and internal references on your outline or written documents. During your speech, you should use oral citations to let your audience know where the information came from.

Identifying Appropriate Supporting Materials

▶ Examples illustrate your point and can be either brief or extended and either real or hypothetical.

▶ Narratives provide extended stories showing how another person experienced something. Narratives often show the emotional or personal impact of something.

▶ Surveys show the opinions of a broad sample of people. Results from credible surveys are effective in showing the magnitude or scope of something.

▶ Testimony involves the use of quotations from experts, celebrities, or peers. The source of the quotation will determine how it will affect your speech.

▶ Numbers and statistics can be used to show the precise magnitude of something, statistical relationships between things, or statistical differences between groups of people.

The Ethical Use of Supporting Material

▶ All speakers have ethical obligations to find and use good information, to cite their sources of information, and to accurately represent sources.

▶ You must not engage in plagiarism.

1. Data on which proof may be based is termed:
   - (A) interviews
   - (B) evidence
   - (C) oral citation
   - (D) periodicals

2. When interviewing others, you should:
   - (A) call the day before to set up a meeting
   - (B) be vague with regard to your purpose and the assignment
   - (C) be conversational by not using planned questions
   - (D) be careful about the tone of your questions and comments

3. Magazines, newspapers, and academic journals are examples of:
   - (A) internal references
   - (B) holdings databases
   - (C) periodicals
   - (D) lay testimony

4. Criteria for evaluating sources include making sure that the source is:
   - (A) subjective
   - (B) irrelevant
   - (C) vague
   - (D) competent

5. The complete citations that appear in the "words cited" section of your speech outline are called:
   - (A) internal references
   - (B) bibliographic references
   - (C) periodicals
   - (D) oral citations

Answers: 1 (B); 2 (D); 3 (C); 4 (D); 5 (B)

pop **Quiz**

APPLICATION EXERCISES

1. Conduct a web search for sites discussing "dangers of cell phones." After locating a website on the topic, do the same search in Academic Search Premier or some other general database. Compare the conclusions of the website and the articles you find. Do the articles provide independent verification of the conclusions stated in the website? Which sources appear most credible? Why?

2. For each of the topics listed here, identify at least three databases that you would use to locate information sources at your library. Briefly explain why you selected each database.

   Stand your ground laws

   High-fructose corn syrup

   Net neutrality

   Economic recession

3. Following is information about a magazine article and a book on the topic of student motivation. For each source, correctly write the citation in both APA and MLA styles.

MAGAZINE ARTICLE	BOOK
AUTHOR: LI JIA, PHD	KIEWRA
MAGAZINE: PHI RHO KAPPAN	TITLE: ENHANCING STUDENT MOTIVATION
ARTICLE TITLE: MAKING LEARNING FUN FOR STUDENTS	EDITION: 2ND
	YEAR: 2012
	PUBLISHER: UNIVERSITY PRESS
YEAR: 2012	
DATE: JUNE	PUBLISHER LOCATION:
PAGES: 34–38	OMAHA, NE

KEY TERMS

Analogy	Holdings database	Plagiarism
Bibliographic references	Internal references	Reference librarian
Celebrity testimony	Lay testimony	Search engine
Content curation	Narratives	Supporting material
Definitions	Numeric literacy	Survey
Evidence	Oral citation	Testimonial evidence
Examples	Periodicals	Two-sided argument
Expert testimony	Personal experience	Virtual library

6

ORGANIZING & OUTLINING

Good organization heightens a speaker's credibility and helps listeners better understand a presentation. In this chapter you will learn principles that should guide the construction of your speech outline, the various types of outlines that you might prepare, and specific strategies for creating the body, introduction, and conclusion of your speech.

YOUR PRESENTATION

Have you ever looked at a particular aspect of your community and thought, "something isn't right"? A fairly natural instinct of humans is to observe their environment and find ways to improve it. Of course, what we define as problems, and what solutions we seek, differ widely from one person to the next. Still, almost everyone has an idea to promote. In Chapter 11, you will learn more about developing arguments, but learning how to properly organize your speech is a first step to making a strong case to others.

In a recent presentation on the fall of adoption rates given before the Royal Society of London, Secretary of State for Education Michael Grove organized his ideas around two statements:

Statement 1: "It troubles me—more, angers me—that so few children are benefitting from that generosity and humanity . . . Adoption rates have fallen by 17 percent over the last decade."

Statement 2: "That is why it is so important that we tackle delay throughout the system. We need to speed up care decisions and work with local authorities to make sure they speed up their processes too."[1]

These two statements illustrate a method of speech organization called *problem–solution*. The problem–solution technique is very useful for persuasive speakers like Grove, who wants to persuade others to help fix a problem he sees in the world.

What kind of organizational pattern would work best with your topic? Organizing and outlining your material is the focus of this chapter. You will learn many possible patterns of organization, and tips about which ones are most appropriate for a particular topic or purpose.

Why Is Organization Important?

You have already found information about your topic; now you need to arrange your message. In Chapter 2, you learned about the second Canon of Rhetoric, organization. This chapter expands on that information by explaining specific ways to organize the introduction, body, and conclusion of your speech. Research on organizing speeches indicates that speakers who give well-organized presentations enjoy several advantages over those who do not. First, audience members understand the organized presentations better.[2] Second, organized presenters appear more competent and trustworthy than speakers who deliver disorganized presentations.[3] Clearly, audiences appreciate well-organized messages.

Speakers themselves also benefit from taking the time to carefully organize their presentations. First, they do not just *appear* more confident when their messages are better organized, they actually *are* more confident.[4] Second, they believe they deliver their presentations more smoothly.[5] Third, researchers found that the more students can learn and master the ability to organize ideas, the better analytical thinkers they become.[6] And good organizational skills you learn in public speaking apply equally well whenever you speak or write in this class or in others.

You will notice that this chapter starts with the body of the speech, then moves to the introduction, and then to the conclusion. Why? In reality, you will follow this approach when planning and organizing your speech. You should begin by organizing the body, then move to the introduction, and then to the conclusion. A well-crafted introduction and conclusion require a very clear understanding of the body of the speech. Consequently, you cannot work on those elements until the body of the speech is complete.

What Are the Principles of Outlining?

The organization of a presentation is generally shown in outline form. Outlining is relatively easy to learn. Three principles of outlining govern the writing of an outline: *subordination*, *division*, and *parallelism*.

Subordination

The **principle of subordination** allows you to *indicate which material is more important and which is less important through indentation and symbols.* The principle of subordination is based not only on the symbols (numbers and letters) and indentations, but also on the content of the statements. The subpoints are subordinate to the main points, the sub-subpoints are subordinate to the subpoints, and so on. Evaluate the content of each statement to determine whether it is broader or narrower, more important or less important, than the statements above and below. Figure 6.1 presents an example of subordination, which will make the idea easy to grasp.

More important materials usually consist of generalizations, arguments, or conclusions. Less important materials consist of the supporting evidence for your generalizations, arguments, or conclusions. By less important, we of course do not mean that your supporting evidence is not vital to your presentation—just that it is more specific and detailed and farther down in your outline. In the outline, Roman numerals indicate the main points, capital letters indicate the subpoints under the Roman numeral statements, and Arabic numbers indicate sub-subpoints under the subpoints. Figure 6.1 shows a typical outline format. Notice, too, that the less important the material, the greater the indentation from the left-hand margin.

Margins and Symbols Indicating Subordination

I. A generalization, conclusion, or argument is a main point.
   A. The first subpoint consists of illustration, evidence, or other supporting material.
   B. The second subpoint consists of similar supporting material for the main point.
      1. The first sub-subpoint provides additional support for B.
      2. The second sub-subpoint also supports B.
II. A second generalization, conclusion, or argument is another main point.

Figure 6.1   **Margins and symbols indicating subordination.**

Subordination	Division	Parallelism
I. _____ A. _____ B. _____ 1. _____ 2. _____ a. _____ b. _____ II. _____	Every "I" must have at least a "II." Every "A" must have at least a "B." Every "1" must have at least a "2." Every "a" must have at least a "b."	Each entry must be either a complete sentence, a phrase, or a word; entries may not be a mix of sentences, phrases, and words.

Figure 6.2   **Outlines should follow the principles of subordination, division, and parallelism.**

Division

The second principle of outlining is the **principle of division**, which states that, *if a point is to be divided, it must have at least two subpoints.* For example, the outline illustrated in Figure 6.1 contains two main points (I, II), two subpoints (A, B) under main point I, and two sub-subpoints (1, 2) under subpoint B. With rare exceptions, such as for a single example or clarification, items will be either undivided or divided into two or more parts.

Parallelism

The third principle of outlining is the **principle of parallelism**, which states that *main points, subpoints, and sub-subpoints must use the same grammatical and syntactical forms.* That means that in a sentence outline you would use all sentences, not a mixture of sentences, dependent clauses, and phrases. If one main point is worded as a question, they all should be questions, or they all should be declarative sentences. The sentences would tend to appear the same in structure, with subject followed by verb followed by object, for instance. Notice how the repeated words in this speech by President Obama energize the language and make it memorable:

    I.   Don't tell me that words don't matter.
       A. "'I have a dream'—just words?"
       B. "'We hold these truths to be self-evident, that all men are created equal'—just words?"
       C. "'We have nothing to fear but fear itself'—just words."[7]

These principles of outlining are not just arbitrary rules. By following these principles, your speech will be clearer and flow better for the audience. Remember, they are watching and listening to you, not reading along on an outline. By following these principles, your audience will be better able to follow your organization and understand your message. To review the information on the principles of outlining, you should examine Figure 6.2, which briefly explains each of the three principles.

What Types of Outlines Will You Create?

In the preparation and delivery of a speech, you generally compose three different but related kinds of outlines. In your course, your teacher will likely instruct you about which of these outlines will be required. Also, your instructor might require another type of outline that is not covered in this text. First, you might create a preparation, or working, outline. Next, you will probably develop a formal outline. Finally, you might want to create a keyword outline on note cards or paper, which you can use when you deliver your presentation. Other sections of this chapter will help you understand what the parts of the outlines are; for now, let's concentrate on the formats of the preparation, sentence, and keyword outlines.

The Preparation Outline

After you have selected the topic, given it a title, developed a specific purpose, written a thesis statement, and gathered information for your presentation, you will begin to sketch out the basic ideas you wish to convey to your audience. The **preparation outline** is *your initial or tentative conception of your presentation*.

For example, imagine that you want to speak about volunteering in your community. You might start by thinking of some main point for which you can provide examples:

I. What volunteer opportunities exist in our community?
   A. Working for the local food bank
   B. Serving as a hospice volunteer
   C. Reading to immigrant children at the grade school
   D. Leading a tour of a museum

As you learn more about opportunities you can refine your list, create more main points, and delete those you deem less important. The preparation outline is an informal draft, a tentative plan for the points in your presentation. This type of outline is sometimes called a "working outline" because it mainly helps you sort out your initial ideas in an orderly fashion.

Organizing: There's an App for That

In this chapter, you will learn about the importance of organizing your speech and creating an outline. Although a traditional word processor might be the most obvious tool to use in accomplishing these tasks, a variety of mobile apps can also help, particularly while you are in the early planning stages of your speech. Mind mapping apps let you create visual flowcharts of how ideas break down. Using a mind map, you can quickly explore topics and subtopics related to a particular issue. Eventually, those topics and subtopics might become main and subordinate points in your outline.

There are many different options for mind mapping apps. One such app, called Idea Sketch, created by Nosleep Software, has a free version that is easy to use and relatively robust. You can create and edit detailed mind maps and then send them to yourself or others as a PDF. This type of application could be useful as you take notes while researching and could even emerge into a visual aid that you use during your presentation.

The Formal Sentence Outline

A **formal sentence outline** is *a final outline in complete sentence form*. Teachers will often require that you turn in your formal sentence outline for grading. An example full sentence outline, prepared by Jenny Smith on the topic of ADHD, appears in Figure 6.3. The formal outline includes the following elements:

1. The title.
2. The specific purpose.
3. The thesis statement.
4. The introduction of the presentation.
5. The body of the presentation in outline form.
6. The conclusion of the presentation.
7. A bibliography of sources and references consulted.

Attention Deficit Hyperactivity Disorder
By Jenny Smith

Topic: Attention Deficit Hyperactivity Disorder (ADHD) in college students.

Specific purpose: My audience will gain a better understanding of what ADHD is, will be able to recognize the impact it has on people's lives, and will be able to explain what kinds of resources and treatments are available to those who suffer from it.

Thesis Statement: ADHD is a prevalent and debilitating disorder among young American adults.

Introduction:

I. **Gaining and maintaining favorable attention:** Imagine what it would be like if you simply were not able to prioritize or organize your life. Envision a world in which you felt as if you were always "driving in the rain with bad windshield wipers"—everything around you seems as if it is happening at once and becomes a blur. This is what the world looks like for the approximately 8 to 9 million American adults who suffer from Attention Deficit Hyperactivity Disorder, or ADHD ("Recommended Accommodations," 2012).

II. **Relating the topic to the audience:** As college students, we often have difficulty organizing our time in order to get everything done. For those who have ADHD, the tasks of daily life can present even more extreme challenges.

III. **Relating the topic to the presenter:** Recently my younger sister was diagnosed with ADHD. Along with the research I have conducted on this topic, I also have had personal experience with ADHD at home.

IV. **Previewing the message:** ADHD is a prevalent and debilitating disorder among both children and adults that can lead to problems in school and in the workplace. Today I will explain what ADHD is and inform you about the ways in which it can impact your life. Additionally, I will provide you with information on the treatment options and resources available.

Transition: I will begin by explaining what ADHD is.

Body:

I. **First main point:** In order to understand the effects of ADHD, first you must know what it means to have this disorder.

   A. One definition for ADHD is "a diagnosis applied to children and adults who consistently display certain characteristic behaviors over a period of time . . .

Figure 6.3 **A sentence outline for an informative speech with title, specific purpose, and thesis statement.**

core features include: distractibility, impulsivity and hyperactivity" ("Recommended Accommodations," 2012, para 5).

    1. It is key to understand that the terms ADD and ADHD are commonly used to talk about the same disorder; the only difference is that hyperactivity is not present in all cases.

    2. While many people believe ADHD to be more common in children, it is also prevalent among adults. In fact, studies have found it to be, potentially, "the most common chronic undiagnosed psychiatric disorder in adults" (Adler, 2008, p.4).

    3. 70% of adult individuals who were diagnosed with ADHD as children stated that they still have the disorder (Spencer, 2008).

B. There are a number of symptoms to look for in making the diagnosis of ADHD, depending on how an individual is classified. Specifically, there are three subtypes:

    1. The first division is primarily focused on inattentiveness, with symptoms including but not limited to: difficulty sustaining attention and maintaining organization, and being easily distracted ("Understanding ADHD," 2012).

    2. The second division focuses on the hyperactivity/impulsivity characteristics and includes the following symptoms: excessive talking/interrupting, difficulty remaining seated, and trouble engaging in activities ("Understanding ADHD," 2012).

    3. The final subdivision includes both symptoms of inattentiveness and hyperactivity.

Transition: Now that you know what ADHD is, who is affected by it, and the common symptoms associated with it, we will take a closer look at how having this disorder can affect your daily life.

II. **Second main point:** The symptoms associated with ADHD commonly have a significant impact on the lives of the individuals suffering with the disorder.

A. Unfortunately, individuals with ADHD tend to have more problems in the work place and at home.

    1. Studies have shown that adults with ADHD are more likely to experience difficulties in the work place, frequent absences from work, and unemployment (Stein, 2008).

    2. Similar research has indicated that these individuals are more likely to experience marital problems, as well as divorce or separation from their significant others (Spencer, 2008).

B. Furthermore, these individuals often experience more difficulty in their academic lives than do those without the disorder.

    1. Recent research has indicated that college students with ADHD often take longer to complete their degrees, if they finish at all (Stein, 2008).

    2. Results showed that these individuals are also more likely to experience school dropout, have below-average grades, and need additional years of schooling. These findings indicate the significant impact ADHD has on education (Newcorn, 2008).

Transition: Now that you have an understanding of what ADHD is, and the impact it can have on your life, I will conclude by describing the ways in which the disorder can be treated and the resources that are available.

III. **Third main point:** There are many ways for sufferers of ADHD to get help.

A. To control their symptoms, individuals with ADHD might choose medication, in the form of either stimulants or nonstimulants.

    1. Stimulant drugs such as Adderall, Focalin, and Ritalin, among other options, are used to improve focus, concentration, and impulsivity ("Drug Treatment," 2012).

    2. While stimulants are more commonly used, there are several nonstimulant drug options that provide the same result, such as Strattera and Intuniv, which are often used when stimulants are found to be ineffective or result in too many side effects ("Drug Treatment," 2012).

B. While many individuals use medications alone to treat their ADHD, studies show that combining this with psychiatric treatment can be more beneficial.

    1. Recent research has indicated that combining medications with psychological cognitive-behavioral therapy (CBT) provides positive outcomes, increases overall functioning, and improves ADHD and comorbid symptoms (Ramsey & Rostain, 2006). Comorbidity simply refers to other, though not necessarily related symptoms, like extreme talkativeness or depression.

Figure 6.3   (continued)

    2. More specifically, results show that combined treatment significantly improves sufferers' attention, affect, effort, and memory (Ramsey & Rostain, 2006).

C. Furthermore, there are numerous educational resources available to students with ADHD, such as accommodations for taking tests and for attending lectures and courses.

    1. Students who apply for these special accommodations have the option to take tests in a quiet, isolated environment; they are often given additional time, as well as the option to take the test in more than one sitting ("Recommended Accommodations," 2012).

    2. Lecture accommodations are also offered in the form of recorded lectures, note-taking aid, and reading groups ("Recommended Accommodations," 2012).

    3. Finally, students are given priority during registration, may receive written instructions, and often have a reduced course load ("Recommended Accommodations," 2012).

Conclusion:

I. **The brake-light function:** Today I informed you on the topic of ADHD in young adults.

II. **The instant-replay function:** It is my hope that after this presentation you will have a better understanding of what ADHD is, how it can affect you, and the treatments and resources available.

III. **The action-ending function:** With this knowledge I urge you to raise awareness of the prevalence of adult ADHD; and if you can relate to any of the symptoms mentioned, consider taking advantage of the many treatments and resources available to you.

References

Adler, L. A. (2008). Epidemiology, impairment, and differential diagnosis in adult ADHD; Introduction. *CNS Spectrums: The international journal of neuropsychiatric medicine, 13(8) Supp 12,* 4–5. Retrieved from http://mbldownloads.com/0808PP_CNS_ERT_ADHD.pdf

Drug treatment of ADHD. (2012, May 11). Web MD. Retrieved from http://www.webmd.com/add-adhd/guide/adhd-medical-treatment

Newcorn, J. H. (2008). Comorbidity in adults with ADH. *CNS Spectrums: The international journal of neuropsychiatric medicine, 13(8) Supp 12,* 12–15. Retrieved from http://mbldownloads.com/0808PP_CNS_ERT_ADHD.pdf

Ramsey, J. R, Rostain, A. L., (2006, November). A combined treatment approach for adults with ADHD: Results of an open study of 43 patients. *Journal of Attention Disorders.* 10(2) 150–159. doi: 10.1177/1087054706288110

Recommended accommodations for college students with ADHD. (2012*). Attention Deficit Disorder Association (ADDA).* Retrieved from http://www.add.org/?page=college_accommod

Spencer, T. J. (2008). The epidemiology of adult ADHD. *CNS Spectrums: The international journal of neuropsychiatric medicine, 13(8) Supp 12,* 6–8. Retrieved from http://mbldownloads.com/0808PP_CNS_ERT_ADHD.pdf

Stein, M. A. (2008). Impairment associated with adult ADHD. *CNS Spectrums: The international journal of neuropsychiatric medicine, 13(8) Supp 12,* 9–11. Retrieved from http://mbldownloads.com/0808PP_CNS_ERT_ADHD.pdf

Understanding ADHD. (2012*). Children and Adults with Attention Deficit/Hyperactivity Disorder (CHADD).* Retrieved from http://www.chadd.org/Content/CHADD/Understanding/Symptoms/default.htm

Figure 6.3   (continued)

You will notice that the formal outline provides an exact blueprint for your speech. The introduction of a presentation should take about 15 percent of the total time and should fulfill four functions: (1) gaining and maintaining attention, (2) relating the topic to the audience, (3) relating the speaker to the topic, and (4) previewing the message by stating the purpose and forecasting the organization of the presentation. Each of these elements of the introduction should be a separate point in the outline of your introduction; they are discussed in more detail later in this chapter.

The body of the presentation is the main part of your message. This main portion generally consists of up to three points that account for about 75 to 80 percent of the entire talk. The body should be outlined using the principles of subordination, division, and parallelism that we discussed earlier. The body of your outline should include all supporting material with internal citations showing the sources. You should also include "cues" to indicate where visual aids or other materials will be used.

The conclusion should be even shorter than the introduction. If the introduction to the presentation is about 15 percent of the entire presentation, then the conclusion should be about 5 percent of the presentation and certainly no longer than 10 percent. The functions of the conclusion include (1) forewarning the audience of the end of the presentation, (2) reminding your audience of the main points, and (3) specifying what the audience should do as a result of the presentation. Each of these functions are discussed later in the chapter, but should be identified as separate points on your outline.

The formal sentence outline includes a **list of references,** or *the sources consulted and the sources actually used in the presentation.* Your instructor will tell you whether you should include all of your sources or only those you actually cite. In any case, you will want to provide them in correct bibliographic form. To help you, you can purchase a Modern Language Association (MLA) or an American Psychological Association (APA) style manual. You can also find examples in Figure 5.4 in Chapter 5 of this text.

The Keyword Outline

If you tried to deliver your speech from your formal sentence outline, you would basically be reading from a manuscript. The purpose of a keyword outline is to reduce your full-sentence outline to a manageable set of cues that mainly remind you of what you are going to say and when you are going to say it. A keyword outline encourages conversational delivery instead of an oral reading of your words. In the next chapter, you will learn that this is called *extemporaneous* delivery.

You might want to make a keyword outline on note cards or on a sheet of paper, whichever your instructor prefers. The **keyword outline** is a *brief outline with cue words that you can use during the delivery of your presentation.* The outline may include words that will prompt your memory, sources that you will cite within the presentation, or even the complete quotations of material you will repeat. The keyword outline may look sketchy to someone other than the speaker. Of course, for the keyword outline to be effective, you will need to practice the speech several times so that the cues are meaningful. Figure 6.4 is an example of a keyword outline.

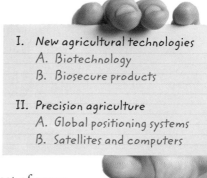

Figure 6.4   **How can a keyword outline help you remember your speech?**

In Chapter 3, you learned about various purposes for speaking and the importance of narrowing your purpose to a specific thesis statement. Those initial steps—selecting the purpose and crafting the thesis—are the foundations upon which your speech is organized. An informative speech will likely result in certain types of main points, whereas a persuasive speech on the same topic will likely result in completely different main points. This section will help you learn how to plan for these differences.

How Should You Organize the Body of the Presentation?

The introduction, body, and conclusion are the three main components of most speeches. You will first learn how to organize the body of the presentation because the body needs to be planned before you can effectively create your introduction and conclusion.

Emphasize Main Points

The first task in organizing the body of the presentation is to identify your main points. Examine the ideas and arguments you have gathered, and consider the key issues you want to address. If you have written down your specific purpose, you may be able to identify your main points easily. For example, Stacey Tischer, a second-year doctoral pharmacy student, gave a presentation on breast cancer[8] with these three main points:

I.   Fifteen hundred men each year contract breast cancer.
II. Black women who are diagnosed die of the disease more often than white women who are diagnosed.
III. Clinical examination can help detect the problem.

By dividing your topic into main ideas, you can better explain and discuss it further. The main points, as we see here, provide the skeleton for the body of the speech. They will be backed up with supporting materials, examples, evidence, and further divisions of subpoints and sub-subpoints. Section III in the preceding list could be further explained with subpoints like these:

A.   Looking and feeling are two parts to breast examination.
B.   Detecting the difference between cancerous and noncancerous irregularities is very important.

As you are considering your topic, your specific purpose, and the main points that you will develop, remember this practical advice:

- Choose two or three main points.
- Choose main ideas that are approximately equal in importance.

Let us consider each of these suggestions in more depth.

Limit Your Main Points to Two to Three Points

Most messages have two to three main points, reflecting what an audience can easily remember. For some topics, you may come up with only two main points. On the other hand, you may find that some topics are more easily divisible into a greater number of points. For instance, if you are talking about a complex process like preparing for an audit, you could divide your talk into the five main steps of the process. Try to present only as much as your audience can remember.

"Most messages have two to three main points, reflecting what an audience can easily remember."

An emergency medical person knows too much about health for a five-minute presentation. He could, however, address what happens in the first minutes of responding to a crisis with three main points in a presentation entitled "First Acts of the First Responder."

I.   Make sure the victim's heart is beating or immediately provide cardiopulmonary therapy.
II. Make sure external blood flow is stopped with pressure or tourniquets.
III. Make sure the victim is breathing or immediately provide oxygen.

Ensure That Your Main Points Are Nearly Equal in Importance

One way that you can check that your main points are of equal weight is to consider how much you subdivide each main point. If one main point has several subdivisions, but the others have none, then the point with many subdivisions must be more important than the others. Merge main points or reduce subdivisions to achieve nearly equal weight. Maybe one of the subpoints is really a main point.

Similarly, when you practice your presentation later on, you may find that you do not spend equal time on each main point. Each main point need not be granted *exactly* the same amount of time, but the time you spend discussing each point should be more or less similar. If you have three main points, you should spend about 30 percent of your time on each.

Determine the Order of the Main Points

Sometimes the order of your main points seems obvious. At other times, the organizational pattern is less clear. Your purpose and topic determine your choice of organizational pattern. In this section we provide you with some alternatives you can consider for the organization of your main points.

The general purpose of your presentation will suggest potential organizational patterns. Among the possible organizational patterns, which we will discuss next, are:

"Your purpose and topic determine your choice of organizational pattern."

1. The time-sequence and spatial relations patterns found often in informative presentations.
2. The cause–effect and topical sequence patterns found in both informative and persuasive presentations.
3. The problem–solution and Monroe's Motivated Sequence patterns found often in persuasive presentations.

Time-Sequence Pattern

The **time-sequence pattern** *states the order of events as they actually occur.* Use this pattern when your primary purpose is to tell your audience how something came about over a period of time. The steps in reducing water pollution, the evolution of sexual harassment policies, and the development of smartphone technology are examples of topics based on time. This pattern is also commonly used in "how to do it" and in "either/or" presentations because the audience will be unable to "do it" unless they follow steps in the correct order. In Figure 6.5, Hannah Back used a time-sequence pattern to explain how to best prepare for an exam. The first main point discusses what to do when taking notes and the second explains what you should do when preparing your review guide. These are in time-ordered sequence because you take notes over class lectures before you prepare your review guide.

The Art of Test Preparation
By Hannah Back

Introduction:

I. Getting Attention: Good morning! Today I will be giving a short presentation, and at the end I will administer a test that will contribute to your grade in this course. I hope you are all ready to take notes! [pause]

II. Relating to Audience: All right, so I am not really giving you an exam on my speech, but how many of you just panicked? Preparing for a test of your knowledge can be stressful, but it does not have to be!

III. Credibility: As a rising junior with a 4.0 GPA, I think I can safely identify myself as a "professional student" who has learned to work within the academic system to achieve success.

IV. Preview: Today I would like to share my expertise with you by walking you through the process of learning and studying that will ultimately, almost certainly, result in a passing grade.

Figure 6.5   **These main points follow a time-sequence pattern because they explain what you do to take notes and, later, prepare for the exam.**

Transition: When your professors tell you that it is important to take notes to do well in a class, chances are they do not tell you exactly what to write down, or how to do it.

Body:

II. During class you need to take good notes so that you can retain and understand information.

    A. According to Makany, Kemp, and Dror, in a study conducted in 2009, note-taking is "a central aspect of a complex human behavior related to information management" (p. 620).

        1. However, a problem addressed in the article is the amount of mental overload experienced by students who only have the time to write and process a small fraction of the information provided in a lecture.

        2. In order to overcome the problem of information overload, Pearson, Nelson, Titsworth, and Harter suggested in 2011 that students try focusing on outlining the main ideas when note-taking. They acknowledged that it might be easier for some students to draw connections between course concepts from broad outlines, rather than from many pages of disorganized but detailed notes.

    B. Note-taking is as important outside of the class as it is during; it is easy to leave important information behind when you exit the classroom.

        1. Reading the textbook before attending class will help tremendously with learning; if something in the book was unclear to you, you can ask your teacher about it in class. In a 2008 US News article about studying in college, college graduates confirmed that "keeping up with the books" was an essential part of their success.

        2. Most educators will recommend that you not only review your notes before the next class period, but that you rewrite and reorganize those notes within 24 hours of first taking them. Muskingum University in central Ohio provided a document of study tips to its students, one tip claiming that if students wait longer than 24 hours to review their notes, they will lose 60–70% of the memory of what they heard in class.

Transition: Once you have taken note of all of the important information from class, it is important to organize it into a study guide, supplemented with notes from your assigned readings.

II. About a week prior to the exam you should begin preparing your review guide.

    A. One way that I choose to prepare for exams is to create a study guide containing all of the most important information from the class and drawing connections to various concepts.

        1. I organize my notes into what was identified by Khogali, Laidlaw, and Harden in 2008 as a timetable-based study guide. Notes from every class and learning activity are arranged in chronological order, after which I identify the main issues and concepts for each class period.

        2. After reading through the notes and highlighting important terms, I usually have a good idea of which concepts I understand, and which concepts are confusing to me. I write these confusing terms on a separate piece of paper and use that document as an additional resource for studying.

    B. The list of difficult terms comes in handy for the last-minute studying that occurs before a test.

        1. Leaving the name of the concept or term a little separate from the detailed information, I will test myself by covering details with my hand to see how much I can remember about each concept without peeking.

        2. Some students prefer flashcards, with the concept on one side and its explanation or examples on the other side. I, however, find it easier to connect ideas when they are also visually connected on a piece of paper.

Transition: I have now walked you through all of the steps it takes to adequately prepare for an examination of your knowledge.

Figure 6.5   (continued)

Conclusion

I. Studying is something that gives a lot of college students a great deal of unnecessary anxiety. Every student has the power to change his or her academic outcomes.

II. Through strategic note-taking, before and after class, the creation of study guides, and the active self-testing of important terms, you can be sure that you will perform to the best of your abilities on test day.

III. So, the next time you leave class with a little extra time, I hope you will use that time to read through your notes. I hope you will take the extra time to understand how the subject you study relates to the world around you. But most of all, I hope that you are now motivated to take accountability for your learning and your success.

References

Khogali, S. O., Laidlaw, J. M., & Harden, R. M. (2006). Study guides: a study of different formats. *Medical Teacher*, 28(4), 375–377. doi:10.1080/01421590600799059

Makany, T., Kemp, J., & Dror, I.E. (2009). Optimizing the use of note-taking as an external cognitive aid for increasing learning. *British Journal of Educational Technology*, (40)4, 619–635. doi:10.1111/j.1467–8535.2008.00906.x

Muskingum College. Learning strategies database: Note taking. Retrieved from http://www.muskingum.edu/~cal/database/general/notetaking.html

Pearson, J. C., Nelson, P. E., Titsworth, S., & Harter, L. (2011). *Human Communication*. Boston, MA: McGraw Hill.

Silver, Marc. (2008, August 21). Advice on how to study in college. *U.S. News*. Retrieved from http://www.usnews.com/education/articles/2008/08/21/advice-on-how-to-study-in-college

Figure 6.5   (continued)

Spatial Relations Pattern

The **spatial relations pattern** *demonstrates how items are related in space.* Examples of presentations that could be organized using a spatial relations pattern would include using a map to show historic conservation sites over a period of time, using a grid to explain choreography in ballroom dancing, or using an architectural model to explain effective kitchen design for people who use wheelchairs. An example of the spatial relations pattern, written by football player Paul Backowski, appears in Figure 6.6.

American Football: A Game of Inches

Introduction:

Three-hundred-pound men in synchronous motion, gracefully grinding their teeth and pushing each other back and forth just to gain a couple inches of earth. Spatial relations in the game of American football is extremely important to the success of opposing players and teams. The offensive line is the group of five players who are typically the largest humans on the field. I will use concepts from the offensive line to explain spatial relations. Why do I know the game from the inside? I was a varsity football player on a major college team.

Figure 6.6   **Spatial arrangements work particularly well when describing activities like playing football or other activities that take place in a defined area like a field, course, or arena.**

Body:

I. I want to begin by describing specific concepts that coaches teach all American football offensive linemen.

    A. Space and distance are extremely important.

    B. Offensive linemen should line up next to each other with at least a two-foot gap between the center, guards, and tackle positions.

    C. Distance between linemen is extremely important because space keeps the linemen from stepping or tripping over each other.

    D. Space allows room for linemen to gather momentum before a collision with opposing defenders, who are less than a foot away.

II. First Steps: Correct spacing is critical to success of individual plays.

    A. After establishing a two-foot gap between each player, the linemen are now ready to execute the designated play.

    B. The first step should be forward 6 inches every time, which allows the player to explode quickly.

    C. American football is a game based on speed and quickness, regardless of size and weight.

    D. The first step is extremely important. If the step is done correctly, the play will be a success. If the step is off, the play runs the risk of being a failure.

III. Practicing the stance and first steps are important to success.

    A. Repetition of stance and steps are the basics to the game of football and are extremely essential to success.

    B. Begin each day by lining up next to a partner and by maintaining a distance of two feet.

    C. Next, practice stepping 6 inches forward. Repeat these two steps over and over until this process becomes natural.

    D. These steps may seem unimportant, but they are integral to the success of every play.

Conclusion:

Spatial relations are extremely important for the success of a football team. Distance and space relationships are constantly being analyzed to increase the efficiency of every play. Stance and length of steps are just two examples of the importance of spatial relationships in the game of American football.

Figure 6.6   **(continued)**

Cause–Effect Pattern

The **cause–effect pattern** of organization *describes or explains causes and consequences.* Actually, the pattern of organization can move from cause to effect or from effect to cause. Examples of effect to cause are the various spinoffs from *Law and Order,* such as *Criminal Intent* or *SVU,* stories in which the narrative begins with the murder (effect) and proceeds to the story explaining why and how the murder took place (cause). In a presentation on the vital topic of health, you might use such a pattern by starting with someone almost miraculously free of pain (effect) and move toward the new drug (cause) that made the person pain-free. Two examples of cause to effect might be how increased exposure to sunshine, medicine, and even lights can defeat SAD (Seasonal Affective Disorder) and how taking a daily vitamin can increase your body's immunity to disease. The speech outline on laughter, written by Hannah Back and shown in Figure 6.7, illustrates a cause–effect pattern.

The Science of Laughter
By Hannah Back

Introduction:

I. Getting Attention: What shakes and twitches and can be found at the bottom of the ocean? [pause] A nervous wreck!

II. Relating to Audience: Of those of you who laughed at my lame joke, how many know what just happened in your bodies? Do you know the effect your giggles had on your mental state?

III. Credibility: I have been laughing for as long as I have been alive. Nowadays, I am often the only one to laugh at my teachers' jokes, or the pedestrian who trips on the sidewalk. I have always loved to laugh, and I know it makes me feel better; but I have never known why.

IV. Preview: I set out on a mission to identify what laughter actually is, mentally and physically, as well as what exactly it does to the body and mind. Today, I share with you my results.

Body:

I. We laugh every day, but few of us could actually explain the physiology behind that simple act.

   A. Physiologically, laughter is your body's response to humor, manifested as a combination of gestures and sounds.

      1. In 2012, the *Encyclopedia Britannica* explained that laughter consists of altered breathing and activity in 15 facial muscles. Muscles in the upper lip are electrically stimulated in varying degrees to produce anything from a faint smile to the variety of facial expressions produced by uncontrollable laughter. Air intake becomes highly irregular, resulting in gasping and the repeated opening and closing of the mouth.

      2. These peculiar gestures are accompanied by a series of repeated sounds, with which we are all familiar. Ha ha ha! Ho ho ho! Cited in Marshall Brain's 2012 article, laughter researcher Robert Provine found that "ha" and "ho" are the two types of laughter we experience, though never simultaneously.

   B. There are many theories that attempt to explain the psychological causes of laughter.

      1. The relaxing effect of laughter halts the body's natural fight-or-flight response. Marshall Brain cites philosopher John Morreall, who theorized that laughter may have originated "as a gesture of shared relief at the passing of danger."

      2. Whatever the origin of laughter in the history of humans, it manifests itself when people are most comfortable around each other. Brain cites studies confirming that people are 30 times more likely to laugh in a social setting than they are to laugh alone.

Transition: The physical and psychological causes of laughter are closely tied to its benefits.

II. Laughter has numerous beneficial physiological and psychological effects.

   A. Recently, more studies have been conducted on the physiological effects of laughter, and how it relates to overall health.

      1. Researchers Michael Miller and William Fry conducted a study on the effects of laughter on the cardiovascular system, for instance, and found that, "mirthful laughter may serve as a useful and important vehicle for the promotion of vascular health."

      2. Ramon Morari's review of research literature on laughter in 2010 concluded with the recommendation that laughter be used as "a complementary/alternative medicine in the prevention and treatment of illnesses." This suggestion is consistent with the idea that laughter is the result of comfortable social interaction. In 2011, Mattson and Hall, in their book *Health as Communication Nexus*, identified several

Figure 6.7   **Laughter is a common behavior that has a variety of health effects.**

key benefits of social support (which could be manifested through shared laughter): improved efficacy, resistance to disease, and recovery from disease are just a few.

B. As you may be starting to see, the physiological effects of laughter overlap with its psychological effects.

1. Laughter can improve individual satisfaction in relationships. Hara Marano of *Psychology Today* wrote in 2003 that laughter is necessary in relationships because it "synchronizes the brains of speaker and listener so that they are emotionally attuned."

2. Laughter can also alleviate discomfort. In 2009, Jude Robinson studied how mothers discuss their unhealthy smoking in relation to their children's health. During the interviews, women used humor and laughter as a "deliberate ploy to prevent other women from letting discussions get too serious." By doing so, they made themselves and others more comfortable while discussing difficult issues.

Transition: We have now thoroughly examined the effects of laughter in relation to both the mind and the body.

Conclusion:

I.   It is easy to get caught up in the stresses of life, and easy to forget to laugh at the little things.

II.   Now that I have explained laughter from a physiological and psychological standpoint, both its causes and its effects, I hope you understand the important impact it can have on your life.

III. So, the next time you are that clumsy pedestrian who trips on the sidewalk, I hope you will be able to take a moment to laugh at yourself. Appreciate how much better your day will be because of it.

References

Brain, M. (2000, April 1). How laughter works. *How Stuff Works*. Retrieved from http://science .howstuffworks.com/environmental/life/human-biology/laughter1.htm

Humour. (2012, May 12). In *Encyclopedia Britannica* online. Retrieved from http://www .britannica.com/EBchecked/topic/276309/humour#ref126128

Mora-Ripoll, R. (2010). The therapeutic value of laughter in medicine [Abstract]. *Alternative Therapies in Health and Medicine* 16(6), 56–64. Retrieved from http://www.ncbi.nlm.nih .gov/pubmed/21280463

Miller, M., & Fry, W. F. (2009). The effect of mirthful laughter on the human cardiovascular system. *Medical Hypotheses* 73(5), 636–639. doi:10.1016/j.mehy.2009.02.044

Robinson, J. (2009). Laughter and forgetting: Using focus groups to discuss smoking and motherhood in low-income areas in the UK. *International Journal of Qualitative Studies in Education* 22(3), 263–278. doi:10.1080/09518390902835421

Marano, H. E. (2003, April 29). The benefits of laughter. *Psychology Today*. Retrieved from http://www.psychologytoday.com/articles/200304/the-benefits-laughter

Figure 6.7   **(continued)**

Topical Sequence Pattern

The **topical sequence pattern**, a highly versatile organizational pattern, *simply divides up a topic into related parts*. Be careful not to treat the topical sequence pattern as a dumper into which you can throw anything. The main points in a topical sequence have to be related to a central idea, and the main points need to be related to each other: three reasons to volunteer at the food bank, two types of hybrid vehicles, or the advantages and disadvantages of jury trials. In Figure 6.8, you will note that Carrie's speech explores three types of alternative energy: sun, wind, and hydro.

Sun, Wind, & Water: The New Green
By Carrie Mackey

Introduction:

I. With the global climate changing, we must begin to turn to renewable energy to reduce or offset our carbon footprint.

II. All of us have a reason to be invested in renewable energy. The use of renewable energy allows us to be less dependent on foreign energy sources (Culley, et al., 2011). In addition, its costs are increasingly competitive with traditional energy sources (Shaw, 2010).

III. I am committed to being environmentally conscious and want to help spread information about these trends in green energy.

IV. A variety of renewable energy sources are being used to supplement more traditional forms of energy production in the United States. I would like to share with you the three most utilized forms of renewable energy: solar, wind, and hydropower.

Body:

I. Hydropower is the most frequently used form of renewable energy.

   A. Hydropower accounts for 6% of the energy consumed in the United States (Energy Information Administration).

   B. Hydropower plants must be located near large water sources. The amount of energy produced is based on the flow of the water. When water pushes on the blades of a turbine, it spins and produces energy.

   C. Hydropower can come in the form of a dam or a reservoir.

   D. Sometimes hydropower plants have negative effects on the ecosystem of the area around the dam or reservoir, though recent efforts have been made to reduce these effects.

   E. A hydropower plant can operate for up to 100 years. The few emissions that are produced when creating the facility, such as from machinery and the production of materials, are offset by the energy the facility produces throughout its operating lifetime (EIA, 2012).

II. Second to hydropower is wind-generated energy.

   A. Wind turbines account for 3% of the energy consumed within the United States—the leader in wind-generated energy.

   B. Similar to a water turbine, the lifting and spinning of the blades of the windmill create energy, and the frequency and speed of the wind turbines impact how much energy is produced.

   C. Windmills can be placed in vast areas from farmland to shorelines.

   D. They are very large machines that have a large visual impact on the area where they're located. At times, the noise the blades make can be an annoyance for people in the surrounding area.

   E. Windmills have a small physical footprint compared to the amount of energy they can produce (EIA, 2012).

III. One of the most recognizable types of renewable energy is solar energy.

   A. Solar energy is converted into various forms.

      1. Heat is one form of energy produced. Solar energy can directly heat water supplies, buildings, and other spaces.

Figure 6.8   **By exploring three sources of alternative energy, Carrie's speech employs the topical sequence pattern of organization.**

2. The thermal energy produced is used as steam heat to power heat-driven generators.

B. When placed on buildings, solar energy panels have minimal impact on the environment.

C. Carbon dioxide and pollutants are not produced by solar energy.

D. On the other hand, solar energy requires a large amount of space to be most effective; moreover, it is dependent on the sun, an unpredictable source.

Conclusion:

I. Together, these three sources of alternative energy—hydropower, wind-generated energy, and solar energy—account for 10% of the energy consumed in the United States (EIA, 2012).

II. As our global climate changes, renewable energy sources like these will become attractive options for providing energy and reducing our carbon footprint.

References

Culley, M. R., Carton, A. D., Weaver, S. R., Ogley-Oilver, E., Street, J. C. (2011). Sun, wind, rock and metal: Attitudes toward renewable and non-renewable energy sources in the context of climate change and current energy debates. *Current Psychology*, 30. 215–233. doi 10.1007/s12144-011-9110-5

Shaw, F. C. (2010). Renewable resources: Energy strategies for education institutions. American School & University 83(3). Retrieved from http://web.ebscohost.com/ehost/pdfviewer/pdfviewer?sid=157c1e83-e6f4-4089-81a5-a7f29b91203d%40sessionmgr15&vid=8&hid=21

United States Energy Information Administration. (2012). Energy explained. Retrieved from http://www.eia.gov/energyexplained/index.cfm

Figure 6.8   **(continued)**

Problem–Solution Pattern

The **problem–solution pattern**, *depicting an issue and a solution*, tends to be used more often in persuasive than in informative presentations. The statement of the problem is difficult without framing the issue in some way that indicates your own perspective, a perspective that you want the audience to adopt. For example, let us say you describe the environmental issue of establishing game preserves. Your position on the issue—that the state should pay farmers to set aside land for wildlife and natural habitat—is the perspective you urge on the audience. Carrie's persuasive presentation about protecting your privacy on Facebook, appearing in Figure 6.9, shows a good example of a problem–solution arrangement. Notice how her call to action in the second point makes this speech more persuasive in nature.

The problem–solution pattern raises three serious questions for the speaker: How much should you say about the problem, how much about the solution, and how ethical is the solution? Usually you can work out a proper ratio based on what the audience knows about the issue. If the listeners are unaware that a problem exists, you may have to spend more time telling them about the problem. On the other hand, if the problem is well known to all, you can spend most of your time on the solution. This pattern lends itself nicely to outlining, with the problem being one main point and the solution the other. Finally, you need to determine if your solution harms anyone.

Monroe's Motivated Sequence

Monroe's Motivated Sequence[9] was developed by Alan Monroe, who applied John Dewey's work on reflective thinking to persuasion. This organizational pattern *includes five specific components: attention, need, satisfaction, visualization, and action.*

Your Privacy and Facebook
By Carrie Mackey

Introduction:

I. **Gaining attention:** As of April 2012, 900 million people were on Facebook (Goldman, 2012).

II. **Relating to the audience:** Do you have a Facebook account? Ninety percent of undergraduate students are Facebook users (Hew, 2011). Many of us use Facebook to stay in touch with friends by posting messages and sharing photos. But how often do we consider the impact these posts might have on us in the future?

III. **Credibility:** As a college student, I have seen firsthand how seemingly harmless disclosures on Facebook can lead to negative consequences, like causing conflicts among friends or even prompting unanticipated questions during job interviews.

IV. **Preview:** Based on my experiences, I am extremely vigilant about the privacy settings on my Facebook account, and I urge you to be as well.

Body:

I. Although millions of individuals have Facebook accounts, many are unaware of the various privacy settings they can use.

    A. The mission of Facebook is to make the world feel more open and connected (Fletcher & Ford, 2010). While there are many benefits to staying connected on Facebook, you should keep in mind that, without the proper privacy settings, your personal information can be viewed by strangers as well as friends.

    B. Some people have a few hundred Facebook friends who can view whatever they post. Often, the larger an individual's network, the more information that person will disclose (Hew, 2011).

    C. By simply changing the default privacy settings on your account, you can limit the number of people that have access to your information. Would you believe that only 20% of users change these settings (Karl & Peluchette, 2011)?

II. Now that we have discussed the importance of insufficient privacy settings on Facebook, let's explore the various ways you can increase your privacy.

    A. The simplest way to ensure your privacy on Facebook is to change your privacy settings (Hew, 2011). To do so, go to "Account" and click on "Privacy Settings" (Peak, 2011). From there you will be able to select who will have access to your profile. For the most privacy, select "friends only," which allows access to only your friends.

    B. Even after selecting "friends only," it is important to be mindful about what you post on Facebook.

    C. Another safety measure you can take is to request that Facebook not share your information with third parties. This is an option within your Facebook page, but it is not in the privacy settings.

    D. In addition to choosing the appropriate privacy settings, you can follow these social networking tips to create a more private Facebook experience for you and your friends.

        1. Create complex passwords and vary the email address used.

        2. Do not install third-party applications from sites you don't trust.

        3. Only accept friend requests from people you know.

        4. Read the privacy statement provided by the company.

        5. Remember that anything can become public on the Internet. Be mindful of what you post on your page (Peak, 2011).

Figure 6.9 **The lack of privacy is identified as a problem in the first point; the second point provides actionable solutions for the audience.**

Conclusion:

While millions of people have Facebook accounts, relatively few take steps to ensure their privacy. By following my suggestions, you can increase your level of privacy on Facebook and enjoy the benefits of a more open and connected world.

References

DiVerniero, R. A. & Hosek, A. M. (2011). Students' perceptions and communication management of instructors' online self-disclosure. *Communication Quarterly, 59*(4), 428–449. doi: 10.1080/01463373.2011.597275

Fletcher, D. & Ford, A. (2010, May 31). Friends without borders. *Time, 175*(21), 32–38.

Goldman, David. (2012, April 23). Facebook tops 900 million users. CNN Money Retrieved from http://money.cnn.com/2012/04/23/technology/facebook-q1/index.htm

Hew, K. F. (2011). Students' and teachers' use of Facebook. *Computers in Human Behavior, 27*(2). doi: 10.1016/j.chb.2010.11.020

Karl, K. A. & Peluchette, J. V. (2011). "Friending" professors, parents, and bosses: A Facebook connection conundrum. *Journal of Education for Business, 86*(4), 214–222. doi: 10.1080/08832323.2010.507638

Peak, Elbert. (2011). Social network privacy: Overcoming Facebook policies that put users at risk. *Army Communicator.* Retrieved from http://web.ebscohost.com/ehost/pdfviewer /pdfviewer?sid=cc324c8b-45e3–4095-b92d-b7c34a6db571%40sessionmgr14&vid=6&hid=14

Figure 6.9 **(continued)**

- First, capture the *attention* of your audience. You want your audience to decide that to listen to you is important.
- Second, establish the *need* for your proposal. You want to describe a problem or show why some need exists. You want your audience to believe that something must be done.
- Third, present the solution to the problem or show how the need can be satisfied. You want your audience to understand how your proposal will achieve *satisfaction*.
- Fourth, go beyond simply presenting the solution by *visualizing* the solution for the audience. You want the audience to envision enjoying the benefits of your proposal.
- Fifth and last, state the behavior that you expect of your audience. In this step, you request *action* or approval. You want your audience to respond by saying that they will do what you have asked. Your presentation should have a strong conclusion that asks for specific, but reasonable, action.

CULTURAL DIFFERENCES IN ORGANIZATION

cultural NOTE

Most North Americans are linear; that is, they like to arrange their thoughts in a line from most important to least important, from biggest to smallest, from tallest to shortest. Other cultures use different organizational schemes. Some East Asian cultures, for example, sound to North Americans as if they are "talking around" a subject instead of getting right to the topic because they expect a rather long "warm-up" of socializing before getting down to business. Also, they may be indirect by suggesting rather than saying something directly. Imagine that you are going to speak to an audience that includes a number of Korean, Chinese, and Japanese people. The audience is predominantly American, however. You will be explaining how to enroll in classes at your college. How will you approach this topic? What adjustments might you make given the composition of the audience?

In the persuasive presentation written by Andrea, shown in Figure 6.10, notice how the five steps of Monroe's Motivated Sequence were integrated into the standard outline format shown elsewhere in this chapter. Whereas the introduction and conclusions fulfill the first and fifth elements of Monroe's sequence, the middle three elements are integrated into main points found in the body of the speech outline.

Incorporate Supporting Materials

The main points create only the skeleton of the body of the presentation. The presenter must flesh out this skeleton with subpoints and sub-subpoints. You need to decide what information to keep and what to discard. You also need to determine where and what kind of visual resources will help your audience understand your message. Refer to Chapter 5 to review how to flesh out the skeleton with supporting materials in the form of examples, narrative, statistics, and evidence.

Now you know organizational patterns from which you can choose to make your presentation effective. You also know that any kind of outline is just the bones of the speech that you have to "beef up" with supporting materials and visual resources.

Table 6.1 shows that each pattern of organization is generally associated with specific purposes you are trying to accomplish in your speech. Time-sequence and spatial relations patterns tend to work well in informative presentations. The problem–solution pattern and Monroe's Motivated Sequence work well in persuasive presentations. And cause–effect and topical sequence patterns work well in both informative and persuasive presentations. Of course, these are not rules, and you may discover ways to creatively break from these traditional trends. Take care, however, that your creativity does not drastically alter the perceived purpose of your speech.

Staying Active to Stay Healthy

By Andrea Vanarsdalen

Introduction:

Attention Step:

I. Thanks to the modern conveniences afforded by technology, life in the twenty-first century seems to be getting easier. However, many years ago, to make up for the lack of convenience, people were more active in their daily lives. For example, people chopped wood for heat, fetched water for drinking and cooking, and traveled by foot instead of by car.

II. Unlike kids today, who sit inside watching television or playing video games, children used to have to entertain themselves by inventing games, which often involved getting fresh air and exercise.

III. Adults spend much of their day driving to work, sitting at their desks, and then coming home to eat dinner and sit on the couch. Should Americans accept this lifestyle as normal?

Body:

Need Step:

I. Unfortunately, many Americans make poor decisions about their health.

    A. In 1960, about 13% of American adults were obese. Today, 66% of adults are overweight and one-third of the population is obese. Children today are also struggling with obesity: 33% of children and adolescents are overweight or on their way to being overweight (Sizer & Whitney, 2011).

    B. Obesity rates are five times what they were fifty years ago—a disheartening trend. In order to ensure that obesity rates do not continue to rise, Americans need to take action by increasing their physical activity.

Figure 6.10 Andrea's speech on staying healthy integrates steps in Monroe's Motivated Sequence into the standard outline format.

C. Adding physical activity to your daily routine will benefit your overall health. For example, it will improve your physical health by decreasing your risk of developing many diseases; your mental health will also improve, as regular exercise can prevent the onset of depression (Sizer & Whitney, 2011).

Satisfaction Step:

II. As you can see, being more active will improve your health. But how difficult would it be for Americans to change their habits?

    A. Exercising doesn't have to be time-consuming.

        1. Choose an activity that fits into your schedule.

        2. Even if you just go for a ten-minute jog or take a half-hour kickboxing class, you will benefit from doing something rather than nothing.

    B. Being active is easy.

        1. Simply going for a walk around your neighborhood or a local park qualifies as healthy, active behavior.

        2. If you don't have enough time in your day to exercise, just do something small: take the stairs at work instead of the elevator; or when you drive someplace, park farther away from your destination.

        3. Encourage children to play outside. A game of kickball with their friends is a healthier option for socializing than an afternoon spent on social media websites.

    C. People often dread exercising because they don't find it enjoyable. But you can make exercise fun by finding things that fit with your personal interests. When your exercise routine is fun, you are more likely to be active and stay active.

Visualization Step:

III. Physical activity is a major factor in America's overall health.

Sizer and Whitney state that, "improvements in health and body composition follow an active lifestyle" (Sizer & Whitney, 2011). A few outcomes of being active are as follows (adapted from Sizer & Whitney, 2011) (Williams & Wilkins, 2010):

    A. Lowered rates of obesity in adults and children.

    B. Lowered chances of developing diseases like type 2 diabetes, cardiovascular disease, and certain types of cancer.

    C. Longer lifespan.

    D. Decreased likelihood of depression as a result of released endorphins.

    E. Reduced stress levels and an improved mental outlook.

Conclusion:

Action Step:

I. America's health is a serious issue. Obesity rates among children and adults are growing rapidly and little action is being taken. The Trust for America's Health Initiatives concludes that, "the country is failing to address the obesity crises with the urgency it deserves" (Trust for America's health: Obesity). You can take steps to improve America's overall health by simply:

    A. Engaging in physical activities every day, even if it's just for a short amount of time.

    B. Asking friends if they will exercise with you. Invite a friend to go for a walk or a bike ride, or to play a game of tennis.

    C. And finally, encouraging family and friends to be physically active.

References

Sizer, F., & Whitney, E. (2011). *Nutrition: Concepts and controversies*. (12 ed., p. 4,325,353,554). Mason, Ohio: Cengage Learning.

Trust for America's health: Obesity. (n.d.). Retrieved from http://healthyamericans.org/

Williams, L., & Wilkins, (2010). *Guidelines for exercise testing and prescription*. (8 ed.). Baltimore, MD: American College of Sports Medicine.

Figure 6.10 **Andrea's speech on staying healthy integrates steps in Monroe's Motivated Sequence into the standard outline format.**

TABLE 6.1 PATTERNS OF ORGANIZATION LINKED TO GENERAL PURPOSES		
USUALLY INFORMATIVE	EITHER INFORMATIVE OR PERSUASIVE	USUALLY PERSUASIVE
Time-sequence	Cause-effect	Problem-solution
Spatial relations	Topical sequence	Monroe's Motivated Sequence

What Holds the Presentation Together?

Your methods of moving from one point to another, of telling the audience where you are in the overall presentation, where you are going next, and where you have been is the "glue" that holds your presentation together. Audience members cannot "reread" a speech as they can reread an essay if they get lost in a disorganized maze. Transitions, signposts, internal previews, and internal reviews are the mortar between the bricks. Together they allow the audience easy access to the information you are presenting.

Transitions are *statements or words that bridge previous parts of the presentation to the next part. Transitions can be signposts, internal previews, or internal reviews.* They almost always appear between main parts of the presentation (introduction, body, and conclusion), when turning to a visual aid, or when moving from an argument to evidence. For instance, transitions might look like this:

- Having explained positive purpose as the first reason for choosing a career as a nurse's aide, let us turn to the second: service to those who are in need. (Review of past point and preview of the next.)
- Now that you have heard an overview of Washington, DC's scenic mall with its reflecting ponds, let me show you a map of the many museums that are free and open to the public. (Move from main point to visual aid.)

Signposts, *like road signs on a highway, reveal where the speaker is going.* Signposts are brief transitions that do not have to point backward and forward; they have only to tell the listener where the presenter is in the message. Some examples include the following:

- My first point is that . . .
- One of the best examples is . . .
- To illustrate this point, I will . . .
- A second, and even more convincing, argument is . . .

Skillful use of signposts and transitions will clarify your organization and help you become a confident presenter.

Internal previews *inform listeners of your next point or points and are more detailed than transitions.* They are similar to the statements a presenter makes in the introduction of his or her presentation, although internal previews occur within the body of the presentation. Examples of internal previews include the following:

- My next point is that education correlates highly with income.
- I now will explain how to build community support for improving our middle schools.

Internal reviews *remind listeners of your last point or points and are more detailed than transitions.* They occur within the body of the presentation. Examples of internal reviews include the following:

- Now that we have covered the symptoms of this disease, let's move to the tests used to diagnose it.
- At this point, we have established that most students are honest when taking tests and writing papers.

Let's turn now to the second major topic of this chapter: outlining the presentation.

How Do You Introduce Your Presentation?

Introductions are very important because they set the tone for your entire presentation. Many audience members will decide whether or not to give you full attention within the first minute of your presentation. Consequently, much care must be given to crafting a strong introduction. Whether you introduce yourself or another speaker introduces you, an **introduction**, *the beginning portion of your presentation*, serves four functions.

1. Gains and maintains favorable attention.
2. Relates your topic to your audience.
3. Relates you to the topic.
4. Previews the message by stating the purpose and forecasting the organization of the presentation.

Gaining and Maintaining Favorable Attention

The first function of an introduction is gaining and maintaining attention. Even if they appear attentive, your audience members may not be completely focused on you or your message when you begin. You need to direct their attention.

Here are 10 possible ways to gain and maintain your audience's attention:

1. *Present a person or object.* A presenter brought a very muscular person to demonstrate safe weight-lifting moves during the presentation, while another student speaking on health food gave everyone a whole-grain granola bar to eat after the presentation. A third student handed out packets of artificial sweeteners. She said, "These sweeteners will not wake us up like sugar would do, but I hope they are a wake-up call. In your hands, you hold the three leading brands of artificial sweeteners."

2. *Invite audience participation.* If you invite **audience participation**, *you make your audience active participants in your presentation*. One student who was speaking about some of the problems of poverty asked his audience to sit crowded elbow-to-elbow during his presentation to illustrate lack of living space. Or you can ask your audience a question and expect and acknowledge a reply.

3. *Imagine a situation.* You might have the audience imagine that they are standing on a ski slope, flying through the air, or burrowing underground. Kelsey Smith began her speech by having her audience imagine that they were in a recent situation:

> Imagine it is a hot summer day. Your mom packs up the car. You and your family drive down to the local pool. Only when you get there you are forbidden to enter the pool and you must go home. This may sound outrageous but to people of color of suburban Philadelphia, this happened. Many of us think that racism is a part of history and that it is not relevant today. However, this incident occurred on July 10, 2009. And, it is only one of the many examples of racism in today's world.

4. *Use audio and video.* A deputy sheriff showed a videotape of a drunken driver being arrested in a presentation on driving while intoxicated. Be sure not to let your audio or visual resource dominate your time.

5. *Arouse audience suspense.* Hannah began her informative speech by saying that at the conclusion she would administer a test that would contribute to students' final grades in the class. Although she quickly told them that they really did not need to worry about the exam and that the goal of her speech was to help them feel more confident about taking tests, her attention-gaining strategy centered on creating suspense for the audience.

6. *Use slides, film, video, or PowerPoint.* A student who was studying big-city slums began with a rapid series of 12 PowerPoint slides showing trash heaps, crowded rooms, run-down buildings, and rats.

7. *Read a quotation.* Gretchen Barker began her speech on music therapy with this quotation: "Music speaks what cannot be expressed, soothes the mind and gives it rest, heals the heart and makes it whole, flows from Heaven to the soul."

8. *State striking facts or figures.* Facts and figures can bore your audience to tears or rouse them out of a stupor. A student speaking about minority students in higher education used Texas as an example because that state requires its 35 public colleges and universities to admit any student in the top 10 percent of his or her class. The result in 2008: The University of Texas–Austin, the largest of the public universities in Texas, attracted more minority students than they used to admit under a race-based system. Today, more than 80 percent of the students at that flagship university have been admitted under the 10 percent rule established when George W. Bush was governor more than a decade ago.[10]

9. *Tell a story.* Telling a story to gain the audience's attention is one of the oldest and most commonly used methods. Your story can be actual (factual) or created (hypothetical), as long as you tell your audience which it is. A well-honed hypothetical story must be realistic and detailed.

10. *Use humor.* Although often overused, jokes or humor to gain and maintain attention can be effective, but only if the humor is related to the topic. Too often jokes are told for their own sake, whether or not they have anything to do with the subject of the speech. Another word of caution: If you are not good at telling jokes, then you ought to practice your humor before your speech in front of the class. If the joke is offensive, you will likely lose your audience altogether. Handled well, an appropriate touch of humor will likely be welcomed by the audience. Noah Nash began his speech on absolute truth by stating, "President James A. Garfield said, 'The truth will set you free, but first it will make you miserable.'"

Relating the Topic to the Audience

The second function of an introduction is relating the topic to the audience. This introductory move assures the audience of a reason for their attention because *there is a connection between them and the topic.* A student presenting on the ethics of changing grades related the topic to her student audience by pointing out that their own university registrar had changed thousands of grades at the request of professors—nearly always raising them. The audience listened to the presentation with more interest because the presenter took pains to relate the topic to both the men and the women in class.

Relating the topic to the audience does not need to be more than one or two sentences in length. For example, Kristen Waldock stated, "According to an article on mercola.com, the average American drinks almost 54 gallons of soft drinks each year, which adds up to a little over a gallon per week." Gretchen Barker said simply, "As college students, we all lead very stressful lives and using music to positively affect our mood is a healthy choice." Both Kristen and Gretchen helped their audience understand exactly how the topics of their speeches were relevant.

Relating the Topic to the Presenter

The third function of an introduction is relating the topic to the presenter. Here are two strategies:

- *Dress for the topic and occasion.* Wear clothing that will signal your credibility on a topic and that shows your relationship to the topic and the occasion.
- *Use self-disclosure* about why or how you have knowledge about the topic. Sometimes self-disclosure, revealing something about yourself that others cannot see, is confessional: "I successfully overcame drug addiction," "I have been a relationship counselor for 10 years," or "I have benefited from affirmative action programs." You do not have to reveal highly provocative or dramatic information. For example, one student shared, "As a health-conscious person, I like to know what I'm putting into my body."

The best advice we can give is to be authentic. Not all college students are experts on topics, and several hours' worth of research does not ensure expertise. However, you can be honest with your audience about why you selected the topic, or why you think it is important. Sincerity is a viable substitute for expertise.

Previewing the Message

Often, the last part of an introduction is a revelation. The presenter reveals the purpose as well as the organization and development of her presentation. **Forecasting** *tells the audience how you are going to cover the topic.* This thesis statement is an example that clearly indicates both the specific purpose and the organization:

> Today I am going to provide three reasons why you should request generic prescription drugs instead of well-advertised, name-brand prescription drugs.

The type of presentation is persuasive. The specific purpose is clear, and the organization ("three reasons") is apparent.

How Do You Conclude Your Presentation?

Just like the introduction, the conclusion of a presentation fulfills certain functions: (1) to forewarn the audience that you are about to stop, (2) to remind the audience of your central idea or the main points in your message, and (3) to specify what the audience should think or do in response to your presentation. Let us examine each of the functions of a conclusion in greater detail.

The **brake-light function** *warns the audience that you are about to stop.* The most blatant, though trite, method of signaling the end of a speech is to say, "In conclusion . . ." or "To summarize . . ." or "In review . . . ." Another way is to physically move back from the lectern. Also, you can change your tone of voice to have the sound of finality. There is a variety of ways to say, "I'm coming to the end." For instance, you have indicated an impending conclusion as soon as you say, "Now let us take my four main arguments and bring them together into one strong statement: You should learn about the candidates before you vote."

The second function of a conclusion—*to remind the audience of the thesis of your message*—is the **instant-replay function**. You could synthesize a number of major arguments or ideas into a single memorable statement. You could simply repeat the main steps or points in the speech. For instance, a student who spoke on the Heimlich maneuver for saving a choking person concluded his speech by repeating and demonstrating the moves for saving a person's life.

The third function of a conclusion is to clearly *state the response you seek from the audience*, the **action-ending function**. If your speech was informative, what do you want the audience to remember? Tell them. If your presentation was persuasive, how can the audience show its acceptance? A student who delivered a presentation on periodontal disease concluded by letting her classmates turn in their candy for a package of sugarless gum.

Once these three functions are completed, many speakers will attempt to find *some artistic way to end the speech*. This is called **closure**. Following are some ideas for closing your presentation. Of course you can think of others that are equally effective. What works for *you* will be best.

- *End with a quotation*. Quotations provide an effective end to your talk. Confine yourself to a brief quotation or two.
- *Ask a question*. Presenters can use questions to invite listeners into their topics; they also can use questions to close their talks, encouraging the audience to learn more about the topic or to take action.
- *Tell a story*. Audience members enjoy hearing stories. Stories are especially apt in a conclusion when they serve to remind the audience of the purpose of a presentation.
- *Close with a striking statement*. In a presentation on using seat belts, the speaker ended by saying: "In an accident, it is not who is right that really counts; it's who is left."
- *Review the central idea and main points*. Remind the audience what you told them.
- *Forewarn the audience that you are nearly done*. Avoid abrupt endings that leave the audience hanging.
- *Tell the audience what you expect*. What do you want them to think or do as a result of your presentation?
- *Refer back to the introduction*. Closing by reminding them how you began is a good strategy. For example, your introduction can be part of a story that ends in your conclusion.
- *End strongly in a memorable way*. You want your audience to remember what you said. Often they remember what you said last best of all.

These tips are just a few of the many ways you can draw your presentation to a close. They are provided here just to jump-start your own creativity in finding ways to end your presentation.

For
REVIEW >>

SUMMARY HIGHLIGHTS

Why Is Organization Important?

▶ Well-organized presentations will help the audience understand the information more easily.

▶ Presenters who are more organized are perceived as more competent and trustworthy.

What Are the Principles of Outlining?

▶ The principle of subordination suggests that you should use indentation and symbols to indicate which information is more important than other information.

▶ The principle of division states that if any main or subpoint is divided, it must have at least two divisions.

▶ The principle of parallelism requires that you use similar grammatical forms when phrasing main points, subpoints, or sub-subpoints in an outline.

What Types of Outlines Will You Create?

▶ The preparation outline is the initial or tentative working draft of your presentation.

▶ The formal sentence outline is a final version of your speech plan and is a formal outline that uses complete sentences and fully develops all aspects of the outline. Although your teacher may require all three types, this outline is typically always turned in for grading.

▶ The keyword outline is a highly abbreviated version of your sentence outline that is used during your presentation.

How Should You Organize the Body of Your Presentation?

▶ Emphasize main points of your presentation by highlighting the primary ideas that you want to develop.

▶ Limit your main points to two or three for most speeches.

▶ You have various options for how to organize your main points:
  • The time-sequence pattern lists main points in an order of events that occur.
  • The spatial relations pattern demonstrates how things are related visually.
  • The cause–effect pattern describes or explains causes and consequences.
  • A topical sequence is highly versatile and simply divides topics into logical related parts.
  • A problem–solution pattern identifies an issue that creates some disadvantageous condition and then ways to remedy that problem.
  • Monroe's Motivated Sequence includes five steps and is particularly well suited for speeches asking for personal action.

▶ Each main point will include two or more divisions that incorporate supporting material.

What Holds Your Presentation Together?

▶ Transitions are statements that bridge from one part of the speech (e.g., the introduction to the body, or between two main points in the body) to another.

▶ A signpost is a brief transition that indicates where you are in the presentation, such as saying, "My second point is that . . ."

▶ Internal previews inform listeners what will be discussed in the upcoming point.

▶ Internal reviews reminds listeners what you just discussed.

How Do You Introduce Your Presentation?

▶ Introductions begin by gaining the audience members' attention.

▶ After gaining their attention, you should relate the topic to them.

▶ You should establish your credibility by relating the topic to yourself.

▶ Your introduction should end with a preview of what your speech will cover.

How Do You Conclude Your Presentation?

▶ The conclusion begins with a specialized transition statement that accomplishes the brake-light function, which signals that the speech is ending.

▶ The instant-replay function reminds the audience of the thesis and main ideas of your message.

▶ The action-ending function of the conclusion is to clearly state what audience members should do with the information you provided.

▶ The closure function simply requires that you find an artistic way to end the speech.

1. The first task in organizing the body of the presentation is to:
   (A) write transitions
   (B) identify subpoints
   (C) determine the order of the main points
   (D) identify the main points

2. The time-sequence pattern:
   (A) demonstrates how items are related in space
   (B) states the order of events as they actually occur
   (C) divides up a topic into related parts
   (D) depicts an issue and a solution

3. If you are giving a speech on different bedroom configurations, the best organization to use is the:
   (A) topical sequence pattern
   (B) problem–solution pattern
   (C) spatial relations pattern
   (D) time-sequence pattern

4. The phrase, "My second point is . . ." is an example of a:
   (A) transition
   (B) signpost
   (C) thesis
   (D) conclusion

5. A final outline in complete sentence form is known as the:
   (A) preparation outline
   (B) formal sentence outline
   (C) draft outline
   (D) keyword outline

Answers: 1 (D); 2 (B); 3 (C); 4 (B); 5 (A)

APPLICATION EXERCISES

1. Think of a topic not mentioned in this chapter that would be best organized into each of the following patterns. Write the topic next to the appropriate pattern.

   ORGANIZATION PATTERN   TOPIC

   TIME-SEQUENCE:

   SPATIAL RELATIONS:

   PROBLEM–SOLUTION:

   CAUSE–EFFECT:

   TOPICAL SEQUENCE:

   MONROE'S MOTIVATED SEQUENCE:

   Can you explain why each pattern is most appropriate for each topic?

2. Go to the library and find the publication *Vital Speeches of the Day*, which is a collection of current speeches. Make a copy of a presentation and highlight the transitions, signposts, internal previews, and internal reviews.

3. Take any chapter in this book and construct an outline from the various levels of headings.

KEY TERMS

Action-ending function

Audience participation

Brake-light function

Cause–effect pattern

Closure

Forecasting

Formal sentence outline

Instant-replay function

Internal previews

Internal reviews

Introduction

Keyword outline

List of references

Monroe's Motivated Sequence

Preparation outline

Principle of division

Principle of parallelism

Principle of subordination

Problem–solution pattern

Signposts

Spatial relations pattern

Time-sequence pattern

Topical sequence pattern

Transitions

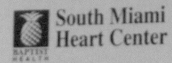

7

BY South Miami Heart Center

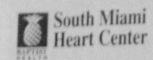
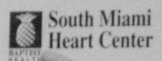

South Miami Heart Center

South Miami Heart Center

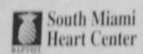

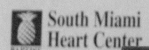

South Miami Heart Center

South Miami Heart Center

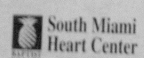

South Miami Heart Center

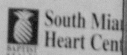

South Miami Heart Center

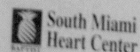

South Miami Heart Center

SISTER TO SISTER
FOUNDATION
sistertosister.org

DELIVERING

Have you observed how skilled presenters seem to know their topic and their audience? The best presenters make delivery look easy. They do so by practicing their presentations until they feel confident, look poised, and sound conversational.

SPEECHES

Every year, college students face the overwhelming challenge of paying for their education. As state funding has disappeared, and healthcare, utility, and personnel costs have increased, public colleges and universities have been forced to raise tuition and fees paid by students—and many students have responded with protest.

Recently, at Ohio University, the Board of Trustees was considering a 3.5 percent increase in tuition. Aware that the decision was imminent, 13 students organized, made posters, and attended the meeting at which the vote was going to take place. If you were one of these students, how would you deliver your message? Would you yell? Would you chant some clever rhyme to ask for a vote against the proposal? The way in which you deliver your message could decide the fate of the vote!

Once discussion of the tuition increase proposal concluded, when the chairperson of the Board of Trustees called the question and prepared to take the vote, all 13 students stood quietly and raised their signs. They said nothing, but their simple nonverbal behavior of standing at the appropriate moment generated immediate energy in the room. The vote ultimately supported the tuition increase. However, nearly every Board member addressed the students directly and thanked them for expressing their views respectfully. They also pledged to continue providing aid to students with need to offset the tuition hike. Although the outcome was not what they wanted, they delivered a message that had clear impact.

What are your strengths in delivery? Do you have an expressive face? Active gestures and movement? Good eye contact? A good voice? Great speakers are able to use these delivery behaviors to enhance their speech without appearing over-the-top. Ray Grigg writes, "Too loud and we are not heard. Too bright and we are not seen. Too fancy and we are hidden. Too much and we are obscured."[1] This is sound advice for any public presenter. If your audience is watching your gestures and your body movements and listening to your pronunciation rather than the content of your speech, you should reconsider what you are doing. Delivery should enhance but not detract from the message. Effective delivery appears conversational, natural, and spontaneous. Your delivery should be comfortable for you and your audience. When you speak in this manner, your audience will be drawn into your speech as if they are having a conversation with you rather than being talked at by a lecturer.

What Is Effective Delivery?

How can you focus on your ideas rather than on your delivery? How can you draw your audience's attention to your message rather than to your delivery? How can you sound conversational and natural? The answer to all these questions is the same. Develop your message first, and then revise your words for delivery.

1. Delivery naturally flows from your message. When you select a topic, pick something for which you have passion or conviction. For any type of speech, informative, persuasive or otherwise, your own conviction for the message will naturally animate your delivery. The natural excitement you have for a topic important to you is much more effective than a rehearsed delivery style over a topic in which you are not interested.

2. Build good delivery on a foundation of the basics. Great speakers are able to polish highly nuanced delivery skills. For most of us, however, we should focus on basic things like maintaining eye contact, avoiding nervous mannerisms (placing our hands in our pockets or on the lectern), and speaking clearly. Perhaps with the help of feedback from friends, you can improve these basic delivery behaviors. Over time, you will naturally begin to use more advanced techniques like movement and more animated gestures.

As you continue to grow in experience and knowledge as a public presenter, you should observe how highly experienced public presenters deliver their messages. How do they appear conversational and yet inviting to their audiences through voice inflection and body movements? What do they do to enhance the impact of their ideas? Which of these techniques can you adopt in your own speeches? Which aspect of other people's speaking styles do you want to avoid? Both positive and negative examples will help you become more effective.

This chapter helps you learn various ways in which you can improve your delivery. To start, you will learn about the various methods for delivering speeches. After that, you will learn specific verbal and nonverbal skills for enhancing your delivery.

The five modes of delivering a presentation are memorized, manuscript, extemporaneous, impromptu, and question-and-answer. While each mode is appropriate for different topics, audiences, speakers, and situations, your instructor will identify which mode is suitable for your assignments.

What Are the Modes of Delivery?

Memorized Mode

The **memorized mode** of delivery is *one in which a presenter has committed a presentation to memory.* This mode entails more than just knowing all the words; the presenter also rehearses gestures, eye contact, and movement, practicing a presentation over and over in much the same way that an actor masters a dramatic script.

Oratory contests, the lecture circuit, and banquet speeches are common places to find the memorized mode. Ceremonial occasions, where little audience or topic adaptation is expected or needed, invite memorization. Politicians usually have a stock presentation they have delivered so many times that they have every word memorized. Some presenters have delivered the same presentation so many times that they even know when and how long the audience is going to applaud, laugh, or respond. In other words, memorization is best when performance to the audience is more important than communication with the audience.

What are the *advantages* of the memorized method of presenting a speech? The main advantage is that this mode permits maximum use of delivery skills: every variation in the voice can be mastered, every oral paragraph stated in correct cadence, every word correctly pronounced at the right volume. With a memorized speech, you have continuous eye contact. Because no notes are used, bodily movements and gestures are freer. While the memorized method does not eliminate the search for the next word, you are simply searching your memory instead of your notes or manuscript.

However, the memorized mode has three *disadvantages*:

1. Memorization permits little or no adaptation during delivery. The presenter is likely to focus more on the internalized manuscript than on the listeners. If the audience appears to have missed a point, the presenter has difficulty explaining the point in greater detail.
2. Recovery is more difficult if you make a mistake. If you forget a line, you have to search for the exact place where you dropped your line.
3. Especially for beginning speakers, the presentation sometimes *sounds* memorized: the wording is too smooth, the pacing too contrived, and the presentation is too much of a performance instead of a communicative experience.

The beginning presenter is more likely to be at a disadvantage than at an advantage by using the memorized method. However, some formal situations, such as commencement addresses, routine political campaign speeches, and repeated rituals and ceremonies call for little adaptation, making memorization a good choice.

Manuscript Mode

The **manuscript mode** of delivering a presentation is *when a presenter writes out the complete presentation in advance and then uses that manuscript to deliver the speech but without memorizing it*. It is most useful when a presenter has to be precise, must avoid error, and must defend every word. A president who delivers a foreign policy presentation in which the slip of a word could start a war, a minister who carefully documents a sermon with biblical quotations, and a politician who releases information to the press are examples of presenters who might adopt this mode.

Some professors lecture from a manuscript. At some point, they probably have written out their lecture. As a student, it is likely that you have seen many manuscript speeches.

What are the *advantages* of the manuscript speech? Generally, the complete manuscript prevents slips of the tongue, poor wording, and distortion. Manuscripts often boost the confidence of beginning presenters who need the security of their manuscript.

The *disadvantages* outweigh the advantages, however. While using a manuscript might make the beginning presenter feel more confident, the delivery often suffers. Among the problems engendered by manuscripts are the following:

1. Manuscripts frequently reduce eye contact because the presenter is reading the script rather than observing the audience.

2. The manuscript method also hinders audience adaptation. The presenter is not watching the audience; to observe and respond to audience feedback is difficult.
3. The presenter may also use fewer gestures. Being bonded to the podium and the script prevents the presenter from gesturing to emphasize or illustrate points.
4. Vocal variety may be lacking as well, because much of the presentation is being read.
5. The pacing of the presentation may be too rapid or too slow for the audience. The presenter will sound inappropriate because written style is markedly different from spoken style. Instead of sounding conversational, the presentation will sound like an essay being read.

To distinguish between extemporaneous and manuscript speeches, select speeches on vital topics given by national political figures. You should select one speech that uses an extemporaneous mode of delivery (House and Senate floor speeches work well) and one that uses a manuscript mode (nationally televised speeches work well). Discuss the reasons for deciding to use manuscript or extemporaneous modes of delivery in these contexts.

Your mode of delivery must be appropriate for you, your topic, the audience, and the situation. Memorizing five pages of print may not be your style. A manuscript presentation is out of place in a dormitory meeting, a discussion among class members, or any informal gathering.

Extemporaneous Mode

In the **extemporaneous mode**, *a presenter often delivers a presentation from a keyword outline or from brief notes.* This mode of delivery is most commonly taught in the public speaking classroom. Its advantages far outweigh the disadvantages for the beginning public presenter. Indeed, for most presenters, this mode is the top choice.

Extemporaneous speaking sounds conversational, looks spontaneous, and appears effortless. However, extemporaneous speaking requires considerable effort. A presenter selects a topic appropriate for the audience; completes research on the topic; organizes the main points and supporting materials; practices the presentation with a working or keyword outline; and finally delivers the presentation with maximum eye contact, appropriate gestures, and motivated movement. The presenter may occasionally glance at notes, but the emphasis is on communicating a message to an audience.

You may have experienced extemporaneous speaking without realizing it. Have you ever read the assignment for a class, caught the drift of the professor's questions, jotted a few words on your notes, and then given an answer in class? Your "speech" was extemporaneous because it included your background preparation, an organization of your ideas, brief reminders, and a conversational delivery.

An extemporaneous presentation is not practiced to the point of memorization. In fact, the presenter rarely repeats the message in exactly the same words, even in practice. The idea is to keep the content flexible enough to adapt to the audience. If the audience appears puzzled by something you say, you can add a definition, a description, or an example to clarify your position. Audience members like to be talked with, not lectured at, read to, or talked down to.

What are the *advantages* of the extemporaneous mode of delivery?

1. This mode is the most versatile: The presenter, using only brief notes, can engage in excellent eye contact. This eye contact allows careful audience analysis and immediate audience adaptation. The presenter can add or delete information based on the audience's responses.
2. Extemporaneous speaking demands attention to all aspects of public speaking preparation. The presenter has an opportunity to consider the important dimensions of selecting a topic, determining a purpose, doing careful research, identifying supporting materials, organizing the presentation appropriately, and using language in a spoken style that best communicates the message. In short, the extemporaneous presentation allows high-quality communication.
3. Extemporaneous speaking invites bodily movement, gestures, and rapid nonverbal response to audience feedback.
4. The extemporaneous presentation sounds conversational because the presenter is not reciting scripted words. The presenter is talking with the audience, not at the audience.
5. An outline is easier to use as a quick reference or guide than is a manuscript of a speech.

"Extemporaneous speaking demands attention to all aspects of public speaking preparation."

What are the *disadvantages* of the extemporaneous speech? If the presenter must be careful with every word, if every phrase needs to be exact, the presenter might more appropriately use another mode of speaking. Under most circumstances, however, the extemporaneous mode is the presentation method of choice.

Can you think of a current presenter who uses the extemporaneous mode of delivery effectively? The speaker who uses the extemporaneous mode of delivery can move away from the podium and walk among the audience as she speaks. Frequently, this type of speaker is given high marks for confidence.

Impromptu Mode

The **impromptu mode** entails *giving a presentation without advance preparation*. Unlike the extemporaneous mode, the impromptu method uses minimal planning and preparation, and usually no practice. You may be ready for an impromptu presentation because of your knowledge, experience, and background, but you do not have any other aids to help you know what to say. The key to effective impromptu speaking is to take a moment to compose your thoughts and to identify important points instead of figuring out what you are going to say as you speak.

You have already delivered impromptu speeches. When your teacher calls on you to answer a question, your answer—if you have one—is impromptu. You were ready because you had read the assignment or had prepared for class, but you probably had not written out an answer or certain keywords. When someone asks you to introduce yourself, explain something at a meeting, reveal what you know about a particular subject, or give directions, you are delivering your answer in an impromptu fashion.

What are the *advantages* of the impromptu method? This mode reveals your skill in unplanned circumstances. In a job interview, you might be asked to answer some questions for which you had not specifically prepared. Your impromptu answers may tell a potential employer more about you than if you were given the questions ahead of time and had prepared your answers. Similarly, the student who can give an accurate, complete answer to a difficult question in class shows a mastery of the subject matter that is, in some ways, more impressive than in an exam or another situation in which the student may give partially planned answers.

Another advantage of the impromptu mode is that it provides you with opportunities to think on your feet, to be spontaneous. As you engage in impromptu speaking situations, you learn how to quickly identify the important points in the information you wish to share or the major arguments in the persuasive appeals you offer. Students might give impromptu speeches when volunteering at events or places such as blood drives or senior centers, while meeting with a student club, or while working.

The impromptu presentation also has *disadvantages.* Spontaneity discourages audience analysis, planned research, and detailed preparation. Most people who are seeking to gain employment, trying to sell a product, or aspiring to academic honors should not risk delivering an impromptu speech. Such circumstances require greater preparation. An impromptu presentation can mean a poor answer as easily as a good one. The lack of planning makes the outcome of the impromptu method of speaking uncertain.

Question-and-Answer Sessions

Some presentations allow for a **question-and-answer session**, which is a *specialized instance of the impromptu presentation approach where the topics of your comments are driven by questions from the audience.* Even if your classroom speeches do not include a question-and-answer period, you may encounter this mode of presentation when you speak in other settings. The question-and-answer session can be among the most difficult speaking situations because you may have no idea what to expect. At the same time, they are very important. A first responder answering questions from a group of reporters during a crisis could be providing information that has life-or-death implications.

In advance of the question-and-answer period, you should consider possible questions that others might ask. If you have friends or classmates who will listen to your speech beforehand, ask them to pose questions that occur to them. Ask other professionals in your field to help you anticipate probable types of questions. Imagine, too, what a critic might say about your presentation. Once you have determined some of the likely questions that others might ask, prepare thoughtful and thorough responses to the questions. From these answers, practice a succinct response that captures the essence of your rejoinder. Although questions can come in any variety, people tend to want to know more about the human-interest elements or potential future impacts of the topics on which you are speaking.

When you actually present your talk, you may be faced with questions that you did not expect. Do not panic. Instead, listen to the question carefully. If the question is not clear, ask the audience member to repeat it or to ask it again in different words. Once you believe you have accurately heard the question, repeat it back to the entire audience: "If I understand you correctly, you are asking about . . . ." This approach will allow all of the members of the audience to hear the question and will also provide you with additional time to formulate an answer.

Even though a question may appear to be antagonistic, do not become defensive or angry. Keep in mind that an audience member has to exhibit a certain amount of courage to ask a question in front of everybody and therefore should be treated with respect. In addition, questions generally signal interest on the part of the audience, which is an indirect sign of a job well done on your part. Be gracious and positive as you respond to what may seem like a critical or hostile question. One approach for answering these types of questions is to respond to the assumptions on which the questions are based. For instance, if you are asked whether you would support energy production from coal or nuclear fuel, you could respond that the question fails to consider alternative energy sources like wind and solar, which you may be more in favor of.

Question-and-answer sessions tend to come across as more candid because they stem from a dialogue. For that reason, observers tend to pick up on more relational aspects of the give-and-take. Be truthful and sincere in your answers. Do not be flippant or sarcastic. Do not fabricate an answer if you honestly do not know information appropriate for the answer. Be straightforward in explaining that you simply do not know the precise answer to the audience member's question.

Finally, be aware that some audience members may have a particular agenda. They may have attended your speech to be heard, rather than to listen. If an audience member raises his or her hand to ask a question, do not be surprised if he or she launches into a long anecdote, reports contrary information, or begins to dominate the question-and-answer period. Be prepared to thank that person for his or her comments in a congenial but clear manner and to move the question-and-answer period to other audience members. As the speaker, you are in charge not only of the presentation but of the question-and-answer period as well.

Ultimately, the method of delivery is not the crucial feature of your speech. For example, in a study to determine whether the extemporaneous or the manuscript method is more effective, two researchers concluded that the presenter's ability is more important. Some presenters are more effective with extemporaneous speeches than with manuscript speeches, but others use both methods with equal effectiveness.[2] See Figures 7.1.a and 7.1.b for a summary of the five modes of delivery. See the Application Exercises at the end of the chapter for an impromptu presentation exercise.

A QUESTION OF OTHER CULTURES

cultural NOTE

As part of a program designed to introduce predominantly white, urban, middle-school students to people from other cultures, seventh-grade social studies students engaged in videoconference dialogues with presenters from Iraq, Kenya, China, Australia, Malaysia, and Egypt. The intended purposes of these dialogues were to help the seventh-graders be reflective on their own culture through the eyes of others and to have a deeper understanding of other cultures as described by the presenters. As reported in a study of this project, many of the dialogues were centered around questions that the seventh-graders asked about the other cultures; most of the questions stemmed from misunder-

standings and stereotypes generated through mass media. For instance, students asked the Chinese presenters about overpopulation, the Egyptian presenters about mummification, the Kenyan presenters about wild animals, and the Australian presenters about dingo dogs that snatch babies. The question-and-answer sessions of these presentations were important to counteract incorrect assumptions about the cultures being presented. These examples show that questions from audience members are often asked from incorrect perspectives driven by outside influences—namely, the media.[3]

Mode of Delivery	Need for Notes	Amount of Preparation Time	Typical Use
Extemporaneous	Low	High 🕐	Situations where delivery and preparation need to be balanced in effectiveness.
Memorized	None	Very high 🕐🕐🕐	Formal situations that call for little or no adaptation.
Manuscript	High	High 🕐	Situations where precision and formality are necessary.
Impromptu	None	None	Situations where planning and practice are not possible.
Question-and-answer	None	None	Situations where audience members are seeking information.

Figure 7.1.a   Five modes of delivery: Need for notes, amount of preparation, and best use.

Mode	Advantages	Disadvantages
Extemporaneous	• Sounds conversational • Looks spontaneous • Appears effortless • Is most versatile • Allows high-quality communication • Invites bodily movement, gestures, and rapid nonverbal response • Easier to use a keyword outline as a quick reference or guide	• Requires lots of practice and effort • Potential for miscommunication because of unpredictable spontaneous word choices
Memorized	• Allows maximum use of delivery skills	• Permits little or no adaptation • To recover from mistakes is difficult • Effective memorization takes substantial time and practice
Manuscript	• Prevents slips of the tongue and poor wording	• Reduces eye contact • Hinders audience adaptation • Could result in less frequent use of gestures • Could affect vocal variety • Pacing and other vocal delivery behaviors could be negatively affected
Impromptu	• Requires minimal planning and practice • Allows for spontaneity • Reveals your skill in unplanned circumstances	• Discourages audience adaptation • Discourages planned research • Has uncertain outcome
Question-and-answer	• Responds to listener's need for information • Can cover a wide range of topics in a short period of time • Encourages audience engagement • Highlights your skill in "thinking on your feet"	• Requires extensive knowledge on multiple topics • Errors are more likely and can have very negative consequences • Lack of control by the speaker creates significant u ncertainty

Figure 7.1.b   Five modes of delivery: Advantages and disadvantages of each.

How Can You Use Your Voice Effectively?

Effective public presenters learn to speak in front of an audience as if they are having a conversation. Their voice and movements are a natural accompaniment for their words. In fact, some teachers believe that the best way to improve delivery is not to emphasize it directly. Instead, they encourage students to let effective delivery flow from the message, the audience, and the situation.

As you study delivery, remember that delivery and the message comprise an organic whole. If what you say is important to you and to your audience, the way you say it will not be a problem for you. You will be so busy trying to communicate your message that you will gesture, move, look, and sound like a very competent presenter. Let's look at eight vocal aspects of delivery.

Adjust Your Rate to Content, Audience, and Situation

Rate, the first vocal characteristic of delivery, is *the speed of delivery*. Normally American speakers speak at a rate between 125 and 190 words per minute, but audiences can comprehend spoken language that is much faster. Speaking with some speed can be beneficial. For instance, studies have shown that rapid speech rate improves a speaker's credibility and results in improved persuasion.[4] In another study students shortened their pauses and increased their speaking rates from 126 to 172 words per minute. The increased rate affected neither the audience's comprehension nor their evaluation of the speakers' delivery.[5] What should you take from this? Faster speaking, up to a limit, can have positive outcomes.

Beginning presenters frequently vent their anxiety by speaking too quickly. A nervous presenter makes the audience nervous as well. Although some speed can be beneficial, increased rate of delivery stemming from nervousness is often accompanied by garbled words, improper pronunciation, and other delivery problems. Fluency comes from confidence, and speed without fluency is impossible to understand. A presenter who is accustomed to audiences and knows the subject matter well may speak at a brisk rate without appearing to be nervous.

The essential point, not revealed by the studies, is that speaking rate needs to be adapted to the speaker, audience, situation, and content of the speech. First, become aware of your natural rate of speaking. If you normally speak rather slowly, you might feel awkward talking like a competitive debater (they can speak close to 200 words per minute or more!). If you normally speak at a rapid pace, you might feel uncomfortable speaking more slowly. As you learn presentational skills, you will probably find a rate that is appropriate for you and for your audience. A great exercise is to record yourself reading a familiar story or passage for 7 to 10 minutes. On average, how many words per minute did you read?

Second, adapt your rate to the audience and situation. A grade-school teacher does not rip through a fairy tale; the audience is just learning how to comprehend words. A public presenter addressing a large audience without a microphone might speak more distinctly and cautiously to make sure the audience comprehends her words. A story to illustrate a point can be understood at a faster rate than can a string of statistics or a complicated argument. Martin Luther King Jr., in his famous "I have a dream" speech, began his address at a slow rate—under 100 words per minute—but as he became more passionately involved in his topic and as his audience responded, he took on a much more rapid pace. The rate should depend on the effect you seek.

Use Pause for Effect

A second vocal characteristic is the **pause**—*a brief silence for effect*. You might begin a presentation with a question or questions: "Have you bought a cup of coffee at a coffeehouse today? [Pause] Have you had two or three? [Pause] Four or five? [Pause] Do you know what your habit is costing you in a year? [Brief pause] A decade? [Longer pause] A lifetime?" The pause allows each member of the audience to answer the question in his or her own mind. These pauses are critical to this opening. Allowing time for the audience to think will mentally engage them; ripping through without pauses will lull them into passive acceptance of hearing another talking head.

Another kind of pause—the **vocalized pause**—is really not silent at all. Instead, it is *a way of delaying with sound*. The "ahhhs," "nows," and "you knows" and "ummmmms" of a novice presenter are annoying and distracting to most audiences. Unfortunately, even some highly experienced presenters have the habit of filling silences with vocalized pauses. Do not be afraid of silence; most audiences would prefer a little silence to a vocalized pause.

Pauses are among the most challenging aspects of your voice to recognize. Our brains are wired to make note of things, not the absence of things. Nonvocalized pauses, as well as the lack of needed pauses, are both exactly that—the absence of things! As a last step in improving your delivery, record your speech and listen to it for pauses. Where should they be inserted? How can pauses, coupled with rate of delivery, be used to affect the tempo of the speech? While these issues are relatively advanced, they really do separate average from extraordinary delivery.

Use Duration for Attention

Duration is *how long something lasts*; in a speech, it can mean how long the sounds last or how long various parts of the presentation last. An anchorperson who says, "Tonight, I am speaking to you from London," is likely to say this sentence by caressing every word but might deliver other parts of the newscast in rapid-fire fashion. Dwelling on the sound of your words can have dramatic impact; the duration gives the words a sense of importance.

Similarly, duration can refer to the parts of a speech: how long you spend on the introduction, the main points, the examples, and the presentational aids. As noted earlier, the duration of most introductions is usually relatively short, the body relatively longer, and the conclusion shortest of all.

Use Rhythm to Establish Tempo

Rhythm refers to *the tempo of a speech*. All the linear arts seem to have this characteristic. A novel or play starts slowly as the author introduces the characters, establishes the plot, and describes the scene. Then the emphasis shifts to the development of the plot and typically accelerates toward a climax, which brings the novel to a close. A musical piece also has some of these characteristics, though music could be said to consist entirely of rhythm.

In a speech, the rhythm usually starts off slowly as the presenter gives clues about who she is and what she is going to speak about. During the body of the speech, the tempo accelerates, with verbal punctuation indicating what is most important. The conclusion typically slows in review as the presentation draws to a close.

We also hear the rhythm of a presentation in words, sentences, and paragraphs. **Alliteration** is *the repetition of the initial sounds of words*. For instance, it is more memorable to say "color, clarity, and carats characterize a good diamond" than to say "brightness, transparency, and weight give a

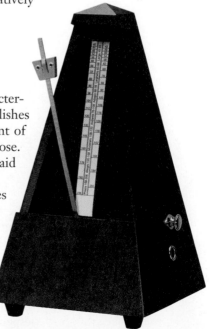

diamond value." Another example of rhythm occurs in sentences when initial words are repeated: "I served my country because I am a patriot; I served my country because I saw it as my duty; and I served my country because its protection is my first concern." Similarly, you can achieve rhythm with rhetorical devices, such as antithesis: "Not because I loved Octavius less, but because I loved Rome more."

Use Pitch for Expression

Pitch is *the highness or lowness of a speaker's voice, its upward and downward inflection, the melody produced by the voice.* Pitch makes the difference between the "Ohhh" from earning a poor grade on an exam and the "Ohhh" you say when you see someone really attractive. Avoid the lack of pitch changes that result in a monotone and the repetitious pitch changes that result in a singsong delivery. The best public presenters use the full range of their normal pitch. They know when to purr and when to roar—and when to vary their pitch between the two.

You learn pitch control by constant practice like an actor does. A public speaker rehearses a presentation in front of a sympathetic audience to receive feedback on whether the words are being understood as she intends them. You may not be the best judge of how you sound to others. Therefore, trust other people's evaluations of how you sound. At the same time, speakers should recognize and develop the individual strengths they already have. For example, when you focus on your message, your pitch will support or match what you say. Compare the pitch in your voice when you tell a friend about something amazing to the pitch when you recite the pledge of allegiance.

Use Volume for Emphasis

A sixth vocal characteristic of delivery is **volume**, *the relative loudness or softness of your voice.* **Projection** means *adjusting your volume appropriately for the subject, the audience, and the situation.* Variations in volume can convey emotion, importance, suspense, and subtle nuances of meaning. You whisper a secret in conversation, and you stage whisper in front of an audience to signal conspiratorial intent. You speak loudly and strongly on important points and let your voice carry your conviction.

Use Enunciation for Clarity

Enunciation, the seventh vocal aspect of delivery, is *the pronunciation and articulation of words.* **Pronunciation** is *the production of the sounds of a word.* **Articulation** is *the physiological process of creating the sounds.* Because your reading vocabulary is larger than your speaking vocabulary, you may use words in your speeches that you have never heard spoken before. To deliver unfamiliar words is risky. Rather than erring in public, first check pronunciation in a dictionary. Every dictionary, on and offline, has a pronunciation key. For instance, the entry for the word *deification* in *Webster's New World Dictionary of the American Language* follows:

> **de·i·fi·ca·tion** (de-e-fe-kka-shen) 1. a deifying. 2. deified person or embodiment.

The entry indicates that the word has five syllables that carry distinct sounds. The pronunciation key says that the *e* should be pronounced like the *e* in *even*, the *i*'s like the *a* in *ago*, and the *a* like the *a* in *ape*. The accent mark indicates which syllable should receive heaviest emphasis. You should learn how to use the pronunciation key in a dictionary, but you can also hear a word pronounced correctly on several online sources. For example, the webpage found at http://aruljohn.com/voice.pl gives you the option of typing in the word and then clicking on the "hear word" option. This feature is especially useful to students who speak English as a second or third language.

Another way to improve your enunciation is to prolong syllables. Such prolonging makes your pronunciation easier to understand, especially if you are addressing a large audience assembled outside or in an auditorium with no microphone. The drawing out of syllables can be overdone, however. Some radio and TV news announcers hang onto the final syllable in a sentence so long that the device is disconcertingly noticeable.

Use Fluency for Fluidity

The eighth vocal characteristic of delivery is **fluency**—*the smoothness of delivery, the flow of the words, and the absence of vocalized pauses*. Fluency cannot be achieved by looking up words in a dictionary or by any other simple solution. It is not necessarily very noticeable, except by its absence. Listeners are more likely to notice errors than to notice the seemingly effortless flow of words and intentional pauses in a well-delivered speech. Fluency can be improved and is related to effective communication.[6]

To achieve fluency, you must be confident in the content of your speech. If you know what you are going to say, and if you have practiced the words, then disruptive repetition and vocalized pauses are unlikely to occur.

See Figure 7.2 for some common articulation problems. Articulation errors are so common that humorous stories are often based on them. Many **malapropisms**, or *mistaking one word for another*, are based on articulation errors. A newspaper article on malapropisms mentioned these:

"Making an obstacle of themselves" for "Making a spectacle of themselves."

"Go for the juggler" for "Go for the jugular."

"He took milk of amnesia" for "He took milk of magnesia."[7]

Addition occurs *when an extra sound is added.* For example, a person says "pic-a-nic" instead of "picnic," "ath-a-lete" instead of "athlete," "real-ah-toor" instead of "realtor."

Deletion occurs *when a sound is dropped or left out of a word.* Examples of deletion are "rassberry" for "raspberry," or "liberry" for "library." Deletion also commonly occurs when people drop the final sounds of words such as "reveren'" for "reverend," "goin'" for "going," or "comin'" for "coming." Finally, deletion occurs when individuals drop the initial sounds of words such as "'possum" for "opossum."

Substitution occurs *when one sound is replaced with another.* For instance, when speakers use the word "git" for "get," "ruff" for "roof," or "tomata" for "tomato," they are making substitution errors.

Transposition occurs *when two sounds are reversed.* College students who call their teachers "perfessor" instead of "professor" or persons who say one "hunderd" instead of one "hundred" are making an error of transposition.

Figure 7.2   **Four common articulation problems.**

How Can You Use Your Body to Communicate Effectively?

Eye contact, facial expression, gestures, movement, and physical appearance are five bodily aspects of speech delivery—nonverbal indicators of meaning—that are important to the public speaker. When you observe two people busily engaged in conversation, you can judge their interest in the conversation without hearing their words. Similarly, in public speaking, the nonverbal aspects of delivery reinforce what the speaker is saying. Researchers have found that audiences who can see the speaker, and his or her behavior, comprehend more of the presentation than audiences who cannot (such as those listening by radio, CD, or podcast, for example).[8]

Use Eye Contact to Hold Audience Attention

Eye contact is *the way a presenter observes the audience while speaking*. With experience, individuals become more capable of using eye contact.[9] Audiences prefer the maintenance of good eye contact,[10] and it improves the credibility of the presenter.[11] Eye contact is one way you indicate to others how you feel about them. You may be wary of a person who will not look at you in conversation. Similarly, if you rarely or never look at audience members, they may be resentful of your seeming lack of interest. If you look over the heads of your audience or scan them so quickly that you do not really look at anyone, you may appear to be afraid. The proper relationship between you and your audience should be one of purposeful communication. You signal that sense of purpose by treating the audience members as individuals to whom you wish to communicate a message and by looking at them for responses to your message. How can you learn to maintain eye contact with your audience? One way is to know your presentation so well and to feel so strongly about the topic that you have to make few references to your notes. A presenter who does not know the material well tends to be manuscript-bound. You can encourage yourself to keep an eye on the audience by delivering an extemporaneous presentation from an outline or keywords.

Other ways of learning eye contact include scanning or continually looking around at your entire audience, addressing various sections of the audience as you progress through your speech, and concentrating on the individuals who overtly indicate whether your message is coming across or not. These individuals usually nod "yes" or "no" with their heads. You may find that you can enhance your delivery by finding the friendly faces and positive nodders who signal when the message is getting through to them.

Use Facial Expression to Communicate

Another nonverbal aspect of delivery is facial expression, using the eyes, eyebrows, forehead, and mouth for expression. Facial expression shows how we feel, and body orientation (leaning, withdrawing, turning) expresses the intensity of our emotion.[12]

"Facial expression shows how we feel, and body orientation (leaning, withdrawing, turning) expresses the intensity of our emotion."

Children between 5 and 10 years of age learn to interpret facial expressions, and those interpretations improve with age.[13] Researchers found male/female differences in expressivity and self-regulation, even at 6 months of age, with males having more difficulty being expressive than females.[14] Some experts believe that the brain connects emotions and facial expressions and that culture determines what activates an emotion and the rules for displaying an emotion.[15] Presenters who vary their facial expression are viewed as more credible than those who do not.[16]

Generally, women use more facial expressions and are more expressive than men; women smile more than men; women are more apt to return smiles; and women are more attracted to others who smile.[17]

Because facial expressions communicate, public presenters need to be aware of what they are communicating. Smiling can indicate both goodwill and a submissiveness. Chimpanzees smile when they want to avoid a clash with higher-status chimpanzees. First-year students smile more than do upper-class students.[18] Constant smiling may communicate submissiveness or nervousness instead of friendliness, especially if the smiling seems unrelated to the presentation's content.

You can practice in front of a mirror, videotape your practice session, or speak in front of friends who will help you. The goal is to have facial expressions consistent with your intent and your message.

Use Gestures to Reinforce Message

Gestures are *motions of the hands or body for emphasis or expression.* Effective use of gestures distinguishes outstanding speaking from the more mundane.[19] Although you probably are unaware of your arms and hands when you converse with someone, they may become bothersome appendages when you stand in front of an audience. You have to work to make public speaking look easy, just as skillful athletes or graceful dancers make their performances look effortless.

Angry workers sometimes appear on television to protest low wages and poor working conditions. Although they are untutored in public speaking, these impassioned people deliver their presentations with gusto and determined gestures. They have a natural delivery because they are much more concerned about their message than about when they should raise their clenched fists. You can deliver the material more naturally if your attention is focused on your message. Self-conscious attention to your own gestures may be self-defeating: the gestures look studied, rehearsed, or slightly out of sync with your message. Selecting a topic that you really care about can have the side effect of improving your gestures, especially if you concentrate on your audience and message.

Gestures differ with the size of the audience and the formality of the occasion. With a small audience in an informal setting, gestures are more like those you would use in ordinary conversation. With large audiences and in formal speaking situations, gestures are larger and more dramatic. In the classroom, the situation is often fairly formal and the audience relatively small, so gestures are ordinarily larger than they would be in casual conversation but not as exaggerated as they would be in a large auditorium.

Another way to learn appropriate gestures is to practice the material in front of friends who are willing to make constructive comments. Actresses and actors spend hours rehearsing lines and gestures so that they will look spontaneous on stage. You may have to appear before many audiences before you learn to speak and move naturally, but with practice, you will learn which natural arm, head, and hand movements seem to help.

Use Bodily Movement for Purpose

The fourth nonverbal aspect of delivery is **movement**, or *what you do with your entire body during a presentation.* Do you lean forward as you speak, demonstrating how serious you are about communicating your message? Do you move out from behind the lectern to show that you want to be closer to the audience? Do you move during transitions in your presentation to signal physically to the audience that you are moving to a new location in your presentation? These are examples of purposeful movement in a public presentation. Movement must occur with purpose. You should not move just to work off your own anxiety.

Always try to face the audience even when you are moving. For instance, even when you need to write information on the board, you can avoid turning your back by putting your notes on the board before class or by putting your visual material on posters. You can learn a lot about movement by watching your classmates and professors when they speak. Notice what works for others (and for you) through observation and practice. Avoid purposeless movement such as rocking back and forth or side to side or the "caged lion" movement in which a presenter circles the front of the room like a big cat in a zoo.

The environment in which you give your presentation helps determine which movements are appropriate. The distance between the presenter and the audience is significant. A great distance suggests presenter superiority or great respect. That is why pulpits in most churches loom high and away from the congregation. A presenter often has a choice about how much to move toward or away from the audience. In the classroom, a presenter who clings to the far wall may appear to be exhibiting fear. Drawing close suggests intimacy or power. Large people can appear threatening or aggressive if they approach the audience too closely, and small people behind large podiums tend to disappear from sight. You need to decide what distances make you and your listeners most comfortable and make you as a presenter most effective.

Wear Appropriate Attire

Clothing and **physical appearance** (*the way a person looks*) make a difference in public speaking situations within and outside the classroom. Following are some suggestions for choosing appropriate attire for the classroom setting:

1. Wear clothing that is typical for your audience, unless you wish to wear clothing that makes some point about your presentation. An international student speaking about native dress could wear clothing unique to his country, for example.
2. Avoid wearing clothing or jewelry that is likely to distract your audience from your message: pants that are cut too low, shirts that are too short, or too many rings in too many places.
3. Wear clothing and accessories that contribute to your credibility, not ones that lower your standing in the eyes of the audience: avoid provocative or revealing clothing.

Public speaking outside the classroom is clearly more complicated because you have to dress for the topic, the audience, and the occasion. Violate audience expectations and they will tend to respond negatively. For example, if you were to wear provocative clothing for a presentation at an assisted-living facility, the audience would likely be distracted from the message by your outfit. When in doubt, ask the people who invited you to speak how you should dress.

Before we conclude this section, we should note that a natural style is important. No one should let public speaking immobilize them; natural instinct is important. If you use many gestures in conversation, you can effectively take it up a notch in public speaking. If you use less bodily movement when you talk, but are very expressive with voice and facial expression, then that may serve you best in public speaking. The information provided in this chapter should enhance, rather than detract from, your natural style.

Delivering on Your Videoconference

According to an industry study reported in *InformationWeek*, upwards of 75 percent of organizations with IT departments could be using videoconferencing to conduct day-to-day business in the near future; 50 percent of them already do! As a college student, you have perhaps taken a class taught by an instructor at a different site, or perhaps you have used Skype or some other peer-to-peer videoconference software to talk with friends. Of course, if you were doing a business presentation or even job interview by videoconference, you would want to make sure that you do not let the electronic medium detract from your presentation. Here are some tips to follow to effectively adapt your delivery to the videoconference environment:

1. Because videoconferencing typically provides a closer image of you, your hand gestures, head movement, and other nonverbal behaviors will be magnified. While you should still act naturally with your nonverbal delivery, softer, more controlled movements will play better on the big screen. Your facial expressions take on even greater importance in this environment because of the relatively close-up view.

2. Avoid wearing stripes when on camera. Stripes on lightly colored shirts, ties, or even blazers can appear to "dance" when on camera. You are better served with solid colors and more patterned ties or other accents.

3. Think about volume. Because you will be speaking into a microphone, one that may not even be visible, watch audience members on the monitor to see how your volume sounds. Depending on the quality of the audio, you may need to be softer than normal in comparison to more conventional speaking situations.

4. Think about other sounds. If you have nervous habits, like playing with pens or pencils, or drumming your hands on a table, try to prevent yourself from engaging in those behaviors. Videoconference tables can act as a great drum and magnify those sounds over the sensitive microphone without you even knowing it. Even a nervous twitching of your leg below the table can be picked up as a "swishing" sound on mics because of your clothing rubbing together.

5. Remember the camera. You will be tempted to maintain eye contact with the monitor. Depending on the configuration of the room, the camera may be slightly above, below or even far away from the monitor. Remember that what they see comes from the camera. When making an important point, answering a question, or making your presentation, look straight into the camera lens. Even if they are close to the monitor, audience members will see if you are not looking directly at the camera.[20]

A student confessed that he had not followed instructions. Told to write a brief outline from which to deliver a speech, the student instead had written out every word. Afraid to speak in front of the class without his manuscript, he practiced by reading it word for word. After rehearsing many times, he wrote the entire speech using a tiny font so it would appear to be delivered from a brief outline on small sheets. However, as he began his speech, he found that he could not read the tiny print so he delivered the whole speech without using any written cues. All the practice had helped him; the small font manuscript had not.

How Can You Improve Your Delivery?

To help you improve your own delivery, you might follow these helpful steps:

1. Start with a detailed working outline that includes the introduction, the body, and the conclusion. Remember to include all main points and supporting materials.

2. Distill the working outline into a speaking outline that includes only reminders of what you intend to include in your speech.

3. Practice your speech alone first, preferably in front of a mirror, so you will notice how much or how little you use your notes. Ideally, you should deliver 80 to 90 percent or more of your speech without looking at notes.

4. Practice your speech in front of your roommate, your spouse, your kids, or colleagues. Try again to maintain eye contact as much as possible. After the speech, ask your observers to explain your message—and seek their advice for improving the speech.

5. Practice your speech with minimal notes in an empty classroom or a similar place that allows you to become accustomed to its size and the situation. Focus on some of the more sophisticated aspects of delivery, such as facial expression, vocal variety, gestures, and movement.

6. Use past critiques from your instructor or classmates to provide direction for improvement on delivery.

7. If possible, watch a recording of your own performance for feedback. If practice does not make perfect, at least the rehearsal will make you confident. You will become so familiar with the content of your speech that you will focus more on communicating your message to your audience.

For REVIEW >>

SUMMARY HIGHLIGHTS

What Is Effective Delivery?

▶ Delivery naturally flows from your message. You should pick a topic for which you have passion and excitement.

▶ Good delivery begins with basic skills like eye contact, use of gestures, and speaking clearly. Once mastered, those skills will allow you to move on to more advanced delivery techniques.

What Are the Modes of Delivery?

▶ The memorized mode is used when a word-for-word manuscript is committed and delivered from memory. Although memorization can allow for very polished and precise speeches when done well, this approach does not allow for responsive adaption to the audience.

▶ The manuscript mode involves speaking from a word-for-word written version of the speech. Like the memorized mode, this approach allows for very precise control of wording and all other aspects of the actual message. Of course, reading from a manuscript can significantly diminish the delivery of the speech.

▶ The extemporaneous mode allows the presenter to deliver the speech from a prepared keyword outline. This mode allows the advantage of thorough preparation while also promoting adaptation to the audience.

▶ The impromptu mode entails giving a speech with little or no preparation.

▶ The question-and-answer mode involves responding to questions posed by audience members, and is very similar to the impromptu mode.

How Can You Use Your Voice Effectively?

▶ Rate is the rapidity with which you speak.

▶ Pauses involve brief moments of silence between words.

▶ You can bring attention to certain terms by extending their duration, or how long you take to say the word.

▶ Rhythm is the tempo of your speech.

▶ Pitch is the highness and lowness created by use of vocal inflections while speaking.

▶ Volume can be used to emphasize certain things.

▶ Enunciation involves the pronunciation and articulation of words.

▶ Fluency is the relative smoothness of your delivery.

How Can You Use Your Body to Communicate Effectively?

▶ You should use eye contact to observe the audience while speaking.

▶ Facial expressions can be used to communicate emotion.

▶ Gestures can help reinforce a message.

▶ Body movement can help you appear relaxed and confident.

▶ Your attire can influence audience members' perceptions of your professionalism.

How Can You Improve Your Delivery?

▶ Be diligent in your preparation so that you feel confident.

▶ Practice your speech often.

▶ Use a recording of your speech to critique your delivery.

pop Quiz

1. Which of the following statements regarding the extemporaneous mode of speaking is *true*?
   (A) The extemporaneous mode allows for very little eye contact.
   (B) An extemporaneous presentation is practiced to the point of memorization.
   (C) The extemporaneous presentation sounds scripted rather than conversational.
   (D) Extemporaneous speaking invites rapid nonverbal response to audience feedback.

2. Writing out the complete presentation and using that text to deliver the speech is speaking using the mode of delivery known as:
   (A) manuscript
   (B) extemporaneous
   (C) impromptu
   (D) memorized

3. An advantage of manuscript speaking is that it:
   (A) sounds conversational
   (B) allows spontaneity
   (C) utilizes a keyword outline
   (D) prevents poor wording

4. If you say that sources should be "current, credible, and comprehensive," you are using:
   (A) alliteration
   (B) pronunciation
   (C) a change in pitch
   (D) transposition

5. The smoothness of delivery, the flow of the words, and the absence of vocalized pauses refer to delivery's:
   (A) fluency
   (B) rhythm
   (C) projection
   (D) pitch

Answers: 1 (D); 2 (A); 3 (D); 4 (A); 5 (A)

APPLICATION EXERCISES

1. Examine the following topics, audiences, and situations and indicate which method of delivery would be most appropriate by placing the letter in the blank. Instead of seeking "correct answers" for these items, you should discuss them with your classmates or teacher and defend your choices based on the message, the audience, and the situation.

   A = Manuscript method   **B = Extemporaneous method**

   C = Impromptu method   **D = Memorized method**

   _____ You have to answer questions from the class at the conclusion of your speech.

   _____ You have to describe the student government's new statement of policy on student rights to a group of high-level administrators in the college.

   _____ You have to deliver the same speech about student life at your college three times a week for 16 weeks to incoming first-year students.

   _____ You have to give parents a "walking tour" of the campus, including information about the buildings, the history of the college, and the background of significant places on campus.

   _____ You have to go door-to-door, demonstrating and explaining a vacuum cleaner and its attachments that you are selling to individuals, couples, and even groups of roommates.

2. Practice impromptu speaking in your class to develop the skills of thinking on your feet, telling illustrative stories, and improving delivery. Prepare by placing topics like the ones listed here on single slips of paper from which the speakers each draw a topic as they would select a playing card from a spread in someone's hand. Then each speaker has 2 minutes maximum to address the topic in front of the class. The best of the presenters stick to the topic and either explain it or develop a narrative about it. The exercise invites you to not only think on your feet but to quickly develop a theme or story from your own experience. Fluency or smoothness of delivery, eye contact, movement, and gesture are other goals for the activity. Here are some possible topics for an impromptu presentation. You and others can think of many more.

   Tell about a person who positively influenced your life

   Reveal your favorite holiday and why

   If you could live anywhere, where would it be and why?

   Where would your dream vacation be and why?

   Do you believe in love at first sight—why or why not?

   What famous person do you most admire and why?

   If you could go back in time, what would you change?

   What do you think are three keys to happiness?

   Describe your ideal home including details

   If you could live in anyone else's shoes for one day, who would it be and why?

   How old should people be to drink or to drive and why?

3. For your next speech, have a classmate, friend, or relative observe and evaluate your speech for delivery skills. Have your critic use this scale to fill in the following blanks.

   1 = Excellent   2 = Good   3 = Average 4 = Fair   5 = Weak

   Vocal Aspects of Delivery

   _____ Pitch: highness and lowness of voice, upward and downward inflections

   _____ Rate: words per minute, appropriate variation of rate for the difficulty of content

   _____ Pause: intentional silence designed to aid understanding at appropriate places

   _____ Volume: loud enough to hear, variation with the content

   _____ Enunciation: correct pronunciation and articulation

   _____ Fluency: smoothness of delivery; lack of vocalized pauses; good pacing, rhythm, and cadence without being so smooth as to sound artificial, contrived, or glib

   Nonverbal Aspects of Delivery

   _____ Gestures: natural movement of the head, hands, arms, and torso consistent with the presenter, topic, and situation

   _____ Facial expression and smiling behavior: consistent with message, used to relate to the audience, and appropriate for audience and situation

   _____ Eye contact: natural, steady without staring, includes entire audience, and is responsive to audience feedback

   _____ Movement: purposeful, used to indicate organization, natural, without anxiety, use at podium and distance from audience

   _____ Physical appearance: appropriate for the occasion, presenter, topic, and audience

KEY TERMS

Addition

Alliteration

Articulation

Deletion

Duration

Enunciation

Extemporaneous mode

Eye contact

Fluency

Gestures

Impromptu mode

Malapropism

Manuscript mode

Memorized mode

Movement

Pause

Physical appearance

Pitch

Projection

Pronunciation

Question-and-answer session

Rate

Rhythm

Substitution

Transposition

Vocalized pause

Volume

8

CHOOSING
YOUR

In this chapter, you will learn how language functions in a public presentation. This chapter will help you avoid word problems, help you choose the right words, and encourage you to use words ethically.

WORDS

Words matter. One reason they do is that what we call things can influence how we think about them. Companies like Walmart that want their employees to feel like valued members of the corporate team call them "associates," for instance, not lowly clerks or cashiers. Researchers who need to establish some distance from the people they study call them subjects and refrain from using their names. Social workers serve clients, not "the poor," and those who use wheelchairs are people with disabilities, not the handicapped. Even the AARP no longer goes by its old name, the American Association of Retired People, because many of its members are only in their 50s and not yet retired.

Words matter, too, when you need to motivate others to work with you and not against you. Consider, for instance, the difference between saying to a fellow team member who's in danger of missing a deadline, "*You* have a problem. What are you going to do about

it?" and saying, "*We* have a problem. What are we going to do about it?" In this chapter, you will learn how language works and how to use words responsibly.

Language is a powerful symbol system used to organize and classify what our senses detect and to shape thought. We will explore the general characteristics of language to better understand its function in our presentations.

What Are the Characteristics of Language?

Central to the understanding of communication and public speaking is knowledge of **semantics**, or *the study of how words come to have meaning*. To study semantics is to observe the ways in which words we already know inform the meanings of new words. For example, when the Internet was first introduced to the public, a new language had to be created for things like network nodes, IP addresses, routers, firewalls, domain names, and other terms whose meaning is unique to the Internet. The creation of this new terminology was based on the language system we all use on a daily basis. For example, the term *web* suggests a spider web, a visual reference that helps us understand how its structure is similar. Other terms like *firewall* and *browser* were also cross-purposed because they provided easy-to-understand references.

This section introduces you to the general characteristics of language as a system of rules. Together, they provide the mechanisms through which words can be adapted, or created, to meet our needs.

Language Is Symbolic

The 19th-century American author Nathaniel Hawthorne once said: "Words—so innocent and powerless as they are, standing in a dictionary, how potent for good and evil they become, in the hands of one who knows how to combine them."[1] Like your name, which is a representation of you, words are **symbolic** in that *they represent the concrete and objective reality of objects and things as well as abstract ideas*. Thus, the word *computer* conjures up a CPU, monitor, and keyboard, and the words *cellular phone* evoke a small handset and tiny screen.

Language Grows and Changes

Some words die from lack of use, like "33⅓," which refers to the slow speed on a record player (another archaic term). Other words change in meaning, like *gay*, which went from meaning "happy" to "homosexual orientation." But our constantly changing language also grows as entertainers, youth, writers, the military, and even gangs add new words to our vocabulary.

In 2008, the *Merriam-Webster Collegiate Dictionary* recognized some of the recent changes in language by introducing more than 100 new words. Here are a few examples, along with the date that the editors found for first use in print:[2]

> *Wing nut*—someone who takes extreme positions politically. The word *wing* refers to "left wing" or "right wing." In use since around 1900, the expression was finally included in the dictionary more than 100 years later.
>
> *Pescaterian* (1993)—a vegetarian whose diet includes fish.
>
> *Pretexting* (1992)—presenting yourself as someone else to gain private information.

Other terms that made the list included *dirty bomb*, *subprime*, and *supercross*, words used by the military, loan officers, and motorcycle racers, respectively.

Language Is Powerful

Diplomats, lawyers, mediators, and negotiators use words to solve the world's political issues, business problems, and legal cases. Speakers, broadcasters, PR professionals, and journalists—the world's communicators—love and depend on words. You will also learn to love words as you learn more about how words work. But first, you may need to be convinced that words are powerful.

Think, for example, of the old saying, "Sticks and stones will break my bones, but words can never hurt me." Although the statement asserts that sticks and stones can be harmful but words cannot, you may remember children using that saying to fend off the sting of words. Actually, you might agree more that "Bones heal, but wounds from words can last forever." You probably remember the words of someone who insulted you, treated you with disrespect, or commented negatively about you in front of others.

Words can cause fights, but they can mend relationships as well. Words like "I'm sorry," "You were right," "I was wrong," and "I did not mean what I said" are mending words. Words like "You did a great job," "I'd hire you any time," and "You have a fine future with this company" are words that most people would like to hear. Words can make you feel wonderful—or awful. Let us see what else words can do.

Words Organize and Classify

Words allow us to organize and classify, to group and cluster individual items into larger, more manageable units. Instead of having to identify every individual thing with a specific word, we cast them into a larger group. So we refer to cars, tables, chairs, houses, cities, states, and countries. We also use words to classify. Imagine you are trying to get your friend to locate someone in a crowd. The conversation might go something like this:

"I just saw a guy from my public speaking class."

"Which one is he?"

"The tall one."

"The blond guy with the red cap?"

"No, the one with a shaved head and sunglasses."

Words quickly allow you to limit your friend's search for your fellow student by gender, height, body type, hairstyle, and accessories.

Your presentations allow you to organize and classify your reality. Examine this excerpt from a talk by varsity basketball player Jason Crawford:

My uncle Johnny grew up in a well-educated family. He moved on to college where he earned a degree in engineering, a profession he pursued to the fullest. This man was alcohol-free the first 23 years of his life. Then one day he decided to pick up a drink. Little did he know that first drink would lead to many episodes down the line.

After a time he became more addicted and became an alcoholic. Johnny found himself driving home from a local bar one night and was pulled over by the police. Unable to function, Johnny decided that he was going to play a little game of cat and mouse. As the police officer approached the car, Johnny sped off. While trying to get away, he crashed into another car, killing two innocent victims. Johnny was also hurt, not physically but mentally. This episode would scar Johnny for the rest of his life. Uncle Johnny is now looking at life from behind bars.[3]

Jason's presentation begins with broad organizational categories—well-educated families, alcoholics, police, and victims—and moves through classifications: an engineer, a nondrinker, a drinker, an alcoholic, an arrest resister, a killer, and a criminal. Your speeches will also use words to organize and classify.

Words Shape Thought

Have you ever thought about how words shape the way you think? We have many more words about war than about peace. D. C. Smith lists some examples: "to beat a hasty retreat," "to get off on the wrong foot," and "to mark time."[4] We have many more words describing violence than describing cooperation. Are we a more warlike culture because our vocabulary reflects more concern for conflict than cooperation?

WORD DIFFERENCES

Not all languages share words with similar meanings or even a word at all for some people or things. Until South Koreans were Westernized (mostly by movies), they had no word for *kiss* and considered such behavior unhygienic. Laplanders have many words to describe snow, but no generic name like the English *snow*. Brazilian Guarani live among palm trees and parrots and have many words for them, but no generic name for all of them as we do in the English language.[5]

In *Prometheus Unbound*, Percy Shelley, the English Romantic poet, says of his hero, Prometheus, who gave humanity fire, culture, and science: "He gave man speech, and speech created thought, which is the measure of the Universe."[6] A similar notion comes to us from the **Sapir-Whorf hypothesis**, a theory that suggests that *our language determines to some extent how we think about and view the world.*[7] Apparently, having a large vocabulary is not only handy when you take a college entrance examination but also when you try to think of an idea and how to express it. The availability of words for a concept speeds up thought and expression, two vital processes in communication.

How Can You Improve the Clarity of Your Language Use?

How you use language will affect the meanings audience members attribute to your message. Thus, one goal for your language use should be to present a clear message to your audience. In this section, you will learn various strategies for improving your clarity through the language you use.

Understand Levels of Abstraction

An **abstraction** is a *simplification standing for a person or thing*. The word *building* cannot capture the complexity of engineering, design, plumbing, electrical networks, glass, and steel that make up a "building." To make sense of these concepts, scholars who study the meaning of language, known as semanticists, refer to particular **levels of abstraction**, or *the degree to which words become separated from concrete or sensed reality*. One prominent semanticist, S. I. Hayakawa,[8] introduced the "ladder of abstraction" to demonstrate that words have degrees of abstractness and concreteness. The ladder of abstraction should look like a stepladder. As an example, see Figure 8.1, where the bottom of the ladder, at the most abstract level, is "living being," followed up the steps by "mammal," "omnivore," "human," "female," "teenager," and "Rebekah." Docs referring to Rebekah as an "omnivore" seem the same to you as calling her by her own particular name, "Rebekah"?

While **abstract words** tend to be *general, broad, and distant from what you can perceive through your senses*, **concrete words** tend to be *specific, narrow, particular, and based on what you can sense*. At a recent class reunion, a classmate described his current occupation by saying "I'm in transportation," encouraging listeners to perceive him as anything from a pilot to a train engineer to a ship's captain—all of whom are "in transportation"—but the more specific and concrete term, *city bus driver*, turned out to be a more accurate representation. When selecting

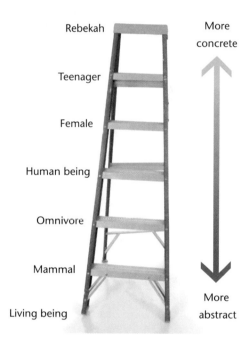

Figure 8.1   **How is Hayakawa's "ladder of abstraction" a useful metaphor for gauging concrete and abstract concepts?**

Abstract	Concrete
I love sports.	I'm a soccer player.
I drive a late-model vehicle.	I drive a Subaru Outback.
Some foods make me ill.	I'm allergic to milk products.
I use drugs.	I take an aspirin each day.
I'm a homemaker.	I stay at home and raise two children.

TABLE 8.1 DENOTATIVE AND CONNOTATIVE MEANINGS OF WORDS		
	DENOTATIVE MEANING	ONE CONNOTATIVE MEANING
Wolf	Wild canine in the dog family	Man who aggressively pursues women
Bigot	Someone who despises people who are different	Someone who despises people that I like
History	A record of human events	A false account of events as depicted by those in power

language for your speech, you may be clearer by trying to avoid overly abstract words, opting instead for more concrete options. Saying that there are five reasons to do annual physical exams with a doctor is more concrete than referencing "many" reasons.

Understand Differences between Denotative and Connotative Meanings

Public speakers need to be aware of the varied meanings evoked by their words. One means of understanding varied meanings is to distinguish between denotative and connotative meanings. **Denotative meaning** is *the direct, explicit meaning or reference of a word*. Dictionary definitions are prime examples of denotative meanings of words. The denotative meaning of the words *college degree* might be "the attainment of a post-secondary degree from an accredited college or university," but to some students, their families, and friends, the term has emotional connotations as well. The **connotative meaning** of a term refers to *the idea suggested by a word other than its explicit meaning*. Connotative meanings often evoke emotional meaning. Thus, the connotative meaning for *college degree* could be, "the attainment of a lifelong dream to be independent."

Table 8.1 compares the denotative meaning with one connotative meaning of several words to help you understand this concept. Notice that you may disagree or agree with the connotative meanings in the right-hand column—that is, words have various connotations for all of us. A practical piece of advice is that in your speeches, you need to consider not only the denotative but also the connotative power of words on your audience. By focusing on only one or the other you can diminish clarity and/or fail to take into consideration how audience members might react to your language use.

Use Descriptive Language

Communicators who are sensitive to others favor descriptive over evaluative language. **Descriptive language** *attempts to observe objectively and without judgment*. **Evaluative language** is *full of judgments about the goodness or badness of a person or situation*.

You can see why evaluative words can invite trouble and how descriptive words can help you avoid negative audience reactions. In public presentations, a speaker is

Descriptive Words

High-energy person

Expensive automobile

Evaluative Words

A person wound too tight

Overpriced, high-maintenance snowmobile

wise not to use hot-button terms that cause a strong, negative reaction in the audience because an outraged listener might very well disrupt your entire presentation. If you want to see how evaluative language promotes dialogue and debate, watch political commercials. If taken to extreme, name-calling and use of hot-button terminology have the potential to diminish clarity and close off dialogue.

Compare and Contrast

Speakers often use comparisons and contrasts to clarify their messages. One beginning speaker, when asked to distinguish himself from others in an "I Am Unique" speech early in the course, first compared and then contrasted his appearance to that of others in the class:

> *Comparison*: I then looked at my physical make-up. I am 5'7" tall, weigh roughly 155 pounds, and have short brown hair. I think I just described 90 percent of the male population at the university.

> *Contrast*: I thought distinguishable marks might help separate me a little. I have more than 70 stitches that have left scars, along with two scars from stab wounds. The most distinguishable mark on me is a tribal tattoo on my back, which I had done in England.[9]

A **comparison** *shows how much one thing is like another*; a **contrast** *shows how unlike one thing is from another*. You can use both for clarification for your audience. Using the power of language is knowing how to use comparison and contrast for clarifying your intended meaning.

Reveal the Origins of Terms

The *origin of a word* is called its **etymology**. Often a word's etymology will help an audience remember the term. For example, the word *psychology* means "study of the mind." Psychology comes from the Greek words *psykhe*, which means "soul," and *logia*, which means "the study of."

Telling a more complete story about a word is more likely to make it more memorable. Every dictionary has a brief etymology of the words, but some sources tell a more complete and compelling story. Books by William Safire[10] and by A. H. Soukhanov[11] reveal the stories behind the words, stories that help an audience remember the meaning and the significance of the words in your presentation. Use etymologies sparingly so you do not sound pedantic.

In this section, you have learned various strategies that you can use to improve the clarity of your language use. Figure 8.2 provides a summary of these strategies.

1. Define terms in your speech so your audience will understand the denotative and connotative meanings of your words.
2. Use descriptive language instead of evaluative language to avoid misunderstanding and conflict.
3. Clarify your ideas by comparison and contrast.
4. When appropriate, reveal the origins of words to help listeners remember your words and their meanings.

Figure 8.2 **Strategies for improving your language clarity.**

How Can You Improve the Style of Your Language Use?

In addition to using language to improve your clarity as a speaker, you can also use language to improve your style. In this section, you will learn about various language-use strategies that focus more on the style of your presentation.

Recognize That Written and Spoken Language Differ

One might assume that the styles of written and spoken language are roughly similar. Such an assumption would be incorrect. Written and spoken language differ enormously; even variations within written or spoken language can be vast. Consider the difference between written language in a book in comparison to written language on Twitter, for instance. Recognizing how expectations between written and spoken language differ can help you be clearer. As a speaker, talking like you would write can cause listeners to be bored, confused, or both; alternatively, writing like you speak can possibly diminish your credibility as a writer. Each mode of communication requires a unique style. Table 8.2 highlights stylistic differences between written and spoken language within the context of relationships between speakers and listeners, and writers and readers.

Use Words That Simplify

You will often know more about your topic than do the people in your audience. However, you must be careful not to use language that reduces understanding. This writer, for example, is describing Senator John McCain, Republican from Arizona:

> He would see the heavens fall rather than court Iowa by supporting ethanol subsidies; who, ever an oak, never a willow, insouciantly goes his own way . . . . The media call McCain a "maverick," even though he seems to be, oxymoronically, a predictable maverick.[12]

George F. Will, a Ph.D. from Princeton, is a politically conservative commentator who, nonetheless, attacks many a Republican. His phrase "ever an oak, never a willow" is a clever way to describe the unshakeable McCain, but many readers may have foundered on "insouciantly" and "oxymoronically," which are designed more to highlight Will's high I.Q. than to enlighten his audience. In this case, Will's stylistic choice of

TABLE 8.2   COMMUNICATION DIFFERENCES AMONG SPEAKERS, LISTENERS, WRITERS, AND READERS

	SPEAKER	LISTENER	WRITER	READER
Sentence length	Uses short sentences instead of long ones	Understands short sentences better than long ones	Typically can use longer sentences than a speaker can	Can read long sentences multiple times to achieve understanding
Pace	Sets the pace	Must adjust to pace	Sets no "real-time" pace	Reads at own pace
Repetition	Reiterates ideas to optimize understanding	Needs repetition to catch meanings	Might reiterate ideas to optimize understanding	Rereads if needed for better understanding
Message transmission	Conveys verbal and nonverbal messages	Receives verbal and nonverbal messages	Conveys verbal messages	Receives verbal messages
Feedback and adaptation	Can adapt immediately to feedback	Sends and responds to feedback	Receives no feedback when writing	Sends no feedback while reading

terms could create a barrier with his audience. Effective public speakers use words that are recognizable to their audience.

Notice how Andrew Robinson, a physiology major and veteran runner, uses simple, everyday words with lots of concrete, specific detail in this health-related presentation.

> You and your friends decide to play a late night game of basketball. You throw on an old pair of tennis shoes and eight of you head to the recreation center. After you have been playing for forty-five minutes or so, sweat is dripping down your face and back, and you are huffing and puffing from running up and down the court. You get stuck guarding this quick kid who moves instantly from one spot to the next before you can react. He drives toward the baseline with you right on him. As he nears the bottom of the key, he crosses over to his left to get around you. You try to stop, but as you plant your left foot, you feel your ankle roll as pain shoots up your leg, and you fall to the ground.[13]

Andrew was warming up to a speech not about basketball but about selecting the correct shoes for the sport. By the time Andrew finished his speech, with more agonizing stories about painful hips, sprained ankles, and sore toes, he had convinced his audience to discard their "old pair of tennis shoes" and buy shoes dedicated to their sport. He accomplished his purpose with simple, direct words.

"The skillful presenter chooses words that listeners will understand."

Use Substitutions and Definitions

Another move toward clarity is to define any language that may seem unfamiliar or potentially confusing to an audience. For example, the term "social justice" could be made clear by describing it as an effort that seeks to establish a society in which basic needs are met and all people flourish.

George Will could have substituted simpler words for "insouciantly" and "oxymoronically." He could have said "indifferently" or "uncaringly" instead of "insouciantly," and he simply could have left out the word "oxymoronically," which means contradictory, or two words with opposing meanings, as in "predictable maverick." The skillful presenter chooses words that listeners will understand or defines the terms so they will understand.

Use Figurative Language

Language can be both literal and figurative. **Literal language** *uses words to reveal facts*, whereas **figurative language** *compares one concept to another analogous but different concept.* To say that a fighter hit his opponent 25 times in a round is literal; to say that he fought like a tiger is figurative. Literal language is what you usually find in news reports in newspapers and magazines or text-based news sources on the Internet. Figurative language is found in the lyrics of songs, in poetry, and in feature articles in magazines. The best speakers know how to use figurative language to add succulent spices to an otherwise bland broth of literal language. If you recall the discussion of style and ornamentation from Chapter 2, figurative language is the substance that improves the ornamentation of your speech. Finding the right balance between literal and figurative language can maintain clarity while also punctuating the interest level of your presentation. A speech without any figurative language can come across as overly simple and boring.

Use Synonyms and Antonyms

Another method of clarifying a word or concept, while also potentially improving your style, is to use **synonyms**, *words that mean more or less the same thing*, or

antonyms, *words that are opposite in meaning. House* and *home, office* and *workplace,* and *film* and *movie* are examples of synonyms. *Beautiful* and *ugly, dry* and *humid,* and *hired* and *fired* are examples of antonyms. Using synonyms and antonyms can open possible wording options for you and help you avoid using similar terminology over and over again. Moreover, using them effectively can help you build and display a broader vocabulary and result in more interesting language options during your presentation.

Use Words That Evoke Images

An effective speaker uses creativity to paint word pictures in the audience's minds. Many speakers have used the following illustration to help their audience understand the world population:

> If we could shrink the earth's population to a village of 100 people and maintain the existing human ratios, the village would look like this:
>
> 57 Asians
> 21 Europeans
> 14 from the Western Hemisphere
> 8 Africans
> 51 females
> 70 non-white
> 70 non-Christian
> 80 living in substandard housing
> 70 illiterate
> 50 suffering from malnutrition, and
> 1 with a college education

These words create a picture in people's minds that makes the concept of "world population" more concrete, specific, and easy to understand.

Doug Burch, an army veteran, had these words to say about his eight years in the armed forces. Notice how his words create images in your mind about his experience:

> I have traveled to and from different countries and have seen the most glorious sunsets. I have watched the sun rise one too many times after being up all night. I have sailed around the Spanish Isles and snorkeled among its reefs. I have shared stories and drink with dockhands along the way. I have sat in pubs and bars with strangers who do not speak English and have tried to carry on a conversation. I have learned about many cultures, and that just because ours is one of the most advanced does not mean it is the best. I am starting to feel unique because I have learned about life, and I can still smile.[14]

Colorful words create vivid images in our minds.

Use Correct Grammar

The way you talk affects your credibility with an audience. Paula LaRocque, writing for *The Quill,* says:

> Language misuse ranks high in terms of the negative reaction and irritation it can elicit from people. Most people give considerable value to their native language and their perceptions of its proper use. Thus, people who mis-utilize language are often accused of maiming, massacring, brutalizing, or butchering it. Society's inherent understanding of being civilized apparently means, in part, the ability to communicate well with grace and accuracy and without offense.[15]

Finding the Right Word

iConnect

In this chapter you will learn about several different strategies for improving your language use. Sometimes the strategy boils down to finding the right word—or finding a better alternative word. Writers can spend hours agonizing over the best wording for a paragraph! At times, it takes disruptive creativity to break you out of a word problem. For that, using a resource like **thesaurus.com** can be invaluable. By searching for a word at thesaurus.com, you can find a definition (just like you would with a dictionary), a list of synonyms, a list of antonyms, and examples of how the word can be used in a sentence. Using synonyms and antonyms, you can often devise alternate word options that can improve your style, clarity, or both. If you find yourself using a particular word over and over in your speech or writing, consider using the-saurus.com to creatively disrupt your approach!

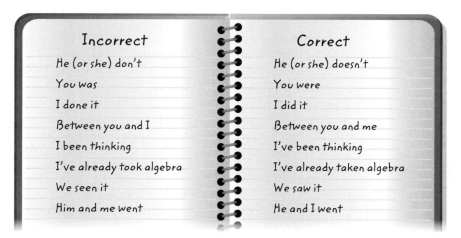

Incorrect	Correct
He (or she) don't	He (or she) doesn't
You was	You were
I done it	I did it
Between you and I	Between you and me
I been thinking	I've been thinking
I've already took algebra	I've already taken algebra
We seen it	We saw it
Him and me went	He and I went

Figure 8.3   **Common grammatical errors.**
Adapted from *Public Speaking for College and Career*, 5th ed. By Hamilton Gregory, 1999. Used by permission of McGraw-Hill.

Bad grammar is much like having a bit of spinach in your front teeth: everyone sees that spinach, but nobody bothers to tell you it is there. Outside your communication class you are unlikely to encounter anyone, including your boss, who will actually say, "We are holding you back from responsible management positions because you constantly misuse the language." Nonetheless, consistent correct use of language gives a speaker credibility because other people assume the person is educated. See Figure 8.3 for some common grammatical errors.

Use Repetition

Repetition, *repeated sounds*, has striking effects in speaking because the audience gets caught up in the cadences, or rhythms, of linguistic structure. Usually, repetition is accompanied by increased volume, increased energy, and increased forcefulness as the repeated forms build toward some climactic ending.

- Recognize that written and spoken language differ.
- Use words that simplify.
- Use substitutions and definitions.
- Use figurative language.
- Use synonyms and antonyms to compare and contrast.
- Use words that evoke images.
- Use correct grammar.
- Use repetition to rhetoric effect.
- Use alliteration to attract attention.

Figure 8.4 **Strategies for improving your language style.**

Observe how repetition works in this speech by Chris Meek, an engineering student and co-owner of Combat Creek Paintball:

> Do you want to get involved in America's fastest growing sport?
>
> Do you want to get involved in a sport in which size, age, and even sex make no difference?
>
> Do you want an ultimate stress reliever in which communication and quick wits make the difference between winning and losing?
>
> Then I have the sport for you, an adult version of capture-the-flag—paintball.[16]

Using repetition makes your speech easier to remember, makes your speech more energetic, and makes your speech more memorable.

Use Alluring Alliteration

Alliteration *means the repetition of an initial consonant.* Professional speakers use alliteration because repeated sounds make words memorable. "The Fabulous Facts about Foster Care" was Lacey Schneider's title. She began her speech by saying "Before I begin my fact-filled speech about fabulous foster care ...."[17] All those repeated "F" sounds are alliteration. Also used in advertising, repeated sounds attract attention and help listeners to remember.

In this section, you have learned several strategies for improving your style through the use of language. Figure 8.4 summarizes those strategies.

What Ethical Considerations Should Guide Your Language Use?

An important aspect of becoming an effective public communicator is to use language ethically and respectfully. That is, you need to use words that include people; that do not establish in-group and out-group identities; and that regard people without negative judgment based on ethnicity, gender, sexual orientation, or worldview. You also know that you should credit the use of other people's words by using oral citations during your presentation. Violating that rule can result in a failing grade for the class or even expulsion from most colleges and universities. These not the only ethical considerations that you should take into consideration. In this section you will learn how exaggeration/oversimplification, inclusive language, use of labels, stereotyping, and perspective taking are all related to the ethics of language use.

Avoid Exaggeration and Oversimplification

Another word for exaggeration in language is **hyperbole** (hi-PURR-bull-ee), which is *a kind of overstatement or use of a word or words that exaggerates the actual situation.* To call a relatively normal fire "the biggest conflagration this city has ever seen" is an example. The ethical speaker exercises care in describing events, people, and situations. You should use vivid, concrete language as long as the words do not overstate or exaggerate. In the heat of a persuasive speech you might be tempted to state your side of the issue with exaggerated or overstated importance.

A second ethical error in language is **oversimplification**, *describing a complex issue as a simple one*. Political campaign speeches are full of examples. The candidate for the Senate says, "We'll solve this crime problem with more prisons." The candidate for the State House of Representatives says, "No new taxes." And the candidate for governor says, "Welfare reform!" Bumper sticker slogans rarely solve problems, and neither do sound bites. The ethical speaker tries to examine issues thoroughly, states them as descriptively as possible, and provides sound reasons for why the audience should adopt a certain position on the issue without exaggeration or oversimplification.

Use Inclusive Language

Another way to articulate this rule of artful and ethical speaking is to say that you should use **inclusive language**, *language that does not leave out groups of people*. When speaking (or writing), you should remember that when you reference others you should not over-emphasize differences, opting instead to emphasize similarity. Referring to "homeless people" highlights differences between people with and without homes; referring to "people without homes" attempts to recognize fundamental similarities. Using inclusive language that recognizes similarities is respectful of all audience members; failing to use inclusive language can create unproductive barriers between you and members of your audience, barriers that can create an insurmountable hurdle for your presentation.

> *"Call people what they themselves want others to call them."*

You can also increase your chances of being inclusive by avoiding slang, because this type of language often is understood only by certain groups of people. When you use slang, you risk alienating those audience members who are not part of the group that typically is acquainted with those words and expressions.

Do Not Label Others

Notice also that the principle says that you should "call people what they themselves want others to call them." Sometimes people within a co-culture call each other by names that are forbidden to people outside that co-culture. Women can call each other "girls," but they probably do not want their employer to call them by that name. African Americans often call each other by names that would be deeply insulting if used by someone else. You are most likely to succeed as a public presenter if you use language that includes, honors, and respects others. Many of our words for others come from those who dominate in a culture. Because men have dominated North American culture historically, you will find many more derogatory words for women than for men. Additionally, Native Americans did not name themselves "Indians." European explorers gave them that name when they mistakenly thought they had reached India. You also can avoid sexist language by using inclusive language. Figure 8.5 shows how you can substitute several of the most common sexist language terms with more inclusive language choices.

Sexist	Inclusive
Mankind	Humankind
Manmade	Handmade
Fireman	Firefighter
Mailman	Mail carrier
Chairman	Chair

Figure 8.5 **Ways to substitute inclusive language for sexist language.**

Stereotypes and Differences

The word *stereotype* was first used in 1922 by Walter Lippmann in his book *Public Opinion*. Lippmann borrowed the term from

ASIAN AND HISPANIC: "BAGGY LABELS"

People in the United States use some terms for others that are "baggy" labels because the words try to include too much: the words are so abstract, so unspecific, that they are not highly useful. The word *Asian*, for example, refers to people from Japan, India, Malaysia, China, Thailand, Pakistan, Bangladesh, Cambodia, and Vietnam; people who are Muslim, Christian, Buddhist, Hindu, and many other religions;

and people who have every possible skin color. All of these varied people—the biggest population groups in the world—we lump under the label "Asian." Similarly, the word *Hispanic* is a baggy label that refers variously to European Americans (e.g., Spanish), "Indians" (another misnomer) who originally inhabited South and Central America, Cubans, Puerto Ricans, Mexicans, and practically anyone else who speaks Spanish and lives in North or South America. What should we call people? *The best advice is to call people what they like others to call them.*

the new machine at the time that printed the same sheet of print over and over, a machine called a "stereotype." Today, **stereotype** has come to mean *the misjudging of an individual by assuming that he or she has the characteristics of some group—that every single individual is just exactly like the others*, as in the case of the stereotype machine.

Every campus has more than its fair share of stereotypes about students who study too much, students who study too little, students who are athletes, and students who are more mature than others. We have stereotypes of professors, accountants, and engineers. But public speakers need to avoid stereotypes to avoid offense.

Similarly, you should avoid calling attention to irrelevant differences. When you describe someone as a *female* judge, a *Hispanic* professor, a *woman* doctor, or the city council member *in a wheelchair*, you are emphasizing irrelevant qualifiers about that person. The implication might be that people who are female are rarely judges or doctors, that people of Hispanic origin are generally not professors, and that individuals in wheelchairs are typically not elected to city council. Or, even worse, a listener might assume that you do not believe that people from such groups ought to be in such positions.

You may be wondering what words you can use in your presentations. Try to use words that explain, clarify, and enlighten the audience by following the advice below.

Language and Perspective Taking

Your words reflect your **perspective**, *your point of view or perception*. The words you choose in public speaking indicate to others how you see the world, whether you intend them to or not.

Imagine you are giving a speech about taxation. If you choose to talk about "rich people," "poor people," and "middle-class people," you are using language that divides America into economic classes. That is a particular perspective. If you talk about the "struggling young people" and "the Social Security set," you are dividing Americans by age—another perspective. Talk of the "marriage penalty" and high taxes on single wage earners divides the adult population into those who are married and those who are not. No matter how you discuss the issue, you use language that indicates your perspective.

How is this concept related to ethical speaking? Consider the connotations of the words that you can use to describe individuals who earn more than $100,000 annually:

"top 10 percent in income," "rich people," "wealthy individuals," "fat cats," or "privileged class." Each description indicates a perspective, but some of them—like the last two—indicate a medium to strong negative connotation that may or may not be fair to high-earning individuals. In other words, the words you choose can indicate prejudice, bias, or unfairness toward individuals or groups. Figure 8.6 lists three ways to make sure you use words ethically.

Figure 8.6   **How to use words ethically.**

- *Avoid exaggeration.*
- *Avoid oversimplification.*
- *Recognize that your language reveals your perspective.*

How Should You Begin to Improve Your Language Use?

After reading this chapter, you have probably concluded that a good deal of thought must go into language use. That assumption is correct, but you must also recognize that language use is a constantly evolving skill. Even the most experienced and thoughtful speakers will make mistakes with their language. Rather than striving for flawless perfection, be cognizant of your language use and always look for ways to improve. Here are some concluding tips to help you grow in your use of language:

1. *Choose language at a level that is appropriate for the specific audience.* Speak with a level of formality that is right for the audience and the situation. Nearly always, the language of public speaking is elevated above that which you would use on the street or in conversation with close friends. You might call it enlightened conversation.

2. *Choose language that the audience will understand.* Words the audience cannot comprehend might impress the audience with your vocabulary, but they neither inform nor persuade. If you must use words that the audience is unlikely to understand, then define, explain, or provide examples.

3. *Choose language consistent with yourself, the topic, and the situation.* If you do not normally use legal or medical terms, you will feel and look uncomfortable using them in a presentation. Your language needs to fit the topic and be consistent with your level of knowledge and experience. Using overly dramatic words unwarranted by the topic constitutes exaggeration; understating complex problems indicates a lack of analysis. The situation or occasion may dictate a certain kind of language—you don't speak the same way in a mosque, synagogue, or church as you do at a football game.

4. *Choose language that meets high ethical standards.* Choose words that neither exaggerate nor oversimplify. Recognize that words reflect a perspective. Avoid language that offends others because of their race, sex, sexual orientation, or physical or mental disability. Your task is to inform, persuade, or entertain, not to offend.

For REVIEW >>

SUMMARY HIGHLIGHTS

What Are the Characteristics of Language?

▶ Language is symbolic, which means that words are used to stand for concrete objects, other aspects of reality, and even ideas.

▶ Language can grow and change over time. Some words are uniquely bound to a culture and/or time period. The rules of each language system guide ways in which new language emerges.

▶ Language is powerful because it provides the mechanism through which many messages are expressed.

▶ Words help us organize and classify. When we describe someone or something, we use classification words like *tall*, *colorful*, *solid*, etc. Those words explicitly provide overlapping linguistic categories to help us organize and subdivide reality.

▶ As demonstrated through the Sapir-Whorf hypothesis, words can help shape how you think about the world.

How Can You Improve the Clarity of Your Language Use?

▶ Understand that words have levels of abstraction. Abstract words are very broad classifications (e.g., "living creature"), whereas concrete words are very specific (e.g., "Rebekah").

▶ The meanings of words can be described as denotative or connotative. Denotative meanings are those that represent the direct or explicit meaning of a word, as you would find in a dictionary. The connotative meaning refers to the ideas suggested by the term.

▶ You should try to use descriptive language—language that provides an objective description of what was observed. The alternative is using evaluative language, which is full of judgment.

▶ By using language to compare and contrast, you can explain how things are both similar and different.

▶ By using substitution and definitions, you can make the terminology you use more straightforward and easier to decipher.

► By revealing the origin of the word, you might be able to help audience members see a more complete picture of what you are talking about. Entire books have been written about the etymology of words used in our popular culture.

How Can You Improve the Style of Your Language Use?

► There are substantial differences between written and spoken style. Failing to recognize those differences can diminish the quality of your speaking and/or writing.

► By using words that simplify, you can often provide a more direct and recognizable message for your audience.

► Figurative language can add intrigue and interest to your message.

► Synonyms and antonyms can provide alternative wording for saying the same thing. Such alternative wordings can often improve the style of your speech wording.

► By using words that evoke images, you can make descriptive statements more vivid. Imagery-oriented words bring pictures of things to people's thoughts while you are speaking.

► Failing to use correct grammar can seriously undermine your credibility.

► Repetition and alliteration are both strategic devices that can affect the rhythm and flow of your speech.

What Ethical Considerations Should Guide Your Language Use?

► You should avoid exaggeration and oversimplification.

► You should use inclusive language.

► You should not label other people.

► You should avoid speaking in stereotypes that emphasize differences.

► You should recognize that your particular choice of language use represents your own unique perspective.

How Should You Begin to Improve Your Language Use?

► Choose language appropriate for your audience.

► Choose language your audience will understand.

► Choose language consistent with yourself, the topic, and situation.

► Choose language that meets high ethical standards.

1. What does "language is symbolic" mean?
   (A) Words allow us to cluster individual items into larger units.
   (B) Words are powerful.
   (C) Words determine how we think about the world.
   (D) Words represent the concrete and objective reality of objects as well as abstract ideas.

2. A theory that suggests that our language determines to some extent how we think about and view the world is called the:
   (A) semantic theory
   (B) Sapir-Whorf hypothesis
   (C) ladder of abstraction
   (D) Hyperbole theory

pop **Quiz**

3. Which of the following terms is the *most concrete*?
    (A) mammal
    (B) carnivore
    (C) Shih Tzu
    (D) male

4. How is spoken language different from written language?
    (A) Spoken language uses longer sentences than the written language.
    (B) Written language needs to repeat phrases so the reader can catch meanings.
    (C) Written language is affected by feedback.
    (D) Spoken language conveys verbal and nonverbal messages.

5. "Exciting" and "exhilarating" are examples of:
    (A) substitutions
    (B) antonyms
    (C) synonyms
    (D) stereotypes

Answers: 1 (D); 2 (B); 3 (C); 4 (D); 5 (C)

APPLICATION EXERCISES

1. Translate the abstract terms in the column on the left into more concrete terms in the blanks on the right.

    a. A recent article   _____

    b. An ethnic neighborhood   _____

    c. A good professor   _____

    d. A big profit   _____

    e. A distant land   _____

    f. A tough course   _____

    g. A tall building   _____

    h. He departed rapidly   _____

    i. She dresses poorly   _____

    j. They are religious   _____

Now examine each of the words you have placed in the blanks and place a check after each one that may be a poor choice because it skews the audience's response in a negative or unduly positive direction. In other words, the word lacks honesty and accuracy.

2. Examine the words in the column on the left. Write in the blank after each word its denotative meaning and its connotative meaning. Remember that the denotative meaning is a descriptive definition; the connotative meaning is the feeling or emotion evoked by the term. In the columns to the right of letters f., g., and h., add three words and establish denotative and connotative meanings for each.

	Denotative Meaning	**Connotative Meaning**
a. Girl	_____	_____
b. Terrorist	_____	_____
c. Environmentalist	_____	_____
d. Developer	_____	_____
e. Senator	_____	_____
f.	_____	_____
g.	_____	_____
h.	_____	_____

3. Using any sources available, see if you can find the story behind the word or phrase.

   a. O.K.

   _____

   _____

   b. Trojan horse

   _____

   _____

   c. Baby boomers

   _____

   _____

   d. Eye candy

   _____

   _____

   e. Curse of the Bambino

   _____

   _____

KEY TERMS

Abstraction	Descriptive language	Perspective
Abstract words	Etymology	Repetition
Alliteration	Evaluative language	Sapir-Whorf hypothesis
Antonym	Figurative language	Semantics
Comparison	Hyperbole	Stereotype
Concrete words	Inclusive language	Symbolic
Connotative meaning	Levels of abstraction	Synonym
Contrast	Literal language	
Denotative meaning	Oversimplification	

9

VISUAL RESOURCES & PRESENTATION

Human beings use multiple senses to learn. From the time of infancy, we utilize combinations of senses to look for patterned regularities in the world. Seeing mom or dad walk from the refrigerator with a bottle or bowl is quickly associated with food; hearing an excited laugh and seeing a smile becomes a signal that someone is happy with what we have done. The list goes on and on. That capacity to use multiple senses is important in speaking situations so long as speakers recognize how to use them effectively. This chapter helps you develop plans for doing just that.

TECHNOLOGY

Adora Svitak is a literary giant and not even in high school. By the age of 7, Adora had already published a book sold internationally, and now, still only a teenager, she is in high demand to speak in front of teachers to help them understand how to instill reading and writing skills in children. Adora reads and writes at a level eclipsing most adults. Her grasp of language is enviable. Adora's body of work as a writer, teacher, and speaker shows that age is less important than determination in predicting success.

In a presentation given for TED (see http://blog.ted.com/2010/04/01/adora_svitak_on/), Adora develops the argument that adults are constrained by their own socially created conventions of rational thought. Adora argues that children are different because they have the "audacity to imagine." She further notes that adults tend to inhibit children from learning because they "don't trust them" and restrict them to learning in the way that adults think children should learn. Her speech is insightful, and it illustrates how our "adult" ways of speaking, teaching, and communicating often result in less creative and less interesting ideas.

Watching Adora's speech, you will notice that her point was explicitly illustrated by the visual aids that she used. Although Adora used a computer and projector to display her visual aids, she did not use lists of bullets on PowerPoint slides like those you

see every day in classrooms and business meetings. Rather, Adora presented creative visual imagery and cleverly designed textual messages to add interest, variety, and emphasis. If you take a few minutes to view her presentation, you will see that visual aids do not need to be confined to predetermined PowerPoint templates. A little creativity and attention to aesthetic design can enhance presentations in ways that make conventional PowerPoint-type presentations look as contemporary as mullets and mood rings.

This chapter teaches you about the use of visual aids, both the conventional and, following the advice of Adora Svitak, the more creative.

Even inexperienced speakers can guess that good presentations consist of more than just the speaker talking. One way to enhance any presentation is to use **sensory aids**, which are *resources other than the speaker that stimulate listeners and help them comprehend and remember the presenter's message.* Although sensory aids can appeal to any of the five senses, the most common ones stimulate sight. These **visual aids** are *any observable resources used to enhance, explain, or supplement the presenter's message.* They include pictures, diagrams, charts, graphs, video, and even demonstrations by actual people. In fact, some might argue that presenters are always visual aids for their messages because they use nonverbal messages to enhance their verbal statements. Nonvisual sensory aids can include music, touchable materials with different textures, and even food—with its pleasant aroma and good taste.

How Can You Benefit from Using Sensory Aids?

You have many good reasons to use sensory aids in your presentation. First, people learn better through **dual coding**, *the use of words accompanied by other sensory stimuli.*[1] Because people learn through each of their senses—seeing, hearing, touching, tasting, and smelling—presentations that use more than one sense can open a completely different channel through which learning can occur.

Second, people remember information better when they use sensory aids. Researchers have found that after listening to presentations in which visual aids are used, audience members remember approximately 85 percent of the content three hours later and 65 percent of the content after three days.[2] The same presentation without visual aids results in lower recall. Audience members remember only 70 percent of the information after three hours and only 10 percent of the information after three days. The lesson of this research is simple: using a visual aid can have a significant impact on whether audiences remember your message.

Third, in addition to helping audience members learn and remember information from your presentation, sensory aids hold their attention and motivate them to listen.[3] Because we think much faster than others talk, much of our mental energy is wasted anticipating or daydreaming during presentations when the speaker talks the entire time. By using sensory aids, you are better able to build interest and maintain audience members' attention.

Finally, effective sensory aids result in clearer messages. Using a picture or model to illustrate a complex idea can do wonders to help audience members understand your point. Moreover, by taking time to carefully locate or create your sensory aids, you will gain valuable knowledge that will help you explain the concept more effectively. In short, sensory aids have the potential to dramatically improve your presentation.

Because the technology has become so accessible, presenters have grown to rely on computers as a primary resource for visual and sensory aids. Computers are particularly useful for presenting **multimedia materials**, which are *digital or electronic sensory resources that combine text, graphics, video, and sound into one package.* Of course, not every multimedia presentation combines all these elements. Presenters commonly use computers to show text and images to the audience; using the computer to present video and sound is less common, although the use of YouTube and podcasts are certainly becoming a viable option for many speakers.

What Type of Visual and Sensory Aids Should You Use?

In addition to multimedia materials, a variety of other sensory resources can be used to supplement and accentuate your message. From a simple costume to a sophisticated scale model, a range of materials might be appropriate, even vital, to a well-planned speech. The following sections describe several of these options.

Slide-Deck Programs

Slide-deck programs like Microsoft's PowerPoint and Apple's Keynote are similar because they rely on a series of slides. *Like cards in a deck, you can arrange slides in a particular order and then display those slides to the audience.* Your job as a speaker is to determine the content on each slide and then arrange the order of slides to fit your presentation. The content of slides can vary widely, although most slides tend to be one of six types: text, tables, charts, flowcharts, pictures, and multimedia. Before discussing the general advantages and disadvantages of the slide-deck approach, we will first explore examples of these types of slides.

Text Slides

How many times have you been in a class where the teacher shows one "bullet" list after another? Are those classes more exciting because of the colorful slides with text? Or not? Were you able to take notes more effectively because of them? Did the teacher seem more spontaneous or more restricted because of the slides? These questions highlight the dilemma presenters face when deciding whether or not to use a substantial number of text slides in their presentations. Simply defined, a **text slide** *relies primarily on words and phrases to show audience members information.*

Figure 9.1 shows how text can be arranged on a slide, in bullet form, to highlight important concepts. If you recall the survey data reported about use of mobile Internet devices in Chapter 5, the bullet slide summarizes the process used to collect data.

Text slides do some things well and other things not so well. Research consistently demonstrates that when written messages accompany oral information, as when text slides are used, people tend to remember the information more easily; however, research also suggests that written messages do little to motivate and inspire listeners.[4] Because too many text slides can actually be distracting for the listener, you should avoid using more than a few during your presentation; you are better off limiting their use to your most important or most difficult information. When using text slides, placing information into "bullet points" is often more effective than using paragraphs and complete sentences. Second, make sure that you spend enough time explaining each point on the slide. Listeners become frustrated if you spend too much time on one bullet and ignore others. Finally, avoid placing extraneous information on your slides. Extraneous material can distract or even confuse listeners, thus counteracting any advantage of using the visual aid in the first place.

Collecting Survey Data

- Surveyed 8 people at work
  - 5 males
  - 3 females
- Average age was 26.75 years old
- Respondents spent average of 3.75 hours per day online

Figure 9.1 **Text slide with bullet list.** Text slides help emphasize key ideas and provide details for audience members.

Tables

Tables *use text and/or numbers to efficiently summarize, compare, and contrast information.* When you insert a table into PowerPoint, you will need to know in advance the number of columns and rows that you need—including any rows or columns for headings and labels. For that reason, we recommend that you draw a rough sketch of your table so that you know the exact dimensions before you attempt to create it on the computer.

Tables combine text and numbers to allow comparisons. The mobile Internet device data from Chapter 5 was used to create the table shown in Figure 9.2. Notice

Mobile Internet Device Use by Males and Females

	Males	Females
Droid	3	0
iPhone	1	0
iPad	1	2
netbook	0	1

Figure 9.2   **Table comparing mobile Internet device use by males and females.** Tables efficiently summarize, contrast, and compare information.

how the table allows easy comparisons between males and females' use of mobile Internet devices.

When using tables, practice discussing the information. As you can tell from the sample table, these types of slides contain a great deal of information, and presenters often underestimate the amount of time necessary to explain them adequately. Limiting your tables to key information and making them well organized can help you explain them more efficiently. As a rule of thumb, plan on spending about two minutes discussing tables.

Charts

Charts are *useful for visually displaying quantitative or statistical informatio*n. Recall from Chapter 5 that numbers and statistics are most commonly used to describe things, show relationships, and show differences. The bullet list slide and table shown previously are useful for describing things; charts are more effective at showing relationships and differences. Using the mobile Internet device survey from Chapter 5, the following charts could be created.

1. *Bar and column charts.* **Bar and column charts** typically *illustrate differences between categories of information.* In the example shown in Figure 9.3 you can see the average time spent online by Droid, iPhone, iPad, and netbook users. In this case, the column chart provides a quick and clear visual indication of that information.

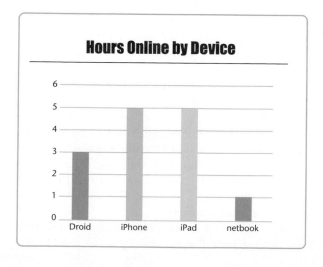

Figure 9.3   **Column chart showing hours online by device.** Column charts help illustrate differences in categories.

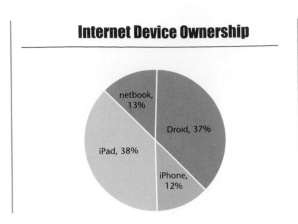

Figure 9.4   **Pie chart showing percentage of sample owning mobile Internet devices.** This pie chart shows that the Droid and iPad are most popular among the sample.

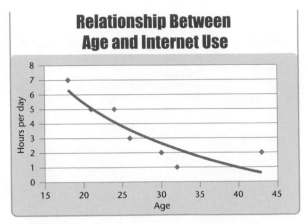

Figure 9.5   **Scatterplot showing relationship between age and Internet use.** A scatterplot is a specialized type of line plot used to show relationships between values.

2. *Pie charts.* **Pie charts** are *used to show percentages of a whole.* In the mobile Internet device data, we know that a total of eight people responded to the survey. The pie chart shown in Figure 9.4 shows the percentage of people who owned each type of device. Information used to create this pie chart came from Figure 9.2.

3. *Line charts.* **Line charts** *show trends in quantitative data.* Line charts could be used to show trends over time. For example, you could plot the number of Internet users each year for the past 20 years to show how Internet use has consistently increased each year. A special type of line chart is called a **scatterplot**, which *plots related values on an X–Y axis and then creates a line showing how those values are related.* Figure 9.5 shows a scatterplot using the mobile Internet device data. Each person's scores for both "hours per day on the Internet" and age were plotted on the chart. If you look at the plots and connect them with a line, you see that younger respondents tend to be online more than older respondents.

Flowcharts

Flowcharts are *diagrams that represent a hierarchical structure or process.* Flowcharts might be used to illustrate various positions within a company or organization. For instance, the organizational flowchart in Figure 9.6 shows the leadership positions within a student club. You might also use a flowchart to represent a process, as in the example illustrating how to use a visual aid during a presentation. This type of flowchart is illustrated in Figure 9.7.

Pictures

Presentations are often enhanced by using pictures to show audience members objects, places, and even people being discussed. However, most public speaking teachers warn students that passing pictures around during a presentation is not a good idea because the activity becomes very distracting. Moreover, most pictures are so small that not everyone can see them if they are held by the speaker. Fortunately, PowerPoint is an easy way to display pictures so that everyone can see them.

Presenters have three basic options for using PowerPoint to display pictures. First, many pictures are available via the Internet. For instance, you can use Google

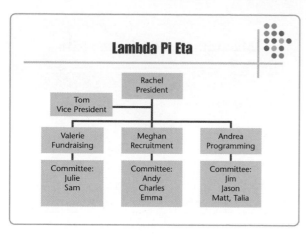

Figure 9.6   **Organizational flowchart for Lambda Pi Eta, the communication studies honor society, sponsored by the National Communication Association.**

.com to search for pictures related to keywords associated with your topic. Remember that using a picture from the Internet is just like using a quotation—you must credit the source for the picture. Another option is to use a digital camera to take a picture. With the price of digital cameras plummeting to less than $100, finding someone with access to one is relatively easy. Finally, if you have conventional photographs and access to a scanner, you can scan photos directly into PowerPoint. If you are unfamiliar with how to work with pictures in PowerPoint, we recommend that you ask your instructor for the location of a lab or resource person on campus. Remember that if you need to find or take pictures for use during your presentation, you will need to build extra time into your preparation process.

Regardless of what type of picture you want to show—photos, computer-generated graphics, or even drawings—the methods of inserting the pictures into PowerPoint remain the same. You can even use PowerPoint to create very basic pictures. Figures 9.8 and 9.9 show two slides used by José, a second-generation "mainlander" of Puerto Rican descent, in a presentation about his grandfather's unit in World War II. The first figure combines the crest of the 65th Infantry Regiment with text that briefly explains the history of the unit. The second picture shows the places his grandfather traveled to during his time in the service.

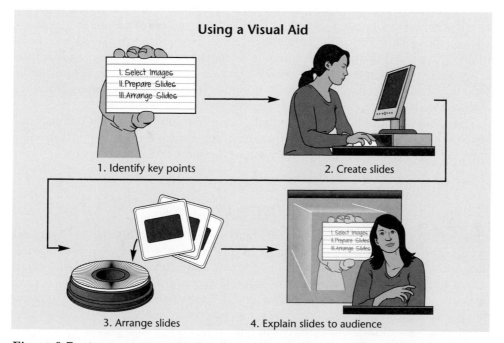

*Figure 9.*7   **A process-oriented flowchart showing use of a visual aid.** Flowcharts help audience members learn step-by-step actions.

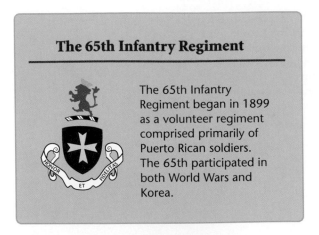

Figure 9.8   **A picture combined with text in PowerPoint.**

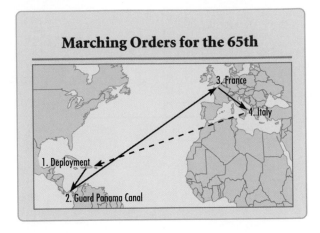

Figure 9.9   **A picture used as a visual aid.**

Multimedia

Presenters have traditionally used DVDs to present full-motion video during their presentations. Of course, this option still exists, and most digital projectors can accommodate input from a DVD, Blu-ray, and perhaps even a mobile device. However, incorporating digital video into PowerPoint is easy, and if the clips are short (which they should be), there are advantages to using PowerPoint to display the video. Gaining access to digital video is easy if you have a digital camcorder or if you have a video converter attached to your computer. Digital camcorders are still somewhat expensive, but digital video converters are typically less than $100. Many campuses have multimedia computer labs equipped to convert standard DVDs or older videotapes to digital video. Of course, you might also have access to a cell phone or tablet that will allow you to shoot and edit your own video clips. Online sources like TED, YouTube, and Vimeo provide access to thousands of videos created by others.

Once you have digital video, incorporating the video into PowerPoint is no different from incorporating a picture. When you play the slide and use the mouse to click on the video, the clip will play automatically. The advantage of using PowerPoint to play the video is that you do not have to worry about switching the projector from PowerPoint (the computer) to the DVD and back again. Also, by creating and editing the digital video, you have complete control over how long the clip is and what the audience is able to see.

Students and teachers are commonly using YouTube and other online video sources during presentations. Remember that using a video is no different than using any other type of Internet-based information: you must take care to ensure accuracy and give proper credit to sources.

General Tips on Using Slide-Deck Programs

Although PowerPoint and similar programs have been available to speakers for decades, relatively little research exists to document how best to use computer-generated presentation aids to promote recall and attitude change. However, a recent study conducted by researchers at the University of Central Florida provides evidence that PowerPoint is, indeed, beneficial. In that study, several groups of students watched a speech where PowerPoint was used and were compared to a control group that viewed the same speech without PowerPoint.[5] The groups viewing the speeches with PowerPoint remembered more than the group viewing the speech without PowerPoint. Of those who viewed the speech with PowerPoint, participants remembered more when the bullets on each slide were shown all at once rather than one at a time using a "build" transition effect.

Much more research must be done to fully understand the effects of PowerPoint and other computer-generated presentation aids in speeches. Until these effects are adequately researched, the following suggestions might help you avoid some of the most common blunders.

1. *Don't overload the number of slides.* Having so many slides that you cannot possibly talk intelligently about any of them is a problem many presenters face. The ease with which we can create slides often makes including "one more" too tempting. As a general rule of thumb, you should not have more than one slide per minute. One slide every two minutes is an even better average.

2. *Don't overload any one slide.* The number of words, figures, or pictures on one slide should not exceed the amount a person can process in 30 seconds. As a practical matter, a maximum of four or five lines of text is a good rule to follow.

3. *Use a large type font.* Slides should never use less than a 28-point font. Smaller type fonts are difficult to see for people sitting more than a few rows back. Also, you should stick to fonts like Times, Courier, or Arial rather than fonts based on script or handwritten typefaces, which are harder to read at a distance.

4. *Select colors with contrast.* Although PowerPoint provides many options for preset templates, take care to use coloring schemes that allow for substantial contrast between text and the background. Also take care when creating graphs and charts so that lines, bars, and pie pieces effectively contrast with the background. Keep in mind, too, that dark slides shown in a darkened room can lull audience members to sleep!

5. *Avoid unnecessary images and effects.* Using too many clipart images or several fancy animation schemes can cause your presentation to appear shallow. Allowing PowerPoint slides to draw attention away from you, the presenter, is a common mistake made by inexperienced speakers. Your message, rather than the PowerPoint slides, should be the centerpiece of your presentation.

> *"Having so many slides that you cannot possibly talk intelligently about any of them is a problem many presenters face."*

6. *Have a backup plan.* Computers fail, files get lost or corrupted, and projectors sometimes do not turn on. Most teachers will expect you to be prepared to make your presentation on the day assigned regardless of whether PowerPoint is cooperating. Taking time to print slides and copy them onto color transparencies is wise.

7. *Do not read slides to the audience.* Inexperienced presenters often forget that the audience can read. Reading text to the audience is time wasted in a presentation. Explaining points on a slide, providing conclusions that should be drawn from information on a slide, and talking about how the information on the slide bolsters your central idea and main points is a much more valuable use of time.

8. *Use blank slides to hide your presentation.* One rule, which we discuss later, is that visual aids should not be visible when you are not referencing them. PowerPoint seemingly makes this difficult because you do not want to turn the projector on and off during the presentation. However, you can easily insert blank slides between slides with content, so that a blank background is being displayed when you are not specifically referencing slides. Of course, these blank slides do not "count" toward the one- to two-slides-per-minute rule.

9. *Practice, practice, practice.* This suggestion is certainly not new, nor will this be the last time you read it. Yet, the importance of practicing your presentation takes on new urgency with the use of PowerPoint. Besides becoming used to the technology, you will want to determine how long you will need to explain and analyze each slide that you present.

Slide-deck programs are common, easy to use, and improve speeches if used effectively. However, these types of programs have disadvantages. Slide-deck programs like PowerPoint and Keynote force the speaker and audience to adapt to a very linear progression of isolated facts, concepts, and ideas. Because each slide is separate from the others, a sense of the whole is lost and information can easily become decontextualized. Think of how often you have become lost when a teacher gets 12 or even 20 slides into a class lecture using PowerPoint! Slide-deck programs also give you very little control over the aesthetics of your presentation. You are generally limited to the templates and layouts built into the program. In essence, you are forced to adapt your presentation to the way Microsoft and Apple programmers built the software rather than using it as a tool for your own creativity.

Alternatives to Keynote and PowerPoint

Whereas PowerPoint and Keynote emphasize the linear progression of discrete ideas, **immersive design programs** *allow you to work from a broader picture down to specific ideas and back again.* Think of these types of programs as giving you a zoom button for ideas. You start with a big picture, zoom in to view details, fly from one detail to the next, and zoom out to see the big picture again. You have probably done this before, but in a different context. As a child, did you ever take a magnifying glass out to explore your yard? Using that simple tool, you were able to explore dimensions from the broad to the micro—think of how different that experience is in comparison to a slide-by-slide PowerPoint. Like a magnifying glass, holistic programs add the dimension of depth. Rather than moving through ideas, you move into ideas.

Although immersive design can be incorporated into a simple graphic or HTML page, the most widely used example of this type of program is Prezi, which can be found at Prezi.com. Prezi is a web-based program that allows you to create "Prezis," allowing

POWERPOINT, LINEAR THINKING, AND BREAKING THE MOLD

Cultural critics have long argued that traditional Western views on rhetoric have emphasized an overly linear progression of ideas during presentations. In this instance, the term *linear* is used with some negative connotation because it implies that information is given in an overly simple and predictable manner. As noted by researchers Ian Kinchin, Deesha Chadha, and Patricia Kokotalio, PowerPoint reinforces this linear approach. As they point out, the use of bullet slides in a relatively linear sequence not only presents information in a linear way, but also segments related ideas across slides. They suggest that to break out of the cultural tendency toward linear thinking teachers and presenters should use PowerPoint in more dynamic ways. For instance, rather than emphasizing bullet lists, focus on models of interactive processes, show visual images that can allow listeners to arrive at multiple meanings, and use concept mapping to show how experts would envision interrelationships among ideas. PowerPoint does much to reflect our cultural comfort with linear thinking, but can also do much to challenge those cultural norms by helping listeners approach ideas from multiple perspectives and meanings.[6]

you to present ideas using depth and simple animation. This sounds complicated, but for most computer users, Prezi is no more or less difficult to use than PowerPoint and Keynote. Students and faculty can obtain free accounts to experiment with and use Prezi. We urge you to take time to visit Prezi's website and watch several of the showcase examples to get a better idea of what they look like and how they might be used to enhance presentations. Also, if you watched the speech by Adora Svitak mentioned at the beginning of the chapter, you saw Prezi in action. Although we are still experimenting with how to best use Prezi during presentations, here are some tips to start:

1. *Think about design.* The exciting potential of Prezi is that the program allows you to make greater use of visual appeal. Communication researcher Dale Cyphert recommends that you use visual images to create a larger visual narrative supplementing your spoken words.[7] Although PowerPoint and Keynote can be adapted for this purpose, Prezi seems more up to the task. For example, you can use Prezi to create a virtual landscape of your ideas. As you walk audience members through the landscape, you narrate what they should learn from what they see. Although Prezis are programmed to follow a linear progression of images, they also easily depart from that script so that you can adapt to audience questions or highlight images out of order. In that sense, the Prezi design allows you to break away from the linear script if necessary.

2. *Emphasize the visual.* PowerPoint and Keynote are visual aids; ironically, they are most commonly used to present words to the audience. In our own experience with Prezi, we have been drawn more toward using images and less toward using bullet points and text. Take time to think about various types of visual images, sometimes enhanced with labels and other text, to emphasize ideas and help you tell a story.

3. *Think about the big picture.* Our biggest concern with slide-deck programs is that they isolate ideas. Prezi allows the holistic picture to drive presentations. For example, much like the details you discovered about your yard with the magnifying glass, you can use Prezi to embed details and other information inside a larger image related to your topic. Use that feature to help your audience remain aware of the big picture of your speech before delving into details.

Prezi and other holistic presentation programs provide an exciting alternative to PowerPoint and Keynote. Prezi is not perfect. Some aspects of Prezi's design options are limited, and the process of creating a Prezi is different from slide-deck-based programs. Some audience members even have the experience of motion sickness because of the way Prezi flies you through images. However, if you take time to learn how to effectively use Prezi, you will perhaps be able to energize your presentations in ways not possible using more traditional approaches.

Other Visual and Sensory Resources

Computers have become very popular tools for use in presentations. Now let's look at other options available to you as a presenter for incorporating visual and sensory aids. Of course, the decision of which type of visual/sensory aid to use should be determined by your specific objective for the presentation. You should avoid using the chalkboard/dry erase board or hand-drawn posters because these types of visual aids often lack professionalism and detract from your credibility as a presenter.

iConnect

Collaborating on Visuals: SlideRocket Saves the Day!

Have you ever worked on a presentation with a group of other students and experienced frustration when trying to collaborate on the PowerPoint or Keynote slides? Typically, one person has to keep the file, and if they try to share it with others to add or edit, multiple versions can exist and chaos can quickly ensue. An effective option for collaborating on visual aids, called SlideRocket (www.sliderocket.com), is similar to Keynote and PowerPoint, but it allows multiple presenters to create individual slides that are part of a group library and can then be integrated into one presentation. If you have multiple people working as part of a team, each person can be assigned to a different aspect of the presentation, including visuals, and their work can be integrated easily into the group presentation. The advantage to SlideRocket over more traditional programs is that if someone changes one of the slides they created, those updates will automatically appear in the group presentation, or any other presentations using those slides. In addition to streamlining collaborative work on presentation aids, SlideRocket also allows for easy integration of multiple-choice and text-based questions. So, during your presentation, you can ask audience members questions to which they can respond, and you can view instant results similar to "student response systems" or "clickers" that you may have used in a classroom setting. Because SlideRocket is web-based, you can use this tool on any web-enabled device, including tablets and even smartphones.

Yourself as a Visual Aid

When presenting on topics with which you have significant personal experience, you are often your best visual aid. Amelia, a public communication student, was a black belt in the martial arts and used herself and a friend to demonstrate simple self-defense techniques. Because her presentation described actions and "moves," such personal demonstration was necessary. Amelia even asked for volunteers from the audience to practice several of the techniques as the presentation progressed.

When you use yourself as a visual aid you are essentially performing a narrative of your experiences for your audience. Amelia, for example, performed a personal narrative of how she learned martial arts as she enacted different moves and behaviors for the audience. When performing your personal narrative, you do have some unique ethical obligations toward your audience. As explained by one scholar, there is a "reportability paradox" with any personal narrative: If the personal narrative is easy to tell it may lack credibility and authenticity with the audience—that is, they may not believe the narrative to be absolutely true.[8] To successfully blend reportability and credibility, speakers must carefully merge their own story or narrative with a more abstract explanation of others' experiences. So, for example, when telling about learning martial arts, Amelia may need to focus on broad principles of how one learns and interject her own experiences as affirming or counter-illustrations of those principles. This balance of particular and universal narratives should be considered whenever you use yourself as a focal point in a presentation, whether you are acting as a visual aid or simply telling a story.

Objects

Any type of physical object can be used as a visual aid. When presenting a speech on percussion in rock music, David set up a drum set to show different pieces of equipment used by modern drummers. Teachers throughout the building were particularly impressed with the solo performed for his attention-getter. Other objects could include tools, historical artifacts, equipment used to play sports, devices like a handheld computer, or water and air filters for the home.

Presenters sometimes pass objects around during their presentation. Although this approach can provide a memorable experience for audience members, you should avoid passing around valuable or breakable objects. Also, remember that objects will not reach all audience members while you are referencing them unless you have several of them. Jamie effectively used this approach during her presentation on the geology of the Flint Hills region of Kansas. She passed around several (10 or more) rocks with fossils. After showing how to identify the fossils, Jamie pointed out that the fossils provided evidence that Kansas was once a thriving seabed. Each audience member was able to see—and feel—what Jamie was talking about because she had nearly enough objects so that each audience member could look at them during her description. Be sure to check with your instructor before planning to pass around objects—some instructors discourage their use because audience members may become distracted.

Use common sense when selecting objects for use in your speech. You should never bring potentially dangerous objects like live animals or weapons. Audience members are always uncomfortable during presentations with live snakes, fencing swords, knives, and firearms. Depending on the expectations of your university, other objects might also be inappropriate. For instance, would displaying a condom be considered acceptable or unacceptable at your university or in your particular classroom? This question reinforces the importance of audience analysis—visual aids require your careful forethought about the audience and the situation.

Models

Sometimes bringing an actual object is not feasible. Very few classrooms can physically accommodate whales, nuclear submarines, cars, homes, cities, ancient ruins, or wind farms. In such cases, a model might be a better option. **Models** are *scaled representations of an actual object or objects*. You encounter models all the time in classes. Rarely do anatomy and physiology students get to play *CSI* on a cadaver; however, models of the human body commonly populate these classrooms. Do you remember the tried-and-true science fair project of building a working volcano out of clay, baking soda, food coloring, and vinegar? These types of models can be both informative and interesting for audiences.

Locating or preparing a model can take a great deal of time and models may be very expensive. Taking time to plan well in advance is therefore necessary for this approach. Even the decision to make your own model (say of a city or of a rainforest ecosystem) is very time consuming. Allow at least a week to plan and prepare such visual aids.

Audio and Video

Computers offer a number of options for finding and playing audio and video. If your classroom does not have a computer or if the computer cannot play your files, you must find other means. And, sometimes it is just more practical to avoid using PowerPoint. Taking time to prepare a PowerPoint presentation when all you want to do is show a 30-second clip from a TV show would be a poor use of your time. Of course, if you intend to use PowerPoint regardless, adding the clips to your PowerPoint file makes sense.

Audio and video can effectively spice up a presentation when used correctly. Joel gave an informative presentation on Led Zeppelin's influence on modern rock and effectively used short clips of songs to introduce unique aspects of Led Zeppelin's music. Joel took care to use only short clips and tried to play instrumental sections of songs so that he could still speak over the music. In her presentation on the formation of black holes, Kim used a short clip from a documentary by astrophysicist Stephen Hawking to explain how black holes are detected.

Avoid using more than a few clips throughout your presentation, and limit the clips to 20 or 30 seconds. Plan in advance how you intend to play the clips. If your classroom is equipped with a DVD player, make sure you know how the unit works—classrooms are often set up differently from your home entertainment system. If you intend to use audio, make sure that you can find a way of playing the clip so that everyone can easily hear the sound.

Slide Transparencies

Although slide transparencies are becoming increasingly outdated because of computer technology, professionals in fields like the sciences, history, and theater often use slides to display pictures and photographs. Other professors might have such resources available if you do not have slides of your own. Trey, a theater major, showed slides obtained from his lighting design professor to illustrate lighting concepts used during the previous theater season at his university. You should follow many of the same suggestions we provided for using PowerPoint if you intend to use slide transparencies.

Handouts

Handouts helped Sally convince audience members to attend a "Race for the Cure" walk held to raise awareness about breast cancer. She provided listeners with information about the event and also gave them the web address for the American Cancer Society. In this case, handouts helped Sally make direct appeals to the audience for their support for breast cancer prevention.

However, presenters must plan carefully when using handouts. Detailed notes and lengthy, technical information can distract listeners from the actual message. Even the act of passing materials around can be distracting for both the presenter and the listener. Hand out materials either right before or right after the presentation. Regardless of when you distribute materials, make sure that you reference them during your presentation. For instance, "The pamphlet that I passed around before identifies the location where the rally will take place," and "At the end of my presentation I will provide you with a flier identifying the web address for the American Cancer Society" are ways to effectively reference your handout while speaking. You should also consider asking one or two members of the audience to pass out the materials so you can concentrate on your presentation.

How Can You Effectively Use Visual and Sensory Aids?

Now that you can identify several options for using visual and sensory aids during your presentation, you should devote particular attention to using them effectively and ethically. This section provides tips and advice for integrating visual and sensory resources into your talk.

1. *Be audience-centered when selecting sensory aids.* When presenting a persuasive presentation on the need to eliminate "junk mail," Katherine passed around several perfume and cologne samples found in popular magazines. Several of the audience members were overwhelmed by the smells—nearly to the point of having to leave the classroom. Katherine unwittingly caused some of the annoyance that she was trying to argue persuasively against.

Remember to think like an audience member when selecting sensory aids for your presentation.

2. *Be ethical.* Using inappropriate, dangerous, or unpleasant sensory aids can detract from your message and destroy your credibility. Indeed, presenters have an ethical responsibility not to use or display dangerous, obscene, or offensive materials. Some teachers require that you get approval for all sensory resources used during your presentation. Even if your teacher does not require formal approval, a short discussion about your plans could help you avoid problems when you give your presentation.

3. *Keep the content of your sensory aid clear and relevant.* Although you are responsible for explaining all visual and sensory aids, most should be easily understood by audience members after a few moments of reflection. Remember that irrelevant sensory aids can do more to confuse, rather than enhance, your presentation.

4. *Explain your visual aids.* The time spent carefully crafting a chart or graph is wasted if you do not explain what the graph means. Presenters often fail to explain what conclusion should be drawn from visual aids. Even pictures should be explained well enough so that audience members understand what they represent. Seeing well-done visual aids and not getting appropriate explanation is frustrating for listeners.

5. *Understand that using sensory aids takes time.* Besides the significant time involved in locating and/or creating sensory aids, such resources take time during the presentation. A 7-minute presentation can easily become a 15-minute presentation with the addition of three or four detailed visual aids. Though different types of sensory aids take different amounts of time to explain, allowing at least two minutes for the presentation and explanation of sensory aids is wise.

6. *Avoid being too simple or too complex.* Sensory aids should be professional, but they should not overwhelm the message. Hand-drawn posters, lists of ideas on the chalkboard, or hastily created PowerPoint slides cause your presentation to appear unprofessional and insincere. Likewise, trying to use every feature in PowerPoint, including animated transitions and the ever-popular "machine gun" sound for list builds, may be entertaining in your dorm room at two in the morning but will do little to impress audience members. Special effects can even be annoying if used to the extreme.

7. *Strive for professionalism.* Take care to ensure that your visual aids are easy to read. If you use audio and/or video, make sure that the audio is loud enough to be heard easily and that the video is of the highest quality possible. Practicing your talk with the sensory aids is essential for giving a professional-looking presentation.

8. *Hide your visual aid when not in use.* Whether you are using an object, PowerPoint file, or even another person to help you demonstrate something, do your best to display the visual aid only when necessary. Asking your partner to step to the side of the classroom, placing the object behind the lectern, or using blank slides in PowerPoint are all ways you can accomplish this. Audience members might be tempted to look at the visual aid rather than at you if you do not remove the temptation.

How Do You Keep Your Focus on the Message?

Although an important skill, using visual and sensory aids is secondary to your main goal of communicating with audience members—such aids are simply one of many means to that end. Remember that your use of visual and sensory aids should not take the place of effective delivery, attention to organization and style, and good research. Presentation aids are just that—they supplement the message that you have already created. Your presentation is likely to be better with them than without them, but good visual aids will do little to make up for an otherwise poorly done presentation.

Rarely will your speech planning begin with a visual aid. Rather, you should follow the advice in this book and from your teacher by devoting specific attention to crafting a strong message. Once done, you should then carefully consider how images or other sensory aids can help you convey and reinforce your message. Although great visual and sensory aids can take a great deal of time to prepare, the message of your speech should still be your primary focus.

If you opt to use visual or sensory aids, make sure you use them to full advantage. Using PowerPoint to display several bullet points is less effective; using something like Prezi to enhance your narrative is more effective. Think about the design and aesthetics of your sensory aids to obtain the greatest impact. This is exactly the principle advocated by Adora Svitak in her speech on creativity mentioned at the beginning of the chapter.

For >>
REVIEW

SUMMARY HIGHLIGHTS

How Can You Benefit from Using Sensory Aids?

▶ Sensory aids are resources used by a speaker to help audience members comprehend and remember key aspects of the speaker's message. Sensory aids can target one primary sense, as with visual aids, or can target other senses such as with an audio recording, or fragrant smell.

▶ Audience members will find messages clearer when sensory aids are used, and as a result, will be able to remember the messages more easily. A theory called dual coding suggests that we learn more easily when we receive information through more than one sense.

What Type of Visual and Sensory Aids Should You Use?

▶ Modern speakers tend to rely on computer presentation software as a primary tool for using sensory aids. Using PowerPoint, Keynote or other programs you can easily integrate a variety of types if information ranging from simple quotations to advanced multimedia.

▶ Text slides simply display bullet points, quotations, definitions or other types of textual information.

▶ There are a variety of tables that can be used to summarize, compare, and contrast both numeric and text-based information.

▶ Charts and graphs are efficient and clear ways to visually display numeric data.

▶ Flowcharts are diagrams that can be used to represent hierarchies or processes.

▶ Pictures, video, and other multimedia can easily be displayed on computer projectors.

▶ There are many tips you should keep in mind when using computers to display information. Perhaps the most important tip is to practice several times with your visual aid to avoid common problems and unintended errors.

▶ In addition to using computers, there are many other types of sensory aids that you might consider for your presentation.

▶ If you are an expert at something, you very well could be your own visual aid.

▶ Depending on your topic, you might be able to bring in specific objects to show during your speech.

▶ If actual objects are not practical to bring, using a model could be a viable alternative.

▶ Audio and video can potentially add multiple senses to your sensory aid plan.

▶ Slide transparencies and handouts may be important alternatives to consider if you do not have access to a computer and computer projector.

How Can You Effectively Use Visual and Sensory Aids?

▶ Be audience-centered when selecting your sensory aids.

▶ Be ethical and do not use sensory aids that are dangerous, inappropriate, or otherwise offensive as perceived by your audience.

▶ Keep the content of your sensory aids relevant to your speech.

▶ Explain your visual and sensory aids to your audience.

▶ Practice, because using sensory aids takes time and could lengthen your speech.

▶ Avoid having sensory aids that are too simple or too complex for your audience.

▶ Make sure that your sensory aids are professional in the way they look, etc.

▶ Hide visual and sensory aids when you are not specifically using them.

How Can You Keep Your Focus on the Message?

▶ Remember that your primary emphasis should be on carefully constructing your message.

▶ Plan and design your visual aids so that they will add impact to your message, not become your message.

pop Quiz

1. The use of words accompanied by other sensory stimuli is called:
   (A) stimuli
   (B) sensory aiding
   (C) confirmatory explanation
   (D) dual coding

2. Charts used to illustrate the differences between categories are:
   (A) pie charts
   (B) line charts
   (C) bar charts
   (D) flowcharts

3. Ryan wants to show how the sale of music CDs has decreased over time. Which type of chart would best illustrate this trend?
   (A) bar chart
   (B) line chart
   (C) flowchart
   (D) pie chart

4. One tip to follow when using Microsoft PowerPoint is to:
   (A) use blank slides to hide your presentation
   (B) use as many slides as possible
   (C) use as many words, figures, or pictures on a slide as will fit
   (D) read the slides to the audience

5. How much time should you allow for the presentation and explanation of a typical visual aid?
   (A) 30 seconds
   (B) 1 minute
   (C) 1 minute and 30 seconds
   (D) 2 minutes

Answers: 1 (D); 2 (C); 3 (B); 4 (A); 5 (D)

APPLICATION EXERCISES

1. Practice creating a PowerPoint presentation that integrates pictures from the Internet. Assume that your task is to create a short, 5- to 7-minute presentation on your university for new students. Using PowerPoint and your university website, locate and integrate pictures and graphics that you could use in your presentation. Remember that the source of each graphic should be identified on the slide where it is used—you can use a text box to create the reference.

2. Using the following data, create an appropriate graph or table to use during a presentation. You may have enough data to create more than one graph or table:

    A poll conducted by a nonprofit group attempted to determine differences in people's perceptions about crime depending on whether they watched more or less than 20 hours of television per week. Those who watched more than 20 hours per week were labeled as high-rate viewers, and those who watched less than 20 hours per week were labeled low-rate viewers. Results of the poll found that 30 percent of the low-rate viewers perceived crime to be increasing, whereas 81 percent of high-rate viewers did. When broken down by age, high-rate viewers over the age of 35 had the highest percentage, believing crime to be on the rise, with 87 percent, followed by high-rate viewers under 35 with 75 percent, low-rate viewers under 35 with 32 percent, and low-rate viewers over 35 with 28 percent. When asked to comment on their perceptions, high-rate viewers typically responded with something like, "Crime is everywhere—you see it every night when you turn on the news." Low-rate viewers typically responded, "I feel safe in my neighborhood—I know everyone and we look out for each other."

3. A necessary skill when creating text slides is identifying key information so that the number of text slides can be limited. Create one or more text slides using the information covered in the sections "General Tips on Using Slide-Deck Programs" on pages 202–204, and "How Can You Effectively Use Visual and Sensory Aids" on pages 208–209.

KEY TERMS

Bar and column charts	Line charts	Sensory aids
Charts	Models	Slide-deck programs
Dual coding	Multimedia materials	Tables
Flowcharts	Pie charts	Text slide
Immersive design programs	Scatterplot	Visual aids

10

PRESENTING

You know a great deal of useful information, and you have a number of useful skills. As you learn more in college and in life, you may find yourself communicating your knowledge to your children, colleagues, clients, or community. The purpose of this chapter is to examine the primary means of communicating information to other people: the informative presentation.

TO INFORM

Do you have a grandparent, or even a parent, who lives in a nursing home? As of 2010, nearly 1.4 million Americans lived in facilities that provide care later in life.[1] In fact, so many people now make use of these facilities that national efforts are being made to provide better care at reduced costs.

In January 2012, Risa Lavizzo-Mourey, president and CEO of the Robert Wood Johnson Foundation, delivered a speech in West Orange, New Jersey, commemorating the 100th Green Home Nursing Facility built by the Green House Project. In her speech, this is how Lavizzo-Mourey described Green House Project's approach:

> The Green House model calms those fears and turns those old stereotypes upside down. They replace large, depersonalized institutional facilities with what look and feel like real homes, because they are real homes. Family room and hearth. Open kitchen and dining area. Private bedrooms and baths. Medical equipment and clinical apparatus that clutter hallways and rooms in the old kinds of nursing homes is tucked away or built into the beds. More important than anything else—Green House residents enjoy all the social and personal benefits of a small home environment without sacrificing the same full range of personal care and quality clinical services offered by large, traditional hospital-style facilities. The difference—literally—is life-giving.[2]

Lavizzo-Mourey informed her audience by describing the history of the Green House Project and explaining how it provides a different type of care at lower cost. Furthermore, she used vivid and descriptive language to help audience members understand the benefits of Green House's unique approach. When preparing to inform on complex issues, like those related to the vital topic of healthcare, maintaining an informative focus rather than a persuasive one can be challenging. This chapter will help you recognize the unique objectives of an informative speech, as well as provide several strategies for improving your presentations.

Two fundamental rhetorical principles should guide your informative presentations: *to relate the presenter to the topic* and *to relate the topic to the audience*. Although they are important to any presentation, these principles require special emphasis in informative presentations because they focus on the relationships between the presenter and the topic and the audience and the topic. Audiences are more likely to listen to a presentation if (1) they believe the speaker is well informed and connected to the topic and (2) the information is relevant to them.

What Principles Should Guide Informative Presentations?

Relate the Presenter to the Topic

The first rhetorical principle states that you, the informative presenter, must show the audience the relationship between you and your topic. What are your qualifications for speaking on the subject? How did you happen to choose this topic? Why should the audience pay particular attention to you on this issue?

In a speech delivered on March 19, 2012, at the University of Chicago, then presidential candidate Mitt Romney related himself to his topic of economic recovery in this way:

> I spent 25 years in business. My work took me to many countries. I was often struck by the enormous differences in the wealth and well-being of people living in different nations. I was interested in how nations that were so close to each other in terms of geography could be so different in terms of prosperity. Take, for example, Mexico and the United States, Israel and Egypt, Chile and Ecuador. I read books that purported to explain the disparities between such nations. Jared Diamond argued it was largely due to their physical differences, their minerals and natural resources.[3]

In this example, Romney connected his experiences in business to his topic; he also related to his audience of university students by discussing the books that helped him gain insight on his topic.

Pat Sajak, the host of *Wheel of Fortune*, gave an address at Hillsdale College in Michigan. He related the topic to himself as he noted,

> I, of course, attended Game Show University. All the great game show hosts did. I lived in the Bob Barker Dorm. I majored in vowels and consonants. It was a tough program. In the Jeopardy course, I had to know the questions instead of the answers. My thesis was called: "Lovely Parting Gifts: Are they really all that lovely?" Of course, the upside was that if I got stumped during finals, I was allowed to use 50/50 or phone a friend.[4]

The point is that you must relate the topic to yourself, so that the audience will respect and apply the information you communicate. Are you giving a presentation about wind farms in central Iowa? Let the audience know that you grew up in that area. Are you giving a presentation on the National Parks Service? If you are a student at San Antonio College, you might connect yourself to your topic by talking about knowledge you have of the ProRanger Law Enforcement partnership with the Parks Service. Are you giving a presentation on the path to U.S. citizenship? At Cal State Northridge, you might share your experience with Project S.H.I.N.E., which links college students with older immigrants and refugees who hope to learn English and become U.S. citizens. Finding ways to talk about direct experience or personal knowledge is the best approach for connecting yourself to your topic.

Relate the Topic to the Audience

The second rhetorical principle of informative presentations is to relate the topic to the audience early in the presentation to ensure their interest and understanding. Again, you must be explicit: specifically tell listeners how the topic relates to them.

Remember, too, that many topics may be very difficult to justify to an audience. An informative presentation on taxes is lost on an audience that pays none. An informative presentation on the farming of genetically modified food could be lost on an urban audience. Analyze your audience to find out how interested they may be in your proposed topic.

This example demonstrates the rhetorical principle of relating the topic to the audience:

> All of us still live in the shadow of the Korean War, with its heroism for sure, but with even more sacrifices and tragedies. A few miles away from here, near the monument to Abraham Lincoln, is the Korean War Veterans Memorial. We have all been there. Even if we visited in hot July, we could feel the American soldiers shivering in their ponchos as a cold Korean day turns to a colder night.[5]

In this speech, a U.S. State Department Foreign Service Minister used vivid language, something you learned about in Chapter 8, to connect the audience to his topic of the Korean War. Notice how his use of vivid language is designed to take audience members' thoughts to the Korean War monument, and then even to battlefields of a distant time.

Audience members want to have some reason to be personally invested in a speech. Finding common ground between the speaker and the audience or the audience and the topic are both effective rhetorical approaches for helping the audience build that investment. The most important question you should begin with for your speech is, "Why should my audience care about this?" If you can answer that question effectively during your speech, the audience will give you full attention. Failing to answer that question will have the opposite effect!

What Are the Purposes of Informative Presentations?

An **informative presentation** is *one that increases an audience's knowledge about a subject or that helps the audience learn more about an issue or idea.* Four purposes of informative presentations are (1) to create information hunger, (2) to help the audience understand the information, (3) to help the audience remember the information, and (4) to help the audience apply that information. These purposes are often interrelated. If you do a good job of helping the audience understand, you will likely also create information hunger, help them better apply the information, and so on.

Create Information Hunger

The first purpose of informative presentations is to *generate a desire for information*—to create **information hunger**. Audiences, like students, are not always receptive to new information. You have observed teachers who were skilled at inspiring your interest in poetry, advanced algebra, chemistry, or physical education. You will have an opportunity to demonstrate whether you are as skilled at communicating information to an audience of classmates.

What are some strategies for creating information hunger? Among the many possibilities are these: arouse audience curiosity, pose a puzzling question for which your presentation is an answer, and provide an explanation for an issue that has confused people.

Arouse Audience Curiosity

A useful strategy for creating information hunger is to arouse audience curiosity about your topic. Consider this speech titled "Competitive Sports: Don't Take Me Out to the Ballgame."

It is a warm, sunny day out on the baseball field. You, playing shortstop, decide to taunt the upcoming batter with such comments as, "Easy out," "This one can't hit," "He runs like a girl," and so on. All of a sudden, there is commotion in the stands. The game is called to a halt as a fistfight in the stands ends with your father in critical condition. Seems the father of the "easy out" started calling you names, and it all spun out of control. Something like this would never happen though, would it? Unfortunately, this is becoming an all-too-common scenario in the area of Little League and high school sports.

In this example, the speaker arouses curiosity by using a detailed example. Narratives and examples are effective strategies for arousing curiosity, particularly if they are based on your own personal experience. Because of their desire to learn more about you, your story might draw them into the speech. However, if your topic or story is too bizarre or disconnected from your actual topic, the audience could lose interest or become distracted. For example, you should not wear a strange costume, behave in a weird manner, or present yourself in a way that is completely out of the ordinary.

Pose a Puzzling Question

One student, Ramona Anderson, induced information hunger this way:

> Have you read your "Mountain Dew" bottle? Your "Diet Pepsi" bottle? Your "Classic Coke" can? If you take the time to read your bottle or can, you will find an interesting message, sometimes in distinctive red print. That message says: "Phenylketonurics: Contains Phenylalanine." Is this a message to aliens who dwell among us? Have you ever personally met a "phenylketonuric"? Today you are going to find out what this label means and why you should read the warning. My presentation is entitled "The Phenylketonurics among Us."[6]

The presenter posed a puzzling question about this mysterious word and its cryptic message. You can start an informative presentation by thinking of other puzzling questions that emerge in everyday life: Who are Sarbanes and Oxley? What is "smart medicine"? What common food is processed with benzene and other chemical solvents? Be sure that your question is truly puzzling and not trite or mundane.

Explain a Confusing Issue

A number of controversies receive considerable news coverage without much explanation of the issues: lots of smoke and fire but little light. For example, how many people really understand what a stem cell is? Why is stem cell research controversial? Who supports stem cell research and who opposes it?

If you can locate controversy and confusion in issues like smokers' rights, privacy concerns, and immigration policies, you have found yourself the topic for an informative presentation. Remember, however, that you are trying to explain an issue—to bring light, not heat and smoke. Your purpose is *informative*, not persuasive.

"A number of controversies receive considerable news coverage without much explanation of the issues."

In the following example, Stephen Coan, CEO of the Sea Research Foundation, explained multiple ways in which the oceans are critical to the economy:

> I need hardly tell you that water is essential to our existence, and that its health is critically important to our health. The health of our oceans and water environments is also critical to our economic well-being in staggering terms. Allow me to provide three examples. First, tourism is the second largest contributor to America's G.D.P., and 85 percent of that tourism is focused on our coastal regions. Last year, the deep water horizon event devastated the tourism economies of four states. Second, deep water ports and major river systems are vital economic engines for our nation. The Mississippi River alone is the highway for more than 470 million tons of commodities annually in just its lower half. That translates into $6 billion in annual revenues and some 30,000 jobs. When a river like the Mississippi is shut down due to flooding, or navigational hazards, including growth of non-native plants or algae blooms, it wreaks havoc. Third, we humans

consume over 100 million tons of food from aquatic environments every year. This translates into 18% of our protein intake. When fish stocks are threatened, and they are, a major source of food is in jeopardy leading to rising poverty and hunger.[7]

In this example, Coan's discussion of potentially intricate relationships between the oceans and the economy were clear and easy to follow. The clear rationale provided for his speech is an effective way to create information hunger for the audience.

Help the Audience Understand the Information

The second general purpose of informative presentations is to increase the ways in which the audience can respond to the world. The kind of knowledge we possess affects our perception of the world. A poet can look at a boulevard of trees and write about her vision in a way that conveys nature's beauty to others. A botanist can determine the species of the trees, whether their leaves are pinnate or palmate, and whether the plants are healthy, rare, or unusual. A chemist can note that sulfur dioxide in the air is affecting the trees and estimate how long they can withstand the ravages of pollution. A knowledgeable person may be able to respond to the trees in all these ways. Acquiring more information provides us with a wider variety of ways to respond to the world around us.

Whether the audience is interested in the topic before you present may be less important than the interest they demonstrate after the presentation. Your audience analysis here should help you find out how much the individuals already know about a subject, so you do not bore the informed or overwhelm the ignorant. Narrow the topic so you can discuss an appropriate amount of material in the allotted time. Finally, apply your own knowledge to the task to simplify and clarify the topic.

How can you encourage the audience to understand your topic? Here are some ideas:

1. Remember that *audiences probably understand main ideas and generalizations better than specific facts and details*. Make certain that you state explicitly, or even repeat, the main ideas and generalizations in your informative presentation. Limit yourself to two to three main points.

2. Remember that *audiences are more likely to understand simple words and concrete ideas than complex words and abstract ideas*.[8] Review the content of your informative presentation to discover simpler, more concrete ways of stating the same ideas.

3. Remember that *early remarks about how the presentation will meet the audience's needs can create anticipation and increase the chances that the audience will listen and understand*.[9] In your introduction, be very explicit about how the topic is related to the audience members. Unless your presentation is related to their needs, they may choose not to listen.

4. Remember that *audience members' overt participation increases their understanding*. You can learn by listening and you can learn by doing, but you learn the most—and so will your audience—by both listening and doing.[10] Determine how to encourage your listeners' involvement in your presentation by having them raise hands, stand up, answer a question, comment in a critique, or state an

opinion. One community member, speaking to potential donors, began her talk by asking if the members of the audience had eaten that day and if they would have a place to sleep that night. All of the audience members raised their hands. She then told them that 1 out of 12 people in their community had neither eaten all day nor had a home in which to sleep. Some pitfalls can occur when you involve the audience by asking them for overt participation. First, their reaction or participation might not be what you have in mind. Second, they might take more time to respond than you had intended. Third, the audience could become unruly when they are given an opportunity to talk or move around. Be aware of these potential consequences if you decide to encourage overt participation.

These four suggestions are powerful. If you observe your best teachers, you will notice that they regularly use these techniques in their lectures.

Help the Audience Remember the Information

The third general purpose of informative presentations is to help the audience remember important points in your presentation. How can you get listeners to retain important information?

One method is to *reveal to the audience members specifically what you want them to learn from your presentation*. A presenter can tell you about the physiology of long-distance cycling and let you guess what is important until you flounder and eventually forget everything you heard. However, if the presenter announces at the outset, "I want you to remember the three measures of athletic performance: peak use of oxygen, power at peak in watts, and average power during a 4- to 6-hour ride," you know what to focus on as you listen. Similarly, a student presenter at West Virginia University might say, "After this presentation, I will ask you to explain the two primary goals of the West Virginia Energy Express, a service program supported by AmeriCorps." Audiences tend to remember more about an informative presentation if the presenter tells them specifically at the outset what they should remember.

The announcement of the topic typically occurs in the introduction of the speech but may not be one of the first things you state. Some topics encourage you to announce them later. For example, if one of your classmates states, "I want to teach you how to knit," he or she might immediately lose the bulk of the audience. By luring them into the topic before telling them what they are expected to learn, the speaker might stir more audience interest. Rather than announcing the topic right away, the student could hold up some attractive products that are the finished result of knitting and ask something like, "Would you like to own this? Would you like to give it as a present to your spouse or a family member?"

A student decided to give her informative presentation on the welfare system as viewed from a single mother's perspective. Although she regularly shared information about being a mother and had shown her classmates photos of her children, she knew that most of them did not realize that she had taken advantage of some features of public assistance in the past. She also felt that the other students probably had little experience with welfare. To be sure that the audience would focus on her specific purpose, she stated in her introduction, "At the end of my presentation, I want you to be able to identify three qualifications to apply for assistance."

A second method of encouraging an audience to remember (and one also closely tied to arousing audience interest) is to indicate clearly in the informative presentation which ideas are **main ideas**, *generalizations to be remembered*, and which are **subordinate ideas**, *details to support the generalizations*. In preparing for examinations many students highlight important points in their textbooks and notebooks with a highlighter pen. You can use the same method in preparing your informative presentation. Highlight the important parts and convey their importance by telling the audience, "You will want to remember this point . . . ," "My second main point is . . . ," or "The critical thing to remember in doing this is . . . ."

"Audiences expect important parts of the presentation to receive more than temporary attention."

A third method that encourages an audience to retain important information includes repeating an idea two or three times during the presentation. Audiences expect important parts of the presentation to receive more than temporary attention. They expect important points to be repeated. An early study demonstrated that if you repeat important matters either infrequently (only one time) or too often (four repetitions or more), your audience will be less likely to recall your information.[11] While excessive repetition can be distracting, a second or third restatement can help the audience understand. You can and should follow the popular saying: "Tell 'em what you are going to tell 'em; tell 'em; and then tell 'em what you told 'em." Research supports the idea that this is a good recipe for the introduction, body, and conclusion of a presentation. A woman who works for the USDA in one of its labs talked to a neighborhood group about vertical farming. Because the concept was new to many in the group, she explained exactly what it was in her introduction, in her body, and in her conclusion. The audience usually expects a summary ending that recaps the main points.[12]

A fourth method of encouraging retention is the nonverbal practice of *pausing or using a physical gesture to indicate the importance of the information*. Just as repetition signals an audience that the thought was important, a dramatic pause or silence just before an important statement is also effective. Similarly, your own energy level signals importance, so using bodily movement, gesture, or facial expression can grab audience attention and underline a statement's importance.

Most of the research on retention has been conducted with middle-class, white audiences. If you are speaking to a more diverse audience, you may want to accept these conclusions cautiously. Some audiences appear to appreciate and learn more from several repetitions. Others may expect a great deal of enthusiasm.[13] How can you ensure that your audience will retain the information that you provide them? In the classroom, listen to your instructors' and classmates' informative presentations and try to determine what these presenters do to inspire you to remember the information. In other settings where you are likely to speak, similarly observe the successful informative presenters you encounter. Then see whether you can apply the same techniques in your own informative presentations.

Help the Audience Apply the Information

The fourth general purpose of informative presentations is to encourage the audience to use or apply the information. An effective presenter determines methods of encouraging the audience to use information quickly. Sometimes the presenter can even determine ways that the audience can use the information during the presentation.

Komiko Tanaka, who was delivering an informative presentation on community engagement, for example, had everyone in class write down where they had engaged in service learning. Another student presenter had classmates taste several kinds of local cheeses. Amanda Agogino invited everyone to go online to determine how many articles they could find about accountability in corporate governance. These presenters were encouraging the audience to apply the information from their presentations to ensure that they retained the information.

Why should the informative presenter encourage the audience to use the information as quickly as possible? One reason is that *information applied immediately is remembered longer.* A second reason is that *an action tried once under supervision is more likely to be tried again later.* To think of informative presentations as simply putting an idea into people's heads, of increasing the amount they know about a topic, is easy. However, the presenter has no concrete indication that increased information has been imparted except by observing the audience's behavior.

Therefore, the informative presenter may seek a **behavioral response** from the audience, *an overt indication of understanding.* What behavioral response should the informative presenter seek? Many kinds are possible. You can provoke behavioral response by inviting the audience to talk to others about the topic, to actually apply the information, or to answer questions orally or in writing. If the audience cannot answer a question on the topic before your presentation but can do so afterward, you have effected a behavioral response in your audience. One woman spoke to a lunch group at her place of work on behavioral changes they could make in "going green." She gave all of them coupons worth 15 percent off at a large department store that features products made of recycled materials and urged them to shop there after work.

The four general purposes of informative presentations, then, are to create a desire for information in the audience, to increase audience understanding of the topic, to encourage the audience to remember the information, and to invite the audience to apply the information as quickly as possible. Next, we will examine five learning principles that relate to informative presentations.

CULTURAL DIFFERENCES IN LEARNING PROCESSES

When speaking to inform, your primary objective is to help audience members learn information in such a way that they are able to think differently about something or take some action as a result of your speech. Should you assume that the way people best learn information is common from one culture to the next? Researchers from a university in Istanbul explored how people from Western and East Asian cultures process information and concluded that there are indeed cultural differences.[14] When presented with two visual diagrams that are identical except for small changes in color, East Asian individuals were slightly slower in identifying the color switch than were Westerners. Based on their experiments, the authors conclude that East Asian individuals may have a preference for, or greater ability in attending to the holistic representation, whereas Westerners perhaps have a preference for, or greater ability to focus attention on specific elements. If these conclusions are accurate, you may want to adapt how you talk about visual aids depending on the type of audience to which you are speaking. Western audiences might more quickly attend to a focal point in a visual, whereas East Asian audiences might start their attention with a more holistic understanding. Either type of audience could require adaptation on your part.

How Can You Help People Learn Information?

Informative speaking is a type of teaching. Listening to informative presentations is a type of learning. If you expect an audience to understand your informative presentation and apply the knowledge gained, you must treat the presentation as an occasion when teaching and learning both occur. Because you, as an informative presenter, are inviting the audience to learn, you can apply these five **principles of learning** to your presentation: *building on the known, using humor and wit, using sensory aids, organizing your information, and rewarding your listeners.*

Build on the Known

One principle of learning is that people tend to build on what they already know and to accept ideas that are consonant with what they already know. An informative presentation, by definition, is an attempt to add to what the audience already knows. If the audience is to accept the new information, it must be related to information and ideas they already hold.

Let us say that you are going to give an informative presentation on the topic of depression. What do most people in your audience know about the subject? Do they know the possible causes of depression? Do they know the difference between "feeling down" or "feeling blue" and clinical depression?[15] Do they know the symptoms of depression? Do they know the profiles of the most likely victims? Your mission is to start with audience analysis to determine what the audience knows, and then build on that knowledge with new information, presented so the material will be attractive to a variety of learning styles.

Use Humor and Wit

A second principle of learning to observe in informative speaking is to use humor and wit. **Humor** is *the ability to perceive and express that which is amusing or comical*, while **wit** is *the ability to perceive and express humorously the relationship or similarity between seemingly incongruous or disparate things*. Informative presentations make the information palatable to the audience. Notice that it does not have to be funny. The principle is "Use humor and wit." Wit and humor are the clever ways you make the information attractive to the audience. Wit and humor are the packaging of the content.

Often, language choices help add wit and vigor to your presentation. Darris Snelling, who was delivering a potentially boring presentation on "TV and Your Child," enlivened his presentation with witty language by beginning this way:

> Within ten years almost everybody in this room will be married with a young one in the crib and another on the way. Do you want your youngster to start babbling with the words sex, violence, and crime or do you want him to say Mommy, Daddy, and pepperoni, like most normal kids?[16]

The presenter hit the audience with the unexpected. The words were witty, and they made his presentation more interesting.

Being humorous or witty is challenging, particularly for inexperienced speakers. However, if done well, these rhetorical devices can help audience members remember information. Research exploring connections between emotion and learning shows that when we experience positive emotions, like humor, those experiences act like mental bookmarks.[17] Because the information we are learning is connected to a distinct emotional experience, we can more easily retain and use that information. Of course, these emotional bookmarks are not limited to instances where humor and wit are involved. Any emotional connection between you and your audience can act in the same way. One word of caution, however: if the emotional content of your speech is too intense, a boomerang effect can occur and audience members could selectively choose to tune you out.

Humor and wit must be used judiciously. Some topics are not appropriate for humor. In addition, simply adding a joke at the beginning of a talk is often misguided. As you can determine from the example just provided, humor and wit must be appropriate for the topic and must be integrated into the entire message.

Use Sensory Aids

A third principle of learning is to *communicate your message in more than one way, because members of the audience have different learning styles*. Verbal/linguistic individuals learn best by listening or reading, while visual/spatial individuals learn best by seeing. Effective informative presenters recognize that different people have varied learning styles. Therefore, such presenters try to communicate their messages in a variety of ways to meet diverse learning styles. In Chapter 9, you learned various ways in which visual aids could be used to help audience members learn information more easily.

If giving a presentation discussing a difficult to understand topic, consider using a diagram or organizational chart; if presenting statistics, use a chart, graph, or table. Visual aids help take complex things and make them clearer for the audience. In fact, well-crafted sensory aids can become the centerpiece of your message for an informative speech.

Organize to Optimize Learning

A fourth principle of learning is to *organize your information for easier understanding.* Organization of a presentation is more than outlining. Outlining is simply creating the skeleton of a presentation. In an informative presentation, consider other organizational possibilities. How can you try to create a proper setting for learning to take place? Where in the presentation should you reveal what you expect the audience to remember? Do you place your most important information early or late in the presentation?

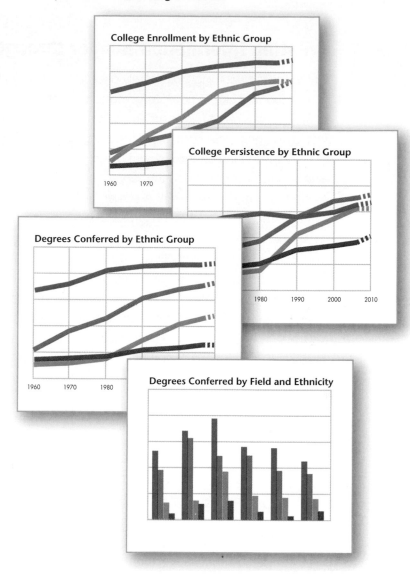

No hard-and-fast answers to these questions exist, but research does hint at some good suggestions:[18]

1. *When do you create a setting for learning?* The earlier you create an atmosphere for learning, the better. Make clear to audience members early in the presentation exactly what you want them to learn from your presentation.

2. *Where should important information be placed?* Audiences remember information placed early and late in the presentation, so avoid placing your most important material in the middle of your presentation. **Primacy**, or *placing the information or main point early in the presentation*, seems to work better in presentations on controversial issues, on topics that the audience cares little about, and on topics highly familiar to the audience. **Recency**, or *placing the information or main point late in your presentation*, seems to work best when audience members care about the issue, when the issue is moderately unfamiliar, and when the topic is not terribly interesting.[19]

3. *How do you indicate which parts of your presentation are main points and which are supporting?* In writing, subordination is easy to indicate by levels of headings, but people listening to a presentation cannot necessarily visualize

Creating Information Hunger through Information Graphics

Our world is becoming increasingly data driven. Being able to find clever ways to display data is an important skill to have. **Information graphics**, or infographics for short, *use principles of graphic design to represent and display complex data or information*. For instance, how would you graphically display information during an informative speech about where members of Congress stand on the issue of global warming? Would you simply show a list of all U.S. Representatives and divide the list by "those who believe" or "those who don't believe" in the existence of global warming? A similar, but perhaps more effective approach, would be to use symbols to represent each congressperson. You could place each symbol into one of those categories to visually represent the division of Congress on this particular issue. You could even color code the symbols to indicate Democrats and Republicans, providing yet another aspect of the data you are presenting.

There are a variety of tools available for you to create your own infographics. Check out the website infogr.am, for example, to create interactive infographics for your presentations. Your visual aids will look more professional and your audience will be more engaged in your message. For more advanced training in infographics, check the course listings in the graphic design or visual communication departments at your college or university.

the structure of your presentation, which is why the effective informative presenter indicates early in the presentation what is going to be covered. This forecast sets up the audience's expectations; they will know what you are going to talk about and for approximately how long. Similarly, as you proceed through your presentation, you may wish to signal your progress by indicating where you are in your organization through transitions. Among organizational indicators are signposts and transitions like the following:

"My second point is . . ."

"Now that I have carefully explained a brief history of democracy in the United States, I will describe how democracy is viewed today."

"This story about what happened to me in Iraq will illustrate my point about obeying orders."

In each case, the presenter is signaling whether the next item is a main point in the presentation or supporting evidence for it. Chapter 6 has a thorough explanation of transitions and signposts.

Reward Your Listeners

A fifth principle of learning is that *audiences are more likely to respond to information that is rewarding for them*. **Reward** in this context means *a psychological or physical reinforcement to increase an audience's response to information given in a presentation*. One of the audience's concerns about an informative presentation is "What's in it for me?" The effective informative presenter answers this question not only in the introduction, where the need for the information is formally explained, but also throughout the presentation. By the time a presenter is in the middle of the presentation, the audience may have forgotten much of the earlier motivating information presented, so the presenter continually needs to remind the audience how the information meets its needs.

One student began her presentation by saying the following:

> Did you realize that, at this very moment, each and every one of you could be and probably is suffering from America's most widespread ailment? It is not a sexually transmitted disease, cancer, or heart disease, but a problem that is commonly ignored by most Americans—the problem of being overweight.

As the presenter proceeded through her information on nutrition, she kept reassuring the audience members that they could overcome the problem in part by knowing which foods to eat and which to avoid. The audience benefited by learning the names of foods that could improve or weaken health.

In this example, the reinforcement was in the form of readily usable information that the audience could apply. But rewards come in many forms. A presenter can use other, more psychological, forms of reward. "Do you want to be among the few who know what a credit card interest rate is?" The presenter who confidentially tells you about credit card debt is doing you a service because you will no longer be ignorant and you will be in the special category of those few "in the know."

Figure 10.1 reviews the five principles of learning. Informative speaking employs a number of skills that help make a presentation effective. In informative speaking, those skills include defining, describing, explaining, and demonstrating. Let us explore for a moment how these skills work in an informative presentation.

1. Build on the known.
2. Use humor or wit.
3. Use sensory aids.
4. Organize your information.
5. Reward your listeners.

Figure 10.1   **Principles of learning.**

Now that you understand the various purposes of informative speaking, as well as some principles to follow so that your audience members can more easily learn information, you should learn specific skills to accomplish those outcomes. Informative speaking generally revolves around these key elements: defining, describing, explaining, and demonstrating.

What Skills Are Important for Informative Speaking?

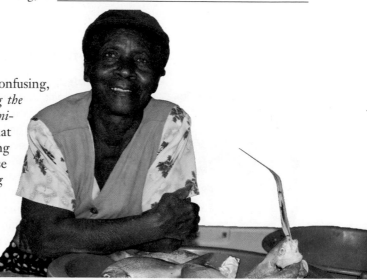

Defining in an Informative Presentation

In Chapter 8, you learned that to be clear, you must define confusing, technical, or otherwise complex terms. **Defining** is *revealing the presenter's intended meaning of a term, especially if the term is technical, scientific, controversial, or not commonly used.* Know, too, that definitions cannot substitute for other appropriate supporting materials. Presenters often forget to define the terms they use in a presentation. If a presenter has mentioned something called a "plah-see-bow" about five times without telling you what a *placebo* is, the presentation has failed to inform.

Three ways to define a word are to reveal its denotation, its connotations, and its etymology. We discussed these different ways of defining a word in Chapter 8, and you may wish to review this material. For instance, the word *patois* (etymology: French, pronounced paa-TWAA) is used for the type of language spoken by many black inhabitants of the island of Jamaica in the Caribbean. A patois is a rare language that does not extend far, in this case not even to the other Caribbean islands, and that is more of a spoken than a written tongue because its grammar and spelling are not standardized. It is an informal sort of language. That would be the word's dictionary meaning, or denotation. The connotative meanings of *patois* are more complex because few white people can speak this form of language, which has been mastered by so many black people in Jamaica. Connotatively, patois suggests a private language, such as the one limited pretty much to black people who grew up in Jamaica. It may be considered less worthy because it is informal, but because it is rich in local associations and folklore, it may also be admired by outsiders.

Because the general function of an informative speech is to help audience members become more familiar and aware of your topic, defining key terms is important. If terminology remains unclear at the conclusion of your speech, your audience members' ability to remember and use information from your speech will likely be very small.

Describing in an Informative Presentation

Describing *evokes the meaning of a person, a place, an object, or an experience by telling about its size, weight, color, texture, smell, or your feelings about it.* Describing relies on your abilities to use precise, accurate, specific, and concrete language to make your audience vividly aware.

Mark DuPont, in a public speaking class at Iowa State University, told his classmates about his hometown of Phoenix, Arizona, using the following descriptive words:

> The heat cannot be escaped. As the sun beats mercilessly on the endless lines of automobiles, waves of shimmering heat drift from the blistering pavement, creating an atmosphere of an oven and making the minutes drag into eternity. The wide avenues only increase the sense of oppression and crowding as lane after lane clogs with rumbling cars and trucks. Drivers who have escaped the heat of the sun in their air-conditioned cars are overwhelmed by the heat of frustration as they do battle with stoplights and autos that have expired in the August sun. Valiant pedestrians wade through the heat, pausing only to wipe from their foreheads the sweat that stings their eyes and blurs their vision. It is the afternoon rush hour at its peak, Phoenix, Arizona, at its fiercest. The crawl of automobiles seems without end as thousands of people seek out their homes in the sweltering desert city.[20]

Explaining in an Informative Presentation

Explaining in an informative presentation *reveals how something works, why something occurred, or how something should be evaluated.* You may explain a social, political, or economic issue; you may explain a historical event; you may explain a variety of theories, principles, or laws; or you may explain by offering a critical appraisal of art, literature, music, drama, film, or presentations. A wide collection of topics may be included in "explaining." You should notice that in offering your opinion, you may come very close to attempting to persuade the audience.

Do you or your classmates understand the concept of minimal tillage in organic farming, how margarine is made, the rules of NASCAR, the qualities of Chateau Malmaison Moulis wine, a shahtoosh "ring shawl," or a lyric opera? The informative presenter takes lesser known words and concepts and renders them understandable to the audience through explanation, as illustrated in the excerpt from a speech provided here:

OEM & Non-OEM: Only Your Body Shop Knows for Sure

Until my daughter wrecked her Honda Civic, I had never thought about what happens at the body shop. In fact, a chance remark alerted me to the problem. When I stopped by the body shop after two weeks to see when the vehicle would be repaired, the person behind the desk said, "This one's going to take a while. Your insurer is recommending non-OEM parts." Probably he was not supposed to make the statement because the repair of that one relatively inexpensive car became a nightmare that revealed the cracks in our insurance/auto repair system.

OEM is an acronym for "original equipment manufacturer." A body shop that completely repairs a Honda with OEM parts is using Honda-made parts to replace the damaged portions of your vehicle. The body shop's other choices are to use salvage, that is, parts borrowed from wrecked vehicles or, more likely, to use non-OEM parts or imitations. The imitation parts could be as good as OEM parts, but they could also be misshapen, inferior in quality, and likely to peel and rust quickly. According to the February 1999 *Consumer Reports*, imitation door shells can be installed without the guard beams, with weak welds on guard beams, or with guard beams made with weaker steel. Similarly, knockoff hoods sometimes come without the crumple initiators that keep sheet metal from crashing straight through the windshield. Imitation bumpers can compromise your headlights, radiator, and even your airbags.

Demonstrating in an Informative Presentation

Demonstrating is *showing the audience an object, a person, or a place; showing the audience how something works; showing the audience how to do something; or showing the audience why something occurs.* For example, a student who was informing her classmates about the features of cellular phones used five cellular telephones as models. To help her classmates see the features on these relatively small objects, she used an instrument called an ELMO (electronic monitor, or document camera, or digital video projector), which magnified each phone on the screen in front of the classroom. Describing can accompany demonstrating.

Consider demonstrating those ideas, concepts, or processes that are too complex to be understood through words alone. In addition, Chapter 9 discussed a wide range of visual and sensory aids that can be used to enhance your demonstration including models, pictures, and even yourself.

Some examples of presentations that invite a demonstration are

- A presentation by a health worker on how to inject insulin.
- A presentation by a civil engineering student on alternate transportation systems.
- A presentation by a library science major about how to find more and better information on the Internet.
- A presentation by a mechanic showing us how to save money on oil changes.

Consider whether your topic would lend itself to demonstration.

Tainted or unethical information is a common problem with people who are less than honest.

What are some guidelines for positive ethical choices in an informative presentation?

What Are the Ethical Principles of Informative Speaking?

1. *Be sure of the quality of your information.*
- Is the information accurate, verifiable, consistent, and placed in context?
- Have you avoided implying that you have information that you lack?
- Have you avoided making up facts or distorting information?

2. *Exercise caution when using the words of others.*
- Have you accurately quoted the sources you have cited?
- If you have summarized the words of others, have you paraphrased accurately?
- Did you cite the sources of your material?
- Have you avoided plagiarism?
- Have you kept all quotations in proper context?

3. *Be careful not to mislead your audience.*
- Have you told the audience of your association with the groups whose work or purpose may be relevant to the topic?
- Have you been honest?
- Did you present all the relevant information?
- Did you tell your audience whether your examples were hypothetical or real?
- Have you used appropriate language to clarify words or concepts that the audience does not understand?

4. *Be sure the audience needs the information.*
- Are you providing the audience with new information?
- Are you allowing the audience free choice to accept or reject the information you provide?
- Can your audience make reasoned choices about the importance and accuracy of the information you are providing?

5. *Be sure that the information you are providing is in the best interests of the audience members.*
- Are you providing information that helps rather than hurts the audience?
- Are you providing information that advances rather than harms our culture and society?

Figure 10.2   **A checklist for the informative speech.**

Ethical choices affect your creddibility as a source. If you are not ethical—if you bend the truth, twist the evidence, and shape information for selfish purposes—then your audience will find you less credible in the presentations that you give in the furture. So be careful, accurate, and honest. The checklist in Figure 10.2 will help you accomplish this.

An Example of an Informative Presentation

Organic Food

Every time I walk into the grocery store I face a dilemma. Most people worry about simple things like Coke versus Pepsi, or vanilla versus chocolate ice cream. Me, I worry about one thing: conventional versus organic. You see, I grew up on a small farm in Southeast Ohio, and on that farm we practiced organic farming. My dad probably wouldn't say that he started farming organically because of a philosophical reason. We have just over 150 acres, which does not make it cost effective to invest in expensive equipment or chemicals. So, growing organic foods allows us to compete against big conventional farming operations in the central United States. This morning you will learn what organic food is as well as some tips for buying organic food. This is important information for you because it will help you make

Using contrasts of familiar objects can arouse curiosity.

Previous experience is used to establish credibility.

The central idea and primary points should be clearly previewed for the audience.

smarter choices at the grocery store—choices that could improve your health and the environment.

First, you should understand what the label "organic" means when you run across it in the grocery store. The organic food market is growing rapidly as a segment of the grocery market. Kathleen Welton, writing in the February 2010 issue of the *Library Journal*, noted that global sales of organic foods exceeded $23 billion in 2008. The United States is a big part of that global organic trend. Dr. Maureen Callahan, a CNN medical correspondent, explained that in America alone, consumers spent $28 million on organic foods in 2008. Why do you think so many consumers are jumping on the organic food cart? An agronomist writing in the *Allelopathy Journal* explained that many consumers recognize the benefits of organic food in comparison to conventional food that may have been treated with pesticides and other chemicals. Also, many assume that using fewer chemicals is a benefit to the environment.

So what exactly does *organic* mean?

The term, as used regarding food, is actually governed through the Organic Foods Production Act. The act oversees national standards for the production, handling, and processing of all foods labeled as organic. Being certified as an organic producer or processor requires certification from the United States Department of Agriculture. Mary Gold, of the Alternative Farming Systems Information Center, explained that the act authorizes food to be labeled as organic when it "promotes and enhances biodiversity, biological cycles, and soil biological diversity." Further, organic foods are based on minimal use of off-farm inputs like fertilizers, pesticides, and growth hormones. The primary objective of the act is to "optimize the health and productivity of interdependent communities of soil life, plants, animals, and people." Of course, the organic label from the FDA is not without some controversy. A 2009 *Washington Post* article explained that lobbyists have successfully gotten the FDA to relax standards on what counts as organic. For example, baby formulas now contain a synthetic additive that reportedly boosts brain power, grated organic cheese contains wood starch to prevent clumping, and organic beer can contain nonorganic hops. The article explains that aggressive lobbying, driven by significant consumer demand, has led the FDA to become more lax in its labeling standards.

There are several reasons why farmers might choose to grow organic crops. First, the organic label tells consumers that farming practices were enacted to minimize the risk of chemical contamination. Although no food can be guaranteed to be 100 percent free of chemicals, organic foods are far more likely to be pure than are conventional foods. This certification provides a certain degree of protection to the consumer, and farmers who are organically certified are proud of the fact that their food is safer for the consumer. Second, farmers have a strong connection to the land. Although organic farming is more labor intensive, harsh chemicals are not used on the land, and more natural crop rotation methods are used to maintain enriched soil. Also, animals produced for consumption by organic farmers are treated humanely. On my family farm we focus a lot of energy on rotating crops through various tracts of land so that the soil can replenish its nutrients. By doing this we do not have to rely on chemical pest controls and fertilizers to maintain production.

In this picture you can see how we use terrace farming. Terrace farming allows us to plant small crops on the side of hills, but the terraces prevent topsoil from washing down the hill. The different terraces also make it easy for us to rotate crops. Terrace farming does not necessarily mean that the resulting crops are organic, but this practice is better for the environment and makes organic farming easier to accomplish.

So now you know that organic food is more natural and probably has benefits for your health. How can you be smart when buying organic food? That's what I'll talk about next.

Because organic food can cost more than conventionally produced food, you need to be smart when shopping. First, look for the organic label. Remember that federal standards must be met before that label can be used. Also, there are no such standards for seafood of any type, so don't bother looking for organic fish, shrimp, or crabs. The vegetable and fruit aisle is where you can make your biggest impact. For fruits and veggies where you eat the outside, like celery and lettuce, buying organic is important. For other foods like bananas and melons, you will discard the outside, so the benefits of buying organic may be less significant. Also, make sure you plan before you even get to the store. If you plan menus that maximize use of organic foods, especially menus that emphasize fruits and vegetables, you can do a better job of transitioning your food consumption away from conventional food where chemicals are more common.

The Sustainable Table website provides some other smart suggestions for consumers. That website encourages us to think local and seasonal. Although not all local food will be certified as organic, because it is local it requires less transportation and does not have to be stored for long periods of time. Both of these factors mean that fewer chemicals are necessary. A trip to your local farmers' market can allow you to buy organic without having to pay higher prices. Also, buying seasonal food means that you are less likely to be eating chemically preserved food. A strawberry in January obviously requires transportation and preservation, whereas most areas of the country have plentiful local strawberries in May and June. As you can guess, the January strawberry is far more likely to be grown and preserved through use of chemicals.

If you make the decision to start buying organic food, there are several possible outcomes. According to an article in *Men's Health* by Maria Rodale, there are many potential health benefits from eating organic foods, including a reduced risk of diabetes, cancer, heart disease, and even autism among children. Margot Pollans, a recognized advocate for sustainable agriculture, also noted that the production of organic food reduces significantly the amount of pollution generated by agriculture. But, there are also drawbacks. Because it is so labor intensive and takes longer in terms of production time, organic food does cost more. A consumer could see prices for organic food that are a few cents or even a few dollars higher than those for their conventionally grown cousins.

As college students we don't often think about what we buy. For some of us a quick trip through the grocery aisles with ramen, pop, and chips defines a typical

When using explanation to analyze complex issues, using signposts (spoken numbers) can help maintain clarity. Visual aids can be integrated to provide even greater clarity of the points.

When integrating visual aids or other supplements, take care to provide adequate explanation so that audience members understand what they are seeing or experiencing.

Transitions between main points should attempt to summarize the previous point and preview the next. This transition could be even clearer if an explicit signpost were added. How could you word that signpost to make it effective?

As your presentation unfolds, help audience members understand how they can use your information in their own lives.

For important information, find stylistic wordings like "local and seasonal" that can be easily remembered by your audience.

Concrete examples can be used to illustrate principles you are trying to teach your audience.

Rhetorical style includes the use of ornamental language. Style can be as simple as using alliteration, as with "conventionally grown cousins."

Close the speech with a clear summary and reminder of how audience members can use the information you provided.

trip to the store. But many of us do try to buy healthier foods. Today you have learned what the "organic" label means on foods as well as some tips for buying organic foods. Organic food could cost a little more, but the benefits, both in terms of your own health and for the environment, could be significant. Regardless of whether you buy all organic or, like many of us, mix things up, you should understand what the label means so that you can make smarter decisions the next time you are at the grocery store.

For REVIEW >>

SUMMARY HIGHLIGHTS

What Principles Should Guide Informative Presentations?

► Your presentation should relate the presenter to the topic.

► State explicitly your qualifications to speak on the topic.

► State what led you to select this topic.

► Your presentation should relate the topic to the audience.

► Be explicit in explaining how your topic relates to your audience.

► Help audience members understand why they should be personally invested in the topic.

What Are the Purposes of Informative Presentations?

► Informative presentations should increase audience members' knowledge about a subject or help them learn more about an issue or idea.

► One purpose of informative speaking is to create information hunger, which is a desire for information. The following strategies can be used to create information hunger:
  • Arousing audience curiosity can be effectively accomplished through using a detailed example or narrative.
  • Posing a puzzling question to audience members will make them want to learn the answer.
  • By explaining a confusing issue the audience might find clarity and want to learn more.

► Another purpose for informative speeches is to help the audience understand information. You can accomplish this by focusing on main ideas and concrete ideas, having a clear introduction, and focusing on audience participation.

► Helping the audience remember information is to be explicit in what you want audience members to remember, and then clearly signposting those points as your speech progresses. Using repetition and pauses are also effective strategies.

► If you want to help the audience apply information, you must identify a clear behavioral objective for the audience members and focus your speech on helping them accomplish that objective.

How Can You Help People Learn Information?

► Build on the known by connecting your topic to things that audience members are already familiar with.

► Use humor and wit so that audience members can connect specific emotional experiences with your message.

► Use sensory and visual aids to help clarify your message and allow audience members to encode information using more than one sense.

► Organize your presentation to optimize learning and be explicit as you explain your organization to audience members through transitions and signposts.

► Reward your listeners by psychologically or physically rewarding them for giving attention to your message.

What Skills Are Important for Informative Speaking?

► Defining involves the speaker providing explicit intended meaning to terms, especially those that are technical, scientific, controversial, or not commonly known.

► When describing, you evoke images of a person, place, object, or experience by providing concrete ways of visualizing the topic.

► When you explain, you reveal how something works, why something occurred, or how something should be evaluated.

► Demonstrating is when you present the audience with an object, a person, or a place, show them how to do something, or illustrate why some action occurs.

What Are the Ethical Principles of Informative Speaking?

► Be sure of the quality of your information.

► Exercise caution when using the words of others.

► Be careful not to mislead your audience.

► Be sure the audience needs the information.

► Be sure the information you are providing is in the best interest of the audience.

pop Quiz

1. Which of the following is *not* a purpose of an informative presentation?
   (A) to shape or influence the audience's thoughts
   (B) to create information hunger
   (C) to help the audience understand information
   (D) to help the audience apply the information

2. Subordinate ideas should be used:
   (A) as generalizations to be remembered
   (B) to link main points
   (C) to introduce ideas
   (D) as details to support generalizations

3. You can help the audience remember information from your speech by:
   (A) letting them guess what you want them to learn
   (B) repeating an important idea two or three times
   (C) avoiding pauses during your speech
   (D) allowing them to differentiate between main and subordinate ideas

4. It is not advisable to place important information:
   (A) at the beginning of the speech
   (B) late in the speech
   (C) in the middle of the speech
   (D) at the end of the speech

5. One guideline to follow to make ethical choices in your presentation is:
   (A) to make up facts if it will make your presentation more interesting
   (B) to cite only important sources
   (C) to present only information that supports your argument
   (D) to keep quotations in the proper context

Answers: 1 (A); 2 (D); 3 (B); 4 (C); 5 (D)

APPLICATION EXERCISES

1. Think of three topics about which you could give a three-minute presentation to inform. List the topics in the blanks at the left. In the blanks at the right, explain how you relate to the topic in ways that might increase your credibility with the audience.

	Topics	Your Relationship to Topic
A.	_____	_____
B.	_____	_____
C.	_____	_____

KEY TERMS

Behavioral response

Defining

Demonstrating

Describing

Explaining

Humor

Information graphics

Information hunger

Informative presentation

Main ideas

Primacy

Principles of learning

Recency

Reward

Subordinate ideas

Wit

11

PRESENTING PERSUASIVE

This chapter defines, analyzes, and helps you create effective persuasive messages. Much of our communication attempts to influence others. At the same time, we are often the targets of persuasion. This chapter shows how to influence others through ethically responsible persuasive presentations.

MESSAGES

Recent political discourse surrounding the 2012 presidential election highlighted a host of ethical issues surrounding persuasion. For example, many pundits spoke to the influence of money on the outcome of the election. Political ads that aired during the campaign presented statements by the candidates and their surrogates that many believe may have misrepresented the actions and views of their opponents. Evidence used to support claims made during debates, speeches, and interviews, and in political ads was likewise called into question. Unfortunately, many observant citizens, regardless of their party affiliations, were led to unflattering conclusions about the ethics that guided candidates in their use of persuasive messages.

The Annenberg Public Policy Center at the University of Pennsylvania created Factcheck.org to help counsel citizens on many of these questions. Analysts and writers for that organization dissect statements by candidates and provide nonpartisan analysis of the accuracy behind claims. If you spend even a few seconds on the organization's website, you will find that inaccuracy (and misrepresentation) is a truly bipartisan issue.

The Factcheck organization highlights both the power and perils of persuasion. Being persuasive is a skill that must be cultivated, but one that must also be guided by strong ethical principles. Do you have an opinion about climate change? Can you make an argument and support it in a way that convinces others to adopt your position? Can you achieve these outcomes in ways that demonstrate high ethical standards? This chapter will show you how to influence others through ethically responsible persuasive presentations.

How Are Persuasive Presentations Unique?

Persuasion permeates our culture so much that we may not be fully aware of its presence. In our democratic society, we send and receive persuasive messages on crucial issues such as war and peace, taxation and representation, freedoms and restrictions, and readiness for natural disasters and terrorist attacks. These messages can be crucial to the formation of our beliefs as well as to our overall well-being. For all of these reasons, it is important that we understand what makes persuasive presentations unique from other types of presentations.

Informative Presentation		Persuasive Presentation
To increase knowledge	**Presenter's Intent**	To change mind or action
To define, describe, explain, or demonstrate	**Purpose of Message**	To shape, reinforce, or change audience response
To know more than before, to advance what is known	**Listener's Response**	To feel or think differently, to behave or act differently, to critically evaluate the message
To willingly gain new knowledge	**Audience Choice**	To change behavior by choice, to be inspired or convinced by credibility, logic, or emotion

Figure 11.1   **How do informative and persuasive presentations differ?**

What Are Persuasive Presentations?

Persuasive presentations are *messages that influence an audience's choices by changing their responses toward an idea, issue, concept, or product.* Let's compare informative and persuasive presentations. Perhaps no message is completely informative or completely persuasive. In fact, persuading and informing may work to reinforce each other, but generally we are trying to do one or the other. Figure 11.1 highlights the characteristics of the two kinds of presentations.

What Are the Elements of Persuasion?

As demonstrated in Figure 11.1, informative and persuasive presentations differ along various dimensions. Because persuasive presentations are designed to influence others, they require more advanced building blocks to achieve that purpose. Aristotle, one of the first people to theorize about persuasive communication, suggested that persuasive messages rest on three elements, or what he called proofs: ethos, pathos, and logos.

When using **ethos**, you attempt to persuade others by *using an authoritative and trustworthy source in support of the message.* Many commercial advertisements attempt to use celebrities, acting as opinion leaders, to support a particular product or service. When you do research for your presentation, you hope to find high-quality sources that you can integrate into your speech; this may be a different tactic than using a celebrity, but in the eyes of the audience, it might work much the same. Of course, you are also a source of ethos. Your credibility, or lack thereof, as a speaker, can dramatically influence how audience members perceive your message.

Pathos involves *appealing to the audience members' feelings.* Using narrative as a type of supporting material is a highly effective way to

bring pathos into your presentation because narratives typically contain natural emotion. Your delivery can also have an important impact on pathos, as perceived by the audience. A sincere delivery of a story will have much more impact than reading that same story in a monotone voice.

Finally, **logos** involves the *use of evidence and reasoning to advance a claim*. A **claim** is simply a conclusion of what the persuader would have the listener believe or do that invites proof or evidence. Dillard and Marshall say that, based on the research, "We may assert with confidence that including evidence in a persuasive message will enhance the performance of the appeal."[1] You will learn more about how to use evidence and reasoning later in the chapter.

What Questions Do Persuasive Presentations Address?

The content of persuasive presentations often revolves around three distinct kinds of questions: questions of fact, questions of value, and questions of policy.

The **question of fact** *means that the persuasive presentation seeks to uncover the truth based on fact*. That truth or fact could be the question of who did something or how or why something was done. For instance, Donald Trump presents a question of fact when he repeatedly questions whether President Obama was born in the United States. People on either side of this controversy have attempted to use evidence to persuade others how to interpret a factual question.

The **question of value** *raises issues about goodness and badness, right and wrong, enlightenment and ignorance*. In the immigration debate, there often arises a question of value surrounding the topic of deportation of illegal immigrants. Is it justifiable to deport individuals who have lived in the United States for several years? Is it ethical to deport parents of children who are born in the United States? How should we balance public policy concerns with moral concerns surrounding human dignity? Do our laws become degraded if the issue of illegal immigration is ignored? All of these questions, in some way, probe values pertinent to the immigration debate.

The **question of policy** *enters the realm of rules, regulations, and laws*. Should state governments be obligated to provide more support for all levels of public education? Would reducing government spending, raising taxes, or a combination of the two serve the nation's future best? Should the United States set a date for troops to be withdrawn from Afghanistan? Should the United States be more active in stopping the Iranian nuclear program? Each of these questions ask audience members to consider the merits of one or more courses of action and to weigh in on what action, if any, should be taken.

How Does Persuasion Affect You?

We use persuasion in everything from sales to civic engagement and public deliberation. Persuasive messages bombard you every day. You are the target of many persuasive attempts. Your mobile phone becomes a mobile billboard where you receive texts, IMs, tweets, and pop-ups urging you to spend money on a product or service. Every few minutes, television and radio programs are interrupted by commercials. Magazines, newspapers, and websites are filled with flashy ads designed to sell you products. Even political parties and charities vie for your loyalty and contributions. Today, more than ever, the traditional media, the Internet, and people compete for your attention, your money, your time, your vote, or your membership. In other words, they all use persuasion.

You are also a producer of persuasive messages. Think about groups and organizations that you belong to. Have you been asked to raise money? Do you support any causes? Even some classes take on projects that are intended to support particular groups or organizations. Those experiences likely require you to engage in persuasion. Perhaps you are even a member of student government or a residence hall association. In those groups, you deliberate on issues of policy. Stated simply, we are all members of many organizations. In nearly every case, our membership implies that we act as an advocate for that organization—or the constituents we represent through that organization. Our membership thus requires that we actively persuade others if we intend to do our jobs effectively.

Your production of persuasive messages is not limited to public arenas involving organizations and groups. In our interpersonal relationships, we often use persuasion to try and influence those with whom we have relationships. A clear example of a simple but important persuasive message is a marriage proposal. But, thinking backward from the actual proposal message, think of all the persuasive messages that must happen for a romantic relationship to develop and grow. You may not think of love as an arena for persuasion, but in reality, romantic relationships involve ongoing negotiations of mutual influence. Persuasion is just as important in our personal lives as it is in our public lives.

Your satisfaction in both private and public spheres is dependent, in great part, on your ability to be both a competent consumer and a producer of persuasive messages. You do not want to be deceived by others. You want to be able to understand why you feel compelled to respond to certain messages while you disregard others. You also want to learn to be an effective and ethical persuader. Our democratic and capitalist culture thrives on persuasion. This chapter helps you to understand and to practice persuasive presentations.

What Are the Types of Persuasive Presentations?

The three types of persuasive speeches are the speech to convince, the speech to inspire, and the speech of action.

The **speech to convince** is *a persuasive presentation delivered with the intent of influencing listeners' beliefs or attitudes.* You may wish, for example, to convince the audience that prayer should be allowed in public schools, that people of the same sex should be allowed to marry, or that tuition should be lower. The issues for which you attempt to convince listeners can be national or local in scope. Although convincing your audience that the United States should have taken greater steps to protect civilians in Syria is very different from trying to convince them that all-terrain vehicles should be banned from local hiking trails, they both attempt to convince the audience of a particular viewpoint; one happens to be in regard to an international issue and the other a purely local issue. The speech to convince encourages listeners to adopt a stronger position on an issue; they are not required to act. You ask your audience only to rethink their beliefs and attitudes. Of course, there could be an implicit assumption that some individuals may decide to act on their convictions, but such action is not explicitly called for in the presentation.

The **speech to inspire** is a persuasive speech, although we do not often think about inspirational messages as persuasive. *The purpose of this speech is to influence listeners' feelings or motivations.* Speeches of inspiration often occur at ceremonial

events. They occur in places of worship, at graduations and rallies, and on holidays or at special events.

Can you inspire your fellow students to join some cause in which you believe? Can you inspire them to be more spiritual, less materialistic, more focused on learning, or more concerned about their own community? Consider opportunities to deliver speeches of inspiration at your place of work. Can you inspire people to create a union, to donate money to a fellow worker who has lost a child, or to adopt more environmentally friendly practices? To experience examples of inspirational speaking, watch live or televised ministers, see politicians during campaigns, or observe individuals who believe strongly about issues related to natural resources, education, gun ownership, health care, and other causes.

The **speech of action** is *a persuasive speech given for the purpose of influencing listeners' behaviors and actions.* The foundation of the speech of action is the changing of listeners' beliefs and attitudes—and then asking them to act on those new beliefs. In many respects, the speech of action combines elements from the other two types of speeches. By first convincing audience members to think differently about a particular issue and then motivating them to act on those beliefs, the call to action in this type of speech is more persuasive. In fact, many of the previous examples in this section could easily be turned into a call to act. After inspiring other students to join a particular organization, you might ask them to commit to attending a meeting later in the day. If you convince audience members that the United States should be tougher on the Syrian government, you might ask them to sign a petition or engage in an email campaign.

How Does Online Persuasion Work?

Social media have become a pervasive platform for persuasion. Most of these messages are relatively obvious. Advertisements on the side of your Facebook timeline, tweets from companies pushing products, and large banner ads on popular websites are all attempts to persuade you to buy some product or service. But what about the more subtle persuasive messages you may encounter? When you search for a product online, how often do you read product reviews? For many products, these word-of-mouth messages actually outpace formal advertising in scope and potentially have far greater impact on consumer behavior. A recent study explored characteristics of word-of-mouth product reviews that had the greatest influence on behavior.[2] That study identified the following characteristics of persuasive reviews:

- They are clearly written and easy to read.
- They explain how the product was used.
- They include supporting evidence (like pictures, detailed examples, etc.) to support their claims.
- They provide positive information about the product.

The last finding is intriguing. How might we account for the appeal of positive messaging in product reviews? One explanation might be that people who read product reviews have already made up their minds to purchase a product and are thus seeking information that affirms their decision rather than contradicts it. As you will learn in a few pages, consistency persuades!

This text emphasizes "vital" topics, because public discussion of important issues—civic engagement—is at the very heart of democracy. However, effective engagement in public discourse requires careful planning. Most experienced speakers will tell you that persuasive presentations are the most difficult to plan and execute. This section helps you understand strategies you should use in planning your speech, beginning with understanding how audiences react to persuasive messages.

How Should You Plan a Persuasive Message?

What Should You Know about Your Audience?

One fundamental task in persuasion is **audience analysis**, *learning enough about the listeners so that you can predict their probable response to your message.*[3] Effective audience analysis begins with the recognition that every persuasive appeal has a relationship dimension. The **relationship** is *how the audience feels about you as the presenter before, during, and after the persuasive appeal.* You are more likely to persuade if your audience respects you, if your integrity remains intact during your presentation, and if the audience continues to believe you are credible after they have heard your presentation. If you are too pushy about achieving your purpose, your audience might resist you more and like you less.

Your audience analysis should also help you predict various ways in which audience members might respond to your message. In general, people react in the following ways to persuasive appeals: critically, defensively, or compliantly.[4]

- A **critical response** *occurs when the audience focuses on the arguments, the quality of the evidence, and the truth or accuracy of the message.* In your pitch for a state-of-the-art playground for physically challenged children, your audience may want to know how many children you are talking about.
- A **defensive response** *occurs when the audience fends off the persuader's message to protect existing beliefs, attitudes, and values.* A person proposing a tax increase for the new library may fare poorly with an audience committed to no new taxes.
- A **compliance response** *occurs when the audience does what is socially acceptable,* including pleasing the persuader or pleasing the other listeners. An audience may go along with the idea of working with Habitat for Humanity just because they do not want to appear insensitive toward their underprivileged neighbors. They comply to be socially acceptable.

Finally, you should recognize that audiences will respond to persuasive messages depending on how motivated they are to process the message.[5] Unmotivated audiences who do not take the topic seriously will respond superficially to the message. For instance, students tend to be motivated more by classes in their major than in courses they are required to complete. On the other hand, motivated audiences who see the topic as important to them will respond by being thoughtful, analytical, and understanding. Audiences who choose to hear a presentation are more likely to respond to a message meaningfully. Audiences will also respond favorably to timely messages. Students about to graduate, for example, will pay more attention to a presentation on job-gaining interview skills than to a presentation on retirement possibilities. A group of people in their 70s will be more interested in ideal places to live, in healthy diets that are linked to longevity, and in Social Security benefits. Consider whether your topic is timely.

What Persuasive Strategies Should You Use?

If you have ever played a competitive sport, or engaged in a competitive game of any type—checkers, chess, cards, etc.—you know that strategy is important. There are many strategies for winning a contest. So too, in persuasion, there are many strategies, or principles, that can help you convince, inspire, or gain action from your audience.

Consistency Persuades

The first principle of persuasion is that **consistency persuades**, meaning that *audiences are more likely to change their behavior if the suggested change is consistent with their present beliefs, attitudes, and values.* Risk takers like daring ideas. Competitive people are most likely to enter still other competitions. People who understand that "we are a nation of immigrants" are unlikely to discourage immigrants from moving into their neighborhood.

"Risk takers like daring ideas."

People tend to be relatively consistent. Past behavior is a good predictor of future behavior. The public speaker uses this notion of consistency by linking persuasive proposals to past consistencies. The presenter promotes change by showing how the promoted activity is consistent with the audience's past behavior. If you are speaking to a group of Republican delegates, you may show how your ideas are consistent with the rights to own guns, to discourage abortions, or to toughen immigration legislation.

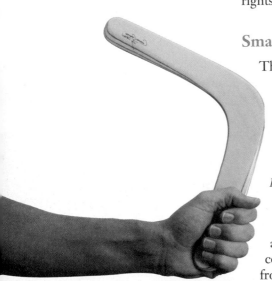

Small, Gradual Changes Persuade

The second principle of persuasion is that small, gradual changes persuade, meaning that audiences are more likely to alter their behavior if the suggested change will require small, gradual changes rather than major, abrupt changes. A common error of beginning persuaders is that they ask for too much change too soon for too little reason. Hostile audiences especially are resistant to persuaders who ask for too much too fast. They might respond with a **boomerang effect** in which *the audience likes the presenter and the proposal even less after the presentation.*

In a presentation on energy conservation, you probably would not succeed with an appeal that bluntly says "Quit using so much electricity." However, a presenter who begins with "Shut off the lights in rooms you are not using" and moves to "turn off the hot water heater when you are gone for more than a couple of days" will more likely accomplish her goal of gaining behavioral change from the audience.

Benefits Persuade

The third principle of persuasion is that *audiences are more likely to change their behavior if the suggested change will benefit them more than it will cost them.* We consider **cost-benefit analysis**, for example, every time we buy something: "Do I want this new jacket even though it means I must spend $150 plus tax? The benefits are that I will be warm and look nice. The cost is that I will not be able to replace my broken cell phone." The persuader frequently demonstrates to the audience that the benefits are worth the cost.

How can you use cost-benefit analysis in your classroom speech? Consider the costs to the audience of doing as you ask. What are the costs in money, time, commitment, energy, skill, or talent? Consider one of the most common requests in student speeches: communicate with your representative or senator about an issue. Many student speakers make that request without considering the probability that nobody in class has ever communicated with a senator or representative. Even if the speaker includes an email address, the message writing will take a commitment of time and effort. Few students are willing to pay those costs. On the other hand, if the speaker comes to class with a letter already composed

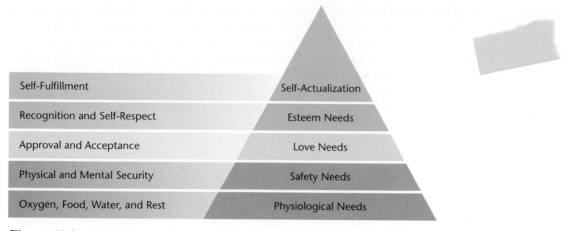

Figure 11.2   **Maslow's pyramid: A hierarchy of needs.**
Can a persuader target particular human needs?

SOURCE: "Maslow's Hierarchy of Needs," from *Motivation and Personality*, 3rd ed., by Abraham H. Maslow, Robert D. Frager, and James Fadiman, © 1987. Adapted by permission of Pearson Education, Inc., Upper Saddle River, NJ.

and simply asks for signatures from the class, then the cost is a few seconds of time, and the speaker is more likely to gain audience cooperation. Whenever you deliver a persuasive speech, consider the costs and how you can reduce them so the audience will feel the costs are worth the proposed benefits.

Need Fulfillment Persuades

The fourth principle of persuasion is that audiences are more likely to change their behavior if the change meets their needs. Psychology scholar Abraham Maslow created an often-cited **hierarchy of needs**,[6] *a pyramid that builds from basic physiological needs like the need for oxygen all the way up to self-actualization needs—the realization of one's highest potential* (see Figure 11.2). Maslow's pyramid makes sense. As a human being, you do need all the items in the hierarchy, though many people never get very far above the second level shown in the figure, and few people think they have achieved complete self-actualization.

Maslow's pyramid is a useful resource for your persuasive presentations. You can analyze your audience for specific needs. Do they need money? Jobs? Day care for their children or elders? Do they need help in dealing with government bureaucracies?

NEEDS DIFFER BETWEEN CULTURES

Scholars who study differences between cultures have suggested that Eastern and Western cultures have very different orientations toward communication. Traditionally, it was thought that Western cultures, like the United States, tended to be oriented toward individualism, whereas Eastern cultures tended to be collectivist in orientations. As the names suggest, individualistic cultures were thought to emphasize the autonomy of the individual, while collectivist cultures tend to emphasize the importance of the whole culture. More recent research, however, suggests that this difference may not be valid. In fact, both Western and Eastern cultures demonstrate collectivist orientations.[7] Western cultures tend to place an emphasis on obedience to group norms, adherence to authority, and subordinating individual interests to the interests of the group—think peer pressure. Eastern cultures, on the other hand, tend to emphasize positive relationships, mutual cooperation and interdependence, and mutual concern among members of a community. How might this knowledge assist you in persuading? When focusing on needs fulfillment for your audience, you may want to provide nuanced messages tapping into these collectivist tendencies, taking into account whether your audience is primarily Western or Eastern. An American audience might be particularly receptive to arguments based on community norms, whereas Eastern audiences might be more persuaded by the potential of positive relationships.

cultural NOTE

Do they need better living conditions? Do they need to learn how to study, how to handle children, or how to live with spouses? Using careful audience analysis, you can determine which needs are most salient to the lives of your audience members and generate appeals targeting those needs. For example, if your audience members tend to be oriented toward love needs, you could tell a narrative about two people establishing a relationship; if your audience is more oriented toward safety needs, you might develop an argument explaining why acting a certain way could diminish or enhance their physical or mental security. In essence, this strategy emphasizes appeals that are directly relevant to the needs of your audience.

Carefully Planned Messages Persuade

Once you have a purpose to direct you and an audience to listen to you, you need to create a message that uses content most likely to gain acceptance. According to current communication research, an effective persuasive presenter will:

- Employ message production *to create, organize, and deliver a persuasive appeal.*[8]
- Use the content of a persuasive appeal *to fulfill the primary goal of influencing the listeners in a predetermined direction.* The content often consists of reasons to adopt the presenter's ideas plus supporting material to bolster those claims.
- Be **explicit**, which is *the extent to which the persuader makes his or her intentions clear in the message.*[9] Often the presenter clarifies intentions at the outset—"After this presentation, you will want a new water supply for our city." But, if the audience is likely to resist the presenter's purpose, then the presenter is better off preparing the audience with reasons first and making the purpose explicit later, after the audience is more prepared—"Now I think you see the need for an expensive cleanup at the site of the old fertilizer plant."
- Use **argument**, which is *the extent to which the presenter furnishes reasons for the message claims.*[10] The skillful presenter finds the reasons, the evidence, and the proof that the audience is most likely to accept.
- Use **testimonial evidence**, *the words of a cited source in support of the presenter's claims*, to produce attitude change and improve source credibility. By quoting sources whom the audience respects, the presenter will increase acceptance.
- Use **complete arguments**, *including all the parts—claims and supporting material— to produce attitude change and improve source credibility.* Audiences want to know as fully as possible why they should comply.
- *Use* **specific numbers**—*percentages, actual numbers, averages, and ranges of numbers*—rather than saying "many," "most," or some other vague quantity. Being specific increases message effectiveness and improves source credibility.[11]

Now that you know more about what communication research reveals about audiences and messages, you are ready to consider particular strategies a presenter can use to influence an audience.

How Can Critical Thinking and Reasoning Improve Your Message?

Earlier you learned that logos, one of Aristotle's three elements of persuasion, is the use of evidence and reasoning to make a claim. This section focuses on logos in more detail by helping you recognize two approaches to reasoning, some ways in which you can use evidence to engage in reasoning, and how to avoid fallacies in your arguments.

Approaches to Reasoning

When you think carefully about the nuances and points surrounding an issue in an attempt to draw a conclusion, you are using reasoning. In other words, the step that occurs when you jump from a piece of information to a conclusion is reasoning in action. There are two general forms of reasoning that guide many of our conclusions: inductive and deductive.

Using Inductive Reasoning

The kind of reasoning in which the *persuader amasses a series of particular instances to draw an inference* is known as **inductive reasoning**. The critical thinker knows that inductive reasoning is vulnerable in several ways. One weakness is that such reasoning involves an "inferential leap" in which the presenter jumps from a series of particulars to some generalization about them—for example, the local banks have unfair rates for students. But were those particulars typical? Were they biased in that the presenter selected them while ignoring others that did not support his claim? Inductive reasoning is like circumstantial evidence: Nobody saw the killing, but the alleged killer's fingerprints were on the gun, witnesses saw him at the scene at the time of the crime, and the killer was having an affair with the victim's estranged sister. We make an "inferential leap" to the probable notion that this particular person did the killing.

Using Deductive Reasoning

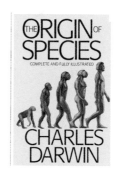

Deductive reasoning *occurs when the presenter bases her claim on some premise that is generally affirmed by the audience.* Notice that the premise does not have to be true; it just has to be widely believed by the audience. So, in some communities, the major premise that "God created human beings" becomes the widely believed idea that moves easily to "human beings inhabit Kansas" (minor premise) and "therefore, God created the people of Kansas" (conclusion). This kind of reasoning is known as deductive reasoning, an argument based on a major premise, a minor premise, and a conclusion.

Like inductive reasoning, the critical thinker can attack deductive reasoning by questioning the premises on which the persuader bases the argument. Look how significantly the argument changes if the major premise is "Evolution resulted in human beings." Whether persuaders use inductive or deductive arguments, they have plenty of generalizations and premises to argue about: life begins at conception, Social Security should be privatized, wealthy people should receive tax cuts, and retirement age should be raised.

Using Reasoning to Make Arguments

Reasoning is a process through which you think critically about an idea—you might think of it as the internal dialogue that leads to your own viewpoint. When you express that reasoning to others, you must communicate your thought process through arguments. In this section, you will learn about six types of arguments that help you express your reasoning on a topic.[12]

Arguments about Causes and Effects

Determining cause can be a challenging task. For example, convincing people that smoking cigarettes is a causal factor in lung cancer took decades. For many social and political issues, the causes and effects can be complex and various. Nonetheless, we use reasoning from cause often and in two directions: Sometimes we move from cause to effect and sometimes we move from effect to cause.

Reasoning from cause means that you have to demonstrate, for example, that the leading cause of lung

cancer is cigarette smoking, not air pollution, not water contamination, not genetics. Causal reasoning also means that the cause must be solidly linked to the effect; otherwise, what we are witnessing would simply be correlation, two unrelated things occurring together. Scientists can prove that smoking cigarettes and getting lung cancer are solidly linked even if every smoker does not die of cigarette use. When reasoning from cause, you must be very careful to (1) show that the cause and effect are solidly linked and (2) eliminate other possible causes. Similarly, when starting with effect, you must be careful to (1) demonstrate that effect and cause are solidly linked and (2) eliminate other possible effects.

Arguments from Sign

He has a backpack and he is walking across campus; therefore, he must be a student. We reason from sign every day, but we may not be correct in doing so: The guy with the backpack turns out to be an unemployed mechanic looking for a warm building for refuge. The best way to reason from sign is to reason from multiple signs. Multiple signs ordinarily lead to a better conclusion. So, if he looks like a student, acts like a student, walks across campus like a student, and appears to know others on campus, the chances are better that he is a student. In reasoning from sign, you need a sufficient number of reliable signs that do not contradict each other and are not accidental or coincidental.

"We reason from sign every day, but we may not be correct in doing so."

Arguments from Generalization

This approach to arguing involves the assumption that a particular example, story, or piece of data can be generalized to a larger population. If you tell an example of what happened to one of your friends who traveled to a foreign country on a study abroad trip, would that example have relevance to other students? If you reason from generalization, the answer (you hope!) is yes. Your reasoning is, essentially, that what happened in one case is likely to be true in other similar cases. This form of argument is inductive in nature and applies best with examples, narratives, and statistical information based on a sample of data.

Arguments from Parallel Case

Similar to reasoning from generalization, an argument from parallel case starts by using an example, story, or piece of data. Through your reasoning, you establish that what was true in the example you presented would also be true of another, similar case. For example, an emerging trend in higher education is to create massively open online courses (MOOCs). These courses are free and designed to attract students who want to improve their skills or knowledge in specific areas. A course in artificial intelligence offered in this format attracted more than 160,000 students from around the world.[13] In making an argument from parallel case, you might assume that if a public speaking class were offered in the same way, an equal number of students might enroll. The key to this type of argument is showing the correspondence between the example of what has already happened and then drawing the parallel to some future example.

Arguments from Analogy

An argument from analogy involves comparing two things that are not obviously similar. For instance, you might argue that public discourse between Democrats and Republicans seems like two ships passing in the night because they cannot find common ground. The analogy between political discourse and the visual image of ships passing unseen by one another helps frame an argument about how to view such discourse. What makes this an analogy, rather than a parallel case, is that the two things being compared are very different from one another. This type of argument is advanced through clear analysis of the analogy. You must carefully describe the two things being compared and must also carefully analyze the implications of the comparison—what should the audience conclude from comparing the two things?

Arguments from Classification

The final type of argument is classification. This type of argument begins with data substantiating a generalization about a class of persons, objects, events, or ideas. For instance, you might begin this type of argument with data about the importance of the free market and capitalism. You might say something like, "Our country was founded upon principles of the free market and capitalism." Then you might apply that classifying statement to a particular instance by saying, "Venture capital firms help free market forces drive productivity and innovation." The argument you are advancing classifies venture capital firms in a certain way in relation to the broad principle you described. This argument could be used as part of a persuasive speech of value trying to convince audience members that venture capital firms are beneficial to the country.

Avoid Fallacies of Reasoning

A **fallacy** is *an error in reasoning that weakens an argument*. Fallacies come in many forms, but those described here are the ones we have found public speaking students to (mis)use the most.

Name Calling.   This fallacy unfairly categorizes people by slapping a label on them. Calling someone a "liberal" may be perceived as a slam, while labeling someone a "conservative" may be perceived as a compliment. As a political candidate, would you perhaps win an election by labeling your opponent as "a liberal"? How can you avoid name calling in a presentation?

- Omit the label and refer instead to the person's record.
- Decide for yourself if an idea has merit without regard for the label.

Glittering Generality.   The technique behind the "glittering generality" is to embrace a word that symbolizes some highly positive virtue. The glittering generality invites us to accept and approve an idea without examining any evidence. For example, "We need to bring democracy to country X" is a statement that exploits our very positive attitude about our form of democracy without analyzing its appropriateness to another nation or region. The critical questions to ask are:

- Does the idea in question (transplanting democracy) have a legitimate relationship to the virtuous word (democracy)?
- Is a misguided plan (transplanting democracy) being advanced simply by linking it to a positive name?

Bandwagon Technique.   With this fallacy, the speaker encourages the listener to do something because "everyone" in the same valued group is doing it. For example, you should vote for a candidate because everyone in our congregation is doing so. The critical questions to ask are:

- What is the evidence for adopting or rejecting this idea?
- Does this idea serve or hinder my interests regardless of who else allegedly is following this idea?

Circular Reasoning.   This fallacy uses two unproven propositions to prove each other. Pit bulls should be outlawed because they are vicious animals. We know they are vicious animals because they should be outlawed.

- Avoid circular reasoning by making certain that your assumptions can be proven.

Either/Or.   This fallacy assumes that everything is binary, that every issue has two opposite positions: Either you are for me or you are against me. However, someone certainly could be fairly neutral, neither for nor against. The fact is that few issues have only two opposite points of view. Most issues have multiple positions. How do you avoid this fallacy?

- Recognize that most issues are complicated enough to have multiple points of view.

Post Hoc Fallacy.   The actual name of this fallacy is "*post hoc, ergo propter hoc,*" an expression that means "after this; therefore, because of this." Fortunately, this fallacy is easier to explain than to pronounce. For instance, I no sooner bought a new battery than my transmission failed; I met her, and my misfortunes began; and I walked under a ladder and almost immediately was splashed by a passing car. This fallacy attributes misfortunes to an event that occurred before the misfortune, even though the event did not actually cause the misfortune. You can avoid this fallacy if you are always aware of the following:

- Just because two things occur closely together in time does not mean that one caused the other.
- Realize that often things occur closely in time by accident or coincidence, not because one caused the other.

What Ethical Principles Should Guide Persuasive Speaking?

Persuasive presentations offer ample opportunities for positive purposes or for ethical mischief. Persuasive speaking can result in the advancement of a good cause or the purchase of a product you do not need, never wanted, and that you will never use. Distinguishing between ethical and unethical persuasive appeals is a challenging task for which the following guidelines apply:

1. *Be careful whom you trust.* The best-looking, smoothest-talking presenter can be a pathological deceiver, while an unattractive, inarticulate person can have your best interests in mind. Listeners need to watch whom they trust, and presenters need to provide credentials to show they are trustworthy. They need to demonstrate their source credibility.

2. *Analyze and evaluate messages for reasonableness, truth, and benefit to you and the community.* Many vendors try to convince you to buy in a hurry because rushing limits your reasoning. They do not want you to carefully consider whether the decision really makes sense. As a critical thinker, you will want messages to meet standards of reasonableness.

3. *You and your messages will be more persuasive if you have a long, positive history.* "The thing you get to lose once is your reputation." If your past invites others to trust you and your word, and if others tend to benefit from your messages as much or more than you do (that is, you do not seek compliance for selfish purposes), you will build credibility. Are you building a history that will help you or harm you when you attempt to persuade others?

4. *Always be respectful of your audience.* If you treat them as you would want to be treated, you will avoid many ethical problems.

5. *Avoid fallacies.* If you always strive to use sound reason tempered by critical thinking, then you will skillfully avoid those short circuits to reasonable thought that we know as fallacies.

See Figure 11.3 for a checklist that reviews the important features of the persuasive presentation, including the ethical dimension.

1. Have you shown how the change you are suggesting for the audience is consistent with their past behavior?

2. Have you kept your requested changes gradual so that the audience does not perceive your request as too much to ask?

3. Have you demonstrated for the audience the benefits received if they do as you request?

4. Have you shown the audience ways that your request will fulfill their needs?

5. Have you approached your suggested change gradually so the audience does not perceive that you are asking for change without sufficient preparation?

6. Have you avoided fallacies in your presentation?

7. Have you embraced the highest standards of ethics in your talk?

Figure 11.3   **Checklist for the persuasive presentation.**
What have you done on this list to help persuade your audience?

An Example of a Persuasive Presentation

Keep the Mekong Free

This is a picture of the Mekong River, on the border between Northeast Thailand and Laos. If you look to the side of the bank you will see a small pipe sticking out of the ground. This pipe is a marker for a proposed dam that will forever change the Mekong River once it is built.

This past summer I had the opportunity to visit Thailand as part of a study-abroad experience. In our program we visited two villages, one on a tributary to the Mekong where a dam had been built and one near the site of the proposed dam on the Mekong itself. In both cases, villagers explained what has happened and what could happen when dams are built.

After meeting the villagers and learning what happened after the first dam was built, I pledged to do everything possible to oppose construction of new dams on the Mekong. I hope that you will join with me in these efforts. First I'll explain why dams are used so extensively to promote economic development. Second, I will explain the scope of the proposed dam projects on the Mekong River. Next I will

Starting with a visual aid using rich verbal description is an effective way to raise audience curiosity and interest in your topic.

The speaker used personal experience to establish goodwill and credibility with the audience and then presented a very clear call to action.

Four main points are a lot for a shorter speech. However, some persuasive speeches may rely on more main points to clearly develop the argument(s) being presented.

describe what happens to the environment and river villages when dams are constructed, and finally I will explain how you can help.

So that you can better understand why I oppose dams on a river so far away, first let's explore why dams have been used so frequently to promote economic development.

This is an example of a well-worded transition statement with a signpost. Clear transitions better help audience members follow the speech as it develops, particularly when this many main points are used.

As a result of the Industrial Revolution, humans have increasingly looked to rivers as sources of raw material to promote economic growth. According to the World Dam Commission, there have been over 4,500 dams at least as high as a four-story building built across rivers worldwide. In fact, humans have dammed over half of the world's rivers. To put this in some perspective, the chairperson of the World Dam Commission explained in the introduction to the 2000 report the following:

These statistics are good for providing perspective on the scope of dams; however, without using a visual aid the intricacy of the explanation could become confusing. Visual aids help make statistics clearer.

> Less than 2.5% of the Earth's water is fresh water; of that, only 33% of the fresh water is in liquid form, and of that water less than 1.7% flows in streams. Why is this important? Basically, a fraction of a percent of the Earth's water flows from town to town, village to village, and country to country. Dams threaten the small amount of naturally flowing water that does exist.

Why do people create dams in the first place?

Here, the speaker uses a source from an academic journal. What more could the speaker say about the source to develop stronger credibility?

In a special issue of the *Journal of Environmental Management*, a group of researchers explained that dams have four primary purposes in terms of development: Dams can provide sources of irrigation; they can help control floods; they can create reservoirs to supply large bodies of water for domestic, industrial, and recreational uses; and dams can be used to create hydroelectric power. On the screen you can see a representation of how a hydroelectric dam works. Water from the artificial reservoir travels through the dam to rotate a turbine, which generates electricity. The river above and below the dam is altered because of the change in water flow. This last use, power generation, is the primary motivation behind most large-scale dam projects such as those on the Mekong River and its tributaries.

Notice how the reasoning develops in this paragraph. To establish the claim that dams require international scrutiny, the speaker presents several reasons why dams have impacts beyond the home country's borders.

The growth of large dams has accelerated at such a large pace that international bodies are now starting to bring greater scrutiny on the practice of damming. Most dams are international concerns because rivers typically flow across national boundaries, so the actions of one country could affect one or more countries downstream. Also, dam projects are so large that they typically always require significant funding from international sources like the World Bank or private, multinational corporations. Because dams are international in scope, the World Commission on Dams was created in 2000 to act as an independent body of academics, policy makers, and other experts who can develop international guidelines for comprehensive assessment and evaluation of existing and proposed large-scale dam projects.

This is the transition and signpost to the second point.

With this understanding of the international significance of dams, the second point explains the proposed dam projects on the Mekong River.

Here, the speaker uses technical language. Using your own knowledge or an online dictionary, what does "metric" mean and how could the speaker have been clearer?

The Mekong River is one of the world's largest rivers. According to the United Nations Environmental Program, the Mekong is between the tenth and twelfth largest river in the world, depending on which metric is used. The 4,200-kilometer Mekong stretches from Southern China south through Myanmar, Laos, Thailand, Cambodia, and empties into the South China Sea in Vietnam. Over 265 million people live in the Mekong River basin, with most living in Vietnam, Thailand, and Myanmar. Although economic development has been substantial over the last fifty years in Southeast Asia, people who live in the Mekong River basin are still among the poorest in the subcontinent, if not the world. Many are indigenous people who have lived along the river for thousands of years.

Notice how the speaker uses style (the third Canon of Rhetoric) in the form of several metaphors. Stylistic devices like these can naturally increase interest in the speech. Can you identify all of the metaphors in the first two sentences of this paragraph?

As explained in a 2007 *National Geographic* story, the threat to the river flows from growing economies, primarily in China, Thailand, and Vietnam. The massive flood of population, supercharged by a thirst for electricity, has led economic and political elites across the subcontinent to target the Mekong as a natural source for hydroelectric power and abundant natural resources. Despite the fact that dams already constructed along the Mekong and its tributaries have had significant negative impacts, as many as sixteen new dams are under construction or planned along the Mekong itself to meet the growing need for development in the region. Of course, my goal, and the goal for all of us, should be to see that those dams are never constructed.

Why should we care about the dam? After all, development is generally seen as good, right? Unfortunately, dams are not the environmentally safe alternative for cheap energy. First, dams catastrophically alter the river ecosystem. Speaking at a 2010 meeting of Southeast Asian leaders of state, Thai Prime Minister Abhisit Vejjajiva warned that the "Mekong River is being threatened by serious problems arising from both the unsustainable use of water and the effects of climate change." Based on experiences from other dams in the Mekong system, scientists have learned that large dams impact the environment in three significant ways.

Here, the speaker uses a direct quotation because the wording is powerful and the source is highly credible. Moreover, using a government source from one of the Mekong countries can add significant power to the argument that dams are not the best source for economic development.

First, when reservoirs are created, silt that normally runs down the river collects behind the dam. This not only places greater strain on the dam itself, but also chokes the ecosystem behind the dam and robs land downstream from its natural replenishment of nutrients. Second, because the riverbank downstream is not replenished with naturally flowing river silt, valuable farmland along the banks of the river will erode away and be unusable for local production of plants and vegetables. Finally, and most dramatically, the natural fisheries along the Mekong will be destroyed. According to a 2008 report issued by a Thai nongovernmental organization called ESCR, the Pak Mun Dam, constructed in the late 1970s on a Mekong tributary, caused significant loss of natural fish species in the Mun River. Of the 265 indigenous species of fish natural to the river, only 45 were present upstream from the dam once it was completed. The problem is so bad that the Thai government has agreed to open the dam for at least four months out of the year to help maintain even a modest fish stock for villagers upstream. Even these steps have been ineffective. Villagers report fish declines of 60 to 80 percent since the dam opened.

Here, the speaker relies on statistics to provide a rationale for the argument about fisheries being depleted. The argument could be strengthened with additional explanation for why a dam would harm fisheries upstream from the dam.

Of course, the impact of damming goes beyond fish and farmland. In these river villages people are connected to the river through generations. When the Pak Mun Dam was erected, small islands and sand bars were destroyed; those high spots in the river were key meeting spots for celebrations and supported active community life tied to the river. When EGAT (Eee-GHAT), the Thai energy authority, offered to relocate villagers displaced by the dam, they were given substandard housing in areas where it was impossible to grow crops or to fish. As a result, villagers lost their primary means of personal and economic prosperity. In this picture that I took, you can see one of the village elders looking over the Mun River below the dam where he used to fish. In the short clip you are about to see, one of the village elders, speaking through an interpreter, explained how the dam has harmed his community.

Here, the speaker uses a picture and actual narrative from a villager to establish pathos, a form of persuasive proof. The video narrative and picture helps audience members identify with the problems faced by the villagers.

Just one dam on one tributary of the Mekong literally destroyed generations of knowledge built up around a small section of one river; imagine the effect if the Mekong itself was forever altered to quench the thirst for electricity in Bangkok, Saigon, and other metropolitan areas. Tilt, Braun, and He, an interdisciplinary group of scholars who study the impact of dams, concluded in a 2009 article that the social impact of dams on indigenous populations is equally as devastating as the ecological impact, both of which are often irreversible.

Here again, the speaker uses a metaphor to add interest to the speech.

So what can we do as Americans, thousands of miles away from the Mekong River? My final point tries to give you some practical steps that you can take to help. First, we need to make sure that our government views the issue of dams as a significant aspect of its human rights policy. We should contact our elected senators to let them know that we oppose dams so that they can take those views into consideration when debating and voting on international treaties. Second, we should contact the U.S. Department of State and encourage our international dignitaries to promote free rivers. The Department of State has significant authority to help promote human rights among indigenous populations, and our nation's diplomatic corps could have a meaningful impact on stopping some of the projects from gaining further traction. Finally, all of us should make a commitment to sign the online

In the final point of the speech, the speaker identifies several specific things audience members can do. Even though some of the actions may seem less effective (e.g., writing government officials), such steps could spur audience involvement, which may allow more robust steps to be taken.

Here, the speaker likely saved the solution step considered most interesting to be the last. Notice how the speaker provided exact information for accomplishing this step, whereas the other steps were more vague. This persuasive strategy is often used to lead audience members to a particular desired action.

The speaker adds impact to the solution step by showing that "protest" has successfully helped in another circumstance. Such explanation may persuade audience members that their actions after the speech could have positive outcomes.

petition opposing dams on the Mekong River. Small steps like these show that free rivers are an international concern and they make it more difficult for economic and political elites to write off opposition to dams as the views of a few uneducated, poor river people. You can sign the petition in just a few seconds by visiting the "Save the Mekong Coalition" Web site. I'll provide you with a small slip of paper with the URL that you can use and pass along to a friend. I'll also send you an email with the URL later today.

In conclusion, you have learned about the practice of damming and the threat that dams pose to the people living along the Mekong River. Unless these dams are stopped, the ecology and communities of people along the Mekong will be lost forever. Luckily, we know that voices like ours can help. In the face of informed protest, the Thai energy authority was forced to open the Pak Mun Dam to help save the threatened fisheries. With more voices from around the world, I hope that we can keep other villages from facing the same problems. You are armed with a simple action—to sign a petition. Use Facebook and email to tell your friends about this problem and get them to sign it, too. If we all voice our concern, hopefully the Mekong can remain free and the people along the river can continue to lead the life that they choose.

For REVIEW >>

SUMMARY HIGHLIGHTS

How Are Persuasive Presentations Unique?

▶ Unlike informative presentations, persuasive presentations are intended to influence audience members' views, feelings, or actions toward a particular issue.

▶ Persuasive presentations are generally built on three forms of proof: ethos, pathos, and logos.

▶ Ethos persuades by using an authoritative and/or trustworthy source in support of a particular view.

▶ Pathos persuades by tapping into audience members' feelings.

▶ Logos persuades by using evidence and reasoning.

▶ Persuasive speeches tend to address questions of fact, value, or policy.

▶ Persuasion is relevant to all of us because we are constantly acting as both producers and consumers of persuasive messages.

What Are the Types of Persuasive Presentations?

▶ A speech to convince attempts to influence listeners' beliefs or attitudes about a particular issue.

▶ A speech to inspire aims to influence or modify listeners' feelings or motivations toward a particular issue.

▶ A speech of action attempts to influence or modify listeners' behaviors and actions. This type of speech may include and add to approaches that would be taken in speeches to convince and/or inspire.

How Should You Plan a Persuasive Message?

▶ Like all speeches, your planning should begin with a careful analysis of your audience. In particular, you should attempt to predict how they might react to your message:
  • A critical response occurs when the audience focuses on the arguments, evidence, and message.
  • A defensive response occurs when the audience ignores the message to protect existing beliefs, attitudes, and values.
  • A compliance response occurs when the audience responds in ways that are socially acceptable.

► There are a variety of persuasive strategies that can be used to improve your message, including promoting consistency; asking for small, gradual changes; showing benefits; fulfilling needs; and carefully planning your message.

How Can Critical Thinking and Reasoning Improve Your Message?

► Reasoning is a mental process of developing your own position on issues.

► Inductive reasoning involves drawing a conclusion based on one or more particular cases.

► Deductive reasoning involves a claim that is based on a universally accepted principle, fact, or condition.

► There are a variety of types of arguments that can be advanced to express your reasoning: arguments about causes and effects, arguments from sign, arguments from generalizations, arguments from parallel case, arguments from analogy, and arguments from classification.

► When using evidence, arguments, and reasoning in your speech, you should avoid fallacies, which are errors in reasoning that weaken arguments. Fallacies discussed include name calling, glittering generality, bandwagon, either/or, and post hoc.

What Ethical Principles Should Guide Persuasive Speaking?

► Be careful whom you trust and show others that you are trustworthy.

► Analyze messages for reasonableness, truth, and benefits.

► You should think of your credibility as a long-term creation and act accordingly.

► Always be respectful of your audience.

1. Beth wants her listeners to volunteer to donate blood. She will be giving a:
   (A) speech to inspire
   (B) speech of action
   (C) speech to convince
   (D) speech of desire

2. If an audience member responds to a persuasive message by doing what is socially acceptable, he or she is employing a:
   (A) critical response
   (B) compliance response
   (C) defensive response
   (D) motivated response

3. To create an effective message, you should:
   (A) use "many" or "most" rather than specific numbers
   (B) employ incomplete arguments
   (C) use testimonial evidence
   (D) avoid being explicit

4. "Should the university require public speaking as a graduation requirement?" is a question of:
   (A) fact
   (B) value
   (C) opinion
   (D) policy

5. An organizational pattern *not* generally used for persuasive presentations is:
   (A) topical sequence
   (B) cause-effect pattern
   (C) Monroe Motivated Sequence
   (D) spatial pattern

Answers: 1 (B); 2 (B); 3 (C); 4 (D); 5 (D)

APPLICATION EXERCISES

1. Persuasive speeches often appeal to an audience's unmet needs. Because needs vary according to the community, college, class, and individual, you can make yourself more sensitive to audience needs by ranking the five unmet needs that you believe are important to your audience.

   a. _____

   b. _____

   c. _____

   d. _____

   e. _____

2. After reading the section on principles of persuasion, you should be able to identify cases in which they are correctly used. Examine the following cases and indicate which of the following principles is being observed:

   C = *Consistency persuades.*

   S = *Small changes persuade.*

   B = *Benefits persuade.*

   N = *Fulfilling needs persuades.*

   G = *Gradual approaches persuade.*

   _____a. To save my audience members considerable time and effort, I am going to provide them with a form letter that they can sign and send to the administration.

   _____b. Because I know most of my classmates are short of cash, I am going to tell them how to make some quick money with on-campus jobs.

   _____c. I plan to wait until the end of the speech to tell the audience members that the organization I want them to join will require two hours of driving per week.

   _____d. My audience of international students already believes in the value of learning public speaking, so I think the listeners will respond favorably to my recommendation for a course in voice and articulation.

   _____e. I would like my audience to cut up all their credit cards, but because they are unlikely to do so, I am instead going to ask that they try for a zero balance each month to avoid interest and fees.

   Answers: a. B, b. N, c. G, d. C, e. S

KEY TERMS

Argument	Defensive response	Question of policy
Audience analysis	Ethos	Question of value
Boomerang effect	Explicit	Relationship
Claim	Fallacy	Specific numbers
Complete arguments	Hierarchy of needs	Speech of action
Compliance response	Inductive reasoning	Speech to convince
Consistency persuades	Logos	Speech to inspire
Cost-benefit analysis	Pathos	Testimonial evidence
Critical response	Persuasive presentations	
Deductive reasoning	Question of fact	

12

SPEAKING

Most of this book is devoted to planning, preparing, and delivering presentations for practical purposes—to teach audience members about a topic or persuade them to change their attitudes, beliefs, or behaviors. Although many of our public presentations are intended to accomplish practical outcomes like these, another common type of speaking situation involves presentations that highlight a special event. These speeches are quite common and are generally referred to as special occasion presentations. In this chapter, we will show how special occasion presentations differ from other types of presentations. We will also describe the various kinds of special occasion presentations and guide you in developing your own.

ON SPECIAL OCCASIONS

Special occasion speeches draw meaningful connections between people and events. Whether a person is being introduced, given an award, or eulogized, the connection between the person and the event is what makes the speech truly special. This relationship was especially apparent when Meryl Streep gave a speech of introduction and tribute for Hillary Clinton at the 2012 Women in the World Summit held in New York. Streep's presentation was notable because of her own celebrity status—think *The Devil Wears Prada* and an astonishing 17 Academy Award nominations—coupled with Hillary Clinton's iconic persona—remember the spring 2012 spoofs of Hillary's texts? The two women coming together in one special event was truly exciting! In this excerpt from her speech, you can see how Streep attempted to mix humor into her purpose of introducing Clinton:

Thank you. I feel like I've been plugged into an energy source that's bigger than the one generated by oil, gas, coal, or nuclear. It's girl power. (Cheers.) This one's going to electrify the next century. . . . It's a great honor for me to be here because we women really do look very hard at each other, like, "Check my jacket." (Laughter.) We can be hard on each other. But we really look so deeply because we want inspiration. . . . We've all spent a lot of time thinking about Hillary Clinton because—poor girl—she represents us, Hillary is us and we are Hillary. But while we're busy relating to her, judging her, assessing her hair, her jackets, supporting her, worrying about her—is she getting enough sleep? She's just been busy working, doing it, making those words "Women's rights are human rights" into something every leader in every country now knows is a linchpin of American policy. It's just so much more than a rhetorical triumph. We're talking about what happened in the real world, the institutional change that was a result of that stand she took, just for one example, a small thing.[1]

Streep's speech is an excellent example of a special occasion speech. Notice how she intentionally interjected humor while at the same time giving honor to Hillary Clinton's efforts on the part of women worldwide. In this chapter, you will learn about the range of ceremonial speeches as well as appropriate ways to adapt your speechmaking skills to special situations.

Special occasion speeches [are] [in their] [n]ature, somewhat different from more traditional informative and persuasive presentations. In this section, you will learn about those differences as they relate to the purposes, style, organization, and formality of these types of speeches.

What Are the Unique Characteristics of Special Occasion Presentations?

Purpose

Recall from previous chapters that the primary purpose of an informative speech is to teach and the primary purpose of a persuasive speech is to change behaviors or beliefs. Although special occasion presentations might try to inform or persuade, these objectives are typically secondary. Rather, the primary purpose of a special occasion presentation is to perform a **ritual**, *a ceremonial act that is characterized by qualities or procedures that are appropriate to the occasion.*

All cultures have ceremonial rituals. Weddings, funerals, grand openings, awards ceremonies, and graduations arc all examples of ritualized events. During such events, public presentations often punctuate important moments. At a wedding reception, for instance, the toasts to the new couple made by the "best man" and "maid of honor" are punctuating moments. The ritualistic nature of special occasion speeches is important. Such rituals help bring certainty and comfort to otherwise stressful events, they help attendees know what to expect, and they help attendees and audience members share in a common collective experience, such as wishing good tidings to a newly wedded couple or dedicating a new building to a devoted teacher. Some scholars go so far as to say that ritualized presentations at special occasions help link together the past, present, and future. That is exactly what Meryl Streep attempted to do in her introduction of Hillary Clinton—she talked about Clinton's prior accomplishments in relation to the Women of the World event.

"Some scholars go so far as to say that ritualized presentations at special occasions help link together the past, present, and future."

Style

Special occasion speeches typically differ in style from more traditional informative and persuasive speeches. Recall from Chapter 2 that style refers to the clarity and ornamentation used during a presentation. Whereas a typical informative or persuasive speech might selectively use stylistic devices like narratives, metaphors, similes, or analogies, special occasion speeches might emphasize such techniques. Because special occasions are highly ritualistic, they invite the use of *highly stylized*, or **ornamental language**.

Organization

When speaking to inform or persuade, you must pay particular attention to how you organize large quantities of information. Because special occasion presentations are less concerned with information dissemination and argumentation and more concerned with setting a particular tone for the occasion, you need to handle the organization of such presentations differently than you would an informative or persuasive presentation. For instance, although special occasion presentations still should have an introduction, body, and conclusion, they typically have less obvious transitions between main points. Instead, their ornamental styling may suggest more subtle and creative ways to signal transitions between ideas. Moreover, special occasion cultural NOTE

WHAT IS THE VALUE OF SILENCE ACROSS CULTURES?

In Western culture, particularly in the field of rhetoric and public speaking, having the ability to talk and be heard is a form of power. Despite some natural tendencies to have some level of anxiousness when speaking, those who speak are viewed as more powerful than those who listen. In fact, the behavior of listening is often viewed as passive, unmotivated, and unengaged—look no further than participation grades in some classes for proof! Being silent is not viewed negatively in all cultures, though. Professor Donald Carbaugh and colleagues told a story of a Finnish foreign exchange student who was puzzled that her host family expected her to talk in the car when traveling on family outings. In Finnish culture, the term *mietiskelä*, which is interpreted as being contemplative and thoughtful, is part of the cultural way of being, according to Carbaugh and colleagues. They describe situations where entire groups of people can be engaged in mietiskelä at the same time. Think about times in American speaking situations when silence is explicitly called upon. At weddings, the hope is that silence prevails when the officiant asks if there are any objections—in fact, silence is usually appreciated. At memorial services, there are often moments of silence to honor those who have passed away. So, even in a talk-centered American culture, silence (or the Finnish concept of *mietiskelä*) often becomes an important marker of special occasion speeches.

presentations often are relatively short, and developing several main points may not be practical. In a presentation to introduce someone, for example, you should have a short introduction, provide a brief biography of the person, conclude by welcoming them, and invite applause or recognition. Taking time to "fully develop" several main points may be unnecessary and inappropriate.

Formality

Based on the previous sections, you might have guessed that special occasion speeches tend to be a bit more formal than traditional informative and persuasive presentations. Because you are taking part in a ritualized event and because you will likely try to make your style more ornamental, your special occasion speeches may appear more formal in tone.

Being formal does not mean being "stuffy." Rather, formality in this context refers more to the degree of professionalism you might use to share your ideas with your listeners. You might practice your presentation so often that you can memorize particular wordings and phrases; you might make extra efforts to use a full array of nonverbal gestures to accentuate your message; you may even, in some situations, go so far as to prepare a manuscript and practice that delivery technique. In sum, special occasion presentations are just that—special. Taking extra efforts to polish your presentation will allow you to have a more meaningful impact in setting the appropriate tone for the situation.

What Are the Types of Special Occasion Presentations?

Although the potential number of different types of special occasion presentations is quite large, you will learn here about nine of the most common purposes for special occasion speaking:

- to welcome
- to pay tribute
- to introduce
- to nominate
- to dedicate

- to commemorate
- to say farewell
- to give recognition
- to entertain

These categories should provide some guidance for almost any special occasion at which you find yourself speaking.

Presentations to Welcome

Presentations to welcome are intended to *set a tone for a larger event by inviting all participants—including other presenters and audience members—to appropriately engage* *the event*. By "engage the event" we mean that events have a certain tone or feel, and the welcome speech should set that tone for the attendees. If the event is joyful, like an awards ceremony, the welcome speech should set a happy tone. If, on the other hand, the occasion is more serious, like an academic conference on your campus, the welcome speech should establish the professional tone necessary for that conference.

Welcome presentations are typically brief. Such presentations might try to accomplish two specific purposes. First, the presenter should welcome any honorees, important guests, or other noteworthy participants in the event. Second, the presenter should provide a brief message establishing the purpose of the event. During this latter stage, he or she should use language, stories, or other stylistic devices to set the appropriate tone for the occasion.

Presentations to Pay Tribute

Presentations to pay tribute are designed to *offer celebration and praise of a noteworthy person, organization, or cause.* Speeches of tribute can be further subdivided into the following: eulogies, celebratory roasts, wedding toasts, retirement addresses, anniversary tributes, and other special events designed to celebrate the life or work of an individual or entity. For example, one of our campuses has a Campus-Community Day, established to celebrate the long heritage of cooperation between the campus and the surrounding community. Speeches at that event are tribute speeches because they honor the combined efforts of the two entities—the campus and the community.

Because tribute speeches include several different types, you should take care to fully analyze the situation to determine what focus would be most appropriate. However, nearly all tribute presentations attempt to provide some biographical sketch of the person/entity being honored. Generally speaking, tributes make extensive use of narratives to tell stories about the honoree. Such stories are effective at evoking emotion while at the same time celebrating the past. In some cases, tribute speeches might end by looking toward the future. For a retirement presentation, you might wish someone well as they take on new adventures in life; for a celebratory roast, you might encourage the honoree to "keep up the great work."

Presentations to Introduce

Speeches of introduction *are designed to tell us about the person being introduced and to help establish their ethos—in this case ethos might include credentials and/or goodwill.* Speeches of introduction usually precede a longer address, which will be presented by the person being introduced, and are typically brief.

Because the primary objective in a speech of introduction is to present information about the speaker, the majority of the speech should be devoted to the person's biography or other information relevant to the speaker's credibility. Depending on the occasion, you might also talk about the reason(s) this person was asked to speak. For this type of speech you may want to adapt the following approach:

- *Introduction*: Use an anecdote or some story to establish audience members' emotional connection with the speaker being introduced.
- *Body*: Discuss the speaker's biography and other qualifications. The focus of this part of your presentation should be on qualifications most relevant to the occasion but should also raise other interesting facts about the person.
- *Conclusion*: Summarize the person's qualifications and use that summary to explain why she/he was asked to speak. End by welcoming the speaker and inviting the audience to join in the welcome by applauding.

Presentations to Nominate

Speeches of nomination *introduce and honor someone you wish to place in contention for an award, elected office, or some other competitively selected position.* In clubs that you belong to, officers and other leaders in the organization may be nominated for their positions through a short speech or presentation. Nomination presentations vary in length depending on the nature of the nomination. In the United States, the Republican and Democratic Party conventions, for example, feature several lengthy speeches to nominate candidates for the national presidential election. For your clubs, a very short speech might suffice to nominate officers.

Speeches of nomination should focus on two things: the qualifications of the nominee and the reason these qualifications match the characteristics of the office, position, or award to be granted. You should think of this speech as an abbreviated oral résumé for the person you are helping to nominate. What has he or she done to deserve being elected or appointed to a particular position? What character attributes does he or she possess that will make him or her trustworthy? If the nomination is for an award, what activities did he or she accomplish that distinguish his or her work from others' work? These types of issues are common in a nomination presentation.

Presentations to Dedicate

A **dedication presentation** *honors someone by naming an event, place, or other object after the honoree.* A dedication presentation could be as simple as a professional athlete saying that he or she dedicated the game to his or her parents, or as elaborate as the dedication of a Navy ship. These types of speeches will vary in length and focus depending on the setting, the honoree, and the event, place, or object being dedicated. Typically, the speaker in such presentations will talk about the dedication and the reasons why the honoree is a worthy namesake. Perhaps the person has some special connection to the object or event being dedicated, or perhaps the person has done extraordinary work for the organization and is being honored by having his or her name placed on a building, room, or some other object. A dedication attempts to honor someone in reference to a specific time or place that is meaningful. The presentation, then, should focus on those two issues.

iConnect

Social Media for Special Occasions

When planning a special occasion, your to-do list might include items like "send invitations" or "hire a photographer." But what about "hire a tweeter"? While watching recent events on television, like the Miss USA Pageant or the Super Bowl, you have probably noticed that Twitter hashtags, like #MissUSA2012 for instance, are displayed prominently enough so that anyone using Twitter can join in an open conversation about the event. Hashtags are now a commonplace feature of events large and small—from an international sporting event, to a national conference, or even a lecture or class. When planning an event, many organizers now recommend that a person be designated, or hired, to drive tweets about what happens moment to moment. Tweeting is also a way of commemorating special occasions. Those who receive awards are just as excited to see themselves honored in tweets and re-tweets as they are having their picture in a newspaper or on a website. Perhaps wedding plans should include hiring a tweeter alongside the photographer!

Presentations to Commemorate

Commemorative addresses are typically speeches that are part of some ritualized event like a graduation, a holiday, or even a unique local occasion like First Amendment Day. **Commemorative addresses** mostly are *designed to set a tone for the event—much like a welcome speech—and also usually are considered the primary, or keynote, presentation for the event.* For example, most graduation ceremonies have a graduation speaker who is supposed to give new graduates advice for their future—such speeches set a tone for the entire graduation ceremony. Of course, the highly ritualized nature of such events means that commemorative addresses are more formal and make greater use of stylistic devices.

When planning a commemorative address, analyzing the audience and situation is very important. You must carefully determine (1) what length and tone the audience expects and (2) how to creatively highlight specific values that capture the essence of the occasion. Commemorative addresses should use subtle transitions and supporting material. Commemorative presentations should also highlight the unique ideas and thoughts of the presenter more than other types of speeches. Nancy Cartwright, an Emmy award-winning actor who is the voice of Bart Simpson and the *Rugrats*, recently gave a college commencement address in which she urged graduates to surround themselves with good people. Although there were other points in her speech, this particular point provided examples of how she had benefited from trying to work with good mentors and creative individuals as she progressed from being a radio announcer near Dayton to an award-winning actress. Her speech, like other commemorative addresses, found ways to highlight key messages to signify values or attributes meaningful for the audience.

Farewell Presentations

Farewell presentations occur in many different types of situations in which a person (either you or someone you know) is leaving. One very specific type of "farewell" might be the eulogy that is presented at a funeral. Other farewell presentations might occur when a longtime employee leaves an organization, when a leader in a community organization decides to step down, or even when a notable community member or church patron moves away. The common feature among all of these **farewell presentations** is that *a person is paid tribute for his or her service before leaving.*

A farewell presentation can be delivered from two perspectives: one from the people who remain behind and another from the person leaving. If you are preparing a speech to say good-bye to someone who is leaving you should (1) create a brief introduction that establishes an emotional tone, (2) orient the body of the presentation around accomplishments and other notable qualities of the person, and (3) wish the person well and say something to maintain an ongoing connection (for example, "we will keep you in our thoughts because . . ."). When saying goodbye to a valued faculty member who is leaving, you might highlight the many ways in which she or he provided assistance to students through her or his teaching, advising, and mentoring. If a co-worker is leaving, you might be slightly more light-hearted, but you would still want to discuss ways in which he or she affected others. In both examples, your goal is to help give meaning to the attributes that made the person special to you and others.

You may find yourself in a situation that calls for you to give a farewell address because you are leaving. Chances are that you will be the last to speak—those who thank and pay tribute to you will speak before you. In such situations, you might begin by discussing what your time with the organization has meant; use anecdotes, stories, and other evidence to explain your feelings toward the organization; mention specific individuals who were meaningful to your experience; and conclude with gratitude (both for your experience and for the tribute) as well as warm wishes for the future. That your colleagues decided to have some sort of event in your honor means that they value their relationship with you. In your presentation, you should highlight the relationships you have cultivated and point out that your transition away from a formal organization does not necessarily mean that those relationships will end.

> *"The sincerity of a well-crafted farewell address can provide lifetime memories for all involved."*

The speech of farewell can be emotional both for those staying behind and for the person leaving. Such feelings are healthy because they provide ritualized moments to be gracious to those around us. The sincerity of a well-crafted farewell address can provide poignant memories for all involved.

Recognition Addresses

Speeches of recognition are typically presented when one or more people are given awards. For instance, many high schools have yearly awards nights during which students receive awards for academic and extracurricular achievements. Another example is the Oscars or other entertainment awards shows. Both of these types of events are similar in that *presenters are asked to give short presentations to introduce an award recipient.*

Speeches of recognition are often very short because they tend to be part of a larger program of events—there may be several other awards being presented. As such, speeches of recognition may not have explicitly developed introductions, bodies, and conclusions. The three key pieces of information necessary in these types of presentations are (1) what the award is, (2) the criteria for being honored with the award, and (3) who the recipient is and why he or she is deserving of the award. The latter point might be the most developed and may use anecdotes, stories, and other forms of support to elaborate on why the person is receiving the award. If only one award is being presented, the presentation can be developed in more detail and might resemble a traditional speech with an introduction, body, and conclusion. In such cases, the organization of the speech might be adapted from that described for the speech of introduction.

Sometimes, award recipients are asked to speak in acceptance of the award. Such speeches should be brief—typically about the same length as the recognition speech. When accepting the award, you should discuss what the award means to you and provide appropriate thanks. People often assume that it is better to list everyone possible when thanking others; in contrast, more effective speeches might explain that there are many people who deserve thanks but then focus on one or two people who were especially critical in supporting your efforts.

Presentations to Entertain

The final type of special occasion speech is a presentation to entertain. As the name suggests, **presentations to entertain** *are designed to make a point in a creative and oftentimes humorous way.* Entertainment speeches are sometimes called "after-dinner speeches" because events often schedule these types of speeches as part of a social time or banquet.

Although the name suggests that the entertainment speech should be all about fun and laughs, presenters should also make some substantive point. In other words, stand-up comedy and speeches to entertain are different from each other. Generally speaking, speakers should plan their presentations by thinking about a more formal, perhaps even serious, message and then finding ways to make that message more humorous. For example, as part of a larger awards ceremony, you might be asked to provide a "keynote" address. If appropriate for the situation, you might approach the keynote address as a speech to entertain. In such a case, your speech to entertain should focus on the topic for the event, but should do so in a humorous or amusing way. In talking about the great work done by your organization over the course of the year, you can interject fun stories about things people did while those activities were carried out. Your humorous stories will entertain, but your larger message about the accomplishments of your organization will not be lost.

If effectively prepared, the difference between the entertainment speech and more traditional informative and persuasive speeches will be less pronounced than between the other types of special occasion speeches. You should have a clear thesis statement as well as obvious main points, although these structural elements may be presented more subtly than one would expect in persuasive or informative presentations. After determining the point you want to make, you should find ways to interject humor that are appropriate to the audience and natural to the situation. Finally, pay particularly close attention to practicing delivery. Whether or not audience members perceive your presentation to be humorous depends on how you "sell" a line. Being able to "sell" a line involves a combination of delivery and timing. Working with others to develop humorous material and to refine your delivery is essential for a successful entertainment presentation.

How Should You Prepare Special Occasion Presentations?

Special occasion presentations vary widely in type, purpose, and setting. As such, no textbook or class could ever prepare you for every possible special occasion speech. At the same time, the success of special occasion presentations, as is the case with other types of presentations, typically centers on one concept: how well you analyze your message in relation to the audience and situation. Figure 12.1 is a brief worksheet you can use to plan your special occasion presentations. In this figure, we use plans to dedicate the grand opening of a new campus sustainable agriculture garden as an example.

When preparing your special occasion speech you should remember that even though this type of speech is special, basic principles of ethics still apply. In fact, there are probably additional ethical principles at play *because* these speeches are special. For instance, if you use quotations or specific ideas, phrases, or even jokes from another person, you should give attribution to the source. You should not lie, fabricate, or misrepresent yourself or another person as part of your presentation. Those and other ethical principles of communication are pertinent to any speech, special or not!

In special occasion speeches, ethics also come into play with regard to adapting your speech to the occasion. Is it ethical for you to give a speech at a wedding if you think the bride or bridegroom is a creep? Would it be ethical for you to voice your opinion during the speech, violating all audience expectations? If you were speaking at a dedication, would it be ethical for you to criticize the namesake of a building because you felt that person was involved in shady business practices? The fit between a speaker, message, and situation is something that sometimes crosses from smart practice to ethical practice in special occasions. If you do something against the norm during a special occasion speech, you should consider whether you are crossing an ethical line.

Finally, those of you who work in government service and some other professions know that special events often involve gifts, and receipt of gifts by government employees can be problematic. For instance, NASA has a policy that employees cannot receive gifts exceeding $20 in value.[2] So, if you receive an award at a conference and it carries a cash honorarium, can you take it? Should you offer gifts as part of a special occasion speech? Could the mere act of honoring someone with a speech be perceived as creating a potential conflict of interest? These examples may seem farfetched, yet they are exactly the type of situations that get people in trouble unexpectedly. When planning a special occasion speech, take care to think through professional codes of ethics related to the event!

Special Occasion Presentation Worksheet

1. Define the Occasion
Describe elements of the speaking situation that will be important to the message you intend to convey in your presentation.

a. the audience:
Approximately 10 members of my class, 5–10 faculty, and 5 or so administrators. Students from other classes could attend, but I have no way of knowing.

b. the event or setting:
To provide opening remarks for the sustainable agriculture garden. The garden will open to the public for the first time after my presentation.

c. other speakers or activities before and after presentation:
Dr. Lehman will provide some introductory remarks and welcome audience members. I will speak next and the ribbon will be cut after my presentation.

2. Define the Message
Describe the ideas, emotions, or attitudes that you want to convey. List any stylistic devices like metaphors or narratives that you want to bring into your message.

a. primary message:
I want to accomplish two purposes: (1) to talk about the process of creating the garden, and (2) to dedicate the garden in Dr. Lehman's name. This will be a surprise to everyone, but the dept. chair said that such a dedication is a great idea.

b. stylistic device ideas:
Use the metaphor of "sustainable growth" to talk about Dr. Lehman as a mentor. Tell the story about how he helped me pass Plant Biology my freshman year by meeting with me and a few other students in the arboretum every Friday.

c. main points (if applicable):
Main points should follow the two parts of the primary message. Should do the dedication last to catch Dr. Lehman by surprise.

Figure 12.1   **Worksheet for planning a special occasion presentation.**

Sample Special Occasion Speech

The following speech of tribute was given at an end-of-year banquet, at which several awards are given to both teachers and students. In this particular speech, an Ohio University professor is being honored for his work as a mentor. Notice how the speech is divided into two basic points: (1) a description of the award and (2) a discussion of the recipient.

Tribute to Jeffrey Redefer

The LJ Hortin Award for faculty mentoring is given to a faculty member who demonstrates outstanding mentoring to students. The award was created by alumnus Tom Kuby in honor of his mentor, Lauren Joseph Hortin, who taught for 20 years as a faculty member from 1947 to 1967. Recipients who are current faculty receive $1,500 in professional development or $1,000 as a cash prize. Emeriti faculty can designate the $1,500 prize to a program of their choice in the college.

The recipient is Professor Jeff Redefer.

Jeff Redefer has been the Associate Director of Undergraduate Studies in the School of Media Arts & Studies for more than 11 years. That means he has greeted more than 1,800 incoming first-year students. Eighteen-hundred. And, for Jeff, that means that he sat with each one of them in the summer and helped them choose classes. It means that he more than likely gave those students and their parents a personal tour of the school, a shoulder to cry on, a desk where they could pound their fists, or a hand to give a high-five.

A former student who nominated Jeff for this award wrote: "Students are more than just passing ships in Professor Redefer's life. He cares about each of them." Remembering her time as both an undergraduate and graduate student at OU, she reflected back on the experiences she gained in studying with Jeff and reflected, "Hardly a day goes by that I don't use some bit of training or wisdom he imparted to me." Now, as a parent, she still uses examples of patience and humor that she learned from Jeff as she raises her own children. And that seems to be a fair comparison. Jeff treats the students of the school as if they were his own children. Jeff is selfless with his time, offering advice, encouragement, or direction to any student who needs it.

For REVIEW >>

SUMMARY HIGHLIGHTS

What Are the Unique Characteristics of Special Occasion Speeches?

▶ Special occasion speeches are unique in their purpose because they are intended to be part of certain rituals or ceremonial occasions.

▶ The style of special occasion speeches are typically more ornate, which involves highly stylized language features. For example, metaphors, narratives, and analogies are common in special occasion speeches.

▶ Many special occasion speeches have an introduction, body, and conclusion. However, the situation, particularly time constraints, could dramatically limit your ability to develop these speech elements in the same way you do in more traditional speeches.

▶ Special occasion speeches tend to be more formal because they are expected to follow certain norms for the ritualized occasions in which they are given.

What Are the Types of Special Occasion Presentations?

▶ A presentation to welcome sets a tone for an event and invites all participants to fully engage the activities associated with the event.

▶ A speech that pays tribute offers a celebratory message and praise for a noteworthy person, organization, or cause. Because there are many types of celebrations, you should carefully analyze the situation to plan your message.

▶ Speeches of introduction tell us about a person who is about to speak and helps establish his or her credibility in the minds of the audience.

▶ Presentations to nominate introduce and honor someone who is being placed in contention for an award, elected office, or some other competitive selection process.

▶ When you do a speech of dedication, you honor someone by naming an event, place, or other object after the honoree.

▶ Commemorative addresses are designed to set a tone for an event and are often thought of as a keynote presentation at the event.

▶ A farewell presentation can be given by a person who is leaving an organization and/or by people who are saying farewell to the person leaving. A eulogy is a special type of farewell presentation.

► Speeches of recognition are given when someone receives an award.

► A speech to entertain, sometimes called an after-dinner speech, makes a serious point about something but does so in a more humorous or entertaining way. Whereas stand-up comedy is primarily meant to be entertaining, a speech to entertain makes a clear point about something but uses comedy or other entertaining material to make the point.

How Should You Prepare Special Occasion Presentations?

► Basic principles of ethics still apply to special occasion speeches. You should not lie or misrepresent information, you should give attribution to sources of information, and you should keep the best interest of your audience in mind.

► You should carefully analyze the situation and understand what is expected of you by your audience. Violating expectations in these types of situations can potentially be viewed as a breach of ethics.

► Some occasions involve gifts, which can potentially pose conflicts of interest for some speakers. Make sure to review policies and laws governing the appropriateness and size of gifts or honorariums before giving or accepting such symbols of appreciation.

1. The primary purpose of a special occasion presentation is:
   (A) to inform the audience
   (B) to change the audience's mind
   (C) to perform a ritual
   (D) to define terms

2. Eulogies, wedding toasts, or retirement addresses are examples of a presentation to
   (A) welcome
   (B) pay tribute
   (C) introduce
   (D) dedicate

3. A graduation speech is a presentation to:
   (A) dedicate
   (B) pay tribute
   (C) commemorate
   (D) entertain

4. Speeches to entertain are also called:
   (A) after-dinner speeches
   (B) farewell addresses
   (C) commemorative addresses
   (D) tribute speeches

5. The organization of a special occasion speech:
   (A) lacks a conclusion
   (B) uses obvious transitions between main points
   (C) allows the speaker to develop several main points
   (D) differs from informative or persuasive speeches

pop **Quiz**

Answers: 1 (C); 2 (B); 3 (C); 4 (A); 5 (D)

APPLICATION EXERCISES

1. Special occasion presentations tend to emphasize the use of stylistic devices. Pick a person whom you would consider a "mentor" for you. This person could be a professor or teacher, a family member, or some other individual who has helped you grow personally. After identifying that individual, create a metaphor describing how that person has helped you. For example, in Figure 12.1, Kim used the metaphor of "sustainable growth" to describe Dr. Lehman, her mentor.

2. To understand how special occasion speeches serve as ritualistic events, look only so far as your campus. Attend an event on campus that involves speeches. The event could be a public lecture, an awards ceremony, or even a commencement. List all of the speeches you heard at the event and analyze how the speeches "fit" into the ritual being enacted. Why do you think speeches are part of our rituals?

3. Practice presenting to nominate through the "class award" activity. Your class will manage an annual "Community Engagement Award." You should be prepared to nominate (and speak in favor of) a person from your community whom you would like to place in contention for the award. The recipient of the award, whom your class recommends, will be given a certificate and be invited to speak to your class.

KEY TERMS

Commemorative address	Presentation to entertain	Speech of introduction
Dedication presentation	Presentation to pay tribute	Speech of nomination
Farewell presentation	Presentation to welcome	Speech of recognition
Ornamental language	Ritual	

APPENDIX

WORKING &
PRESENTING

Business and professional speaking situations rarely involve just one person presenting to a large audience. Especially for many entry-level and mid-management positions, most public communication involves a team or group. Although group-based presentations have many benefits, they also require greater coordination and planning. This appendix teaches you how to work in groups to prepare a high-quality presentation.

AS A GROUP

In the recent 2012 presidential bid, American Republican politician and three-time presidential candidate Ron Paul failed once again to secure the GOP nomination. Nevertheless, he was credited widely for having a very strong "ground game."[1] But what exactly does that mean? You may remember that supporters of Ron Paul described themselves as spearheading a movement with the intent to change the nature of the Republican Party. Through use of social media, personal contact, and active mobilization of supporters, Ron Paul's advocates worked to gain key leadership positions in the Republican Party's organization. Those efforts did not result in a presidential nomination, but they did ensure that aspects of Paul's political philosophy would shape the stance taken by the Republican Party at its summer nomination convention.

The approach taken by Paul's supporters relied on an intricate web of small groups. Organized as a social movement, supporters in local communities banded together and worked to influence state

delegations. Using groups whose core messages centered on the role of government, Paul achieved success that few thought possible for a "fringe" candidate on the Republican slate of nominees. The lesson here is simple: when people work in groups they can accomplish significant outcomes. As you read this appendix, you will learn more about ways in which groups can be used to carry out meaningful dialogues that have influence.

How Are Small Groups and Public Communication Connected?

Small groups are a common format in which we communicate. Indeed, much of what we accomplish on a daily basis involves working with others in groups. In this section, you will learn about the characteristics of small groups as well as various benefits for using groups for presentations.

What Are Small Groups?

Small group communication is *the interaction among three to nine people who are working together to achieve an interdependent goal.*[2] The definition of small group communication establishes *communication* as the essential process within a small group.

Communication creates a group, shapes it in unique ways, and maintains it. Like other forms of human communication, small group communication relies on verbal and nonverbal signals that are perceived, interpreted, and responded to by other people. Group members pay attention to each other and coordinate their behavior to accomplish the group's assignment. Perfect understanding between the person sending the signal and those receiving the signal is impossible; in a group, members strive to have enough understanding so that the group can achieve important objectives.

Why Are Small Groups Used for Presentations?

Increasingly, small groups are used to facilitate public communication. For example, important business presentations are often organized so that people with different backgrounds and skills discuss issues with which they are each familiar. Student groups often divide responsibility for various tasks among group members based on personal interest. For a presentation on designing homes for people with developmental disabilities, for instance, Tom might enjoy talking about electronics while Debra might prefer talking about design. These types of presentations are so common because many companies and organizations use **self-managed work teams**, or *groups of workers with different skills who work together to produce something or solve a problem*, to handle important issues like new product development, quality control, and human resources.

A second reason small groups are often used for public presentations is that they can make the process of preparing and presenting less stressful for everyone. Groups can help counteract many of the difficulties we face during public presentations because they satisfy our need for inclusion, affection, and control. **Inclusion** suggests that people need to belong to, or be included in, groups with others. As humans, we derive much of our identity, our beliefs about who we are, from the groups to which we belong. Starting with our immediate families and including such important groups as our church, mosque, or synagogue; interest groups; work teams; and social groups—all these help us define who we are. During public presentations, this need for inclusion might be particularly important because of the vulnerability that many of us feel. **Affection**, another essential need, means that we humans need to love and be loved, to know that we are important to others who value us as unique human beings. The emotional support from group members sharing similar experiences can make us feel more comfortable working as part of a group. Finally, we have a need for **control**, or the ability to influence our environment. We are better able to exercise control if we work together. Preparing a good public presentation is challenging, but groups let us accomplish the task more effectively, thus satisfying our desire for control.

Although the content and format for group presentations differ, each has the following common elements:

1. *Group members share in responsibility.* Regardless of how the presentation is formatted, all group members share the task of preparing and, to some extent, presenting the information. Even if some group members are not responsible for the delivery of information, they might be responsible

for preparing and controlling multimedia resources like PowerPoint or videos.

2. *Group members are interdependent.* As discussed at the beginning of the appendix, small groups are interdependent in the sense that all group members are essential to positive outcomes for the group. In most presentations, this interdependence is enhanced because each group member typically adds unique and necessary information about a topic. If one group member does not do his or her job, the audience will not have a complete understanding of the topic.

3. *Group presentations are more interactive.* When one presenter talks to an audience, norms and implicit rules often prevent audience members from asking questions or interrupting the speaker. Group presentations are inherently less focused on one-way transmission of information. Because multiple people speak and share ideas, a "democratic spirit" ensues, and discussion in and among presenters and audience members flows more freely.

4. *Group presentations are coordinated.* Rather than having the right and responsibility of worrying about only your own message, as a member of a group you must be concerned about how your message fits within the context of other presenters' ideas. Such coordination takes careful planning.

Group presentations are enjoyable, and in many cases more productive than individual presentations.

What Skills Do You Need for Effective Group Presentations?

Although group presentations differ from traditional informative and persuasive individual presentations, there are similarities. For instance, your individual component of a group presentation should be well researched, effectively organized, and compellingly presented. For the sake of clarity, however, here are some of the unique skills that may be required for a group presentation.

1. *Creativity.* The real benefit of working on presentations as part of a group is the chance to capitalize on the collective creativity of many people. Your ability to do good research and use a clever approach for discussing your topic will be greatly enhanced through group dialogue. This implies that groups working on a presentation should devote enough time to brainstorming and discussion of the topic(s) being addressed in the presentation.

2. *Coordination.* Group presentations should be well coordinated. For instance, there should be smooth transitions from one speaker to the next; visual aids should be coordinated as a group, rather than each individual having her or his own approach (for instance, using one PowerPoint file rather than several separate files); all group members should dress professionally; and group members should have a plan for where those who are not presenting should stand or sit. In short, for group presentations, every small detail should be planned in advance to demonstrate a well-coordinated effort.

3. *Identification and quick resolution of conflicts.* Because group efforts of any kind—presentations included—require that members work together, identifying and resolving conflict is essential for group success. To

identify and manage conflict, group members should engage in open dialogue where they can explain and check their perceptions. If conflict is actually present, all group members should take part in talking through potential causes and solutions for the conflict. Conflicts surrounding group presentations typically stem from workload distribution, scheduling, and personality clashes among individual group members.

4. *Ability to incorporate discussion.* Group presentations typically invite dialogue among presenters and between audience members and presenters. When planning group presentations, you and your team members should carefully discuss how and when to invite audience participation. You may decide to prepare questions—perhaps in the form of a brief handout—that you want audience members to react to as the presentation progresses.

WHAT PROMOTES DIVERISTY IN GROUPS?

Scholars who study group interaction point to several advantages of diverse groups. Primarily, those advantages flow from the assumption that greater diversity among group members will generate richer dialogue because of the variety of viewpoints that will be shared. A challenge for many college campuses, however, is encouraging diversity among groups. A study conducted by students and faculty at California State University, San Bernardino, concluded that the following characteristics could contribute to greater diversity among student groups on that campus:

- CSUSB has a highly diverse population of students, increasing the likelihood that particular groups of students will be more diverse.
- Because it is a commuter campus, students are less likely to become accustomed to congregating within culturally divided groups.
- Students belong to a similar social class, which increases the likelihood that common ground will be shared among cultural groups.
- The surrounding community is likewise very diverse, meaning that interracial communication is more common.

Not every campus is as culturally diverse as CSUSB. However, whatever the cultural makeup of your campus or community, it is important to find ways to integrate diverse viewpoints. When applied to a group presentation, these viewpoints can improve the quality of dialogue in meaningful ways.[3]

cultural NOTE

How Should the Group Plan Its Workflow?

As you will learn, group presentations come in multiple forms. Common to each of these types of group presentations is a need for shared work and coordination. This section discusses strategies that you and your group members should use to effectively plan for any type of group presentation. Specifically, you will learn about four stages that your group should go through when preparing your presentation: agreeing on a topic, dividing responsibilities, assigning presentation roles, and enacting quality control.

Agreeing on a Topic

Previous chapters have discussed the challenges that students face when selecting topics for presentations. Although some of those problems are overcome by groups, other types of problems emerge. Groups of people are effectively suited to overcoming

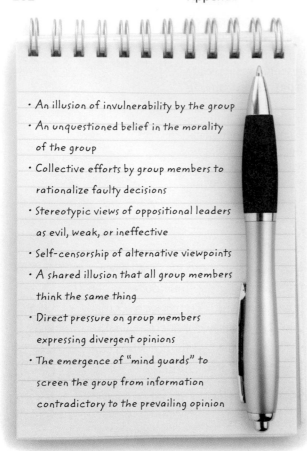

- An illusion of invulnerability by the group
- An unquestioned belief in the morality of the group
- Collective efforts by group members to rationalize faulty decisions
- Stereotypic views of oppositional leaders as evil, weak, or ineffective
- Self-censorship of alternative viewpoints
- A shared illusion that all group members think the same thing
- Direct pressure on group members expressing divergent opinions
- The emergence of "mind guards" to screen the group from information contradictory to the prevailing opinion

Figure A.1   **Observable signs of groupthink.**

ill-defined problems, which can include any task with undefined objectives and outcomes. For instance, groups are very good at brainstorming ideas and coming up with unique and creative ways of presenting issues to audience members. Because they allow us to feel included, groups also help us manage some of the nervousness that we naturally encounter when "flying solo" on a speech.

Although groups help us to be more creative and comfortable, those same characteristics can cause problems. Because groups tend to become highly cohesive when working on a task, groupthink can occur. **Groupthink** is when *members of the group become locked in on one way of thinking about something or carrying out a task and ignore viable (and perhaps better) alternatives.* Also, the comfort and creative energy of a group can cause members to think they are on the same page, when in fact they are not. Figure A.1 lists observable signs that a group is at risk of engaging in groupthink.

To maximize the benefits of working in a group while also minimizing the dangers, the first task of group members should be to carefully evaluate and agree upon a topic (or topics) for the group presentation. If you return to the discussion of the invention canon in Chapter 2, you will recall several questions that you can ask to improve topic selection; those same questions are relevant to group discussions. Another thing that should be discussed by the group is the intended outcome of the presentation. For instance, in a persuasive presentation, is the group trying to advance arguments about fact, value, or policy issues? Table A.1 shows examples of fact, value, and policy questions.

Once the group has sufficiently discussed potential topics and objectives, the group should write down an agreed-upon central idea and objective statement for the overall presentation. By taking time to discuss and record the focus of the presentation, you can be sure that all group members have a clear understanding of what needs to be accomplished when working individually.

Division of Labor

One of the benefits of working in groups is that multiple people can bring skills and assets to the task at hand. Perhaps one person in the group is great with multimedia; another is a whiz at research; and another likes to coordinate and put finishing touches on outlines, visual aids, and other materials. Part of your group discussion should be devoted to finding out what skills, resources, and interests each group member has in relation to your assignment. Taking a few minutes after discussing a topic to have each group member create a personal inventory is wise.

Of course, you should not assume that division of labor means that each person has one task and works in isolation to accomplish that task. Taking such an approach does not capitalize on the benefits of group work and tends to result in poor products that lack cohesive vision. Rather, you should use the personal inventories to select task leaders who are in charge of coordinating efforts on that particular task with the help of other group members. For instance, the library

TABLE A.1 QUESTIONS OF FACT, VALUE, AND POLICY

FACT

How has the divorce rate changed in the past 15 years?

How many Hispanic students graduate from high school each year?

What percentage of college students graduate in 4 years?

How often, on average, does a person speak each day?

What occupations earn the highest annual incomes?

VALUE

Why should people seek higher education?

How should Americans treat international students?

Does our legal system provide "justice for all"?

How should young people be educated about AIDS?

What is the value of standardized tests for college admission?

POLICY

What courses should students be required to take?

Should the state's drunk driving laws be changed?

What are the arguments for and against mandatory retirement?

Should the United States intervene in foreign disputes for humanitarian reasons?

What advantages should government provide for businesses willing to develop in high-risk areas of a city?

expert could assign each member of the group to conduct research for different types of information or different topics related to the overall presentation. As the research coordinator, that person could provide suggestions and help manage the overall effort of all people assigned to the research group. In essence, groups need to have many people using their expertise to take on leadership roles at various stages of the project. In so doing, the group is better able to get maximum productivity out of all group members.

Assigning Presentation Roles

Just as each person needs an assigned task during the planning of your group presentation, each group member needs to have a clearly defined task during the presentation itself. In addition to determining who will speak when, your group should also carefully plan transitions between speakers and from one section of the presentation to the next. Typically, transition periods are where a lack of coordination becomes apparent to audience members. Your teacher or the situation may dictate whether all members need equal speaking time or whether some can be involved in speaking while others take on support roles like managing visual aids, coordinating handouts, and so on.

Quality Control

Earlier in this section, you learned that one of the problems with groups is the possibility of groupthink. Although groups are generally better than individuals at making good decisions, groupthink can erode that advantage. Groupthink occurs when groups become so cohesive that they fail to consider alternative viewpoints. Figure A.2 shows steps groups can take to try and reduce the possibility of groupthink. In addition to

- Seek all pertinent information that can guide group deliberation on an issue
- Carefully assess and discuss the credibility of information relevant to the group's task
- Assign members to pose counter-arguments to fully test the positions taken by the group
- Maintain a commitment to basing decisions on evidence rather than unsupported opinions

Figure A.2 **Actions to reduce the potential for groupthink.**

these steps, there are other actions the group should take to ensure quality control of its work.

Perhaps the most natural method of quality control involves constant and open communication among group members. You should plan to have group members provide daily or periodic reports on their activities. The reports should be detailed in the sense that others know exactly what was done and what was accomplished. These reports might be done orally during scheduled group meetings, by email, or even on Facebook. The reports will encourage a greater sense of responsibility to get work done, and mistakes will be caught more quickly.

A second method of quality control is to be ethical when giving and receiving constructive criticism and feedback. When giving feedback, you should be honest and avoid making unintended attributions for behaviors. People do make mistakes, and in fact, that is part of the learning process in highly hands-on classes like public speaking. Just because someone makes a mistake does not mean he or she is a poor group member. You must also commit to giving good feedback. Telling people that their work is not up to par is hollow unless you can provide authentic help to improve it. When receiving critical feedback, you should make an effort to learn from the experience. Even if you disagree with the feedback, learning why another person perceives things a certain way can potentially teach you how to present your work to avoid such misperceptions.

A third approach to quality control involves assigning people specifically to that task. Some groups appoint members to be "process observers" who are charged with monitoring group communication and outcomes to make sure that the group is working effectively and accomplishing desired outcomes. Process observers might also be charged with playing devil's advocate to ideas to help ensure that multiple views are considered, thereby reducing the chances of groupthink.

What Are the Types of Group Presentations?

A wide variety of group presentations exists. At the annual convention of the National Communication Association (www.natcom.org), faculty and students from around the country give presentations—in groups—using one of these formats: panels, discussion groups, roundtable discussions, town hall meetings, and debates. Members of a law firm trying to land a big client might use four or five representatives to carefully overview the services and expertise of the firm—following more or less a panel discussion format. At Pace University in New York, a group of students in a computer science course might prepare and present a multimedia symposium discussing and demonstrating website design for nonprofit organizations in their lower Manhattan community. Let's look at several common approaches to group presentations: symposia, panel discussions, and debates.

Symposia

A **symposium** is *a type of group presentation where individual members of the group divide a large topic into smaller topics for coordinated individual presentations.* Typically, one of the group members acts as a moderator for the symposium and provides an introduction and conclusion for the group in addition to brief transition statements

Using the Internet to Help Your Group Work

As Internet technology has advanced, many tools have become available to help support the work of groups. Consider how the following free resources can help groups work more efficiently:

- **Facebook**. Besides helping group members stay connected as friends, Facebook allows you to create a group page for any group to which you belong. On the group page, you can post messages, links to resources, agendas, and other information that may help group members stay prepared. You can also create events to alert group members to upcoming meetings.

- **Dropbox**. Dropbox is a free file-sharing service that allows you to create shared folders so that all group members can store, have access to, and edit group documents like word processing files, presentation files, and other documents.

- **Evernote**. This free resource can be used for content curation, or the collection and storage of information from across the web. Your group might locate several webpages, videos, and other resources from the web and use Evernote to maintain a research file in shared notebooks. Evernote is also a powerful note-taking tool, so you can use the service to record and publish notes from meetings.

- **Google Documents**. Google provides a free version of office programs used for word processing, spreadsheets, and presentations. You can even create, collect, and analyze online forms using Google Documents. As with Dropbox, all files can be shared and edited by other members of your group.

These are just a few of the resources available on the web that can be used to facilitate the work of groups. Of course, how you use the web for group work is limited only by your imagination. A variety of services and social media sites can be readily adapted to support the work of your group.

introducing each individual presenter. The moderator might also be responsible for fielding questions from the audience.

Groups preparing for a symposium presentation must initially decide on a topic and then discuss how specific aspects of the topic can be addressed by individual presenters—taking care to ensure that each presenter has a roughly equal amount of information to cover. Consider a group choosing to do a symposium on the topic of water shortages. With five people, one person will act as a moderator. The remaining four members of the group must decide who will handle specific aspects of this relatively broad topic. After doing initial research, the group can compile a list of topics and subtopics related to water shortages. Then, after preparing a working outline of those ideas, the group can divide areas of responsibility and prepare a tentative schedule for the presentation. Figure A.3 provides a sample schedule for a 40-minute symposium.

Presenter	Time	Responsibility
Leslie	00:00–03:00	Opening Remarks • Attention getter • Listener relevance link • Preview the objectives of the symposium
David	03:00–09:00	Causes of Water Shortages • Increased Population • Increased Development • Drought
Karla	09:00–15:00	Current Policies Governing Water Shortages • Mandatory Rationing • Federal Policies • Treaties with Other States
Todd	15:00–21:00	Effects of Water Shortages • Diminished Water Quality • Economic Harms • Damage to Ecosystems
Alane	21:00–27:00	Potential Solutions • Recycling Storm Runoff • Desalinization • Cloud Seeding
Leslie	27:00–40:00	Concluding Remarks and Audience Questions • Summary • Call to Action • Questions (10 minutes)

Figure A.3 **Schedule for symposium on water shortages.**

Depending on your teacher's preference, you might be asked to do a particular type of symposium. Although each type has different content, the general format for each type is typically the same as that illustrated in Figure A.3.

Current Issue Symposium

The water shortage symposium in Figure A.3 is an example of a current issue group presentation. The objective of this presentation is to provide a coordinated and detailed analysis of some current event or significant issue. Much of the group's effort for this type of presentation must be devoted to brainstorming, researching, and outlining potential topics. Typically, though not always, a current issue symposium tackles topics that are somewhat broader than in an individual presentation. In addition, your teacher will probably expect you to address topics in more depth because you can draw on the research and ideas of other group members.

Multimedia Symposium

Because groups are often better at producing creative solutions to problems, some teachers assign a special type of symposium asking group members to pay particular attention to the use of multimedia resources. Angela Garcia, a sociology professor at the University of Cincinnati, asks her students to prepare multimedia symposia discussing aspects of a culture from outside the United States, including language, ethnicity, and communication.[4] Garcia requests that students incorporate music, video, art, and other multimedia resources as part of their presentations. Similar approaches could be used to examine any variety of topics.

For this type of symposium, group members should think creatively when brainstorming for multimedia resources to use and should also practice several times to coordinate all aspects of the presentation. For instance, you want to avoid playing long clips from songs or movies. Longer clips (more than 30 seconds) take attention away from the message(s) you want to relay and can actually confuse listeners. Because using multimedia resources tends to take a great deal of time, practicing the entire presentation is recommended—otherwise, one person might take substantially longer than expected and the entire time allocation plan could be destroyed. Remember that multimedia resources also take much longer to prepare than other types of presentation resources—you might need to edit video or audio, and you might need to combine your resources into a PowerPoint or Keynote presentation. Finally, emphasizing creativity is important. Students often assume that showing video is the best form of multimedia. Music, art, pictures, and even people to interview are all potential resources for a multimedia presentation.

Cultural Symposium

A third type of symposium asks each group of students to pick a unique culture or co-culture to analyze. One group of students chose to analyze the Native American co-culture for their symposium. One student in the group discussed origins of several Native American tribes; another analyzed how various bands developed unique customs, rituals, and beliefs; another traced what happened to many of the larger tribes during the 1800s when westward expansion of the white population caused many conflicts and forced evacuations; and a fourth student analyzed the current status of many of the tribes, including the issues of casino gambling on reservations and Native American mascots of sports teams. As you can see, the group analyzing Native American issues used a basic chronological arrangement to divide responsibilities among group members. Although some of the individuals used PowerPoint and other multimedia resources, others did not—but the same project could have been done as a "multimedia presentation," where all group members would have been required to use multimedia.

Teaching Symposium

Groups are particularly effective at taking complex ideas and determining how to present them to audiences. For that reason, some group assignments are designed as teaching presentations. A common approach is to ask a group to choose topics from a textbook chapter or some other resource or reading assigned by the teacher and then to present information from that resource to the class. The objective of the group is to teach the class important information, skills, and strategies discussed in the chapter or reading. Although the teaching symposium is similar to the other types of symposia discussed, group meetings should pay particular attention to the best ways to teach the assigned material. Group members should discuss how to combine activities, discussion questions, multimedia, and traditional lectures so that the material will engage audience members. Although you are students, you should think like a teacher for this assignment.

Panels

Symposia are more or less similar to other types of presentations you might prepare in your class—like an informative or persuasive presentation. Symposia differ from those presentations because a group of people must coordinate their individual presentations around a common topic. **Panels** differ from symposia because they *rely less on the transmission of information between the presenter and the audience and focus more on interaction and dialogue in and among presenters and audience members.* A typical panel presentation begins with a moderator introducing a topic for discussion, followed by brief introductory statements by panelists, and then time for interaction between and among panelists and audience members. Figure A.4 provides a basic outline for a panel discussion on the topic of student-managed farmers' markets.

As you can see, this panel format builds in time for audience members to discuss issues raised by the panelists in small groups. Then, after short group discussions, the entire class returns to a general discussion of whether to propose a student-managed farmers' market. Using small groups to generate audience participation is wise if the panel is presenting on a topic that is controversial or that many audience members might wish to discuss. As an alternative to using small group discussions, presenters can make longer opening statements, and some of the time devoted to small group discussions could be redirected to time for audience questions.

Panel discussions are particularly effective for topics that are controversial and/or are very relevant to most audience members. These types of presentations work less well for topics about which

Presenter	Time	Responsibility
Rob	00:00–03:00	Opening remarks
Natalie	03:00–06:00	Defining student-managed farm markets
Suchita	06:00–09:00	Working with the college farm
Chris	09:00–12:00	The costs and benefits for students
Brian	12:00–15:00	How students can participate in the decision-making process
Chris	15:00–17:00	Discussion group directions Answer the following questions: • What benefits do you see for a farm market? • What drawbacks do you see in the plan? • What would you like to see in a farm market? • Other questions
	17:00–27:00	Group discussions led by members of the panel
Rob	27:00–37:00	Group reports, audience questions, and concluding remarks

Figure A.4 **A panel presentation on the plan for a new student-managed farmers' market.**

audience members know little. They may not have enough background to effectively discuss issues or ask questions. Consequently, groups planning for a panel presentation format should carefully consider whether this format is appropriate for the audience and topic.

The moderator is very important to a panel discussion format. Besides introducing speakers, the moderator must field audience questions and know to which member of the panel to direct questions. The best moderators are those who know a great deal about the material and who are able to think on their feet quickly. Watching Sunday morning political talk shows is an excellent way to see panel discussions in action—nearly all use this format.

Debates

In a **debate**, *members of the group divide responsibilities to prepare both "pro" and "con" presentations on a controversial issue or question.* Consider this question: "Should the city create new ordinances to enact tougher penalties for individuals who have nuisance parties in their apartment or house?" Various cities have such policies. Nuisance parties are typically defined as parties with excessive noise, underage alcohol consumption, and/or excessive public intoxication. These types of parties are most problematic in neighborhoods where "locals" and students live close together.

If your group wanted to debate the effectiveness of nuisance party ordinances, you would first need to divide group members into pro and con sides. Those individuals assigned to the "pro" side might interview local citizens, law enforcement officers, and university administrators to determine arguments in favor of such ordinances. Those on the "con" side would surely interview students and might interview local attorneys and civil rights leaders to get opposing arguments. For many debate topics, including nuisance party laws, a great deal of information is available at the library and on the Internet.

Debate formats typically include two types of presentations: constructive presentations and rebuttal presentations. In **constructive presentations**, *you initially present arguments—both for and against an idea.* In **rebuttal presentations**, *presenters respond to arguments raised by the opposing side.* If you are a "con" presenter making a rebuttal, you will analyze and critique the arguments in favor of nuisance ordinances. One additional principle in debates is that the side in favor of changing the **status quo**—*the way things are currently done*—typically gets the first and last word. Figure A.5 provides a sample format for a group debate over nuisance party laws.

Notice how each side in the debate has equal time to present its ideas. In addition, notice that the amount of time devoted to James's presentation is the same as everyone else's, but that his time is divided into a first rebuttal and a concluding rebuttal. This division of time allows the "pro" side to speak first—to lay out its case for change—and last in the debate. The format described in Figure A.5 also includes a moderator and time for questions from the audience. Some teachers may require groups to build in time for members from each side to cross-examine the other side rather than having time for audience questions. Finally, some teachers may have the audience "vote" for a winner of the debate after the last presentation has been made.

Presenter	Time	Responsibility
Doug	00:00–03:00	Introduce topic and preview format
Steve	03:00–09:00	Constructive speech in favor of nuisance ordinance
Becky	09:00–15:00	Constructive presentation against nuisance ordinance
James	15:00–19:00	Rebuttal of Becky's "con" presentation
Andi	19:00–25:00	Concluding "con" rebuttal
James	25:00–27:00	Concluding "pro" rebuttal
Doug	27:00–40:00	Summary of key arguments and time for audience questions

Figure A.5   **Debate over nuisance party laws.**

Public debate is likely one of the most challenging presentations you will make. The experience is worth the effort. Students often comment that these presentations were more enjoyable in the long run than most other types. Successful debaters know much about the topic in question so they can think on their feet. In addition, debate arguments are always based on good evidence and audience adaptation.

How Should You Evaluate Group Productivity?

Using groups to accomplish any task—whether the task is organizing a dance for local seniors, planning a community health fair, or raising awareness of environmental issues on campus—involves risk. The group can fail to become interdependent and work together, or one or more members can fail to accomplish their assigned duties adequately. For that reason, observation of, reflection upon, and evaluation of group behaviors is important. Some teachers even include your reflection on group activities as a component of your grade in the course.

Observing and reflecting on your group's activities requires careful evaluation of the group as a whole as well as individual members' contributions to group tasks. Figure A.6 provides a sample progress evaluation form that your group can use to track work on your group presentation. Before adjourning each meeting, your group should discuss responses to the questions on the form. One form should be completed for each meeting.

In addition to evaluating the progress of your group as a whole, you might also be asked to evaluate the individual contributions of group members. Taking time to review previous information on leadership and group communication skills will help you complete this reflective evaluation. Figure A.7 provides an example of an evaluation sheet based on leadership behaviors and group communication behaviors. Notice that you rate each person, including yourself, and provide brief comments. When commenting on member performance, take care to provide descriptive feedback. Notice how Andrea provided descriptive comments about both her and Keran's behaviors during group meetings. Descriptive rather than exclusively evaluative feedback is more productive in helping people understand how others perceive their behaviors. Although the sample shows evaluations only for Andrea and Keran, your evaluation should be of each group member.

In closing, you should understand that group presentations should follow the principles and practices presented throughout this book for individual presentations. Accordingly, group presentations involve research and audience analysis. They should be organized, supported, rehearsed, and delivered effectively. The overall group presentation should also have an introduction and conclusion, which follow the guidelines provided for individual presentations. And to ensure professional delivery, groups should plan and practice how to make smooth transitions from one speaker to another and coordinate their visual aids. Group presentations do require planning and cooperation; however, the format also allows presenters to capitalize on the talents of multiple individuals. Consider this quote by U.S. anthropologist Margaret Mead: "Never doubt that a small group of committed individuals can change the world. Indeed, it's the only thing that ever has."

Group Progress Form

Group Members: Sue, Jim, Andrea, Lau, and Keran

Presentation Topic: Still deciding

Meeting #1   Date: Nov 3   **Members Present:** All

Objectives for Meeting: Talk about assignment
Brainstorm initial topics

Outcomes of Meeting:

We brainstormed an initial list of 12 topics. After thinking about them and combining some topics, we narrowed the list to 3 good topics: the environment, health and wellness, and seniors in our community.

Assignments for Next Meeting Scheduled for: Nov 5

Each person is supposed to find one article (or book) on each topic. At the next meeting, we will discuss the articles and select a final topic. Everyone is supposed to e-mail article citations to the rest of the group so that we do not duplicate research.

Figure A.6   **Example of a group progress form.**

Group Evaluation Form

Your name: <u>Andrea</u>

Directions: Rate each member of your group on how well they display leadership qualities and how well they engage in group communication behaviors. Use the following scale for numeric responses and provide comments as necessary. Remember that "Self-Centered Functions and Statements" are undesirable qualities of group communicators. Consequently, a rating of "5" would indicate that the person avoids those behaviors. Write "NO" if you did not observe the person using a particular category of behaviors.

1 = Very Ineffective

2 = Ineffective

3 = Neither Effective nor Ineffective

4 = Effective

5 = Very Effective

Group Member Name	Task Functions and Statements	Maintenance Functions and Statements	Self-Centered Functions and Statements	Leadership Behaviors and Qualities
Andrea (me)	4	3	3	4
Comments: I was the person who tried to keep the group on task. I most often used opinion giving and coordinating statements during discussions. I need to work on getting along with other group members when we have disagreements—should avoid dominating discussion. I tended to use status seeking comments because I wanted to get things done.				
Keran	4	4	4	5
Comments: Keran was the real leader of the group. She handled conflict between Lau and me when it came up. Keran took care to schedule meetings and take notes. Keran was really good at initiating discussions and harmonizing. She was an effective leader because she made sure all of us had a say in group decisions and did not try to boss people around.				

*Figure A.*7   **Group member evaluation example.**

For REVIEW >>

SUMMARY HIGHLIGHTS

How Are Small Groups and Public Communication Connected?

▶ Small group communication involves interaction between, typically, three to nine people who are working together to achieve goals that are interdependent.

▶ Small groups are commonly used to make coordinated presentations on topics ranging from business proposals to politics.

▶ Groups are common in all of our lives because they help us meet our needs for inclusion, affection, and control.

▶ Group presentations are unique because they require group members to act in an interdependent, coordinated way and can promote greater interactivity with the audience.

What Skills Do You Need for Effective Group Presentations?

▶ Creativity allows the group to benefit from multiple viewpoints and ideas for getting tasks accomplished.

▶ Group members must carefully coordinate who will be charged with specific tasks necessary for accomplishing the group's goals.

▶ Group members must take care to identify and resolve potential sources of conflict among members of the group.

▶ Both within the group and when the group interacts with others, members must creatively invite participation and dialogue.

How Should the Group Plan Its Workflow?

▶ Initial group discussion should focus on identifying the task facing the group and selecting discussion topics that help accomplish those tasks. When discussing tasks and outcomes of the group, members should be aware of the possibility of groupthink and take steps to reduce its likelihood.

▶ After identifying tasks, group members should divide areas of responsibility among all members.

▶ Specific assignments for the actual group presentation should be negotiated and settled upon by all group members.

▶ To achieve the best possible outcome, the group should agree upon quality control measures that will be enacted as all members carry out their assigned tasks. These measures include ethical standards for communication, enacting ways to avoid groupthink, and assigning a process observer to keep the group focused.

What Are the Types of Group Presentations?

▶ In a symposium, group members divide a larger topic into smaller topics for a coordinated presentation. There are various types of common symposia:
- A current issue symposium focuses individual presentations around a topic area that is currently part of a larger public dialogue.
- A multimedia symposium emphasizes creative approaches to addressing a topic using multimedia resources.
- A culture symposium focuses presentations on elements of another culture.
- A teaching symposium involves individual presentations related to a general topic area often related to a class reading or class topic assigned by the professor.

▶ A panel is similar to a symposium but emphasizes greater interaction with the audience.

▶ A debate involves multiple participants discussing opposing sides of a controversial issue.

How Should You Evaluate Group Productivity?

▶ Group presentations involve more risk because members must rely on one another to get individual tasks accomplished.

▶ Evaluation of group performance must include two elements:
- An evaluation of how well individuals accomplished assigned tasks.
- An evaluation of the overall group performance with respect to planning and coordination.

▶ When providing feedback to the group as a whole, or individual members, comments should be descriptive rather than evaluative. Descriptive comments help members of the group understand areas for improvement without creating an overly antagonistic tone.

pop Quiz

1. How many people generally comprise a small group?
   (A) 1 to 2
   (B) 3 to 9
   (C) 9 to 11
   (D) more than 15

2. The three needs that groups can help meet are:
   (A) intelligence, desire, liking
   (B) organization, power, direction
   (C) influence, time-management, entertainment
   (D) inclusion, affection, control

3. Which of the following is *not* a common element of a group presentation?
   (A) Group members are independent.
   (B) Group members share in responsibility.
   (C) Group presentations are coordinated.
   (D) Group presentations are more interactive.

4. The question "Should State University lower tuition?" is a:
   (A) question of fact
   (B) question of value
   (C) question of policy
   (D) question of community

5. Tanner and his group decided to work on separate parts of their topic. Each person then presented his or her part of the presentation in a coordinated manner. What type of group presentation did Tanner's group use?
   (A) panel
   (B) seminar
   (C) debate
   (D) symposium

Answers: 1 (B); 2 (D); 3 (A); 4 (C); 5 (D)

APPLICATION EXERCISES

1. Take a moment to list the various groups you belong to and select one that illustrates the role of communication in groups. Using that group as a focal point, explain through examples and analysis how communication has both enabled and constrained the group's ability to meet its objectives. In retrospect, what advice would you give to the group to improve its communication?

2. Using one of the topics identified in the following list, write questions of fact, value, and policy relevant to that topic. Each question should be accompanied by a brief explanation of what issues would be addressed to answer that question as well as an explanation of why your question appropriately illustrates the form of question you intended (that is, how does your question illustrate what a question of fact is supposed to address?).

   - severe weather
   - flu pandemic
   - music file sharing
   - hybrid cars
   - plagiarism

3. Using a topic of interest, plan a symposium, panel, or debate. You should select a format for the presentation and briefly explain what each speaker should do during his or her part of the presentation. Finally, explain why you chose the format (debate, symposium, or panel) that you did. Why was your choice of formats best in light of the other options?

KEY TERMS

Affection	Groupthink	Self-managed work teams
Constructive presentations	Inclusion	Small group communication
Control	Panel	Status quo
Debate	Rebuttal presentations	Symposium

[Glossary]

A

abstract words 179
Words that are general, broad, and distant from what you can perceive through your senses.

abstraction 179
A simplification standing for a person or thing.

action-ending function 145
The third function of a conclusion, to state the response you seek from the audience.

addition 163
An articulation problem that occurs when an extra sound is added.

affection 279
Humans need to love and be loved, to know that we are important to others who value us as unique human beings.

alliteration 161, 186
The repetition of an initial consonant, a repeated sound.

analogy 111
A comparison of things in some respects, especially in position or function, that are otherwise dissimilar.

antonyms 184
Words that are opposite in meaning.

argument 248
The extent to which the presenter furnishes reasons for the message claims.

articulation 162
The physiological process of creating the sounds of a word.

audience adaptation 77
Making the message appropriate for the particular audience by using analysis and applying its results to message creation.

audience analysis 64, 245
(1) Discovering as much as possible about an audience to improve communication with them. (2) Learning enough about listeners to be able to predict their probable response to your message in a public speaking situation.

audience participation 142
The speaker makes the audience active participants in the presentation.

B

bar/column charts 199
Visual aids used to illustrate quantitative differences between categories of information.

behavioral response 223
An objective of a presentation to inform that is met when the audience shows an overt indication of understanding through action.

bibliographic references 104
Complete citations that appear in the "references" or "works cited" section of your speech outline.

boomerang effect 246
A phenomenon in which the audience likes the presenter and the proposal on the issue less after the presentation than they did before it.

brainstorming 48
Generating as many ideas for topics as you can in a limited period of time without pausing to evaluate them for quality.

brake-light function 144
Warns the audience that you are about to stop.

C

categorical brainstorming 48
Approaching the brainstorming process by beginning with categories that prompt you to think of topics.

cause–effect pattern 132
An organizational arrangement in which part of the speech describes or explains causes and consequences.

celebrity testimony 109
Statements made by a public figure who is known to the audience.

channel 9
The means of distributing your words, whether by coaxial cable, fiber optics, microwave, radio, video, or air.

chart 199
A visual aid used to visually display quantitative or statistical information.

claim 242
A conclusion of what the persuader would have the listener believe or do that invites proof or evidence.

closed or closed-ended questions 74
Questions that force a decision by inviting only a yes-or-no response or a brief answer.

closure 145
An artistic way to end a speech.

commemorative address 267
Designed to set a tone for an event—much like a welcome speech—and usually considered the primary, or keynote, presentation for the event.

common ground 16
Features you share with your audience.

communication 11
A transaction in which speaker and listener simultaneously send, receive, and interpret messages.

communication apprehension (CA) 18
An individual's level of fear or anxiety associated with either real or anticipated communication with another person or persons.

comparison 181
Shows how much one thing is like another by highlighting similarities.

competence 16
A thorough understanding of your topic.

complete arguments 248
Include all parts of the argument—claims and supporting material—to produce attitude change and improve source credibility.

compliance response 245
The audience does what is socially acceptable based on the persuader's message.

concept maps 29
Pictures or diagrams that allow you to visualize main and subordinate ideas related to a more general topic.

concrete words 179
Words that are specific, narrow, particular, and based on what you can sense.

connotative meaning 180
The idea suggested by a word other than its explicit meaning.

consistency persuades 246
The concept that audiences are more likely to change their behavior if the suggested change is consistent with their present beliefs, attitudes, and values.

constructive presentations 288
Debate presentations in which arguments for both sides of the debate are initially presented.

content curation 100
The process of finding and sorting through large amounts of information on the web and organizing it for public display around a specific theme.

contrast 181
Shows how unlike one thing is from another by highlighting differences.

control 279
The ability to influence our environment.

conventional wisdom 65
The popular opinions of the time about issues, styles, topics, trends, and social mores; the customary set of understandings of what is true or right.

cost-benefit analysis 246
The idea that members of an audience are more likely to change their behavior if the suggested change will benefit them more than it will cost them.

critical response 245
The audience focuses on the arguments, the quality of the message, and the truth or accuracy of the message.

current topics 49
Topics that are of interest today because they are in the news, in the media, and on the minds of people in your audience.

D

debate 288
Members of a group divide responsibilities and present both "pro" and "con" sides of a controversial topic.

dedication presentation 266
Honors someone by naming an event, place, or other object after the honoree.

deductive reasoning 249
The presenter bases his or her claim on some premise that is generally affirmed by the audience.

defensive response 245
The audience fends off the persuader's message to protect existing beliefs, attitudes, and values.

defining 227
Revealing the presenter's intended meaning of a term, especially if the term is technical, scientific, controversial, or not commonly used.

definitions 111
Determinations of meaning through description, simplification, examples, analysis, comparison, explanation, or illustration.

degree questions 74
Questions used in interviews and in audience analysis; questionnaires that ask to what extent a respondent agrees or disagrees with a question.

deletion 163
An articulation problem that occurs when a sound is dropped or left out of a word.

delivery 33
The verbal and nonverbal techniques used to present the message.

demographics 66
Audience characteristics such as gender composition, age, ethnicity, economic status, occupation, and education.

demonstrating   229

Showing the audience an object, person, or place; showing the audience how something works; showing the audience how to do something; or showing the audience why something occurs.

demonstration presentation   39

A talk intended to teach audience members how something works or how to perform some task.

denotative meaning   180

The direct, explicit meaning or reference of a word.

describing   228

When the presenter evokes the meaning of a person, place, object, or experience by telling about its size, weight, color, texture, smell, or his or her feelings about it.

descriptive language   180

Attempts to observe objectively and without judgment.

dual coding   197

Because people tend to learn words separately from other sensory stimuli, presenters can use words as one channel, and other senses as another channel through which information can be presented.

duration   161

The amount of time devoted to the parts of a speech (e.g., introduction, evidence, main points) and the dwelling on words for effect.

dynamism   16

The energy you expend in delivering your message.

E

enunciation   162

A vocal aspect of delivery that involves the pronunciation and articulation of words; pronouncing correctly and producing the sounds clearly so that the language is understandable.

ethnicity   67

People who are united through "language, historical origins, nation-state, or cultural system."

ethos   241

Use of an authoritative and trustworthy source in support of your message.

etymology   181

The origin of a word.

evaluative language   180

Language that is full of judgments about the goodness or badness of a person or situation.

evidence   92

Data on which proof may be based.

examples   106

Specific instances used to illustrate your point.

expert testimony   109

Statements made by someone who has special knowledge or expertise about an issue or idea.

explaining   228

Reveals how something works, why something occurred, or how something should be evaluated.

explicit   248

The extent to which the persuader makes his or her intentions clear in the message.

extemporaneous mode   155

A method of speech delivery in which the presenter delivers a presentation from a keyword outline or from brief notes.

eye contact   164

A nonverbal aspect of delivery that involves the speaker's looking directly at audience members to monitor their responses to the message; in public speaking, eye contact is an asset because it permits the presenter to adapt to audience responses and to assess the effects of the message.

F

fallacy   251

An error in reasoning that weakens an argument.

farewell presentation   267

A person is paid tribute for their service before leaving.

feedback   9

Verbal and nonverbal responses by the audience.

figurative language   183

Comparing one concept to another analogous but different concept.

Five Canons of Rhetoric   27

The essential skills associated with public dialogue and communication that Roman scholars synthesized from the teachings of Greek philosophers and teachers. The Five Canons are invention, organization, style, understanding, and delivery.

flowcharts   200

Visual diagrams representing hierarchical structures or sequential processes.

fluency   163

A vocal aspect of delivery that involves the smooth flow of words and the absence of vocalized pauses.

forecasting   144

Tells the audience how you are going to cover the topic.

formal sentence outline   124

A final outline in complete sentence form, which includes the title, specific purpose, thesis statement, introduction of the speech, body of the speech, conclusion of the speech, and a bibliography of sources.

G

gestures 165
A bodily aspect of delivery that involves motions of the hands or body to indicate emphasis, commitment, and other feelings about the topic, audience, and occasion.

groupthink 282
When members of a group become locked in on one way of thinking about something or carrying out a task and ignore viable (and perhaps better) alternatives.

H

hearing 17
Receiving sound waves.

hierarchy of needs 247
A pyramid that builds from basic physiological needs like the need for oxygen all the way up to self-actualization needs—the realization of one's highest potential.

holdings database 93
An organization system used by libraries that indexes all books, journals, periodicals, and other resources owned by the library.

humor 224
The ability to perceive and express that which is amusing or comical.

hyperbole 186
A kind of overstatement or use of a word or words that exaggerates the actual situation.

I

immersive design programs 204
A presentation program that visually takes listeners inside holistic pictures to see specific ideas or concepts.

impromptu mode 156
A method of speech delivery in which the presenter has no advance preparation.

impromptu presentation 37
A type of talk that does not allow for substantial planning and practice before the presentation is given.

inclusion 279
People need to belong to, or be included in, groups with others.

inclusive language 187
Language that does not leave out groups of people.

inductive reasoning 249
The persuader amasses a series of particular instances to draw an inference.

information graphics 226
Also known as infographics, these use principles of graphic design to represent and display complex data or information.

information hunger 218
The presenter generates a desire in the audience for information.

informative presentation 218
A presentation that increases an audience's knowledge about a subject or that helps the audience learn more about an issue or idea.

inside informant 73
Someone who belongs to a group who can tell you what the group stands for.

instant-replay function 145
The second function of a conclusion, to remind the audience of the thesis of your message.

internal previews 141
Statements that inform listeners of your next point or points and are more detailed than transitions.

internal references 104
Brief notations of which bibliographic reference contains the details you are using in your speech.

internal reviews 141
Statements that remind listeners of your last point or points and are more detailed than transitions.

interviews 73
Inquiries about your audience directed at an audience member.

introduction 142
The beginning portion of your presentation.

invention 27
The art of finding information.

K

keyword outline 127
A brief outline with cue words created for you to use during the delivery of your presentation.

L

lay testimony 108
Statements made by an ordinary person that substantiate or support what you say.

levels of abstraction 179
The degree to which words become separated from concrete or sensed reality.

line charts 200
Visual aids that illustrates trends in quantitative data.

listening 17
Interpreting sounds as a message.

list of references   127
The sources consulted and the sources actually used in the presentation.

literal language   183
Words used to reveal facts.

logos   242
Use of evidence and reasoning to advance a claim.

M

main ideas   222
Generalizations to be remembered in an informative presentation.

malapropism   163
Mistaking one word for another.

manuscript mode   154
A method of speech delivery in which the presenter writes out the complete presentation in advance and then uses that manuscript to deliver the speech but without memorizing it.

memorized mode   153
A method of speech delivery in which the presenter commits the entire presentation to memory by either rote or repetition; appropriate in situations where the same speech is given over and over to different audiences.

message   9
The facial expressions seen, the words heard, the visual aids illustrated, and the ideas or meanings conveyed simultaneously between source and receiver.

models   207
Scaled representations of an actual object or objects.

Monroe's Motivated Sequence   136
An organizational arrangement based on reflective thinking that includes five specific steps: attention, need, satisfaction, visualization, and action.

movement   165
A nonverbal aspect of delivery that refers to a presenter's locomotion in front of an audience; can be used to signal the development and organization of the message.

multimedia materials   197
Digital or electronic sensory resources that combine text, graphics, video, and sound into one package.

N

narratives   107
An extended story showing how another person experienced something.

noise   10
Interference or obstacles to communication.

nondominant groups   67
Groups that are similar to the larger culture but are distinguished by background, beliefs, and behaviors.

nonverbal messages   9
Movements, gestures, facial expressions, and vocal variations that can reinforce or contradict the accompanying words.

numeric literacy   109
The ability to understand, interpret, and explain quantitative information.

O

observation   72
A method of audience analysis based on what you can see or hear about the audience.

open-ended questions   74
Like essay questions, questions that invite an explanation and discourage yes or no responses from the person being questioned.

oral citation   105
Tells the audience who the source is, how recent the information is, and the source's qualifications.

organization   30
The arrangement and structure of a presentation.

ornamental language   263
Highly stylized and artful uses of words to convey meanings.

ornamentation   30
The creative and artful use of language.

oversimplification   187
A complex issue described as simple.

P

panel   287
Group presentations that utilize short introductory statements from panel members and then provide time for interaction and dialogue between the presenters and audience members.

pathos   241
Appealing to the audience members' feelings.

pause   161
An intentional silence used to draw attention to the words before or after the interlude; a break in the flow of words for effect.

periodicals   93
Sources of information that are published at regular intervals.

personal experience   91
Using your own life as a source of information.

personal inventory   48
Trying to determine a topic by considering features of your life such as experiences, attitudes, values, beliefs, interests, and skills.

perspective   188
Your point of view; the way you perceive the world, reflected in the words you choose.

persuasive presentations   241
A message delivered to an audience by a speaker who intends to influence audience members' choices by changing their responses toward an idea, issue, concept, or product.

physical appearance   166
The way we look, including our display of material things such as clothing and accessories.

pie charts   200
Visual aids illustrating percentages or components of a whole.

pitch   162
A vocal aspect of delivery that refers to the highness or lowness of the speaker's voice, its upward and downward inflection, the melody produced by the voice.

plagiarism   13, 112
(1) A speech, outline, or manuscript from any source other than you. (2) The intentional use of information from a source without crediting the source.

preparation outline   123
The initial or tentative conception of a speech in rough outline form.

presentation to entertain   268
Designed to make a point in a creative and oftentimes humorous way.

presentation to pay tribute   265
Designed to offer celebration and praise of a noteworthy person, organization, or cause.

presentation to welcome   264
Intended to set a tone for a larger event by inviting all participants—including other presenters and audience members—to appropriately engage the event.

primacy   225
Placing your best argument or main point early in the presentation.

principle of division   122
An outlining principle that states that every point divided into subordinate parts must be divided into two or more parts.

principle of parallelism   122
An outlining principle that states that all points must be stated in the same grammatical and syntactical form.

principle of subordination   121
An outlining principle that states that importance is signaled by symbols and indentation.

principles of learning   223
Principles governing audience understanding by building on the known, using humor or wit, using presentational aids, organizing information, and rewarding listeners.

problem–solution pattern   136
An organizational arrangement in which part of the speech is concerned with the problem(s) and part with the solution(s) to problem(s).

process of communication   10
The dynamic interrelationship of source, receiver, message, channel, feedback, situation, and noise.

projection   65, 162
(1) The belief that others believe as you do when they may not. (2) Adjusting your volume appropriately for the subject, the audience, and the situation.

pronunciation   162
The production of the sounds of a word.

Q

question-and-answer session   157
A specialized instance of the impromptu presentation approach where the topics of your comments are driven by questions from the audience.

question of fact   242
The persuasive presentation seeks to uncover the truth based on fact.

question of policy   242
The persuasive presentation enters the realm of rules, regulations, and laws.

question of value   242
The persuasive presentation raises issues about goodness and badness, right and wrong, enlightenment and ignorance.

questionnaires   73
Surveys of audience opinions.

R

rate   160
A vocal aspect of delivery that refers to the speed of delivery, the number of words spoken per minute; normal rates range from 125 to 190 words per minute.

rebuttal presentations   288
Debate presentations where one side presents points in response to arguments advanced by the other side.

receiver   9
The individual or group that hears, and hopefully listens to, the message sent by the source.

recency   225
Placing your best argument or main point late in the presentation.

reference librarian   92
A librarian specifically trained to help find sources of information.

relationship 245
How the audience feels about you as a presenter before, during, and after the persuasive appeal.

repetition 185
Words repeated exactly or with slight variation.

reward 226
A psychological or physical reinforcement to increase an audience's response to information given in a presentation.

rhythm 161
The tempo of a speech, which varies by part (e.g., introductions are often slower and more deliberate) and by the pacing of the words and sentences.

ritual 263
A ceremonial act that is characterized by qualities or procedures that are appropriate to the occasion.

S

Sapir-Whorf hypothesis 179
Our language determines to some extent how we think about and view the world.

scatterplot 200
A special type of line chart that plots related values on an X–Y axis and then creates a line showing how those values are related.

search engine 95
A website on the Internet that is specially designed to help you search for information.

self-managed work teams 279
Groups of workers with different skills and duties who work together to produce something or to solve a problem.

semantics 176
The study of how words come to have meaning.

sensory aids 197
Resources other than the speaker that stimulate listeners and help them comprehend and remember the presenter's message.

signposts 141
Direct indicators of the speaker's progress; usually an enumeration of the main points: "A second cause is. . . ."

situation 10
The time, place, and occasion in which the message sending and receiving occurs.

slide-deck programs 198
Computer-generated programs that allow the user to arrange slides in a particular order and then display those slides to the audience.

small group communication 278
Interaction among three to nine people working together to achieve an interdependent goal.

source 8
The originator of the message; the speaker.

source credibility 16
The audience's perception of your effectiveness as a communicator.

spatial relations pattern 131
An organizational arrangement in which events or steps are presented according to how they are related in space.

special occasion speech 55
A presentation that highlights or punctuates a special event, situation, ceremony, or occasion.

specific numbers 248
Percentages, actual numbers, averages, and ranges of numbers used instead of "many," "most," or some other vague quantity.

specific purpose 55
A statement that reveals precisely what you want the audience to know or believe as a result of your presentation.

speech of action 244
A persuasive speech given for the purpose of influencing listeners' behaviors and actions.

speech of introduction 265
Designed to tell us about the person being introduced and to help establish their ethos.

speech of nomination 266
Introduces and honors someone you wish to place in contention for an award, elected office, or some other competitively selected position.

speech of recognition 268
Typically presented when one or more people are given awards.

speech to convince 243
A persuasive presentation given for the purpose of influencing listeners' beliefs or attitudes.

speech to inform 54
A speech that seeks to increase the audience's level of understanding or knowledge about a topic.

speech to inspire 243
A persuasive speech given for the purpose of influencing listeners' feelings or motivations.

speech to persuade 54
A speech that seeks to influence, reinforce, or modify the audience members' feelings, attitudes, beliefs, values, or behaviors.

status quo 288
The way things are currently done.

stereotype 188
A hasty generalization about an individual based on an alleged characteristic of a group.

style 30
The use and ornamentation of language.

subordinate ideas 222
Details that support the generalizations in an informative presentation.

substitution 163
An articulation problem that occurs when one sound is replaced with another.

supporting material 106
Information you can use to substantiate your arguments and to clarify your position.

survey 107
Study in which a limited number of questions are answered by a sample of the population to discover opinions on issues.

symbolic 177
Words that represent the concrete and objective reality of objects and things as well as abstract ideas.

symposium 284
A group presentation in which individual members divide a large topic into smaller topics for coordinated individual presentations.

synonyms 183
Words that mean more or less the same thing.

T

tables 198
Visual aids that combine text and/or numbers to efficiently summarize, compare, and contrast information.

testimonial evidence 108, 248
Written or oral statements of others' experience used by a speaker to substantiate or clarify a point.

text slide 198
A visual aid that relies primarily on words and phrases to present and summarize information.

thesis statement 56
A forecast of your speech in the form of a complete sentence that reveals the content of your presentation.

time-sequence pattern 129
An organizational arrangement in which events or steps are presented in the order in which they occur.

topical sequence pattern 134
An organizational arrangement in which the topic is divided into related parts, such as advantages and disadvantages, or various qualities or types.

transitions 141
Statements or words that bridge previous parts of the presentation to the next part. Transitions can be signposts, internal previews, or internal reviews.

transposition 163
An articulation problem that occurs when two sounds are reversed.

trustworthiness 16
The degree to which the audience perceives the presenter as honest and honorable.

two-sided argument 112
A source advocating one position will present an argument from the opposite viewpoint and then go on to refute that argument.

U

understanding 32
The fourth Canon of Rhetoric (originally called memory) requires speakers to have a strong mental awareness of the messages they intend to present and know how to interpret facts and ideas for an audience.

V

verbal messages 9
The words chosen for the speech.

virtual library 95
Websites that provide links to sites that have been reviewed for relevance and usability.

visual aids 197
Any observable resources used to enhance, explain, or supplement the presenter's message.

vocalized pause 161
A nonfluency in delivery characterized by such sounds as "Uhhh," "Ahhh," or "Mmmm" or the repetitious use of such expressions as "okay," "like," or "for sure" to fill silence with sound; often used by presenters who are nervous or inarticulate.

volume 162
A vocal characteristic of delivery that refers to the loudness or softness of the voice. Public presenters often project or speak louder than normal so that distant listeners can hear the message; beginning presenters frequently forget to project enough volume.

W

wit 224
The ability to perceive and express humorously the relationship or similarity between seemingly incongruous or disparate things.

[References]

CHAPTER 1

[1] Phillips, M. (No date). "The four most career enhancing skills you can have." *Corporate Heights*. Retrieved from http://www.corporateheights.com/important-career-enhancing-skills/.

[2] http;//www.nytimes.com/2010/03/03/us/03scotus.html.

[3] Savage, D. (2011, May 26). "Supreme Court upholds immigration law targeting employers." *Los Angeles Times*. Retrieved from http://articles.latimes.com/2011/may/26/nation/la-na-court-immigration-ruling-20110526.

[4] Santos, F. (2012, April 18). "In Arizona immigrants make plans in shadows." *New York Times*. Retrieved from http://www.nytimes.com/2012/04/19/us/arizona-illegal-immigrants-adapt-to-a-crackdown.html?partner=rss&emc=rss.

[5] Churchill, W. Retrieved from http://www.brainyquote.com/quotes/keywords/listen.html.

[6] McCroskey, J. C. (1997). Oral communication apprehension: A summary of recent theory and research. *Human Communication Research, 4,* 78.

[7] Greene, J. O., Rucker, M. P., Zauss, E. S. & Harris, A. A. (1988). Communication anxiety and the acquisition of message production skill. *Communication Education, 47,* 337–47.

[8] Daly, J. A., Vangelisti, A. L. & Weber, D. J. (1995). Speech anxiety affects how people prepare speeches: A protocol analysis of the preparation processes of speakers. *Communication Monographs, 62,* 394.

[9] Berger, C. R. (2004). Speechlessness: Causal attributions, emotional features, and social consequences. *Journal of Language and Social Psychology, 23,* 147–69. See also Dwyer, K. K. (1998). Communication apprehension and learning style preference: Correlations and implications for teaching. *Communication Education, 49,* 137–50.

[10] MacIntyre, P. D., & MacDonald, J. R. (1998). Public speaking anxiety: Perceived competence and audience congeniality. *Communication Education, 47,* 359–65.

[11] Ayres, J. (1996). Speech preparation processes and speech apprehension. *Communication Education, 45,* 228–35. See also Menzel, K. E., & Carrell, L. J. (1994). The relationship between preparation and performance in public speaking. *Communication Education, 43,* 17–26.

CHAPTER 2

[1] Kienpointner, M. (1997). On the art of finding arguments: What ancient and modern masters of invention have to tell us about the "ars inveniendi." *Argumentation, 11.2,* 225–37.

[2] Rowan, K. E. (1995). A new pedagogy for explanatory public speaking: Why arrangement should not substitute for invention. *Communication Education, 44.3,* 236–50.

[3] Hirst, R. (2003). Scientific jargon, good and bad. *Journal of Technical Writing & Communication, 33.3,* 201–29.

[4] Keesey, R. E. (1953). John Lawson's lectures concerning oratory. *Speech Monographs, 20.1,* 49.

[5] Kopp, W. (2008). Remember the contributions you can make. *Vital Speeches of the Day, 74.7,* 311–14.

[6] Booth, P., & Davisson, A. (2008, Spring). Visualizing the rhetorical situation of Hurricane Katrina: Photography, popular culture, and meaning in images. *American Communication Journal, 10.1,* no page numbers.

[7] Detz, J. (2009). A thorough speech on brief speechmaking. *Vital Speeches, 75,* 447–50.

[8] Paul Begala, "Elitists for President: Which candidate will stoop to connect with the middle class?" *Newsweek*, April 23 and 30, 2012, p. 21.

[9] Ibid.

CHAPTER 3

[1] Facebook website retrieved from http://newsroom.fb.com/content/default.aspx?NewsAreaId=22.

[2] Press Trust of India (2011, March 24). "FB deletes 20,000 underage profiles daily." Retrieved from http://ibnlive.in.com/news/facebook-deletes-20000-underage-profiles-daily/146972–11.html.

CHAPTER 4

[1] Samovar, L. A., & Porter, R. E. (2003). *Communication between cultures* (5th ed.). Belmont, CA: Wadsworth.

[2] Judy, R. W., & D'Amico, C. (1997). *Workforce 2020: Work and workers in the 21st century*. Indianapolis, IN: Hudson Institute.

[3] Lustig, M. W., & Koester, J. (2003). *Interpersonal competence: Interpersonal communication across cultures*. Boston: Allyn & Bacon.

[4] Carbaugh, D. A. (1998). 'I can't do that' but 'I can actually see around corners': American Indian

students and the study of public communication. In Martin, J. N., Nakayama, T. K., & Flores, L. A. (Eds.), *Readings in cultural contexts*. Mountain View, CA: Mayfield.

[5]These figures are based on data from 2004.

[6]Maurer, M. (1989). Language and the future of the blink: Independence and freedom. *Vital Speeches of the Day, 56(1),* 16–22. A speech delivered at the banquet of the annual convention, Denver, Colorado, July 8, 1989.

[7]Behnke, R. R., O'Hair, D., & Hardman, A. (1990). Audience analysis systems in advertising and marketing. In O'Hair, D., & Kreps, G. L. (1990). *Applied communication theory and research*. Hillsdale, NJ: Laurence Erlbaum Associates, pp. 203–21.

[8]Welton, M. (2002). Listening, conflict, and citizenship: Towards a pedagogy of civil society. *International Journal of Lifelong Education, 21,* 197–208.

CHAPTER 5

[1]Dominick, J. R. (1996). *The dynamics of mass communication* (5th ed.). New York: McGraw-Hill.

[2]Bourhis, J., Adams, C., & Titsworth, S. (2008). Style manual for communication studies. New York: McGraw Hill.

[3]Hornikx, J., Hendriks, B., & Thijzen, D. (2010). The effects of cultural adaptation in fundraising letters: The case of help-self and help-others appeals in a feminine culture.

Communications: The European Journal of Communication Research, 35(1), 93–110. doi:10.1515/COMM.2010.005.

[4]Polnac, L., Grant, L., & Cameron, T. (1999). *Common sense*. Upper Saddle River, NJ: Prentice Hall.

[5]Broeckelman-Post, M. (2008). *Two years later: What we can learn from the third academic integrity study at OU*. Athens, OH: Ohio University School of Communication Studies.

CHAPTER 6

[1]Grove, M. (2012, April). Why are adoption rates falling? *Vital Speeches of the Day, 78,* 107–12.

[2]Thompson, E. C. (1990). An experimental investigation of the relative effectiveness of organizational structure in oral communication. *Southern Speech Journal, 26,* 59–69.

[3]Sharp, H., Jr., & McClung, T. (1966). Effect of organization on the speaker's ethos. *Speech Monographs, 33,* 182–83.

[4]Greene, J. O. (1984). Speech preparation processes and verbal fluency. *Human Communication Research, 11,* 61–84.

[5]Ibid.

[6]Fritz, P. A., & Weaver, R. L., II. (1986). Teaching critical thinking skills in the basic speaking course: A liberal arts perspective. *Communication Education, 35,* 177–82.

[7]http://usatoday.com/oped/2008/03/post-6.html. Accessed July 18, 2008.

[8]Tischer, S. (2004, October). Presentation, North Dakota State University, Fargo, North Dakota.

[9]http://blogs.abcnews.com/politicalpunch/2008/02/Obama-echoes-de.html. Accessed July 18, 2008.

[10]http://usatoday.com/oped/2008/03/post-6.html. Accessed July 18, 2008.

CHAPTER 7

[1]Grigg, R. (1988) *The tao of relationships*. New York: Bantam Books, p. 15.

[2]Hildebrandt, H. W., & Stevens, W. (1963). Manuscript and extemporaneous delivery in communicating information. *Speech Monographs, 30,* 369–72.

[3]Lee, M. (2010). "We are so over Pharaohs and Pyramids!" "Re"-presenting the "othered" lives with young people through an International Studies Program." *International Journal of Qualitative Studies in Education, 23,* 737–54.

[4]Miller, N. (1976). Speed of speech and persuasion. *Journal of Personality and Social Psychology, 34,* 15–24.

[5]Diehl, C. F., White, R. C., & Burk, K. W. (1959). Rate and communication. *Speech Monographs, 26,* 229–31.

[6]Chirumbolo. A., Mannetti, L., Pierro, A., Areni, A., & Kruglanski, A. W. (2005). Motivated closed-mindedness and creativity in small groups. *Small Group Research, 36.1,* 59–82. See also Nakatani, Y. (2005). The effects of awareness-raising training on oral communication strategy use. *Modern Language Journal, 89.1,* 76–91.

[7]Harden, M. (1999, April 18). Making the grade. *The Columbus Dispatch*, p. 1D.

[8]Hall, E. (1959). *The silent language*. New York: Fawcett Publications.

[9]Venezia, M., Messinger, D. S., Thorp, D., & Mundy, P. (2004). The development of anticipatory smiling. *Infancy, 6.3,* 397–406.

[10]Napieralski, L. P., Brooks, C. I., & Droney, J. M. (1995). The effect of duration of eye contact on American college students' attributions of state, trait, and test anxiety. *Journal of Social Psychology, 135,* 273–80.

[11]Beebe, S. A. (1974). Eye contact: A nonverbal determinant of speaker credibility. *Speech Teacher, 23,* 21–25.

[12]Ekman, P., & Friesen, W. V. (1967). Head and body cues in the judgment of emotion: A reformulation. *Perceptual and Motor Skills, 24,* 71–74.

[13]Gosselin, P., & Simard, J. (1999). Children's knowledge of facial expressions of emotions: Distinguishing fear and surprise. *Journal of Genetic Psychology, 160.2,* 181–93.

[14]Weinberg, M. K., Tronick, E. Z., & Cohn, J. F. (1999). Gender differences in emotional expressivity and self-regulation during early infancy. *Developmental Psychology, 35.1,* 175–88.

[15]Ekman, P. (1969). Pan-cultural elements in facial displays of emotion. *Science, 164*, 86–88.

[16]Burgoon, J. K., Birk, T., & Pfau, M. (1990). Nonverbal behaviors, persuasion, and credibility. *Human Communication Research, 17*, 140–170.

[17]Pearson, J. C., West, R. L., & Turner, L. H. (1995). *Gender and communication*. Dubuque, IA: Wm. C. Brown Publishers.

[18]Ibid.

[19]Movshovitz-Hadar, N., & Hazzan, O. (2004). How to present it? On the rhetoric of an outstanding lecturer. *International Journal of Mathematical Education in Science & Technology, 35.6*, 813–27. See also Singer, M. A., & Goldin-Meadow, S. (2005). Children learn when their teacher's gestures and speech differ. *Psychological Science, 16.2*, 85–89.

[20]Source for statistics in first paragraph (the rest is original): Barrett, L. (2011, April 25). 75% of enterprises to use videoconferencing by 2013. *InformationWeek Online*. Available: www.information week.com

CHAPTER 8

[1]Lederer, R. (1991). *The miracle of language*. New York: Pocket Books.

[2]New words in the *Merriam-Webster Dictionary*. (2008, July 7). Accessed July 12, 2008, at http://www.boston.com/news/local/Massachusetts/articles/2008/07/07/new_words_in_the_merriam_webster_dictionary/.

[3]Crawford, J. (1999). Killing us one by one. An unpublished presentation delivered in Interpersonal Communication 103, Public Speaking, Ohio University, Athens, Ohio.

[4]Smith, D. C. (1997, July/August). Is the use of metaphors innocuous or cause for concern? *Peace Magazine*, http://www.peacemagazine.org. See also Lakoff, G., & Johnson, M. (1981). *Metaphors we live by*. Chicago: University of Chicago Press; and Rothstein, L. (1999). The war on speech. *Bulletin of the Atomic Scientists, 55.3*, 7.

[5]Brown, R. (1968). *Words and things*. Glencoe, IL: The Free Press.

[6]Shelley, P. B. (1960). Prometheus unbound. In *John Keats and Percy Bysshe Shelley*. New York: Modern Library, p. 260.

[7]http://venus.va.com.au/suggestion/sapir.html.

[8]Hayakawa, S. I. (1978). *Language in thought and action*. Orlando, FL: Harcourt Brace Jovanovich.

[9]Burch, D. (1999). I am unique. An unpublished presentation delivered in Interpersonal Communication 103, Public Speaking, Ohio University, Athens, Ohio.

[10]Safire, W. (1972). *The new language of politics*. New York: Collier Books.

[11]Soukhanov, A. H. (1995). *Words watch: The stories behind the words of our lives*. New York: Henry Holt.

[12]Will, G. F. (1999, August 25). Giddy over McCain. *The Washington Post*, p. A17.

[13] Robinson, A. (1999). If the shoe fits. An unpublished presentation delivered in Interpersonal Communication 103, Ohio University, Athens, Ohio.

[14]Burch, D., op. cit.

[15]LaRocque, P. (1999). Between you and I, misutilizing words ranks high pet-peevewise. *The Quill, 87.3*, 31.

[16]Meek, C. (1999). Aspects of paintball. An unpublished presentation delivered in Interpersonal Communication 101, Public Speaking, Ohio University, Athens, Ohio.

[17]Schneider, L. (2004). Fabulous facts about foster care. An unpublished presentation delivered in Communication 110, Public Speaking, North Dakota State University, Fargo, North Dakota.

CHAPTER 9

[1]Gellevij, M., et al. (2002). Multimodal versus unimodal instruction in a complex learning context. *Journal of Experimental Education, 70.3*, 215–41.

[2]Zayas-Baya, E. P. (1997). Instructional media in the total language picture. *International Journal of Instructional Media, 5*, 145–50.

[3]Alley, M. (2003). *The craft of scientific presentations: Critical steps to succeed and critical errors to avoid*. New York: Springer.

[4]Kiewra, K. A. (1985). Students' notetaking behaviors and the efficacy of providing the instructor's notes for review. *Contemporary Educational Psychology, 10*, 378–86.

[5]Katt, J., Murdoch, J., Butler, J., & Pryor, B. (2008). Establishing best practices for the use of PowerPoint™ as a presentation aid. *Human Communication, 11*, 193–200.

[6]Kinchin, I. M., Chadha, D., & Kokotalio, P. (2008). Using PowerPoint as a lens to focus on linearity in teaching. *Journal of Further and Higher Education, 32*, 333–46.

[7]Cyphert, D. (2007). Presentation technology in the age of electronic eloquence: From visual aid to visual rhetoric. *Communication Education, 56*, 168–92.

[8]Halverson, E. (2008, January). From one woman to everyman: Reportability and credibility in publicly performed narratives. *Narrative Inquiry, 18*, 29–52.

CHAPTER 10

[1]National Center for Health Statistics. (2011). *Health: United States, 2011: With special feature on socioeconomic stats and health*. Hyattsville, MD: National Center for Health Statistics.

[2]Lavizzo-Mourey, R. (2012, January). The Green House revolution in nursing homes. *Vital Speeches of the Day, 78,* 28–31.

[3]Romney, M. (2012, May). Freedom to dream. *Vital Speeches of the Day, 78,* 165–67.

[4]Sajak, P. (2002, August 15). The disconnect between Hollywood and America: You possess the power. *Vital Speeches of the Day, 68(21),* 701–05.

[5]Bishop, D. M. (2012, February). Bonds that sustain us to this day. *Vital Speeches of the Day, 78,* 58–59.

[6]Anderson, R. (1999). The phenylketonurics among us. An unpublished presentation delivered in Interpersonal Communication 101, Public Speaking, Ohio University, Athens, Ohio.

[7]Coan, S. M. (2012, February). The future of our oceans. *Vital Speeches of the Day, 78,* 66–68.

[8]Goh, C. C. M. (2002). Exploring listening comprehension tactics and their iterative patterns. *System, 30,* 185-206. See also Walker, I., & Hume, C. (1999). Concrete words are easier to recall than abstract words: Evidence for a semantic contribution to short-term serial recall. *Journal of Experimental Psychology: Learning, Memory, and Cognition, 25,* 1256–71.

[9]Kardash, C. M., & Noel, L. K. (2000). How organizational signals, need for cognition, and verbal ability affect text recall and recognition. *Contemporary Educational Psychology, 25,* 317–31.

[10]Springer, L., Stanne, M. E., & Donovan, S. S. (1999). Effects of small group learning on undergraduates in science, mathematics, engineering and technology: A meta-analysis. *Review of Educational Research, 69,* 21–52.

[11]Ehrensberger, R. (1945). An experimental study of the relative effectiveness of certain forms of emphasis in public speaking. *Speech Monographs, 12,* 92–111.

[12]Baird, J. E. (1974). The effects of speech summaries upon audience comprehension of expository speeches of varying quality and complexity. *Central States Speech Journal, 25,* 124–25.

[13]Perry, R. P. (1985). Instructor expressiveness: Implications for improving teaching. In Donald, J. G., & Sullivan, A. M. (Eds.), *Using research to improve teaching.* San Francisco: Jossey Bass, pp. 35–49.

[14]Boduroglu, A., Shah, P., & Nisbett, R. (2009). Cultural differences in allocation of attention in visual information processing. *Journal of Cross Cultural Psychology, 40,* 349–60.

[15]Beating the blues: Dealing with depression. (1999, Fall). *Inova Health Source,* 9.

[16]Snelling, D. (1999). TV and your child. An unpublished presentation delivered in Interpersonal Communication 103, Public Speaking, Ohio University, Athens, Ohio.

[17]Titsworth, S., Quinlan, M. & Mazer, J. (2010). Emotions in teaching and learning: Development and validation of the Classroom Emotions Scale. *Communication Education, 59,* 431–52.

[18]Ehrensberger, R. (1945). An experimental study of the relative effectiveness of certain forms of emphasis in public speaking. *Speech Monographs, 12,* 94–111.

[19]Janis, I., & Feshbach, S. (1953). Effects of fear-arousing communication. *Journal of Abnormal and Social Psychology, 48,* 78–92.

[20]DuPont, M. (1980, Spring Semester). Phoenix, Arizona: My hometown. An unpublished manuscript presented in Honors Public Speaking course, Iowa State University, Ames, Iowa.

CHAPTER 11

[1]Dillard, J. P., & Marshall, L. J. (2003). Persuasion as a social skill. In Greene, J. O., & Burleson, B. R. (Eds.), *Handbook of communication and social interaction skills.* Mahwah, NJ: Lawrence Erlbaum, p. 481.

[2]Li, J., & Zahn, L. (2011). Online persuasion: How written word drives WOM. *Journal of Advertising Research, 51,* 239–57.

[3]Dillard & Marshall, op. cit., pp. 479–513.

[4]Based on Chaiken, S., Liberman, A., & Eagly, A. H. (1989). Heuristic and systematic processing within and beyond the persuasion context. In Uleman, J. S., & Bargh, J. A. (Eds.), *Unintended thought.* New York: Guilford Press, pp. 212–52.

[5]Ibid.

[6]Maslow, A. H. (1943). A theory of human motivation. *Psychological Review, 50,* 370–96.

[7]Lim, T., Kim, S., & Kim, J. (2011). Holism: A missing link in individualism-collectivism research. *Journal of Intercultural Communication Research, 40,* 21–38.

[8]Dillard & Marshall, op. cit., p. 481.

[9]Blum-Kulka, S. (1987). Indirectness and politeness in requests: Same or different? *Journal of Pragmatics, 11,* 131–46.

[10]Dillard, J. P., Wilson, S. R., Tusing, K. J., & Kenney, T. (1997). Politeness judgments in personal relationships. *Journal of Language and Social Psychology, 16,* 297–325.

[11]O'Keefe, D. J. (1998). How to handle opposing arguments in persuasive messages: A meta-analytic review of the effects of one-sided and two-sided messages. In Roloff, M. E. (Ed.), *Communication yearbook, 22.* Thousand Oaks, CA: Sage, pp. 209–49.

[12]Brockriede, W., & Ehninger, D. (1960). Toulmin on argument: An interpretation and application. *Quarterly Journal of Speech, 46,* 44–54.

[13]Lewin, T. (2012, March 4). Instruction for masses knocks down campus walls [online]. *New York Times.* Available: http://www.nytimes.com/2012/03/05/education/moocs-large-courses-open-to-all-topple-campus-walls.html.

CHAPTER 12

[1]Streep, M. (2012, March 9). Meryl Streep hails Hillary Clinton. *The Daily Beast*. Available: http://www.thedailybeast.com/articles/2012/03/09/women-in-the-world-highlights-angelina-jolie-madeline-albright-more-video.html.

[2]National Aeronautics and Space Administration (2010). Ethics frequently asked questions. Accessed May 5, 2010, at http://www.nasa.gove/offices/ogc/general_law/ethicsfaq.html.

APPENDIX

[1]Desjardins, L. (2012, May 15). Ron Paul backers' plan: Transform the GOP. *Cable News Network*. Available: http://www.cnn.com/2012/05/15/politics/ron-paul-plan/index.html.

[2]Galanes, G., Adams, K., & Brilhart, J. (2004). *Effective group discussion: Theory and practice*. New York: McGraw-Hill.

[3]Apacible, C. F., Schmidt, L., Alvarez, M., & Perez, G. (2012, June 14). Interracial interactions at a racially diverse university. California State University San Bernardino. Available: http://thewasc.csusb.edu/repository/Inter-racialRelationsSurvey.htm.

[4]Garcia, A. (2001). Group multi-media presentations in "the sociology of language and ethnicity." *Radical Pedagogy, 3.3*, NP.

Photos

p. i (bottom): © BananaStock/JupiterImages; **p. i. (middle):** © Paul Burns/Getty Images; **p. iii:** © PhotoDisc/PunchStock; **p. iv:** © PhotoDisc/PunchStock; **p. vi:** © Ryan McVay/ Getty Images; **p. vii:** © Tetra Images/Getty Images; **p. viii:** © Stockbyte/PunchStock; **p. x:** © BananaStock/JupiterImages; **p. xi:** © Amos Morgan/Getty Images; **p. xiii:** © Rubberball/ PunchStock; **p. xiv:** © PhotoAlto/PunchStock; **p. xv:** © iStockphoto.com/Cat London; **p. xvi:** © Jose Luis Pelaez Inc./Getty Images; **p. 1:** © Comstock Images/Superstock

Chapter 1, pp. 2–3: © David Young-Wolff/PhotoEdit; **p. 4:** courtesy of Danny Wong and Blank Label; **p. 5:** © Flying Colors Ltd/Getty Images; **p. 7:** © ColorBlind Images/ Blend Images LLC **p. 8:** © Ambient Images Inc./PhotoEdit; **p. 10:** © Comstock Images/ JupiterImages; **p. 11:** © FWilliam Thomas Cain/Getty Images; **p. 12 (top):** © Don Bayley/ Stockphoto (audience) and Michael Kemter/Stockphoto (young man); **p. 12 (bottom):** Library of Congress, Prints and Photographs Division (LC-USZ62-13016); **p. 14:** © Digital Vision/Punchstock; **p. 15:** © FPG/Getty Images; **p. 16 (top):** © Pixtal/age Fotostock; **p. 16 (bottom):** © Cheryl Graham/iStockphoto; **p. 17:** © Getty Images/Digital Vision; **p. 18:** © liquidlibrary/PictureQuest; **p. 22:** © Goodshoot/Punchstock

Chapter 2, pp. 24–25: © Colin Young-Wolff/PhotoEdit; **p. 26:** © Rick Friedman/Corbis; **p. 27:** © Bettmann/CORBIS; **p. 29:** © Izabela Habur/iStockphoto; **p. 31 (top):** © Royalty-Free/CORBIS; **p. 31 (bottom):** © Royalty-Free/Corbis; **p. 33:** © Getty Images/Digital Vision; **p. 35:** © Ian McDonnell/iStockphoto; **p. 36:** © Stockbyte/Getty Images; **p. 37 (top):** © Fuse/Jupiter Images/Getty Images; **p. 37 (bottom):** © Izabela Habur/iStockphoto; **p. 38:** © Getty Images/Photodisc; **p. 40:** Reed Kaestner/Corbis; **p. 41:** © Philadelphia Inquirer/ MCT./Landov; **p. 42:** © HBSS/Corbis

Chapter 3, pp. 44–45: © Veer; **p. 46:** © The McGraw-Hill Companies, Inc./John Flournoy, photographer; **p. 48:** © Image100/Corbis; **p. 49 (left):** © Creatas/PunchStock; **p. 49 (center):** © David Becker/Getty Images; **p. 49 (right):** © Photodisc/Getty Images; **p. 49 (bottom):** © Getty Images; **p. 49:** © Jon Feingersh/Blend Images LLC; **p. 51:** © ColorBlind Images/ Getty Images; **p. 52:** © Bonnie Kamin/PhotoEdit; **p. 53:** © Ana Sousa/Stockphoto; **p. 54:** © Royalty-Free/CORBIS; **p. 55 (top):** © Creatas/PunchStock; **p. 55 (bottom):** © Bonnie Kamin/PhotoEdit; **p. 57:** © Image Source/PunchStock; **p. 58 (left):** © Creatas/PunchStock; **p. 58 (center):** © AFP/Getty Images; **p. 58 (right):** © Rosanne Olson/Getty Images; **p. 59:** © Image100/Corbis

Chapter 4, pp. 62–63: © AP Images/Charles Dharapak; **p. 64:** © Stewart Cohen/Pam Ostrow/Jupiter Images; **p. 65:** BananaStock/JupiterImages; **p. 66:** © Jeff Greenberg/The Image Works; **p. 67 (top):** © Digital Vision/Getty Images; **p. 68:** © Digital Vision/Getty Images; **p. 69 (top):** Digital Vision/PunchStock; **p. 69 (bottom):** Purestock/SuperStock; **p. 71:** © Digital Vision/PunchStock; **p. 72:** © Comstock Images/Alamy; **p. 75:** © Angela Wyant/Getty Images; **p. 76:** © McGraw-Hill Companies, Inc./Lars A. Niki, photographer; **p. 79:** © Andersen Ross/Getty Images; **p. 81:** © Peter Mlekuz/iStockphoto; **p. 83:** © Getty Images; **p. 84:** BananaStock/JupiterImages

Chapter 5, pp. 88–89: © Comstock/PunchStock; **p. 90:** © Karl Weatherly/Getty Images; **p. 91:** © Ingram Publishing/Alamy; **p. 92:** © Hill Street Studios/Blend Images LLC; **p. 93:** © iStockphoto; **p. 95:** © Veer; **p. 96:** © Dan Wilton/iStockphoto; **p. 101:** © LWA/Getty Images; **p. 104:** © STEVE MARCUS/Reuters/Corbis; **p. 106:** © TANNEN MAURY/epa/ Corbis; **p. 111:** © Comstock Images/JupiterImages; **p. 112:** © Royalty-Free/Corbis; **p. 113:** © iStockphoto.com/fotek; **p. 114:** © Hill Street Studios/Blend Images LLC

Text